HISTORY'S GREAT UNTOLD STORIES

LARGER THAN LIFE CHARACTERS & DRAMATIC EVENTS THAT CHANGED THE WORLD

JOSEPH CUMMINS

HISTORY'S GREAT UNTOLD STORIES

LARGER THAN LIFE CHARACTERS & DRAMATIC EVENTS THAT CHANGED THE WORLD

JOSEPH CUMMINS

NATIONAL GEOGRAPHIC

WASHINGTON, D.C.

History's Great Untold Stories
Joseph Cummins

Published by the National Geographic Society

John M. Fahey, Jr., President and Chief Executive Officer
Gilbert M. Grosvenor, Chairman of the Board
Nina D. Hoffman, Executive Vice President;
    President, Books Publishing Group

Book Division Staff

Kevin Mulroy, Senior Vice President and Publisher
Leah Bendavid-Val, Director of Photography Publishing
    and Illustrations
Marianne R. Koszorus, Director of Design

Barbara Brownell Grogan, Executive Editor
Elizabeth Newhouse, Director of Travel Publishing
Carl Mehler, Director of Maps
Gary Colbert, Production Director

Manufacturing and Quality Management

Christopher A. Liedel, Chief Financial Officer
Phillip L. Schlosser, Vice President
John T. Dunn, Technical Director
Vincent P. Ryan, Director
Chris Brown, Director
Maryclare Tracy, Manager

Staff at Murdoch Books

Chief Executive: Juliet Rogers
Publishing Director: Kay Scarlett

Publisher: William Kiester
Editor: Scott Forbes
Concept and design: Peter Long
Photo researchers: Anne Burns and Amanda McKittrick
Maps: John Frith, Flat Earth Mapping
Production: Megan Alsop
Proofreader: Bronwyn Sweeney
Indexer: Meryl Potter

Founded in 1888, the National Geographic Society
is one of the largest nonprofit scientific and
educational organizations in the world. It reaches
more than 285 million people worldwide each month
through its official journal, NATIONAL GEOGRAPHIC, and
its four other magazines; the National Geographic
Channel; television documentaries; radio programs;
films; books; videos and DVDs; maps; and interactive
media. National Geographic has funded more than
8,000 scientific research projects and supports an
education program combating geographic illiteracy.

For more information, please call
1-800-NGS LINE (647-5463)
or write to the following address:

National Geographic Society
1145 17th Street N.W.
Washington, D.C. 20036-4688 U.S.A.

Visit us online at
www.nationalgeographic.com/books

For information about special discounts
for bulk purchases, please contact
National Geographic Books Special Sales:
ngspecsales@ngs.org

First published in 2006 by Pier 9, an imprint of
Murdoch Books Pty Limited

Library of Congress Cataloging-in-Publication Data
available upon request.

ISBN-13: 9781426200311

Printed by Midas Printing (Asia) Ltd. in 2006.
Printed in China.

To Dede and Carson: together, the greatest story in the world.

CONTENTS

INTRODUCTION

WHY ARE HISTORY'S GREAT UNTOLD STORIES UNTOLD?

The stories in this book span more than one thousand years and take you to North and South America, Europe, Australia, Japan, Korea, China, the Philippines, Russia, Africa, the Caribbean, the Middle East, Malaysia, and remote Pacific islands. They are full of lunacy, lust, greed, murder, extreme myopia, and raw ambition—the very stuff of which history is made. They are amazing and moving. And yet they have faded from view.

One reason for this is that many of them take place in exotic locales where they were never written down, or were only written in the poetic—mythic form of ancient documents such as "The Secret History of the Mongols." Other tales here—like the story of a courageous seventeenth-century Japanese peasant boy who led a powerful revolt against the shoguns—occurred in cultures shrouded in secrecy.

Another reason is the failure of the human imagination to contemplate violence on a large scale, such as that of the Taiping Rebellion, which devastated central China for a hundred years. Such horrors slip away from human comprehension and memory.

Aside from bringing to life history not found in standard history books, *History's Great Untold Stories* explores the intriguing effect on human history of the Law of Unintended Consequences, which states that the actions of people, and of governments, always have effects that are unanticipated. We know about this law in our own lives. Events over which we have no control and of which we are often completely unaware affect our very existence. I was born because my father and mother leaned over a lunch counter at a restaurant and reached for the same straw at the same time. You are alive today, perhaps, because, unbeknownst to you, that car that would have hit an icy patch, spun, and killed you as you were crossing the street had a flat tire a mile down the road.

On a larger scale, as *History's Great Untold Stories* relates, historical events unknown to us affect us in myriad ways. Remember that piece of direct mail you received today requesting contributions to your favorite political cause or charity? That technique was pioneered by men desperately seeking to free slaves in Britain in the late eighteenth century. When the plague of AIDS struck America in the early 1980s, the public health system in San Francisco was better prepared for it because of a completely forgotten epidemic—that of the dreaded bubonic plague—that hit the city in 1900. You may have marveled at the so-called Remote Operated Vehicles, or ROVs, created by undersea explorer Robert Ballard, which took pictures of the long-sunken Titanic, but chances are you didn't know that the first vessel able to descend to the depths of the ocean was created by an odd couple of quarrelsome adventurers off Bermuda in the 1930s, who revolutionized underwater exploration.

A corollary to the Law of Unintended Consequences is that the consequences that seem most reasonable and likely to occur often fail to materialize. *History's Great Untold Stories* illuminates this, as well. In 1709, Sweden was the premier military power of northern Europe. When its ruler, King Charles XII, followed the defeated Russian army of Czar Peter the Great to an obscure part of the Ukraine, it was to destroy the Russians and continue Sweden's rise to European domination. Then the unexpected happened, and Sweden's time in the sun (militarily, in any event) was over for good. In early-nineteenth-century Tasmania, a well-meaning Englishman named George Augustus Robinson attempted to save the lives of the island's remaining indigenous inhabitants—and ended up nearly killing them off instead. British and American farmers in the mid-nineteenth century found that bird droppings imported from Peru made a wonderful fertilizer; but the search for a better wheat harvest turned into an aggressive and often bloody competition for the world's supply of guano, as the fertilizer became known.

Yet despite all this, you will also encounter here a good deal of grace and courage. A wronged Filipino of the seventeenth century—now so obscure that no likeness of him even exists—set off a rebellion against a repressive Spanish regime that lasted for nearly ninety years. A nineteenth-century Canadian explorer and mapmaker named David Thompson, who should be as famous as Lewis and Clark, and upon whose maps all subsequent maps of western Canada were based, died blind and forgotten—but still gazing blankly upward at the stars that had once guided him. And an autocratic, but brave and intelligent Korean queen who refused to give up fighting for her way of life, even as she faced Japanese assassins who had come to destroy her and her country.

If *History's Great Untold Stories* has one intended consequence, then it is to discover, for good or ill, what the Scottish philosopher David Hume once called "the constant and universal principles of human nature."

THE CADAVER SYNOD: THE MOST CONTROVERSIAL TRIAL IN HISTORY

Read—How there was a ghastly Trial once
Of a dead man by a live man, and both, Popes.
Robert Browning, *The Ring and the Book*

DURING 1868 AND 1869, ENGLISH POET ROBERT BROWNING PUBLISHED *The Ring and the Book*, a long dramatic narrative poem—twenty-one thousand lines in all—in four installments. Sadly neglected by modern readers, *The Ring and the Book* tells the powerful story of a real-life murder in Rome in 1698. However, about 130 lines of the poem hark back to a much earlier Rome, the Rome of the ninth century. These lines describe the Cadaver Synod, one of the strangest trials ever to take place, in which one pope, Stephen VI (VII), exhumed the body of a predecessor, Formosus, tried it for perjury and other offenses, and, having found it guilty, passed sentence on it.

The Vatican does not officially discuss the Cadaver Synod, which scholars call by the equally ominous-sounding title *Synod horrenda*. With a little prompting, it will admit to popes who were less than paragons of holiness—even murderous popes, sexually licentious popes, popes who succeeded their own fathers on the papal throne. But over the Cadaver Synod—over the vicious, possibly insane, raving of Pope Stephen VI (VII) at the putrefying body of Formosus—a shroud is thrown.

This may be partly because madness is less acceptable than murder or sexual malfeasance—we may talk about our outlaw ancestors, but we tend to keep the crazy ones in the closet. But it is also because the episode throws into doubt the whole issue of papal succession and raises awkward questions regarding one of the papacy's most treasured doctrines, papal infallibility.

THE DARK CENTURY

Being a pope in the ninth century was a far different matter from being pontiff today. To begin with, the Vatican City state, which guarantees the pope's physical independence, was not established until 1929. So for most of the papacy's history, the pope has been a ruler among rulers. In the early middle ages, especially, that meant making alliances to protect your turf; and such alliances would dramatically alter the nature and role of the papacy.

At the beginning of its history, the church was persecuted by Roman emperors such as Nero. But the Christians subsequently managed to make friends with, and even convert, some Roman rulers. In particular, the conversion of Emperor Constantine in AD 312—following a vision he had of a cross of light just before he went into battle—was particularly important, for almost immediately Constantine issued the Edict of Milan, banning persecution of Christians and decreeing Sunday a Christian holy day. However, in the early fourth century, Constantine transferred the capital of the Roman Empire to the city of Constantinople. The popes were left relatively unprotected and had to endure the invasions of Germanic tribes, led on by the vacuum of power in Rome, while meeting the oppressive demands of Constantinople, which attempted to rule Rome and the papacy from afar.

In the early 750s, as the Byzantine Empire began to crumble, the papacy came under threat from the Lombard king, Aistulf, who had taken over nearby states and was eyeing up Rome as another potential fiefdom. Aistulf began to demand taxes from the city—essentially, protection money. So Pope Stephen II (III) was forced to turn to Pepin, King of the Franks, and request protection. He got it; what's more, Frankish protection continued under Pepin's son Charlemagne, who created what became known as the Carolingian Empire.

Leo III was elected pope in 795, but he had made a good many enemies among a powerful Roman family who had supported his predecessor, Hadrian I. One day on his way to mass, a mob in the pay of this family attacked him and tried, unsuccessfully, to gouge out his eyes and cut off his tongue. He managed to escape to the protection of Charlemagne's court, but it was an entire year before he felt safe enough to return to Rome. Leo repaid his debt in 800, when, during mass at St. Peter's tomb in Rome, he crowned Charlemagne as emperor—something he had no legal right to do. The coronation created a western empire to rival the eastern Byzantine Empire, and bolstered papal influence throughout Western Europe; however, it became apparent that Charlemagne felt his role as "protector of the Roman church" gave him certain

After the death of Charlemagne in AD 814, the Carolingian Empire, or Frankish Kingdom, began to fragment, and the papacy turned to local feudal states for support.

prerogatives, which included commissioning his own theologians to settle doctrinal matters where he disagreed with the pope. As often happened, the papacy's alliance with a temporal ruler resulted in an unequal bargain. Moreover, Carolingian backing did not fully protect the pope from other political forces in Rome.

After the death of Charlemagne in 814, the alliance began to fall apart. Faced with many threats to their power that included an Arab invasion of Sicily, subsequent popes turned more and more to powerful Roman families for support. The papacy became, as historian Eamon Duffy has written: "the possession of great Roman families, a ticket to local dominance for which men were prepared to rape, murder, and steal."

The ninth-century papacy is a rogue's gallery filled with portraits of corruption, shame, and malfeasance. Sergius II (844–47) ran an extremely corrupt papacy and became the first pope to swear allegiance to a temporal ruler, in this case King Lothair of the Franks. Hadrian III (884–85) supposedly had a noblewoman whipped naked through the streets of Rome, and also ordered the blinding of a local official. He may have been assassinated; the church made him a saint. Boniface VI (896) was the first pope to be elected after twice being defrocked for immorality. At least five of the century's popes were murdered in office, the first being John VIII, in 882, who was poisoned then clubbed to death by associates, possibly even by his own relatives. Overall, the ninth century saw the rule of twenty popes, compared to only eight in the twentieth century—and that includes the thirty-three-day reign of John Paul I in 1978.

THE UNFORTUNATE FORMOSUS

Pope Formosus I reigned from 891 to 896. It is one of history's ironies that the name of the pope who is chiefly known for his corpse means "good-looking." No reliable portraits of the living Formosus survive to attest to his handsomeness, but it seems that he was actually an able and moral pope, one of few among his contemporaries. He was seventy-six by the time he was elected, and had already had a distinguished career, working successfully as a missionary in Bulgaria and then as a church diplomat in Constantinople, trying to patch up relationships with the Eastern church.

One glitch in his prepapal career would later be held against Formosus—or, rather, his corpse. A contemporary canonical law prevented a bishop moving from one diocese to another or ruling over more than one diocese at a time—this was a way of keeping prelates from hopping to a district they thought might be a little more profitable, or building a little fiefdom out of a number of dioceses. Technically, when Formosus was elected Bishop of Rome (a prerequisite to becoming pope), he was still Bishop of Porto, Italy. But no one seemed to be bothered by this at the time.

As pope, Formosus shored up the church in Germany and England, and continued to try to make peace with Constantinople. But he also made political enemies. One such enemy—and a powerful one—was the Spoleto family. Guido, Duke of Spoleto, had been crowned Emperor of Rome by Formosus's predecessor, and Formosus had been pressured into crowning Guido's son Lambert as co-emperor in 892. But when Guido died in 894, Formosus had Arnulf, King of the Franks, crowned emperor at St. Peter's in mid-896—to the rage of Lambert.

TRYING TO KEEP THE STEPHENS STRAIGHT

If Dante didn't allot a circle in Hell to church bureaucrats, he should have, and the dual numbering of Pope Stephens, beginning with Pope Stephen II (III), is the reason why. The mixup over whether Pope Stephen II (III) (AD 752–757) was the second or third Stephen resulted from the fact that an elderly Roman priest named Stephen was elected pope on March 22 of 752, but died two or three days later of a stroke—before he had been consecrated as Bishop of Rome.

Then, as now, to be a pope in the line of Petrine succession, you must first be Bishop of Rome, as Peter was considered to be. The *Annuario Pontificio*, the official Vatican directory of popes, traditionally included the original Stephen in its list of popes. But the Second Vatican Council of 1962–65 decided he wasn't a pope, after all, and gave all subsequent Stephens dual numbering. Fortunately, no pope has taken the name Stephen since Stephen IX (X) in 1057.

Opposite: Charlemagne's Christian forces fought fierce battles against so-called "barbarians," including the Tartar tribes of the east and the Saracens in the south.

The Church of St. John Lateran in Rome, as depicted in 1840. It is considered, as the inscription on its facade attests, "of all the churches in the city and the world, the mother and head."

Soon, however, Arnulf had a stroke, which left him partially paralyzed, and he was forced to withdraw his army from Rome, to Germany. The Spoletos saw their chance for revenge on Formosus. But before they could act, the pope died, of natural causes, on April 4, 896. He was succeeded by the aforementioned, twice-defrocked Boniface, whose papacy lasted only fifteen days before he died, wracked with gout.

TRIAL OF A CORPSE
In May of 896, Stephen VI (VII) was elected pope, due to the intercession of the Spoleto family, in particular Lambert. Lambert's anger at Formosus's death knew no bounds, for the pope, by dying, had eluded his revenge. And so he set in motion the most horrifying episode in church history—the trial of Formosus's corpse. In this, he had a willing accomplice in Stephen, who, like Formosus, had become Bishop of Rome while serving as bishop of another diocese; in fact, Formosus had consecrated him as bishop. If Formosus could be discredited, if Formosus's acts could be annulled, Stephen would be safe from any subsequent charges regarding *his* simultaneous control of two dioceses; at the same time, he could curry favor with the powerful Lambert.

Nine months after the death of Formosus, Stephen convened a synod. In church history, a synod is an important occasion, a gathering of church leaders to address matters of concern in the life of the church. In order to make this unprecedented trial palatable, Stephen and Lambert first stirred up the Roman citizenry and nobility against Formosus, sending criers through the streets to say that Formosus had been guilty of terrible crimes. Stephen than gathered together a panel of "judges," pulled from those bishops who supported him and those who were simply too afraid to oppose him. It is possible that this puppet panel—as powerless as any jurists at a Stalin show trial—thought that the former pope was simply going to be tried in absentia, as it were, to have his reputation degraded. If so, it must have been a horrible surprise, in January of 897, to walk into the Church of St. John Lateran, the first church built in Rome, considered the holiest, and find the rotting corpse of Formosus propped upright in a chair. In *The Ring and the Book*, Robert Browning described it thus:

> The great door of the church
> Flew wide, and in they brought Formosus' self
> The body of him, dead, even as embalmed
> And buried duly in the Vatican
> Eight months before, exhumed thus for the nonce.
> They set it, that dead body of a Pope
> Clothed in pontific vesture now again
> Upright on Peter's chair as if alive.

Some of the few eyewitness accounts of the trial that survive also have Formosus wearing papal vestments; others have him dressed in a hair shirt. All agree that standing behind the reeking corpse was a terrified teenage deacon who would act as Formosus's "voice," answering the questions that were put to him.

Sitting on his papal throne, Stephen read the three charges against Formosus. The dead pope was accused of perjury in that he lied to become pope by not admitting he was already a bishop; "ambition to seek the papacy," an obscure church crime of which almost every nobleman in Rome at the time was probably guilty; and violating church canons after he had become pope, especially the one that forbade the transfer of a bishop from one diocese to another.

Records of the trial speak of Stephen working himself up into hysterical rages, hurling curses at the corpse and mocking its silence. Occasionally, the trembling young deacon would attempt to make a few mumbled replies from behind the corpse, but was shouted down every time by Stephen.

At one point, in the midst of this travesty, a violent earthquake shook the church, severely damaging it. Since no transcript of the trial proceeding exists, it is hard to know what kind of omen this was considered. Stephen might have been wise to heed it, but instead he instructed the judges to convict Formosus on all counts.

He then passed the sentence. All of Formosus's acts as pope and bishop were invalidated, including every clerical appointment and ordination he had made; three fingers of his right hand were cut off—the ones used to give blessings; and his corpse was ignominiously buried. Shortly thereafter, Stephen and the Spoletos thought the better of the burial, perhaps deciding that those faithful to Formosus might use the grave as a shrine. So they dug up the corpse again and had it thrown into the Tiber. There is a legend that a hermit retrieved the remains from the river and gave the pope a proper burial in an old catacomb; however it happened, Formosus's body was reburied.

THE GREAT AND THE GOOD

There have been many bad popes, but many others have done wonders for the church and the world. Among the most notable are:

St. Gregory the Great (590–604). Gregory was only the second pope in church history to be called "Great" (Leo I was the other). He cared so deeply for the well-being of his flock that he went among them while they were suffering from the plague. He was also an energetic promoter of the liturgy as a way for Catholics to become closer to God in their church services, and he established the Gregorian chant. He was a practical leader as well, organizing and helping to pay an army which kept the Lombard kings from moving against Rome.

Leo XIII (1878–1903). Leo has been called "the workers' pope." He was probably the first pope in modern history to bring about an awareness of the plight of the modern worker and to call for change in social thought. He also promoted the study of natural sciences and opened Vatican archives to scholars, claiming that "the church has nothing to fear from the truth."

Blessed John XXIII (1958–1963). In the early 1960s, John called the Second Vatican Council, bringing the church into the modern world by instituting a series of liturgical reforms—including the replacement of Latin with the vernacular—addressing the fundamental rights of people, and issuing encyclicals that called for Christian unity.

POSTHUMOUS EXECUTION

"How long is this posthumous life of mine to last?" the poet John Keats wondered as he was dying a drawn-out death from tuberculosis. The same question, in a different way, might be applied to Pope Formosus and others like him. For posthumous execution has long been a favorite punishment for those who have died without being, according to others, punished sufficiently for their crimes.

The Englishman John Wyclif (c. 1330–84) was dug up and burned as a heretic twelve years after his death. The warlord Vlad the Impaler, source of the Dracula myth, was beheaded after his assassination in 1476. King Richard III of England was hanged by King Henry VII following his death at the battle of Bosworth Field in 1485. And many of those who had brought about the execution of Charles I of England and died before the restoration of Charles II were later dug up on Charles's orders so that their bodies could be hung, drawn, and quartered—including Oliver Cromwell. More recently, in 1986, the body of François Duvalier, the Haitian dictator known as "Papa Doc," who died in 1971, was exhumed and ritually beaten by opponents of him and his son "Baby Doc."

Previous pages: A dramatic rendition in oils of the Cadaver Synod, painted by French artist Jean-Paul Laurens in 1870.

It is possible that, in trying Formosus's corpse, Stephen had rational motives: a desire, born of self-preservation, to please the powerful Spoletos, and a strong wish to make sure his own position as pope was secure, since he had essentially committed the same "crime" as Formosus had. But his eerie decision to put the dead pope's corpse on trial, his maniacal conduct during the proceedings, and his grisly sentence all indicate that he might have been insane.

Following the trial, Stephen required all clergy ordained by Formosus to submit letters renouncing their own ordinations as invalid. This, plus the macabre nature of the trial, now began to turn the Roman people against Stephen. In an attempt to distance themselves from the events, the Spoletos withdrew their support of Stephen. He was captured by a mob, stripped of his vestments, and thrown into prison. In August of 897, he was strangled in his cell.

In November, Pope Theodore II, a member of a pro-Formosan faction, held a synod invalidating the Cadaver Synod, announced that all of Formosus's ordinations were valid, and ordered that Formosus be dug up once again. The corpse was then dressed in papal vestments, brought to St. Peter's Church, and reburied with full honors.

That was where the matter stood until the pontificate of Sergius III, which began in 904. Sergius, along with Alexander VI (1492–1503), is considered one of the most corrupt popes in history. He not only had his predecessor, Leo V, murdered, he also murdered the antipope Christopher, who had been Leo's rival. (He had them both strangled, a common method of murder in Rome at the time.) Now "elected" to the papal throne, Sergius made a good deal of money for the noble families who were his friends, particularly the family of an official named Theophylact. (In fact, Theophylact's fifteen-year-old stepdaughter became Sergius's mistress; her son by Sergius would later become Pope John XI.)

Sergius had taken part in the Cadaver Synod as a judge and was a supporter of the murdered Stephen VI (VII). Once in power, he convened another synod that invalidated the previous reinstatement of Formosus and reaffirmed the acts of Stephen and the Cadaver Synod. Once again, all of Formosus's ordinations were declared invalid. Formosus's corpse was not dug up again, but Sergius did have an admiring verse placed on the tomb of Stephen VI (VII).

A BROKEN CHAIN?

Sergius III's decisions were never reversed—they have simply been ignored by the Roman Catholic Church. Many scholars within the church consider the Cadaver Synod to be an anomaly, something that stands entirely outside church experience, and which, therefore, theologically speaking, never happened. However, dissenters outside the church have argued compellingly that the "nullification" of Formosus's ordinations has never been reversed and that this raises momentous and troubling questions for the present-day papacy.

In particular, it challenges the whole notion of papal infallibility. Defined during the nineteenth-century reign of Pius IX, but held to apply to popes throughout history, this doctrine asserts that the pope, under the guidance and protection of the Holy Spirit, is incapable of making an error when pronouncing on matters of faith and morals *ex cathedra*, or "from the chair." This is a matter of vital importance to millions of Catholics who wait to hear what their leader has to say on subjects such as birth control, women in the priesthood, homosexuality, and the like.

Popes selling indulgences or plotting with political conspirators are not generally held to have been speaking *ex cathedra*. But in the case of the Cadaver Synod, Stephen can be seen to have been acting in an official capacity. And Stephen not only declared the entire reign of his predecessor void, he even proclaimed every priest ordained by Formosus to be invalid.

As a result, some commentators hold that Stephen's actions call into question the entire doctrine of infallibility and thus the bedrock of the modern church. Some even say that the Cadaver Synod casts doubt on the belief in apostolic succession.

A line of 263 popes leads all the way back to St. Peter, the first Vicar of Christ. According to Catholic beliefs, the popes do not *replace* Peter, the way a president or prime minister replaces another; they can only *succeed* Peter. Each of them is to carry on the work of Peter, to bring "truth and unity" to their flocks. The nullification of Formosus's ordinations could be seen to break this apostolic succession, since we can no longer be sure which bishops, and, consequently, popes, were ordained by "nullified" priests. If this is true, the sanctity of Petrine succession, which reaches all the way back to Jesus Christ himself, has been broken.

These are questions that scholars will continue to debate. It is no mistake, however, that there has never been another Formosus. No matter how good-looking a newly elected pope might consider himself to be, that name brings along with it just a little too much baggage from beyond the grave.

PORTRAIT IN COURAGE: THE LEPER KING OF JERUSALEM

To be deprived of the use of one's limbs is of little help in carrying out the work of government. If I could be cured of the disease ... I would wash seven times in [the] Jordan, but I have found in the present age no Elisha who can heal me.

King Baldwin IV, letter to King Louis VII of France, c. 1178

THE AUTHORITY OF LEADERSHIP IS AS SYMBOLIC AS IT IS ACTUAL. IN OTHER words, human beings like their kings, presidents, prime ministers, and princes to look the part. A firm, high brow, erect carriage, unblemished skin, and an unflinching gaze are all part of the act, no matter how much a leader might quail and quiver in private. Those with physical imperfections need not apply. There have been exceptions, of course: Franklin Delano Roosevelt became a three-term American president, despite the fact that polio had left him unable to walk. But he carefully hid his infirmity from the public gaze.

So imagine what it would be like if the ruler of your country was afflicted with a disease which caused his face to ooze with raw ulcers, turned his hands and feet into little more than suppurating paws, and struck him blind. Imagine that the disease he had was communicable, as well, so that if any of his subjects came into contact with him they might catch it. And imagine that the nation depended on this ruler to be battlefield commander in chief at a time when its land was threatened on three sides by a fierce, wily, and tenacious foe.

If you are able to imagine all of these things, then you have some idea of what it was like to be an inhabitant of the Crusader States in the latter part of the twelfth century, with Baldwin IV, Leper King of Jerusalem, as your sole hope and succor.

THE CRUSADER STATES

For centuries after the rise of the Muslim religion in the Middle East, it had been a goal of the papacy and the Holy Roman Empire to win back the so-called Holy Land for Christendom. At last, in 1095, Pope Urban II preached a great crusade against the infidels, one which, he proclaimed, would achieve full remission of sins for any man who took part in it. European royalty responded to the call, a great army was raised, and the Holy Land was won back. The First Crusade was capped in 1099 by the capture of Jerusalem—and the bloody massacre of its Jewish and Muslim inhabitants—by Godfrey of Bouillon, Duke of Lorraine, and the establishment of the Kingdom of Jerusalem. Godfrey became the first king (although he refused the title, instead taking the name "Defender of the Holy Sepulcher") and went on to expand the kingdom by defeating Egypt in a momentous battle a month later.

Subsequent rulers of Jerusalem—who had no problem being called "king"—expanded the Kingdom of Jerusalem to include the port cities of Acre, Beirut, and Sidon, as well as the principalities of Antioch and Tripoli. But for its entire two-hundred-year history, the kingdom was confined to a long, narrow strip of land between the Mediterranean Sea and the Jordan River and open to the threat of invasion by the Fatimid Caliphate of Egypt and the Seljuk Turks who controlled Syria.

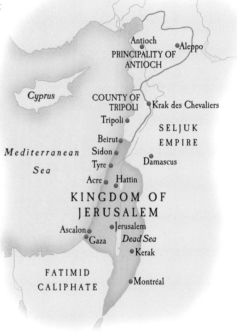

Even so, a thriving and diverse society grew up in the Crusader States. Pilgrims flocked to the shrine churches built at sacred sites, particularly in Jerusalem itself, and this brought prosperity to those who lived there. Despite the massacre of 1099, other religions were tolerated: Jews were not allowed to live in Jerusalem, but they could do business there and worship at the Wailing Wall, and many Jewish synagogues and rabbinical schools existed in other parts of the kingdom. Muslims, too, were afforded the right to practice their religion as they saw fit, even to make the pilgrimage to Mecca.

Jerusalem and the Crusader States, c. 1174. These Christian enclaves clustered along the coast, and on land were surrounded by enemies.

This tolerance was the result of simple demographics. By the mid-twelfth century, there were roughly 620,000 inhabitants of the Kingdom of Jerusalem, of which only 120,000 were Franks or of Frankish origin. The rest were Muslims, in the main, followed by Eastern-rite Christians and Jews. Vastly out-numbered, the Franks pursued the only sensible course when it came to other religions. To some extent, they also adapted to life overseas, wearing cotton and silk as a concession to the climate—fabrics that were far too expensive to wear at home—using public baths, and eating local foods (although the Franks would not touch rice, which they considered simply far too exotic).

Even so, the Franks of the Kingdom of Jerusalem remained Westerners and practicing Catholics, and spoke French among themselves. And they lived out their lives in towers and in walled and castled towns under constant threat of

The battle of Ascalon in 1099 represented the culmination of the First Crusade. The Christians, led by Godfrey of Bouillon, overwhelmed the Muslims and sent them reeling back to Egypt.

Muslim attack—for to the Muslims the Franks were the infidels. Because there was a shortage of able-bodied Christian knights, international orders of knights came into being, including the Knights Templars and the Knights Hospitallers. These orders held huge grants of lands and had their own fortresses all over the kingdom. Their members, financed from Western Europe, were highly autonomous—the King of Jerusalem could not command their allegiance, for instance—and were fierce religious zealots, especially trained to kill Muslims. Their Islamic counterparts, the Assassins, waged an unrelenting war against them.

Such was the kingdom inherited by the thirteen-year-old King Baldwin IV in 1174, only a few short years after it was discovered that he was in the early stages of leprosy.

THE DISEASE TAKES HOLD

Baldwin IV was the son of King Almaric, Count of Jaffa, and Agnes of Courtenay. Almaric had succeeded his childless brother King Baldwin III, in 1163, two years after the future Baldwin IV was born. Agnes, however, had powerful enemies in Jerusalem's establishment, who did not want her to become queen. Almaric was allowed to inherit the throne only on condition that he annul his marriage, on the almost certainly false grounds that he and Agnes were related within prohibited degrees. Almaric did so, and took his son to be raised in Jerusalem, without his wife, a circumstance that would soon leave young Baldwin without a protector.

Baldwin was, however, fortunate in his father's choice of tutors for him. The historian William of Tyre, who was later to be named Archbishop of Tyre and Chancellor of the Crusader States, was one of the most learned men of his day. He was also closely observant. One day, he later noted in his chronicle of the era:

> It happened that, as [Baldwin] was playing with some boys of noble birth who were with him and they were pinching each other on the arms and hands with their nails, as children often do when playing together, the others cried out when they were hurt whereas he bore it all with great patience. When this had happened several times, and I was told about it, I thought it was a consequence of his patient disposition ... [but] finally I came to realize that half of his right arm and hand were dead, so that he could not feel the pinchings at all or even if he was bitten ... His father was told, and after the doctors had been consulted, careful attempts were made to help him with poultices, ointments, and even charms, but all in vain.

As William of Tyre and King Almaric knew all too well, the symptoms the nine-year-old Baldwin was displaying were the classic signs of the earliest stages of one of the most dreaded diseases in the world: leprosy.

AN AGE-OLD PLAGUE

At the time of King Baldwin's diagnosis, leprosy had been present in the eastern Mediterranean for at least a millennium. It was generally thought that the disease, or any other disfiguring skin disease for that matter, was a mark of God upon sinners. Lepers in all societies—Christian, Jewish, or Muslim—were isolated in special hospitals (leprosaria) or reduced to beggary. The disease was thought to be far more contagious than it actually is: although leprosy is passed from person to person by respiratory drops, one has to be in close contact with a leper for a long time to have any chance of catching the disease. In medieval times, leprosy was also thought to be passed by sexual contact and lepers were assumed to be wildly promiscuous. One of the urban myths of the time told of bands of lepers roaming the countryside, seeking to rape young women wherever they could find them.

It's not known how Baldwin became ill with leprosy. No close relatives had the disease, but obviously someone with leprosy—possibly a wet nurse or servant who then left or died before her or his symptoms emerged—spent a great deal of time with him. However he contracted it, Baldwin developed lepromatous leprosy, the worst form of the disease. It proceeds in stages, beginning with the loss of sensation at the nerve endings, which causes people to lose the automatic withdrawal mechanisms that protect them against hot or sharp objects; burns or other wounds then become infected and gradually the bones in the hands and feet are eroded, often leading to amputation. The leprosy bacilli also enter the mucous lining of the nose, eating away at it, and eventually the nose itself collapses. In the final stages, the nerve endings of the face are affected, causing a person to lose the blinking reflex of the eye, which in turn leads to dryness, ulceration, and, eventually, blindness.

All this was well known to William of Tyre and King Almaric, and it was equally well known that there was no cure. Despite this, like any desperate father, King Almaric did his best. He called in the finest physician in the land, an Arab Christian named Abu Sulayman Dawud, who prescribed ointments of quicksilver mixed with herbs and fats, as well as enemas and bloodletting. Nothing worked. And although the nine-year-old heir to the throne displayed no outward symptoms as yet, aside from numbness in one arm, he soon would.

To make matters worse, the kingdom was facing a challenge from its most dangerous enemy in its sixty-year existence: Salah Ad-din Yusuf Ibn Ayyub, otherwise known as Saladin, possibly the greatest warrior of the age. The Kingdom of Jerusalem, despite constant attacks on its borders, had long benefited from the fact that its enemies were not united. To the southwest was Egypt, to the north and east Syria; these countries, despite being Muslim, were ruled by factions who warred with each other almost constantly—until Saladin came along.

Born into a Kurdish family in Tikrit, Saladin was educated in Damascus and fought in the Syrian campaigns against Egypt under King Nureddin. Nureddin named him Vizier of Egypt in 1169; while paying lip service to his role as Nureddin's vassal, Saladin evaded a summons from the latter to march with his forces against the Crusader castles at Kerak and Montréal, almost certainly because he wished to keep

THE ASSASSINS

The Assassins are one of those mythical groups that actually live up to their billing. They were a Shiite sect who followed the teachings of a grand master, or imam, who lived in a castle in Persia. They were essentially the Middle Eastern terrorists of the mid-twelfth century. They wanted everyone to follow the imam and attempted to bring this about by assassinating key religious and secular leaders in the Islamic world, which, they hoped, would foment chaos and revolution.

Although this goal was never achieved, they were extremely good at what they did. Their enemies coined the name "assassin," deriving it from the Arabic word for hashish, because it was believed that the imam kept them hopped up on dope (although the kind of careful planning and stealth that goes into achieving a successful assassination makes this unlikely). They were so powerful that Saladin, after several attempts on his life that nearly succeeded, finally paid them off to leave him alone.

The only group that would take them on was the Knights Templars, who were as fanatical about Christ as the Assassins were about their imam. One chronicler of the time writes: "[The Assassins] knew it was a useless act ... to kill a Master of the Temple, because they would soon appoint another one, who would strive more fiercely to avenge the death of his predecessor."

the Crusader States as a buffer between Egypt and Syria. Nureddin was considering sending an army to oust Saladin from Egypt when he died, in 1174. At which point Saladin marched on Damascus and conquered Syria. Only then did he turn his eyes fully on the Crusader States, beginning a bloody war that would end only after the battle of Hattin in 1187.

QUIET DIGNITY In 1174, returning from a campaign against the Muslims, the thirty-nine-year-old King Almaric died unexpectedly of a fever, leaving his thirteen-year-old son as heir to the throne. Because the age of majority in the kingdom was fifteen, Raymond III of Tripoli was named as regent until such time as Baldwin was able to ascend the throne. But something extraordinary happened here. Instead of extending the regency because of Baldwin's illness, as might have been expected, the Franks went ahead with the coronation when Baldwin

Salah Ad-din Yusuf Ibn Ayyub, more commonly known as Saladin (1138–93), was one of the most ferocious champions of Islam and an extraordinary political and military leader.

reached the required age, in 1176. Why did the court allow him to become king at this most important time, as Saladin moved to invade? And why had he not been isolated when, by this time, although his symptoms were only starting to advance, it was known throughout the kingdom, and beyond, that he suffered from leprosy? The Muslims themselves were surprised. "In spite of [Baldwin's] illness, the Franks were loyal to him, they gave him every encouragement," wrote a Muslim scholar. "They were anxious to keep him in office, but they paid no attention to his leprosy." Why was this?

One reason is that Baldwin seems to have been an extraordinary young man. William of Tyre called him "a good-looking child," a boy "full of hope," who became "more skilled than men who were older than himself in controlling horses and riding them at a gallop." Tyre described how Baldwin tenaciously learned to ride a horse using only his knees, so that he could carry his sword in his left hand, his right already being unable to hold anything.

Baldwin also impressed people by his quiet dignity and courage. It was not just his skills at martial arts that were so amazing, but his equally important ability to make compromises and negotiate between bickering factions in his kingdom. In this he had the help of his mother, Agnes, who had returned to the court. Baldwin had maintained good relations with her, and now that Almaric was dead she grew in influence over her son. Almost certainly with help from Agnes, Baldwin chose the advisers who would help him rule—men like Prince Reginald of Châtillon, who felt that peace with Saladin was impossible.

Herein lies one of the controversies surrounding the reign of King Baldwin IV. For a long time, many historians believed that Baldwin had been unable to rule because of his illness, and that his advisers had simply taken over the kingdom and thrown the Christians into an unwise war against Saladin and his legions. But recent research has shown that the young king, despite his illness, was a capable leader who not only managed to win the support of the rival and often antagonistic orders of Christian knights, but also realized one critical thing: that Saladin could not be appeased, that he was a menace who would have to be faced—at once.

There is another, fascinating explanation for why Baldwin was permitted to stay on as king: Baldwin had remained chaste. Lepers were seen as wildly lecherous; and second only to lepers in their lustfulness were kings. For a leper who was also a king to remain chaste was therefore a sign of extreme favor from God—and celestial favor appeared to have only increased as Baldwin began to beat Saladin in battle after battle.

THE BATTLE OF MONT GISARD

In November of 1177, Saladin launched an invasion of Jerusalem with thirty thousand of his fierce Muslim warriors. Times in the city were so dark that a terrified population took refuge wherever they could find it, often in caves and cellars, awaiting the worst. Baldwin and Prince Reginald set out to attack Saladin with only five hundred knights and a few thousand infantry, all that could be mustered at short notice. Arriving at Ascalon, on the east coast of the Mediterranean just north of Gaza, they

Overleaf: While this nineteenth-century painting of the battle of Mont Gisard shows Baldwin being carried on a litter, in reality he managed to continue fighting on horseback until at least 1182.

sallied forth to meet their foe, but, realizing the futility of attempting to attack such overwhelming forces, retreated back into the city. Saladin bypassed Ascalon and headed directly for Jerusalem, his army plundering and looting as it went, as well as capturing any knights who had set out to try to join Baldwin.

But the sultan made a critical mistake. Assuming that Baldwin's army was far too small to harm him, he failed to leave a detachment behind to block the king in Ascalon. While Saladin advanced on Jerusalem, Baldwin, Prince Reginald, and their men joined forces with about eighty Knights Templars who had come from Gaza. Together, they surprised Saladin's army not far from Jerusalem, at a small hill called Mont Gisard. Many of Saladin's men were out raiding the countryside when the Franks, under the direct command of Prince Reginald, attacked. The result was complete defeat for Saladin. His army was scattered, one of his great-nephews was killed, and he himself was nearly slain by Frankish knights. When darkness fell, the Muslims were unable to reorganize themselves. Meanwhile, the Franks hunted down, isolated, and killed the raiding parties of Egyptian troops which had earlier been sent out. As Saladin fled back to Egypt, he was harassed on his flanks by Bedouin tribes who had heard of his defeat; by the time he arrived home, only a tenth of his army survived.

Mont Gisard was a great victory for the Franks. Just as things had looked darkest, it seemed almost as if there had been divine intervention on behalf of the Christians. The Franks and the young leper king certainly thought so. A legend sprang up that St. George had been seen on the field of battle, and the Franks built a monastery on the site. Just as impressive was the fact that King Baldwin had ridden into battle at the head of his men, despite the fact that, if he had been unhorsed, he would have been unable to get back on his steed. The Kingdom of Jerusalem desperately needed heroic and inspirational leadership at this time and King Baldwin, all of sixteen years old, had provided it.

A BRIEF RESPITE
The battle of Mont Gisard provided Jerusalem with a year or so of relative peace, the first in a long time, while Saladin regrouped. Baldwin was now revered for his great victory, but his symptoms were growing worse. William of Tyre wrote: "[The leprosy] grew more serious every day, specially injuring his hands and feet and his face, so that subjects were distressed whenever they looked at him." It is not known just how Baldwin interacted with those close to him or what precautions would have been taken to prevent the spread of the disease, but he was certainly concerned enough about the progression of his illness to take steps to preserve the future of the kingdom.

Baldwin arranged for his sister Sibylla to marry Guy of Lusignan, with a view to having Guy take over as regent when he, Baldwin, became completely incapacitated. He explained his actions in a letter he sent to King Louis VII of France—which is one of only a few documents we have in Baldwin's voice—saying "it is not fitting that a hand so weak as mine should hold power when fear of Arab aggression daily presses upon the Holy City."

Unfortunately, many of the barons of the Kingdom of Jerusalem were hostile to Guy, whom they saw as an opportunist. So, to avoid dissension and possible civil war, Baldwin continued to reign. In the spring of 1179, he led a small party of raiders into the forest of Banias to steal the cattle Saladin's men had set out to graze there, and was attacked by forces under Saladin's nephew. Baldwin's horse started and the king was very nearly killed before being rescued by his brave constable, Humphrey of Toron, who himself was mortally wounded.

A short while later, Saladin sent forces to pillage the Christian lands near Sidon, and Baldwin rode out to meet them. During the battle that followed he was unhorsed and was unable to get back up on his steed. A Frankish knight had to carry him from the field on his back.

THE SECOND CAMPAIGN OF THE LEPER KING

By late summer, Saladin was ready for a resumption of full-scale warfare. He marched his army against the supposedly impregnable Christian fortress Le Chastellet, quickly breached its walls, and forced its defenders to surrender. He then razed the fortress to the ground and poisoned its wells by throwing Christian bodies into them. After this, Baldwin arranged for a two-year truce with Saladin, which both sides violated. Reginald of Châtillon raided Saladin's communication lines between Syria and Egypt, not only pillaging supplies but capturing Islamic couriers carrying information on Saladin's plans. For their part, the Muslims seized a vessel full of Christians bound for the Holy Land, imprisoning over sixteen hundred passengers.

In July of 1182, Saladin was poised once again to invade Jerusalem. He began by laying siege to a castle in southern Galilee. Baldwin went to intercept him and a battle ensued on July 15, near the town of Le Forbelet. It was a chaotic, bitter fight in a sun so hot that many on the field died of sunstroke. No one knows how many troops Saladin had, but the Christians, with seven hundred knights, were outnumbered once again. Nonetheless, they managed to rout Saladin's forces and send them back across the Jordan. Baldwin was present on the field, despite his illness and the fierce heat, directing his troops. He then set off on a remarkable foray, riding over two hundred miles to attack the Muslim fortress of al-Habis Jaldak, successfully laying siege to it, and forcing its inhabitants to surrender.

All the while, Baldwin was seen not only as a unifying force in his kingdom, but as an almost Christlike figure, one who by his suffering had earned the right to lead his people. Yet it was apparent that, possibly due to the strain of this latest campaign, the king's illness had worsened, as William of Tyre recorded:

> The leprosy … became much worse than usual. He had lost his sight and the extremities of his body became completely diseased and damaged, so that he was unable to use his hands or feet. [Yet] although his body was weak and powerless, he was strong in spirit, and made superhuman effort to disguise his illness and shoulder the burdens of kingship.

ERADICATING LEPROSY

Although leprosy has been around for thousands and thousands of years, it was only in 1873 that the Norwegian scientist Gerhard Hansen discovered *Mycobacterium leprae*, the bacillus that causes the disease. And it wasn't until 1940 that an effective cure was developed using the drug dapsone and its derivatives. Even then, leprosy—also known as Hansen's disease—quickly became drug-resistant, and now must be treated with a cocktail of three or four different medicines.

Today, the disease is most common in tropical and subtropical countries, in particular Brazil, India, Madagascar, Mozambique, and Myanmar. Although leprosaria still exist (the last one in the United States closed in 1999), it is now understood that leprosy is not as virulently contagious as it was once thought to be, and so patients are no longer forcibly confined.

While leprosy has not disappeared, the World Health Organization says that, as of 2005, there was less than one case for every ten thousand people, bringing the disease to a level of near extinction.

In 1183, Baldwin, now twenty-two years old, officially named Guy of Lusignan as regent. Guy did not prove to be a successful leader. In a campaign against Saladin, he maneuvered his army so as not to meet his enemy, and eventually Saladin withdrew to Damascus. Some historians have written that this was a successful stratagem for conserving Guy's much smaller forces, but it was not exactly the kind of campaign that might inspire a kingdom. Worse was yet to come.

Baldwin's half sister Isabella, aged twelve, was to be betrothed that autumn in a grand wedding feast at the fortress of Kerak. Preparations had been going on all year for the celebration, and naturally Saladin had heard about it. So when the wedding guests showed up, so did Saladin—with a large army and eight mangonels, or siege catapults.

At first, chivalry prevailed. Food was sent out to Saladin during the wedding feast, and he instructed his engineers not to aim his mangonels at the tower where the bride and groom were staying—which may have been less out of courtesy than from not wanting to hurt two prime hostages who were worth, almost literally, a king's ransom. But Guy, who was a guest at the wedding, refused to sally forth to meet Saladin. When he heard of this, Baldwin, then in Jerusalem, deposed Guy as acting king, then accompanied a Christian army to relieve the siege of Kerak. By this time, he was too ill to ride, and had to be carried in a litter strung between two horses. Nevertheless, his arrival caused Saladin to break off his siege, and Baldwin, king once more, was able to enter Kerak at the head of a triumphant army.

BALDWIN'S LEGACY

Two years later, by late 1184, it was evident that King Baldwin IV, incapacitated by leprosy and stricken with numerous fevers resulting from opportunistic infections, was dying. He arranged for his succession by naming his five-year-old nephew, also called Baldwin, as heir to the throne, and his own former regent, Raymond of Tripoli, as his nephew's regent. It is an example of Baldwin's strength of will and his utter devotion to duty that, to make sure all might see what he wished, he had his young nephew anointed at a crown-wearing ceremony at the Church of the Holy Sepulcher. Then, ready to die, the king summoned his lords to his bedside so that they could pay their respects. He passed away sometime in mid-May, 1185, a few months shy of his twenty-fourth birthday, and was buried in a cemetery near Mount Calvary.

The Kingdom of Jerusalem would not survive long after his death. His young nephew, King Baldwin V, died in 1186, of an unknown illness (although there was speculation at the time that Raymond of Tripoli had had him poisoned). In a power play, his sister Sibylla and her husband Guy took over the throne from Raymond of Tripoli. This left the kingdom deeply divided between their forces and those of Raymond. Saladin, never one to ignore an opportunity, took advantage of the situation and invaded again. This time, in July of 1187, he inflicted a mortal blow against the Christians at the battle of Hattin. King Guy was captured and held for ransom. The Muslim troops also caught Prince Reginald of Châtillon, who was personally executed by Saladin. Raymond of Tripoli survived the battle but died the following September

THE EVIL PRINCE AND THE HONORABLE SULTAN

It has come down in history that Prince Reginald, King Baldwin IV's chief general and adviser, was a brutal, grasping robber baron who provoked the great Saladin into destroying the Crusader States by continually raiding Muslim caravans from Egypt to Syria. Saladin, on the other hand, is portrayed as an honorable man, forced to destroy the Crusaders because of the actions of Reginald and others like him. Like much in history, there is a little truth here, but also much exaggeration.

Reginald was from a noble French family who came to the Holy Land after joining the Second Crusade, in 1147. In 1160, he was captured by Syrian Muslims during a battle and spent ten years in a prison in Aleppo; after finally being ransomed, he married well, became lord of the great castles at Kerak and Montréal, and vengefully waged war against Muslim caravans, even in times of

truce. He was known for treating prisoners savagely. However, modern historians have speculated that far from being a rogue commander motivated by a hatred of all things Muslim, Reginald was the knight most feared by Saladin, and that this was one reason why Saladin personally beheaded him after capturing him during the battle of Hattin. Like Baldwin, Reginald, although in his own way a racist and autocratic man, understood that the only war possible against Saladin was total war.

Many now think that Saladin's well-documented courtesy to the Crusaders—which extended to providing Richard the Lionheart with aid and succor when the Christian king was suffering in the desert—disguised a steely determination to banish the Christians from his holy lands, and that his jihad would have taken place with or without Reginald of Châtillon.

of illness, dogged by probably unfair accusations that he had abandoned King Guy on the field. Saladin ordered that every captured member of the Knights Templars be executed in a particularly brutal way: they were given to civilians who were encouraged to hack the men to death with swords and knives.

The city of Jerusalem fell to Saladin toward the end of 1187; in fact, the sultan overran most of the kingdom. The Third Crusade under Richard the Lionheart managed to recapture some lost ground, most notably the city of Acre, and in much diminished form the Kingdom of Jerusalem hung on for another hundred years, until Acre was captured by Sultan Khalil in 1291.

King Baldwin IV is known to us as the Leper King, but his disease was a disguise, a mask, if you will. It keeps us from seeing who he really was: one of the finest and most able leaders in history. Despite having a disease that should have turned him into a pariah, he became the beloved leader of a nation. Not only was he a brave military commander, but he seems to have understood something all great leaders of countries at war understand: that it is the spirit that leads, as much as the flesh. And—like Winston Churchill or George Washington or Nelson Mandela—King Baldwin IV was a living symbol of courage for an entire people.

SUBOTAI
THE VALIANT: GENGHIS KHAN'S GREATEST STRATEGIST

N THE BITTER EARLY SPRING OF 1203, A MONGOLIAN GENERAL NAMED Temujin led a ragtag band of officers and men through a remote forest to a muddy lake named Baljuna. Temujin's small army was retreating after a terrible battle at a place called the Red Willows, where Temujin had clashed with the forces of his rival, Jamuka. Temujin had started the battle with twenty thousand men. Now only 2,500 remained.

In a warrior society that esteemed victory at arms above all else, it was accepted as customary that the followers of a defeated general would abandon him. But gathered around Temujin that harsh spring day on the shore of Lake Baljuna was a small cadre of men who refused to leave him. So moved was their leader that he scooped a cup of dirty water from the lake, shared it with his lieutenants, and swore that in the future great glory and wealth would be theirs.

Less than a year later, Temujin swept back against Jamuka with howling vengeance, destroying his forces and capturing and executing his rival. The men and boys of Jamuka's clan were subjected to "measuring by the linchpin"—that is, they were passed in front of the wheel of a wagon, and all those whose heads rose above the linchpin were immediately beheaded. The women and small children were assimilated into Temujin's tribe. In effect, Jamuka's tribe ceased to exist.

Soon, after annihilating his rivals and unifying the disparate clans of an entire country, Temujin would be known as Genghis Khan, the "Great Lord," the man before whom the known world would very shortly tremble. Standing right by his side would be one of the officers who had refused to leave him at Baljuna, a courageous and forceful young man known to his fellow Mongols as Subotai the Unfailing, to his tory as Subotai the Valiant, and to his enemies as one of Genghis Khan's dreaded "Dogs of War." Subotai would become Genghis Khan's greatest *orlok*, or field marshal, and lead campaigns against the Chinese, the Muslims of Eastern Europe, the Russians, and, after the death of the Great Khan, Europe itself.

Although overshadowed by Genghis Khan, Subotai has been compared by modern historians to Napoleon, Hannibal, and Alexander the Great. Napoleon fought in ten campaigns and thirty battles over sixteen years, but in the end lost his major conflicts. Not so Subotai. By the time of his death, according to British historian Sir Basil Liddell Hart, he had conquered thirty-two nations and won sixty-five pitched battles. Yet for centuries, Subotai was virtually unknown, his battle tactics ignored by almost all military academies. Today, however, his strategies, including his lightning strikes and his use of intelligence and psychology, are studied in many military schools. Furthermore, a direct line can be drawn between Subotai's tactical and strategic genius and standard modern theories of how to wage a land war.

As much as we might admire Subotai's skill as a tactician and strategist, those who opposed him felt another emotion: sheer primal terror. *The Secret History of the Mongols*—an extraordinary document written in the thirteenth century that is the *Iliad* of Mongol culture—depicts a fearful general asking, "Who are these people who charge us like wolves pursuing sheep?" He receives the following reply:

> They are the Four Dogs of Temujin. They have
> foreheads of brass, their jaws are like scissors,
> their tongues like piercing awls, their heads are
> iron, their whipping tails swords … In the day of
> battle, they devour enemy flesh. Behold, they are
> now unleashed, and they slobber at the mouth with glee.
> These four dogs are Jebe, and Kublai, Jelme, and Subotai.

By the time Genghis Khan died in 1227, the Mongol Empire stretched from Siberia to Central Asia, from the Pacific Ocean to the doorstep of Europe, forming the world's largest empire.

SUBOTAI'S APPRENTICESHIP
One proof in support of the contention of some historians that the Mongol Empire was a meritocracy was that Subotai was not even a Mongol. Rather, he was a member of the Uriangkhai tribe, the so-called Reindeer People, who lived along the shores of Lake Baikal. While the nomadic clans of the steppe Mongols moved from pasturage to pasturage with their horse and cattle herds, the Uriangkhai were forest hunters who dwelled in mud and wood huts, skated across the frozen expanse of Baikal with sharpened bones attached to their shoes, and tended to specialize as metalsmiths. Subotai's father, indeed, was a blacksmith, and a widower with two sons: Jelme, the eldest, and Subotai, born in 1175. The Uriangkhai traded furs with the steppe Mongols, and their metalsmiths often set up shop in the nomads' seasonal camps. This was probably how Subotai's father met the young Temujin.

Born in 1162, the son of a tribal chief, Temujin was introduced to violent clan rivalry at an early age, when his father was poisoned by enemies and he inherited feuds with several Mongol clans. At the age of nine, he became an outcast, forced from the steppes to the harsh upper regions of the Onon River, where he, his five brothers and his mother ate roots and berries and small creatures like dormice just to stay alive. As he grew older, his father's old rivals sought to kill him; at one point, he was captured and nearly executed, but he managed to escape by crushing the skull of his guard with the wooden collar that had been yoked around his neck. In 1188, when he was sixteen years old, Temujin mounted a campaign to crush his enemies. He was aided not only by other clans who swore him fealty, but by Jelme and Subotai, who

had been given to Temujin as servants by their father. Despite starting from this humble position, both rose within a few years to become Temujin's top lieutenants and "dogs of war," Jelme assuming command of Temujin's bodyguards. Since Subotai and Jelme were Uriangkhai, they did not initially know the tricks of the Mongol trade: how to spend days at a time on horseback, to whistle herds of ponies along after them as if they were dogs, to distinguish man from animal on the steppes at a great distance—often a lifesaver. The fact that they were placed in such positions of trust shows that Temujin, when it came to soldiering, valued ability over blood ties.

By 1206, Temujin had conquered all the tribes of Central Asia: the Naimans to the west, the Merkits to the north, the Tatars to the east. It was in these tribal

This medieval manuscript shows a battle between Mongol armies in the thirteenth century. Before Genghis Khan could conquer the world, he first had to bring rival Mongol clans into line.

AN EPIC HISTORY

Although not well known in the West, *The Secret History of the Mongols* is a truly astonishing document. Part *Iliad*, part factual history, it was probably written a few decades after the death of Genghis Khan in 1227. The original text was in the Uighur script that the Mongols had borrowed from the Turks; the only copies that now survive, however, are Chinese transliterations found in the archives of the Ming dynasty. No other nomadic people has ever created an epic poem of this nature. Blending fact and fiction, it describes the Mongol world in rich detail, starting well before Genghis Khan's conquest, with the creation myths of the tribes: "At the beginning there was a blue-grey wolf, born with His Destiny ordained by Heaven Above. His wife was a fallow doe." Without *The Secret History*, we would know little, if anything, about the early Mongol wanderings and Genghis Khan's struggle for power.

conflicts that Subotai gained valuable military experience. In one battle against the Merkits he traveled alone to the enemy camp, where he pretended that he was a traitor to Temujin's cause and convinced the Merkits to let down their guard, at which point Temujin struck. In 1205, Subotai was given his first solo command, assigned to track down the surviving Merkit princes and their men and destroy them. Subotai dispatched his task brilliantly, utterly destroying his enemy.

In May of 1206, all the Mongol clans gathered at the head of the Onon River, and proclaimed Temujin the Great Khan, or "Great Ruler." He immediately proclaimed the "four dogs" *orloks* and set about building a national army that would become the most efficient killing machine of its time. The army's smallest unit was comprised of ten men and called an *arban*. Ten *arbans* made a squadron called a *djaghoun*, ten *djaghouns* became a *mingan* of one thousand troops. And ten *mingans* became the largest Mongol combat unit, the *touman* of ten thousand men. Soldiers did not move back and forth between units, but spent all their time with the comrades of a single *argan*, thus fostering extreme esprit de corps.

The army was really a cavalry, made up almost entirely of horsemen. It was capable of traveling sixty miles or more in a day, and was superbly disciplined—necessarily so, since the Mongols were almost always outnumbered and operating in enemy territory. The soldiers lived off the land they passed through and whatever they could catch. The standard drink of a Mongol warrior was *kumis*, an alcoholic beverage made from fermented mare's milk and blood. Mongols packed meat under their saddles, where it was rendered tender by the heat of the horse's body and the movement of the animal. A Mongol warrior, still in the saddle, would simply reach under with his knife and tear off a strip, chewing as he rode. It was widely known that Mongols would eat anything: lice, rats, even animal afterbirths. One habit that made foreign chroniclers retch was the Mongol practice of consuming the raw intestines of animals they had killed, after squeezing out the fecal matter, like sausage from its casing.

A GLORIOUS SLAUGHTER
Genghis Khan initiated a number of improvements in the newly united Mongolian Empire: women could no longer be kidnapped or sold into marriage, for instance; lost property was always to be returned; records were now kept; and the position of chief law magistrate created. But Genghis Khan was first and foremost a warrior, as were Subotai and all the khan's men. War was what they did best, and Genghis Khan knew that without a campaign to wage, the Mongols might easily dissolve into quarreling clans.

The khan's first target was northern China, then ruled by the Jin dynasty (the south was ruled by the Song). It didn't seem to matter to him that the Jin population was far greater than that of the Mongols or that the country was filled with city fortresses bristling with armed men. In 1210, he gathered his commanders in preparation for an invasion. Subotai, now in his mid-thirties, was given an extraordinarily important task: to feign an attack on the Great Wall, so that the Jin would think that the main Mongol thrust was coming in that direction. Subotai did this to perfection.

A stone tortoise marks the site of Karakorum, Genghis Khan's capital, which was destroyed by the Chinese in 1388. Nearby are the walls of the sixteenth-century monastery of Erdeni Dzu.

First, he and his army crossed the Gobi Desert—in early spring, when there was sufficient food and water for the horses. Ahead of them was the Great Wall and, to the south of it, on the site of present-day Beijing, was Zhongdu, the capital city. When at last the Jin became aware of Subotai and his thirty thousand cavalry, they sent troops to strengthen the wall against his expected attack. And attack he did, drawing the Jin's full attention to the north, while Genghis Khan and the rest of his troops—some ninety thousand strong—attacked from the west.

Too late, the Chinese commanders realized the trick, and deployed to meet Genghis's troops in a set-piece battle on an open plain near the Shanxi Mountains. The Jin army outnumbered Genghis's men, and fought fiercely, so that the battle swayed back and forth for half a day. Then, Subotai and his three *toumans* appeared and charged into the Chinese flanks. Incredibly, after their feint against the Great Wall, they had disappeared from view, raced to catch up with Genghis's army and now pounced on the Jin army, which was surrounded and destroyed.

What then befell Zhongdu was, in the words of *The Secret History*, "a glorious slaughter." Palaces were razed and most of the citizens killed. Travelers to the city a year later found a ghastly memorial: a huge mound of horse bones and human skeletons. While not alone in their use of terror in the medieval world, the Mongols made it an art form.

Although Zhongdu had fallen, the war against the Jin would drag on for years, as the Chinese simply retreated from the Mongols into their enormous territory. It was not until 1234, after the Mongols captured the new Jin capital city of Kaifeng, that the Jin dynasty capitulated. Subotai would be responsible for the fall of that city, but first he had another role to play in history: the bloody conquest of a Muslim empire.

THE CONQUEST OF KHWAREZM

By 1217, Subotai and Jebe, a former rival of Temujin's who had surrendered to him and was now one of his most faithful "dogs," were the two preeminent leaders of the Mongol forces. In that year, the Great Khan's eyes were fixed to the south and west, on the Muslim state of Khwarezm, governed by Shah Ala ad-Din Muhammad. Because of Mongol conquests there were no buffer states between the empire of the khan and the state of Khwarezm, a fact of which both Genghis Khan and Shah Ala were acutely aware. Not widely known today, Khwarezm was actually a vast holding encompassing parts of Persia and Afghanistan to the south, Transoxania and Samarkand to the north, and the eastern shore of the Caspian Sea in the west. The shah's forces numbered perhaps four hundred thousand, many times those of Genghis Khan.

At first, peace overtures were made by the khan, who sent a caravan of merchants to trade with the shah. But the latter, suspecting the merchants were in reality spies, had the entire group murdered. This affront made Genghis Khan furious and he decided to wreak his revenge on Khwarezm. Raising an army of some two hundred thousand men, the Great Khan marched toward Khwarezm, with Subotai as his field commander. The only approach to the country was through the Zungarian Gate, the so-called Gate of the Winds, a high plateau where the Mongols would be spotted coming for miles. Once inside the country, Subotai would have to contend with heavily fortified cities and miles of protective walls.

Subotai solved these problems in an extraordinary way. First, in the midwinter of 1218, he sent Jebe and thirty thousand men through an obscure pass the Mongols had discovered between the Pamir and Tian Shan mountains. Thousands froze to death, horses died standing up, men began to eat their dead comrades, but three months later, Jebe and the remnants of his army made it through the pass. The shah found out and immediately engaged the weakened Jebe with an army of fifty thousand men. Even so, Jebe nearly beat him before disengaging. Furthermore, the shah was almost murdered by one of the Mongol's special assassination units—akin to today's SAS or Delta Force units—whose job it was to track down and assassinate enemy generals in the midst of battle. Sometimes these hunters traveled a hundred miles to find their retreating quarry, for another rule of Subotai's was never to let an escaping enemy live to fight another day.

Using Jebe's force as a diversion, Subotai then marched around the shah's defenses, going through the four-hundred-mile-wide Kyzylkum Desert, which the shah thought impassible, and coming upon Samarkand from the west. It was a move worthy of a mechanized division during a battle in Africa in World War II—except that it was performed on horses, and in a week.

Completely surprised, the shah began to retreat and never stopped. In the next two years, the Mongols under Subotai and Jebe advanced rapidly. Their success was due in part to their innovative use of massive siege engines—including catapults that shot giant boulders, huge crossbows mounted on vertical stands that shot tree trunks, and even tubes that fired gunpowder. In another example of how quickly the Mongols learned from their opponents, they had adopted Jin siege

THE GREAT HUNT

One of the most extraordinary features of Mongol society was the annual winter hunt instituted by Genghis Khan. Lasting as long as three months, it was intended to train soldiers for battle and provide food for the entire army.

Spread out in a line sometimes a hundred miles long, the soldiers moved across the steppe, driving all animals before them. Gradually the ends of the line closed until a circle was formed, trapping all game within. At a signal from Genghis Khan himself, the soldiers dismounted and attacked the animals, locking bears, tigers, and wolves in mortal combat. After facing a charging bear with only a lance and a knife, so the thinking went, a soldier would have little fear of human opponents.

Opposite: Part of a fourteenth-century Persian manuscript, this illustration shows Temujin having himself proclaimed Genghis Khan, or "Great Ruler."

technology—even employing ten thousand Jin siege engineers—and made it portable. They became the first army in the world to use such weapons in attacks against troop positions, rather than just in static siege situations.

In their attacks, the Mongols destroyed city after city, killing millions of people. The war against the shah's empire was, some historians claim, a genocide: nearly four-fifths of the population of the empire was killed or sent into slavery. In certain cities that had resisted the Great Khan, even the dogs and cats were slaughtered. As they had done in their first campaign against the Jin, the Mongols used the art of terror to instill fear in their opponents. They were saying, in effect: if you resist, you and everything you love will be turned to dust; if you surrender, we will give you your lives. It was a deliberate strategy, and could even be compared to President Truman's thinking when he dropped the first atomic bomb on Hiroshima, and hoped that Japan would then surrender.

Finally, only the shah and his small group of bodyguards were left. Under direct orders from the khan, Subotai and Jebe, with thirty thousand men, followed them all the way west to the Caspian Sea. The shah escaped to a small island, but was isolated there and died alone, his empire destroyed. The Mongols were always determined that enemy leaders should not escape to inspire their people to fight another day, and always pursued them relentlessly. Similar strategies are pursued by many special operations units today, especially in unconventional wars, such as those waged by Israel and occasionally the United States. Subotai would probably have shuddered had he seen Saddam Hussein being allowed to continue as Iraqi leader after the Americans had crushed his forces during the First Gulf War. Had a Mongol been in charge, Saddam would have lost his head forthwith.

WESTERN RECONNAISSANCE
With Khwarezm destroyed, Subotai now set his sights on much greater prizes. In February of 1221, having heard rumors of rich lands to the north and west, he, Jebe, and twenty thousand men headed off on the longest cavalry raid in history, a 5,500-mile sweep west then north into Russia, while the Great Khan returned to Mongolia. Subotai first led his forces around the southern end of the Caspian Sea, then moved north toward the Caucasus Mountains and the city of Tiflis, in Georgia. Here, he was met on the Kura Plain by thirty thousand men under the Christian king George the Brilliant.

The Mongol cavalry first rode back and forth across the front of the Georgian line, firing heavy, armor-piercing arrows that killed and wounded many. Enraged, the Georgian knights charged, at which point Subotai employed a favorite tactic: he had his troops feign a retreat. With the Georgians in pursuit, the Mongols fell back, then launched a sudden counterattack with fresh troops. This was a regular ploy of the Mongols, although not necessarily an original one (Hannibal loved to use it, too). It works especially well in cavalry battles, when passions run high and pursuit is swift.

The badly mauled Christian forces fell back to the city of Tiflis, expecting an attack which never came—for Subotai and his Mongols had retreated once again to

replenish supplies. But then, in the late fall of 1221, when no European army would be setting out to campaign, Subotai roared back toward Georgia, taking George the Brilliant completely by surprise. In the second battle of Kura Plain, George was killed and his army destroyed.

Moving north, Subotai continued his incredible march. He crossed the Caucasus during the bitter winter, started down a rocky pass to the Fergana Valley, and found an enemy army, fifty thousand strong, waiting for him. This was a coalition force of the mountain people of the region, Orthodox Christians, the remnants of the Georgian army, and the Cuman people, whose close relatives had all been slaughtered by Genghis Khan and Subotai during the Khwarezm campaign. The coalition knew how the Mongols fought and surprised Subotai, trapping him as he emerged from a narrow mountain pass. But he refused to be drawn into battle, being content to wait until he was forced to attack. In the meantime, never at a loss, he found another option. Sending secret messengers into the Cuman camp,

The Mongol attack on Liegnitz, in Poland, shown in this fourteenth-century illustration, was a critical phase in Subotai's two-pronged thrust into Eastern Europe.

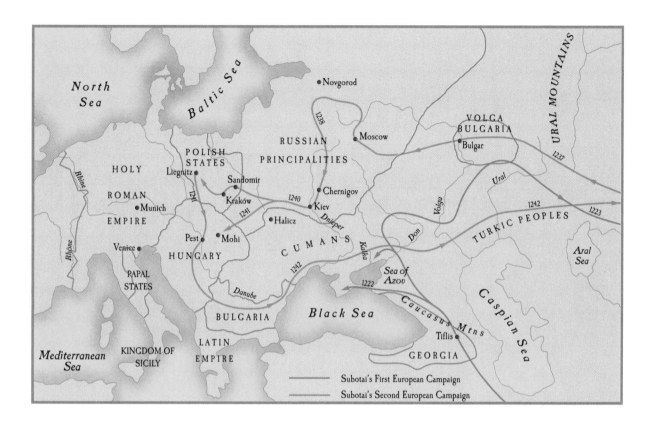

Map labels:
North Sea · Baltic Sea · Novgorod · URAL MOUNTAINS · VOLGA BULGARIA · Bulgar · 1238 · Moscow · 1237 · RUSSIAN PRINCIPALITIES · POLISH STATES · HOLY · Liegnitz · Sandomir · Chernigov · ROMAN · Kraków · 1240 · Kiev · Ural · Munich · Halicz · Dnieper · 1242 · 1223 · EMPIRE · 1241 · Volga · TURKIC PEOPLES · Rhine · Pest · Mohi · C U M A N S · Don · Aral Sea · Venice · HUNGARY · Kalka · Rhône · 1242 · Sea of Azov · 1222 · Caspian Sea · PAPAL STATES · Danube · Caucasus Mtns · BULGARIA · Black Sea · Tiflis · LATIN · Mediterranean Sea · KINGDOM OF SICILY · EMPIRE · GEORGIA

Legend:
— Subotai's First European Campaign
— Subotai's Second European Campaign

Exploiting knowledge gained during his first European foray some twenty years earlier, Subotai advanced into the heart of the continent in 1241.

Subotai bribed their leaders into abandoning the Christians. As soon as the Cumans left, Subotai and his army defeated the Christians—then marched furiously after the Cumans, caught up with them, and slaughtered them. The Mongols now headed toward Russia. As they rounded the Sea of Azov, they encountered Venetian traders—their first meeting with men from Western Europe.

Subotai invited the traders to the Mongol camp and wined and dined them. Both sides saw this as an advantageous encounter, the Venetians recognizing a potentially rich trading market, and the Mongols seeing a new source of military intelligence. Spies were widely used in Europe at the time, notably in the Holy Roman Empire, but the Mongols were the first to place a premium on intelligence gleaned by spies sent to cities they planned to attack, as much as a year in advance.

This is comparable to the "moles" of the Cold War and the sleeper spies sent into America by the Nazis before World War II. Among Subotai's staff were Chinese intelligence officers, who sketched crude maps of Hungary and Poland after conversing with the Venetians, even taking notes on the climate and crops. Before the Venetians left, they signed a secret trade agreement with Subotai, promising to send intelligence reports on the countries they visited. In return, Subotai and his men agreed to help

Venice achieve a monopoly by destroying any other nations' trading posts they happened to encounter.

In the winter of 1222, Subotai and his men crossed the Don River. Arrayed against them near here was an eighty-thousand strong army led by the Prince of Kiev. The Mongols sent an ambassador to bribe the Prince; but he didn't fall for the ruse, and had the ambassador beheaded. The two armies closed in on each other. Then, suddenly, Subotai executed a strategic retreat on a grand scale, falling back fifty miles to the east, with the Russian armies spread out over a wide front chasing him. The retreat lasted nine days; then, when Subotai reached suitable terrain near the Kalka River, he turned on his enemies. Under cover of a screen of black smoke created by huge charcoal smudge pots—a tactic, once again, which the Mongols had picked up from the Jin and which became a staple of later armies—Subotai turned and attacked. The Russians were slaughtered, the Prince of Kiev captured. For his murder of the ambassador, the prince was placed in a box and suffocated. (The Mongols did not believe in shedding royal blood in battle, and so either strangled or suffocated captured princes and kings.) After this, Subotai, Jebe, and his men headed home, although Jebe was to die of a fever along the way.

INTO THE HEART OF EUROPE
In 1227, Genghis Khan died, having bequeathed his kingdom to Ögödei, his son. Ögödei continued the Mongol expansion, occupying northern China, subjugating Korea, opening hostilities against the Song leaders of southern China, and campaigning through Persia in preparation for attacking the Muslim Middle East. Subotai was in the thick of this fighting—it was he who occupied the city of Kaifeng.

In 1236, Ögödei decided to invade Eastern Europe. Genghis Khan's grandson Batu would be nominally in charge of these forces, for the prestige his blood connection would bring, but he was considered too inexperienced to lead such a large military enterprise. Ögödei therefore turned to Subotai, who was then sixty-one years old. The Mongols assembled an army of 150,000 men, including captured Chinese engineers and Turkish mercenaries. Subotai put together intelligence reports, as well. He knew that the European powers would be divided because of the bitter conflict between the Holy Roman Empire, King Frederick II, and the papacy, and he hoped to be able to drive right through Russia and Hungary into the heart of Europe. Heading north and west, Subotai and Batu defeated the Bulgars and the Cumans, their old rivals, before pressing into central Russia. In a lightning winter attack in early 1238, they conquered and destroyed Moscow; after pausing to rest and regroup, the Mongol horde attacked and destroyed Kiev in 1240.

The Mongols were now at the gates of Europe. Rumors of their ferocity had preceded them. So awful was their reputation that the Europeans called them Tartars, inhabitants of *Tartarus*, or Hell. The chronicler Matthew of Paris wrote, in prose as purple and inaccurate as any modern propaganda: "For touching upon the cruelty and cunning of these people, there can be no infamy great enough … The Tartar chief, with his dinner guests and other cannibals, fed upon the carcasses [of their enemies] ... Virgins were raped until they died of exhaustion; then their breasts were cut off, to be kept as dainties."

The Mongols advanced westward through Hungary. Batu sent an ultimatum to King Béla IV, giving him a chance to surrender, but Béla refused, instead sending knights riding through the countryside brandishing bloody swords, a traditional Hungarian rallying symbol. In February of 1241, Batu and Subotai left their winter base in southern Russia and, crossing frozen rivers, entered Central Europe. In typical fashion, Subotai divided his army, seeking to fool his enemy. He sent a force of twenty thousand men north into Poland to quell any Polish support for the Hungarians. Then, at the head of fifty thousand men, he and Batu crossed the Carpathian Mountains into Hungary, arriving in mid-March. While the smaller Mongol force engaged and defeated the Poles at the battle of Liegnitz, King Béla left Pest with an army of seventy thousand and moved to confront the Mongols on the Plain of Mohi, near the Sajo River.

In the battle of Mohi, two differing ideologies and ways of fighting came together. The Mongol forces, highly unified, almost entirely cavalry, commanded by a firm tactician, met Western Christian forces made up of knights who responded to a feudal lord, but not necessarily to an overall commander. The knights were trained for close combat with sword and lance, the Mongols for fighting on horseback and loosing arrows at their enemy. Christian leaders, brave in the extreme, were expected to fight in the midst of their men; Mongol commanders in chief could be anywhere, though they usually occupied an elevated position from where they could view and direct the battle.

At Mohi, Subotai summoned all of his expertise, all the tactical knowledge and strategy gained through nearly a half century of warfare. The result was a battle that would have done any great commander, from Hannibal to Patton, proud. During the night of April 10, Subotai sent out thirty thousand men to secretly flank the Hungarian encampments.

On the morning of April 11, the Mongols opened up on King Béla and his men with mobile artillery fire—stone-hurling catapults, flaming tar, even Chinese firecrackers, the flashes and bangs of which panicked the Hungarians, who had never heard them. Then Subotai sent in his flankers, while attacking directly from the front himself. By 7 a.m., the Hungarians were in a rout. Pressed on every side, and bewildered as to which way to turn, they suddenly saw what appeared to be a Mongol-free avenue of escape to the west. Immediately, they began to flee.

Of course, it was another masterful trick by Subotai: a way to channel the retreating Hungarians so they could be killed more easily. This was a classic Mongol ruse, which depended on an understanding of the human psyche: give an enemy a seeming avenue of escape and they won't fight to the death. Of course, as soon as the knights got through, the Mongols closed in and the killing began in earnest. Riding down the Christians, the Mongols killed at least forty thousand men—some sources say sixty thousand. By noon, the Hungarian army had ceased to exist. Pursued by Mongol assassination units, King Béla had to flee as far as an island on the Adriatic Sea before he found safety.

And then … it ended. Just as Europe opened before the Mongols, as the first Mongol scouts were reconnoitering Vienna, news came that Ögödei had died in Asia. A new leader needed to be elected, according to the law laid down by Genghis Khan, and so the Mongols rejoined forces and headed back into Asia, never to return, but having left a legacy of terrifying nightmares in Europe's collective unconscious—indeed, for centuries to come, mothers would warn their children to watch out, or the Tartars might get them. Subotai died in 1248 at the age of seventy-three. At last tired of war and of the political maneuvering at the Mongol court, he apparently went to a distant encampment where he spent his remaining days tending his herds—and, like many another old general, simply "faded away."

It is interesting to speculate on what might have happened had Ögödei not died, for there was nothing to stop Subotai from heading straight through Western Europe with his forces. The continent was already in crisis: Frederick II had been excommunicated in his battle with Rome; Pope Celestine IV had died in November 1241 and the church remained without a leader, due to factional infighting, until June of 1243. Given that eighteen-month window of opportunity, Subotai could easily have led a takeover of Italy and Europe by Mongol forces. And the Mongols normally stayed and colonized. So today's Western culture might have been very different.

LEARNING FROM SUBOTAI
The first soldier to study the Mongol way of war was a lieutenant-general in the Russian army named Mikhail I. Ivanin. He had fought in a nineteenth-century campaign against the seminomadic Uzbeks in Central Asia, who used the same tactics as Genghis Khan's armies. In 1846, Ivanin published a book called *The Art of War of the Mongols and the Central Asian Peoples*, which subsequently became a textbook in the Russian Imperial Military Academy.

After World War I, British and French military historians recommended that there might be a lesson to be learned from the Mongols. For the most part, this line of thought was ignored, except by the Soviets, who based their strategy in World War II on the Mongol-inspired concept of "deep battle"—the tactic of conducting long-range attacks on the rear of the enemy to disrupt their supply lines and communications so that they are paralyzed when a larger force attacks from the front. The Mongols' policy of marching in smaller units that rapidly came together to strike at an enemy force was also seminal, and not just for the Soviets. Today, the U.S. Army also follows a doctrine of rapidly concentrating forces, now usually by helicopter or armored carrier, to strike as quickly as possible. And the campaigns of Subotai are today studied in military academies such as West Point.

The use of special forces units, to achieve deep penetration and swift, silent strikes, is a mainstay in armies around the world. And Subotai, who depended so deeply on good intelligence, would no doubt have been pleased to see the spy satellites and covert operations run by every sizable country on the globe. In fact, his many victories against larger forces are perfect examples of the asymmetrical warfare being waged across much of the world today.

THE MONGOL KIT
The Mongol soldier was a cavalryman—infantrymen need not apply—and their ability to move fast, to get there "fustest with the mostest," in the immortal words of Confederate cavalryman Nathan Bedford Forrest, was predicated on the speed of their hardy Mongolian ponies.

The Mongols picked up a lot from their opponents. Before their war with the Jin, Mongol armies had only chain-mail armor and probably only fire-hardened wood and bone points for arrows and lance heads. Afterward, they replaced these with metal points and the heavy cavalry began to wear metal-plate armor made for them by captured Jin armorers.

After fighting the Jin's neighbors, the Xi Xia, in 1207, Genghis Khan had his troops adopt the silk undershirt the Xi Xia wore. Some historians have compared this innovation to the introduction of the flak jacket to modern armies. When an arrow hit a silk undershirt, the twisting motion of the missile caused the silk to wrap around the arrow, driving the material into the wound and reducing the depth of penetration. The undershirt also made it easier to remove the arrow by pulling on the undershirt itself. Unfortunately, Mongol hygiene was such that the undershirt was worn until it fell off, so, while it could also have helped prevent infection, it often didn't, and may even have increased the chance of a dirty wound.

RABBAN SAUMA: THE MARCO POLO OF THE EAST

■ N THE LATTER PART OF THE THIRTEENTH CENTURY, THERE LIVED AN INTREPID traveler who journeyed vast and dangerous distances, over mountains, through deserts, and across seas, encountering unknown and exotic cultures. He left behind a manuscript which told not only of his adventures, but of a secret mission he was undertaking, a mission which, if successful, would change the balance of power in the world for centuries to come.

You can be forgiven for thinking that this man's name was Marco Polo, because Polo lived at roughly the same moment in history and also left a fascinating record of his travels. But our traveler is far less well known, partly because he journeyed, initially, as a monk and for spiritual reasons, and partly because the manuscript he wrote was lost to history for almost six hundred years. Yet his journey was, potentially at least, much more significant than that of Marco Polo, and his achievements were even more impressive.

Our traveler was Rabban Sauma. He was a Nestorian monk who lived in the Mongol realm of Kublai Khan. And he was the first Chinese-born man to traverse the known world from east to west, all the way from the capital city of Dadu (later Beijing), to Rome, Paris, and beyond.

SON OF THE FAST Rabban Sauma was born Bar Sauma—Rabban means "master" and was an honorific given Sauma later in life—of Onggud Turkic stock, in eastern China in 1225, not far from the capital. He was the son of Nestorian Christians, a sect which at the time was the ascendant Christian religion in China and Persia. From the point of view of the Roman and Byzantine Catholic churches, however, Nestorianism was a heresy. It was named after Nestorius,

Bishop of Constantinople in the fifth century, who held that in Christ there are two persons, one human and one divine, and that Mary was mother of only the "human" Christ. The Roman Catholic Church, which claims that Christ's divine and human natures are one and that Mary is Mother of God, condemned this heresy at the Council of Ephesus in 431. Thereafter, Nestorian Christians were forced to leave Roman and Byzantine centers of worship.

As a result, the Nestorians became great travelers and adventurers, who soon established themselves in areas of the Middle East and Central Asia that are today almost totally devoted to Islam. Subsequently, they spread all the way to China and Mongolia. By the time of Sauma's birth, many Mongols, especially women in elite Mongol circles, had abandoned their belief in shamans and woodland spirits and joined the Nestorian Church. One reason for the Nestorians' success was that they were prepared to adapt their practices to local cultures. They held popular festivals, incorporated animist rites into Nestorian services, even supported the Mongol practice of polygamy. Also, Nestorian priests often did double duty as doctors, ministering to their flocks physically as well as spiritually.

Bar Sauma was drawn to the religion and decided to become a Nestorian monk, which caused his mother and father great grief. He was an only child, born after his parents spent much time praying and fasting (his name means "son of the fast"), and they did not want him to leave them for a monastery and the celibate life of a monk. In his journal, Sauma quotes them as protesting: "How can it possibly be pleasing to thee for our seed and name to be blotted out?" Sauma delayed for a few years, but finally gave away all his possessions, left home, and, in 1248, joined a Nestorian monastery. But even that proved too busy for the young man, who had a meditative inclination. In 1255, he removed himself to the Fang Mountains, about thirty miles away, where he became a religious hermit famed locally for his piety and kindness, a man who desired only to spend the rest of his days in one spot, in isolated contemplation of the wonders and mystery of God.

Europe and Asia in the twelfth century, at the time of Rabban Sauma's extraordinary journey.

THE FANTASTIC PILGRIMAGE
And that is probably what would have happened, except for the arrival of a boy named Marcus. The boy was from a Nestorian Christian family in northern China, where the holy man Sauma's fame had spread. Against the advice of his family, the fifteen-year-old Marcus took a solitary two-week journey to the Fang Mountains; on finding Sauma, he asked him to be his spiritual mentor. Sauma attempted to turn down the request, but the boy had piety and single-mindedness unusual in one so young, and Sauma eventually relented. Within three years, Marcus was accepted into the community as

a monk. But it was not in his nature to remain contemplative. He began to try to convince Sauma to take a journey with him to Jerusalem so that they might see the holy places sacred to their religion. Sauma, as he recorded, tried to acquaint Marcus with the "terror of the ways and the tribulations that would beset him" on such a trip, but Marcus, who had youthful energy on his side, would not be dissuaded. By 1278, which was about the time the young Marco Polo arrived in China, he had convinced Sauma to accompany him on this fantastic pilgrimage.

Merchants had been traveling along the so-called "Silk Road" for almost two thousand years, but these eastern and western traders normally met halfway, somewhere in Central Asia, and then turned back. After the Mongol invasion of Eastern Europe, however, many Europeans found themselves wondering about these barbarous peoples and where they came from. Pope Innocent IV, whose reign lasted from 1243 to 1254, sought to establish peaceful contact by sending a priest, John of Plano Carpini, to Karakorum, the Mongol capital, to meet with the Great Khan Güyük, Genghis's grandson. This mission, which occurred in 1246, was not successful, mainly because John of Plano carried a letter to the khan urging him and all his people to convert to Christianity, something to which the Great Khan did not take kindly. He sent John back with a letter to the pope which stated that if the Christians did not submit to the Mongols, "we shall know for certain that you wish to have war."

King Louis of France tried his luck in 1253, sending a Franciscan friar named William of Rubruck to speak with the new Great Khan, Mongke, Güyük's first cousin. William was too zealous in his attempts at religious conversion and did not get far with the khan; however, he did leave behind interesting descriptions of Mongol life.

But no one, as far as we know, had yet gone all the way from east to west, which is some measure of what a truly radical idea young Marcus was proposing. To understand the epic scope of this journey, imagine walking or riding on horseback across

the United States, in a period of civil unrest, plagued by bandits, and at a time when the vast majority of people rarely traveled even twenty miles from their homes. You would need to be brave, hardy, and smart—and also in love with an idea, as Marcus was. It is intriguing that Sauma, with his naturally meditative personality, was willing, under these circumstances, to put his spiritual faith into this form of action.

THROUGH REALMS OF WAR

At this time, all of Asia, including Russia and Persia, was part of the Mongol Empire, created as a result of the conquests of Genghis Khan in the early thirteenth century. After Genghis and his son Ögödei died, the empire was divided into four khanates: the Kipchak Khanate of Russia, also known as the Golden Horde; the Il-Khanate, which controlled Persia; the Chagatai Khanate of Central Asia; and the Great Khanate, which controlled China and Mongolia and, in theory, the other khanates. In reality, since the death of Ögödei, the khanates had been warring with each other.

As a result, the Khan of the Golden Horde had decided to make an alliance with the Egyptian Mamluks, which, in turn, threatened to undermine the Mongol Empire. For if the Golden Horde, strengthened by its alliance with the Muslims, attacked the Il-Khanate in Persia, it would almost certainly be triumphant. And the Great Khan, Kublai, was too busy completing his conquest of China and constructing glorious palaces to prevent any of this happening.

The Mongols of the Il-Khanate were not the only ones threatened by the proposed alliance. The Crusader States had lost Jerusalem in the late twelfth century and barely clung to a sliver of ground in the Holy Land. A coalition of the Golden Horde and the Muslims was bound to destroy them, too.

For a journey through such territories, a journey that could take at least six months, Sauma and Marcus needed to be well provisioned. They had to have expensive camels—creatures far more suited than horses to their journey, much of which would

The expansion of the Mongol Empire led to the creation of trading routes, along which Mongol convoys like this one traveled significant distances.

49

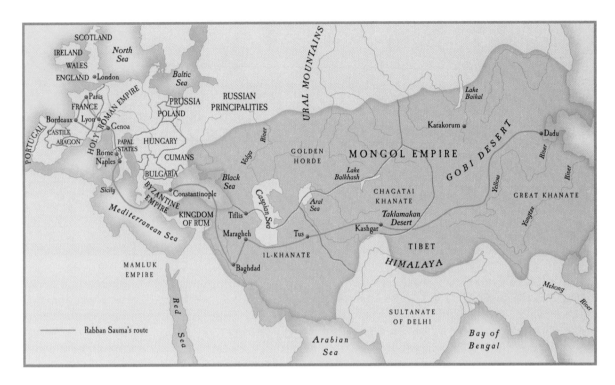

Rabban Sauma's route

Spanning much of what was then the known world, Rabban Sauma's journey constituted the first recorded crossing of Asia and Europe from east to west.

be through arid lands—as well as ample supplies and guides. Some of this was provided by the Nestorian community, but Sauma and Marcus also appealed to the Great Khan, Kublai, in Dadu, the new capital he had built on the site of Zhongdu. From him, they received funding and something equally important: letters of safe passage through the various khanates they would cross.

Interestingly, Sauma's journals do not record his dealings with Kublai, perhaps because of their secret nature; this has led to much speculation as to what service the khan wished of the two monks in return for the favor he was giving them. Some historians theorize that he was planning a military expedition against the Mamluks and wanted information, but this seems unlikely, given the fractious state of the Mongol Empire at the time. It seems more probable that the khan wanted to the two monks to act as emissaries to the Christian world, to show how tolerant the Great Khan was of all religions. He had, after all, recently sent Marco Polo's father and uncle back to Europe with a request that they bring one hundred Christians to convert the Mongols. (Instead, they brought back young Marco Polo.)

Armed with their provisions and safe-passage letters, Sauma and Marcus set out, probably in 1279. They aimed to head south and west from Dadu, following for a time the course of the Yellow River, before skirting the Taklamakan Desert, moving through the Chagatai Khanate of Central Asia and finally stopping in the Il-Khanate, at the town of Tus, a center of Nestorian Christianity.

It was a journey difficult for a modern traveler to imagine. Although the Mongols had improved some highways—even planting trees along them for shade and to make the routes visible from a distance—and established postal stations, some of the roads were little better than tracks. Sauma and Marcus would often lose their way and have to backtrack. Although they only passed along the edge of the Taklamakan Desert, a placed dreaded by travelers, they were still subjected to its heat, shifting sand dunes, and hallucinatory mirages.

They also stepped into the middle of a war. Khaidu, Kublai Khan's cousin, had broken from him and the armies of the two men had made Central Asia a charnel house. "The caravan roads and ways had been cut and grain was scarce … and many died of hunger and perished from want," Sauma wrote in his journals. Arriving at Kashgar, which had been a major trading city along the path of the Silk Road, as well as a center of Nestorian Christianity, they found it devastated.

The next stage of their journey was, if anything, even more perilous. They were heading towards Khwarezm, the former Muslim state so ruthlessly conquered by Genghis Khan in 1218 and now part of the Il-Khanate. To get there, Sauma and Marcus had to cross the high mountain ranges of modern-day Afghanistan, fighting off debilitating injury due to frostbite and altitude sickness. The mountains were so notorious for banditry that Mongol law mandated that travelers form caravans in order to fight off robbers. Even so, Sauma and Marcus traveled a landscape liberally sprinkled with the skeletons of human beings and their animals.

CHANCE MEETING IN MARAGHEH
Arriving in Khwarezm in the spring of 1280, having already traveled several thousand miles, the two monks went to the town of Maragheh, then the site of an observatory built by the Il-Khan for the renowned astronomer Nasir al-Din Tusi, and a remarkable library containing four hundred thousand volumes and a sophisticated array of astronomical instruments. At Maragheh, they were delighted to meet with the head, or patriarch, of the Nestorian Church, Mar Denha. It was an emotional meeting, each of the travelers weeping profusely as they met the holy man. Mar Denha welcomed them with open arms, noting how unusual it was for visitors to come from as far away as China—and he was even more impressed when he learned that the two monks intended to travel all the way to Jerusalem. Mar Denha invited them to visit him once they reached Baghdad, which was the center of the Nestorian Church at the time.

The two set off with renewed energy and reached Baghdad, the last major city on their way to Jerusalem. They were happy to visit Nestorian shrines in the area, but disturbed by what they heard of the Nestorians' situation in Baghdad. The Nestorians had been alienated from the city's much larger Muslim community, partly as a result of the behavior of Mar Denha. He had ordered the drowning in the Tigris of Nestorians who had converted to Islam and, in response, the Muslims had nearly assassinated him.

To make matters worse, Sauma and Marcus now heard that travel to Jerusalem was almost impossible, given the current political situation: the Golden Horde controlled the route to Jerusalem, and the Mamluks the Holy Land itself. Disillusioned, Sauma

THE LOST MANUSCRIPT OF RABBAN SAUMA

But for a fluke, it's quite possible Rabban Sauma's journeys would have come down to us only as references in the archives of the Vatican and the royal courts of France and England. Sauma left his history, which was written in Persian, in the hands of a Nestorian monk, who, after Sauma's death, translated it into Syriac, the language of the Nestorian Church. But then both the original document and the translation disappeared for almost six hundred years.

In 1887, a Nestorian Christian Turk showed an expert an ancient manuscript written in Syriac, which turned out to be the translation of Rabban Sauma's journals. Unfortunately, the translator had excised much of Sauma's writing, in the interest of focusing on the religious themes of the narrative, and the Persian original was never found.

Despite this, Rabban Sauma's journals make fascinating reading. They were translated into English by British scholar Sir Wallis Budge in 1928, and, although out of print, can be found online (at sites including the Unofficial Website of the Nestorian Church and that of Colorado State University–Pueblo).

and Marcus prepared to retrace their route to Khwarezm, and spend time meditating in a monastery there. But Mar Denha attempted to curry favor with them, as important emissaries of the Great Khan, by giving them both the title of *rabban*, or "master." The man's machinations were distasteful to Sauma and Marcus, but they accepted, not knowing what else to do.

Then, as fate would have it, Mar Denha died of a sudden illness. Impressed by the integrity of these visitors from China, the Nestorian faithful elected Marcus as their new patriarch, giving him the name Mar Yaballaha (*Mar* meaning "Your Worship," *Yaballaha* "God-given"). Mar Yaballaha was astounded by his selection, but we can surmise that with Mongols controlling the state, the Nestorians felt that having a Mongol-speaking patriarch from China would give them a real advantage.

With Marcus taking on his new duties as patriarch, their travels came to an end. Sauma settled into life in a monastery and a few years passed in the kind of quiet contemplation that suited him. However, in 1287, politics intervened once again. The new Il-Khan of Persia, Arghun, was feeling a good deal of pressure from the Golden Horde and its Mamluk allies. With the Great Khan in China too far away to help, he knew that his only hope of holding his own in Central Asia and Syria lay in an alliance with Christian Europe.

Seeking a person to lead a mission to the West, he approached Mar Yaballaha, who naturally thought of his old traveling companion. Rabban Sauma was learned, wise, fluent in Persian—which a few Italian merchants now knew, so that one could be hired as a translator—and totally trustworthy. As a Christian, even if from a heretical sect, Rabban Sauma might also be able to influence the pope and the European rulers. Mar Yaballaha thought, too, that Sauma might even succeed in bringing about a rapprochement between the Catholic and Nestorian churches (a vain hope: it was not until 1994 that the Catholic Church and the Nestorian Church signed a doctrine in which each recognized the other's doctrines). No doubt leaving his contemplative life was difficult for Sauma, but this was also an opportunity to see Rome and to visit the great cities of Europe, with their cathedrals. It could hardly be passed up.

ACROSS A TERRIBLE SEA Carrying letters to be delivered to the pope and the kings of France and England, and given thirty horses, a large sum of money, and numerous attendants, Sauma set off early in 1287. After a stop at Constantinople to pay his respects to the patriarch of the Orthodox Church, Sauma and his party boarded a ship to cross the Mediterranean to Naples. He was now making history as the first man from China ever to travel to Europe. Sauma was probably unaware of his status as the first of his countrymen to visit these lands. But he would certainly have made a bit of a sensation among those with whom he traveled.

Although he had crossed the Black Sea earlier to reach Constantinople, the Mediterranean voyage was an ordeal for him. He called it a "terrible sea," an ocean wherein "thousands had perished." During his crossing, he wrote, he saw in the middle of the sea "a mountain from which smoke ascended all the day long and in the night time fire showed itself on it. And no man is to approach the neighborhood of it because of the stench of sulfur." This was almost certainly an eruption of Mount Etna in Sicily. Sauma recorded that he passed his time on the ship delivering daily lectures on the finer points of the Nestorian faith—one way to help transcend any fear he might have been feeling.

Ever a magnet for disaster, Sauma landed in Naples in the middle of a battle between rival political factions, much of which he watched from the roof of a house. He seems not to have been too worried, possibly because he noted that these soldiers, unlike the Mongols he was familiar with, seemed not to be making war on civilians. Still, he did not tarry long. He had learned that Pope Honorius IV had died in April and that the cardinals in Rome were in the process of picking a new pope. By July, he had made his way to the Holy City, hoping to present his letters from the Il-Khan to the new Catholic leader, whoever that might be.

Unfortunately, the cardinals were taking their time—ultimately they would deliberate for eleven months, including a fiercely hot summer during which six cardinals died of heatstroke. Sauma sent word that he was an emissary of the Il-Khan, and the cardinals invited him to speak with them. He told them of his mission, and, perhaps exaggerating, claimed that the Mongols viewed the Christians with great favor and that an alliance would be an opportunity for the Christians to bring the word of God to an entire, vast nation. But the cardinals paid little heed to his appeals and appeared more interested in querying Sauma about his heretical religion. Sauma stood his ground, then told the cardinals he would return once a new pope had been elected.

In the meantime, he set off for France, arriving in late August of 1287. He was now sixty-two years old and his long journey, and chilly reception in sultry Rome, must have exhausted him, yet France held out new hope. Its ruler was the twenty-year-old King Philip the Fair, whom it was rumored, had piety, energy, and crusading fervor. The king had heard of Sauma and his party and sent troops to meet them as they crossed the French border and escort them to Paris. After allowing the cleric to rest and gain his strength, Philip summoned him and rose to greet him, treating him as an equal. Sauma then described the reasons for his journey and presented gifts Arghun had sent, which included jewels and valuable silks.

Sauma felt that the king was moved by and open to his entreaties to join with the Mongols on a crusade against Islam. But what Sauma did not know (or failed to write) is that Philip was embroiled in local difficulties, which included trying to oust the English, under Edward I, from eastern France, and a dispute with the pope over the flow of money collected by French priests to Rome.

Before leaving Paris, Sauma walked about the streets, awestruck by the cathedrals and the sheer number of people, particularly the large number of students. He wrote that there were thirty thousand of them. Modern medieval experts claim that this number is excessive—it would have been a quarter of the population of Paris—and put the figure at three to five thousand. Still, Sauma's descriptions say something about how important education was to him, especially as he went on to describe how the students learned not only scriptures, but grammar, law, rhetoric, and Aristotle's works on logic and science—a liberal arts education, in other words.

There would be one last meeting with King Philip, in which the pious king showed Rabban Sauma an object that was literally priceless: Christ's crown of thorns, which he claimed had been obtained in the Holy Land during the Crusades. Sauma does not speculate as to why it was shown to him—it may have been simply to impress a holy visitor—but he could have been excused for taking it as an indication of France's willingness to help the Mongols reclaim the land of its origin.

Sauma then traveled southwest to meet King Edward I of England, who happened to be visiting one of his French domains in Gascony. Edward was stunned to hear that an emissary from a great Mongol khan had sought him out. He accepted Sauma's presents and, like Philip, listened carefully to what he had to say. He agreed that Islam had to be defeated. "We, the kings of these cities, bear upon our bodies the sign of the cross," he told Sauma, "and we have no subject of thought except this matter." Yet he, too, had other concerns, including his conflict with the French.

Philip IV of France. Rabban Sauma tried unsuccessfully to persuade Philip the Fair, as the king was also known, to unite with the Mongols against Islam.

MISSION ACCOMPLISHED?

Feeling he had accomplished a good deal of his mission, Rabban Sauma returned to Rome in March of 1288 to meet with the new pope, Nicholas IV. Unlike the cardinals the previous summer, the pope received Sauma graciously, insisting that Sauma spend Easter with him. Rabban was amazed at the multitudes that flocked to Rome during Holy Week, and, despite himself, awed by the great power of the Roman church. His description of just one garment the pope wore—"a red vestment with threads of gold and ornamented with precious stones"—and his taking note of the fact that the pope's sandals were studded with pearls, shows his understanding of the huge differences between the Roman and Nestorian churches.

In the end, although the Pope somewhat grudgingly gave him a relic to take back to Asia—a piece of cloth purported to come from Christ's cape—Nicholas IV did not respond to Sauma's appeal. He wrote a letter to the Il-Khan praising him for his religious tolerance (and hinting that Arghun should submit to papal authority), and he congratulated him on his desire to regain the Holy Land. But he did not promise an alliance, and was, in reality, in no position to do so, as his relationships with European rulers were fraught with tension at that time.

Sauma left for Persia in the summer of 1288, arriving back in the Il-Khanate in September. Along the way, he paused in Constantinople to view holy sites such as the Hagia Sophia, the incredible church built by the Emperor Justinian to replace a smaller church that had been destroyed by fire in AD 532. Sauma notes in his journals the overarching dome—it rose to a height of 180 feet—and the beautiful colors of the walls, which were made of red, green, and white marble.

Arghun was happy to see him on his return and thought that his mission had been a great success: after all, even if the pope had not agreed to an alliance against the Mamluks, the kings of France and England had. Arghun even sent a letter the

THE SILK ROAD

The Silk Road wasn't just one road but a four-thousand-mile network of interconnected roads along which East met West for two thousand years. It probably began to take shape about 300 BC as a series of caravan routes from China to Central Asia. Eventually these routes were extended to meet the Middle Eastern road system, and led all the way to the Mediterranean.

The name "the Silk Road" was coined by a German geographer in the nineteenth century. The Chinese called the eastern portion of the road "the road south of the celestial mountains"; the western part was "the Imperial Highway." The first Westerner to travel into China on the Silk Road was probably another Nestorian priest, named Olopun, whose name is found inscribed on a stela at Sian-Fu (now Xian), the ancient Chinese capital located in what is now northwest China. The stela dates back to AD 635 and describes Olopun arriving with "true sacred books." The road was much improved by the Mongols, but even then very few people ever traveled its full length, and exchanges of goods normally took place at midway points.

It wasn't just silk that was traded on the Silk Road, of course. From the West came glass, grapes, cotton, wool, gems, ivory, and larger breeds of horses. From the East came silk, jade, spices, ginger, tea, peaches, paper, printing methods, and gunpowder. And from both directions came ideas: Buddhism and Islam and Christianity from the West; philosophies of mathematics, astronomy, and medicine from the East. The Silk Road began to decline after the fourteenth century, mainly due to the fall of the Mongol Empire and the creation of sea routes, but the name is still synonymous with adventure.

following year to Edward I and Philip the Fair:

> Under the power of the eternal sky, the message of the Great King, Arghun, to the King of France: I have accepted the word you forwarded by the messengers under [Rabban Sauma] saying that if the warriors of the Il-Khaan [sic] invade Egypt, you would support them … If you send your warriors as promised and conquer Egypt, worshipping the sky, then I shall give you Jerusalem.

But nothing of the sort happened. Both Phillip and Edward replied to Arghun in vague terms, Edward suggesting that the Il-Khan should once again contact the pope about a crusade. Then the Golden Horde Mongols to Arghun's north began raiding his lands and he became preoccupied with that. And in 1291 he grew ill and died.

From this point on, Europe was simply too disunited to make another serious attempt to wrest the Holy Land from Islamic grasp.

WHAT MIGHT HAVE BEEN In the years after his return to Persia, Rabban Sauma built his own church with the help of funds from Arghun's brother, the new khan, and settled there to do what he had always wanted to do: pray and meditate. Late in 1293, however, he fell ill with a fever on a visit to Baghdad; he rallied, briefly, but was stricken again.

Although he was wracked with pain, he was able to see his friend Mar Yaballaha again—the latter had been away on business but had hurried back to Baghdad upon hearing of Rabban Sauma's illness—before dying in January 1294, at the age of sixty-nine. Mar Yaballaha was in great grief for some time afterward, but lived on

commence li lines du granut Caam qui parole de la granut Ermeine de perfee
defcrtatis et dijnde. Et des œaux merueille qui p le monde sont.

This painting from a fifteenth-century illuminated manuscript shows **Marco Polo** sailing from Venice in 1271, at the start of his long eastward journey to the court of Kublai Khan.

THE MYTH OF MARCO POLO?

Marco Polo was one of the greatest travelers of his century. Or was he? There are some historians who believe Polo was not all he pretended to be. Polo's father, Niccolò, and uncle, Maffeo, were Venetian traders and the first Polos to reach China, traveling from their trading outpost in the Crimea. They arrived at the court of the Great Khan in Dadu sometime in the 1260s. Kublai received them and then sent them back to Europe as his emissaries, asking them to bring Christians to convert his Mongols (in reality, Kublai was more interested in finding educated people to help run his empire). When the Polos returned to Dadu in 1275, they brought young Marco with them, and he stayed on for seventeen years.

After arriving back in Venice in 1295 or so, he caused a sensation by publishing an account of his travels, *Il Milione*. He had obviously been in China, but just how much he had traveled around is open to question, since, for all his detailed observation, he did not describe basic Chinese customs such as footbinding or tea drinking, nor did he make any reference to phenomena such as the Great Wall. He also claimed to have served as a special emissary for Kublai Khan, but Chinese records of the time, which were usually kept with extreme exactitude, do not mention this. Still, Marco Polo's influence was far-reaching. His description of the riches of the Far East inspired many a future explorer, Christopher Columbus among them.

until 1317. During that time, the Nestorian Church entered a decline, partly because the new Il-Khan converted to Islam. Today, however, there are still Nestorian Christians in Iraq, Iran, India, and other countries, with numbers worldwide totaling about 175,000.

What might have been is an interesting, if obviously highly speculative, question. What if Sauma's mission had been successful? What if the pope and Christian rulers of Europe had joined with the forces of the Il-Khanate to attack and drive Islam out of the Middle East? There was no guarantee of victory—Mongol armies were consistently defeated by Mamluks in this period, notably at the battle of Horns in 1281 in Syria—but consider for a moment what might have followed a Christian Mongol victory in the Middle East. Denied a power base, Islam might have withered, while the way to Africa would have been laid open to the combined European and Mongol forces. Mongol culture and rule might have spread far and wide. This would have made the Mongols and Europeans rivals for global domination—and then who knows what might have happened? Perhaps a vast war, a precursor of the world wars of the twentieth century, might have been played out between these two great superpowers, some time in the early fourteenth century, in the sands of the Middle East or on the vast plains of Central Asia.

But, despite the best efforts of an extraordinary traveler named Rabban Sauma, history did not take this turn in the thirteenth century, and the Middle East is as we know it today. Still, Rabban Bar Sauma made an extraordinary and unprecedented journey. He traveled thousands of miles, saw sights few living men had seen, and, in the end, brought two dissimilar cultures closer together, if only for a short time.

WHEN CHINA RULED THE WAVES: THE TREASURE FLEET

That our sails may meet favorable winds
That the sea lanes be peaceful and secure
That gold, pearls, wealth, and valuables fill our ships full with glory
With pious hearts do we offer up this excellent wine.

THE TONE OF THIS FIFTEENTH CENTURY MARINER'S PRAYER—EXPERTLY mixing godliness and greed—is quite familiar, is it not? Surely it was offered up by a chaplain blessing a Spanish crew, say, or by a Portuguese explorer about to set foot in his caravel. In fact, it was the seagoing incantation proffered to the heavens—along with smoky incense and strong, dark wine—by Chinese adventurers about to embark, one autumn day in 1405, on the greatest voyage the world had ever known. They were 27,000 strong, inhabiting at least 317 ships—a vaster armada would not be seen on the ocean waves again until World War I—and they were about to make history, a history of which many Westerners remain unaware.

By 1415 or so, just as Europe was beginning to emerge from the Dark Ages, China stood on the brink of becoming the foremost power in the world. Literally half the globe was within her grasp. Had she chosen to reach farther, the great European explorers of Spain, Portugal, and England might merely have been foreign visitors to Chinese fiefdoms in the New World, much as Marco Polo was when he arrived at the Chinese court in the thirteenth century. But, in the short space of fifteen years, China's great fleet would be dismantled. In a hundred years, Chinese global power would be only a distant memory and China would gradually sink into the mystery and isolation for which it was known until quite recently.

What happened?

FAR-FLUNG JOURNEYS AND A YEARNING FOR HOME
Far from being an isolated and land-based people, the Chinese were for millennia the most far-reaching seafarers in the world. Chinese ingenuity in shipbuilding and navigation led to voyages as far as Madagascar in the fifth or sixth century BC. Most scholars now believe Chinese sailors reached Central and South America prior to the birth of Christ. By the seventh century AD, Chinese merchants had usurped the sea trade in the Indian Ocean from the Arabs; fine Chinese porcelain—the world's first true porcelain—became a much-desired commodity across the eastern world.

Yet, after the birth of Confucius in the sixth century BC, and the subsequent spread of his religion, another factor came into play. Confucius considered China the center of the world—"the Middle Kingdom" and "All Under Heaven," he called it—and thought that the mercantile world, although necessary, was common and debasing. He also taught that foreign travel detracted from familial obligations—that a man who undertook a long journey while his parents were alive failed in his filial duties. This philosophy would have far-reaching effects on China and, consequently, the rest of the world.

By the latter part of the fourteenth century, the Yuan Dynasty—founded, following the Mongol invasion of China in 1281, by Kublai Khan, grandson of Genghis Khan—had weakened, and the Chinese, led by Emperor Zhu Yuanzhang, were beginning to reclaim the Middle Kingdom for the new Ming Dynasty. During one of his bloody incursions into the Mongol province of Yunnan, Zhu Yuanzhang captured a Muslim boy named Ma He.

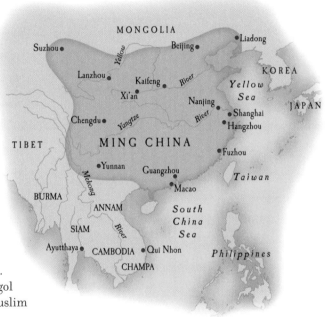

Ming China, c. 1400, when the Ming dynasty was poised to send forth its great treasure fleet.

It had been Chinese custom for at least a millennium to castrate young male prisoners, and Ma He was no exception. Under normal circumstances, he would have been assigned to the Chinese court to wait attendance on the emperor's concubines, perhaps, or to assist some royal bureaucrat. Instead, for reasons unknown, the thirteen-year-old was made the servant of twenty-five-year-old Prince Zhu Di, the emperor's fourth son.

Zhu Di took Ma He along on campaigns against the Mongols on the northern steppes, and Ma He became practiced in the arts of war. The two young men grew to be close companions as well as master and aide de camp. Zhu Di was handsome, aggressive, mercurial, and a brilliant and daring military leader. Ma He, whom the prince renamed Zheng He after the eunuch's horse was killed beneath him in a fierce

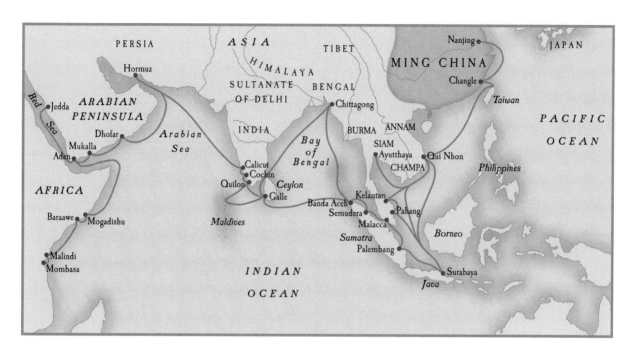

This map shows the routes sailed by Zheng He and his fleet over the course of their epic voyages.

battle near a place called Zhenglunba, was also a striking figure. Nearly seven Chinese *chi*, or feet, tall (approximately six and a half feet in Western measure), he had "glaring eyes … and a voice as loud as a huge bell." But he was also intelligent and had, perhaps at the behest of the prince, learned to read—a privilege not always afforded eunuchs.

When Zhu Di's father died in 1398 and named a nephew, Zhu Yunwen, as his heir to the throne, Zheng He stood by Zhu Di as the latter provoked a civil war, slaughtered his opposition, and drove Zhu Yunwen out of the imperial city of Nanjing.

Zhu Di had himself crowned emperor in 1402. He was a rebel who had usurped a throne, and his grand projects—he rebuilt the Great Wall and constructed a new capital at Beijing—can be seen as those undertaken by a man driven to prove his legitimacy.

One of his very first imperial edicts ordered the building of a fleet of treasure ships—not just any ships, but the biggest ships the world had ever known. They would spread the word of his mighty "Dragon Throne" far and wide, revive the glory of China's ancient seafaring traditions, open Chinese trade to new markets, and bring tribute back to a treasury depleted by years of war.

There may have been another reason why Zhu Di created the treasure fleet. There were rumors that the previous emperor, Zhu Yunwen, had escaped overseas. It is possible that Emperor Zhu Di built the mighty fleet so that he could track down the only man—the legitimate king—who might challenge his rule. However, no trace of Zhu Yunwen was ever found, although Zhu Di would spend twenty years following up every wild rumor of his whereabouts.

LAUNCHING THE TREASURE FLEET

From 1403 to 1405, shipyards up and down the coast of China and in the principal naval works in Nanjing rang with frenzied activity. Special care was lavished on the *bao chuan*, the treasure ships, themselves. And no wonder. They were reportedly 160 feet wide and at least 400 feet long. Indeed, the *bao chuan* were described in Chinese histories as being so large that many modern historians thought the writers were exaggerating. That is, until the day in 1962 when a rudder post from one of the ships was discovered at the site of a Ming shipyard near Nanjing. It was more than 36 feet long. When that measurement was reverse-engineered to typical proportions, it put the treasure ships at well over 400 feet long, and possibly as much as 500 feet long. As a point of comparison, Columbus's *Santa Maria* was just 85 feet long.

It took between twenty and thirty thousand skilled craftsmen—including sailmakers, ropemakers, and carpenters—to construct the fleet. The quantity of raw materials needed was so great that it strained the Chinese economy, as vast amounts of nails, pots, iron wire, and hemp for rope were constantly sought. Trees were in such demand that the coastal provinces could not fill the need and lumber had to be harvested inland and floated down the Min and Yangtze rivers.

As the fleet was being made ready for its first voyage, Zhu Di named his boon companion, the eunuch Zheng He, as Admiral. This was a historic stroke, for never before in Chinese history had a eunuch held such high military command. The degree of trust the emperor placed in Zheng He can be shown by the fact that he presented the eunuch with blank scrolls stamped with his imperial seal so that Zheng He could be his official surrogate at sea.

Zhu Di's trust was not misplaced. Zheng He took care to fill his ships with the right people—not just with experienced ship's captains, who had the emperor-given right to "kill or let live," but also with seven eunuchs who would act as ambassadors of the Imperial Court. There were also official astrologers and geomancers responsible for forecasting the weather and keeping the calendar. And because Zheng He respected other cultures, he made sure to bring along with him ten tutors—including Arabic-speaking translators—whose title was "teachers who know foreign books."

Zheng He set out on his first voyage in the fall of 1405, accompanied by 317 ships and a crew of 27,000. The fleet first headed 400 miles south to the island of Formosa, now known as Taiwan, where the admiral waited out the winter monsoons. As soon as the spring winds began to blow steadily from the southeast, the treasure fleet set sail through the Formosa Strait and across the South China Sea, heading for the ancient country of Champa, now southern Vietnam.

The old Chinese histories describe the fleet as looking like "giant houses" sailing over the water, and it must have been quite a sight. Accompanying the treasure ships were huge eight-masted horse ships some 340 feet long, tanker ships filled with fresh water, countless food supply ships (on which vegetables grew in huge tubs of earth), troop transports, and fierce warships that could disgorge armed men as well as employ a lethal array of the latest "fire weapons." This was no silent passage,

THE UNKINDEST CUT: CHINESE EUNUCHS

Unlike European castrati or harem eunuchs in Persia, Chinese eunuchs lost both penis and testicles. The procedure was gruesome: tight bandages were wound around the lower thighs and abdomen of the boy or young man and he was given a cup of herbal tea, which supposedly had a calming influence. Then his private parts were desensitized by a bath of hot pepper water and swiftly detached with a sharp, curving knife. The urethra was plugged with metal and the eunuch was not allowed to drink any liquid for three days (since urinating might cause an infection). At the end of three days, the bandages were removed and the plug pulled out. If the boy could urinate, he would usually live. If not, he died an agonizing death.

Court eunuchs were an integral part of the Chinese bureaucracy. They ran the imperial household, guarded the emperor's harem—the emperor's companion for the night rode to and from his bedchambers on the back of a eunuch—and advised on matters of protocol and etiquette. Yet as much as the Chinese ruling class depended on eunuchs, they also despised and mistrusted them.

Most emperors tried to keep eunuchs illiterate, and they were forbidden, on pain of beheading, to intervene in government affairs. This did not prevent them becoming powerful, especially during the early years of the Ming Dynasty and the ascendancy of Zheng He.

either, as all these ships communicated with each other through the use of bells,
gongs, carrier pigeons, and flapping banners. In good weather, the fleet could sometimes travel as much as two hundred miles a day.

The holds of the treasure ships were filled with the best trade goods China had to
offer: thousands of bolts of the finest silk and brocade, ceramics from the imperial
porcelain works at Jingdezhen. There was gold and silver, iron tools, and copper
kitchenware. The Chinese also brought with them the coarse but long-lasting cotton
cloth known as nankeen, which was made in Nanjing, and which proved a particular
favorite with foreign traders.

In essence, each treasure ship fleet was a small, floating city, complete unto
itself. In contrast, Columbus's three ships carried only the cheapest of trinkets for
trade, such as scissors, knives, bells, beads, needles, and pins; their entire crews
would have perished had they been forced to stay at sea much longer than they did.

IN THE HANDS OF THE GODDESS
Zheng He proceeded with caution when
he arrived at Champa—the country was
notorious for its pirates and slavers—and the fleet did not stay long. What interested the Chinese the most were the country's timbers, especially its ebony, an
unusual black bamboo, and a rare aloe wood from which the Chinese made
incense. Leaving Champa, the fleet set course for Java, where the Chinese traded
porcelains and silks for spices and copper coins. They witnessed a traditional
Hindu burial, during which a woman, wearing a wreath of grass and flowers,
joined her husband in death by leaping onto his flaming funeral pyre. And,
sounding not unlike some of the first Christian visitors to America depicting the
customs of "savages," they were appalled at an upland aboriginal tribe they
encountered, whom they described as "snake-eaters and devil-worshipers."

After taking his leave of Java, Zheng He sailed across the Indian Ocean to Calicut, a
prosperous city-state in "the great country on the Western Ocean," India ("discovered"
by the Chinese overland explorer Hsuan-Tsan in the seventh century.) Calicut was
the ultimate destination of the first voyage. Zheng He arrived in December 1406, and
the fleet remained until the spring of 1407, in order to take advantage of the rich
trading opportunities the city offered. While the Chinese considered most foreigners
to be barbarians, they had a great deal of respect for the citizens of Calicut, for their
efficient bureaucracy and civil service, and for their honesty in trading. Once an
agreement was reached—and the Chinese mainly traded for precious stones, pearls,
corals, and pepper—it was never repudiated. Too, the Chinese, who counted on abacuses,
were impressed by the Indians' ability to do complicated sums—and never make a
mistake—using only their fingers and toes.

In the spring, the Chinese headed back across the Indian Ocean, and the trip
home proved to be an eventful one. In the Strait of Malacca, near Sumatra, Zheng
He and his ships were attacked by the forces of a powerful pirate chief named Chen
Zuyi, and were forced to do battle for several months. Chinese naval tactics
involved maneuvering warships upwind so that incendiary fire-weapons could be

hurled on the enemy. The chief weapons were mortar-like tubes that sent sprays of gunpowder and flaming paper to burn sails, and "fire-bricks," lethal grenades made of gunpowder and paper soaked in burning, acidic poison.

When Chen Zuyi was finally captured, he was taken back to Nanjing to be executed as an example to future enemies of the emperor. The fleet set sail once again, but somewhere along the way—possibly in the South China Sea—a powerful storm arose without warning. The waves were so monstrous the crewmen believed that an awful dragon was beneath the sea, churning it up with its powerful claws. Together with Zheng He, they prayed to the goddess Tianfei, the Celestial Consort who protected sailors, and, suddenly, a "magic lantern," a sort of blinding white light, appeared on the mast of Zheng He's flagship, and the winds dropped. What the sailors had experienced was the electrical phenomenon known as St Elmo's fire—a discharge of static electricity at the top of a mast. But to Zheng He and his men it was a miracle. In a fitting end to the first grand voyage of the treasure ships, he returned home and set up a temple to honor Tianfei and implore her help on future voyages. The Emperor Zhu Di was so pleased with the results of the voyage that he immediately ordered a second one.

A GOLDEN AGE OF EXPLORATION
The treasure fleet under Zheng He made seven historic voyages from 1405 to 1433, spreading Chinese goods and knowledge to far-flung parts of the world and bringing foreign trade, medicines, and geographic knowledge back to China. On the fourth voyage, in 1413, the fleet reached Hormuz, in the Persian Gulf, and detachments sailed south along the east coast of Africa almost as far as modern-day Mozambique.

Interestingly enough, the Chinese learned a good deal about western Europe from Arab merchants they encountered on their journeys, but had little desire to go there. It sounded to them like a poor place, offering only wool and wine for trade, neither of which the Chinese needed. It is ironic that Columbus later went looking for a new route to China and bumped into America, when China knew where Europe was all along—and chose not to visit.

On the treasure ship voyages, the Chinese traded their silk and porcelain for all manner of goods. From Sumatra they received mahogany for ships' rudders; Siam provided aloe, incense, and tin. Malacca, on the west coast of Malaysia, was a prime source of seed pearls, bird plumes, and batiks.

The treasure ships brought doctors and pharmacists along to collect chaulmoogra-seed oil, used to treat leprosy; volcanic sulfur for skin ointments and as a cure for lung ailments; rhinoceros horn as an antitoxin for snake bites; and all manner of plants and herbs, most of which were boiled or steamed and dried for later use.

The Chinese, like their Western counterparts a hundred or so years later, were fascinated by the curious customs they encountered. Siamese men, who gladly offered up their wives for the pleasure of the Chinese sailors, made a curious tinkling noise when they walked. This was due to the custom of sewing dozens of gold beads partially filled with sand into their scrotums. Muslim women in Aden, on the Red Sea, were bedecked with jewels, from head to toe. In Bengal, the king presented the

Chinese with a strange, long-necked creature with two horns, which the Bengalese had in turn received from the ruler of Kenya. Never having seen a giraffe before, the Chinese mistook it for the mythical *qilin*, one of the four sacred animals of China, along with the phoenix, dragon, and tortoise. This was considered a wondrous sign, since the *qilin* was a symbol of peace, prosperity, and good fortune.

During his treasure voyages, Zheng He, who was born a Muslim, displayed a tolerance for the religious traditions of other countries that put Columbus and his contemporaries to shame. When Zheng He visited Ceylon—a place so beautiful it was rumored to be God's consolation prize to Adam and Eve for having been driven out of Eden—he brought with him a tablet honoring the country's religions: Buddhism, Hinduism, and Islam. In any place with a large Muslim population, Zheng He burned incense and worshiped at mosques. (He was aware of Christianity, but mistakenly believed it was a religion that had originated in western India.)

Hand in hand with the religious tolerance displayed by both Zheng He and his emperor came a belief that China could win other countries over without colonizing them. In fact, the Chinese had a radically different idea of "colonization" than later European powers, one based to no little extent on Middle Kingdom arrogance and self-centeredness. If China was "All Under Heaven," what, really, was the point of conquering other, inferior countries? The Chinese also realized how hard it was to continuously resupply garrisons in distant outposts. It was far wiser to subjugate through trade, to let prosperity be the reward for allegiance to the Dragon Throne. This was a lesson it took Western colonial powers another four hundred years to learn.

FORTUNE ABANDONS THE EMPEROR
The treasure ship voyages established China as the preeminent power of its time. But for a variety of reasons, this power did not last. In part, this was because the empire overreached itself. In 1407, the Chinese invaded Annam (northern Vietnam) in an attempt to put a puppet ruler on the Annamese throne. China became bogged down there, like other great powers centuries later, as imperialist forces battled guerillas for some twenty years.

Then there was Zhu Di's preoccupation with Beijing, the magnificent capital he was erecting in his old age as a monument to his reign. Construction required that more than 130 miles of canal be built or repaired, and that a palace compound be constructed with more than eight hundred rooms, the so-called Forbidden City. Between 1417 and 1420, one in fifty people in China (out of a total population of sixty million) worked on the Forbidden City, further taxing an economic system stretched to its limits by the war and the treasure fleet.

Finally, just as the Forbidden City was dedicated in 1421, the stars themselves turned against the emperor. To begin with, two of his favorite concubines were found to be having an affair not only with a court eunuch, but with each other. Zhu Di had everyone involved executed—and many more women whom he thought were plotting against him—but the whole matter cast a pall over the opening of his magnificent city. The pall became more than symbolic when lightning struck the newly completed palace. The ensuing fire destroyed three great ceremonial halls and killed scores of people. Famine and epidemics further weakened the country, as did a vainglorious war Zhu Di began against the Tartars on the Mongolian border.

On August 24, 1424, the sixty-three-year-old emperor died of natural causes while pursuing his enemies. His son Zhu Gaozhi, an unenergetic young man, took over the empire and surrounded himself with traditional Confucians. Military campaigns were banned (China withdrew from Annam) and the new emperor decreed that "all voyages of the treasure ships are to be stopped … Those officials who are currently abroad on business are ordered back to the capital immediately … and all those who had been called to go on future voyages are ordered back home." In other words, inward-looking Confucian teachings had once again come to the fore.

Admiral Zheng He was recalled home to become military commander of Nanjing and, it seemed, to end his illustrious career on land. But then, unexpectedly, Zu Gaozhi died nine months into his reign. The new emperor, Zhu Zhanji, a more adventurous type, commissioned another voyage of the treasure fleet. This seventh voyage, in 1433, was the largest of all, with well over three hundred ships and some twenty-eight thousand men.

It is possible that Zheng He, now in his sixties, had a premonition that this would be his last voyage. Before leaving on this journey, he stopped in Fujian province and had a tablet erected that told how the Emperor Zhu Di had ordered him to sail to countries beyond the horizon as a display of Chinese power. He wrote:

> We have traversed more than one hundred thousand *li* of immense water spaces and have beheld in the ocean huge waves like mountains rising sky high, and we have set eyes on barbarian regions far away hidden in a blue transparency of light vapors.

Zheng He took his place at the helm once again. The great fleet coursed to Champa, Sumatra, Ceylon, and India, to Hormuz again, and down the East African coast as far as modern-day Kenya. The Chinese were fascinated by Africa, by the array of animals they found there—not just the *qilin* but also ostriches, lions, and leopards—and by the people, who lived in houses of brick, wore their hair in rolls, and offered up a lovely, deep gold amber to trade.

Sadly, sometime on the voyage home, Zheng He succumbed to old age and was buried at sea.

THE END OF AN ERA
When the Emperor Zhu Zhanji died suddenly in 1435, he left only a seven-year-old heir. During the years of this child's reign, eunuchs took over the secret police and treasury and generally acted in such a vicious and corrupt fashion that a backlash ensued. Power once again shifted to the Confucians, shipyards were shut down, and merchants were forbidden to trade overseas under penalty of death. During this internal struggle, in a tragic desecration, the logs of all seven of Zheng He's voyages were destroyed, by an official who

CHINESE MARITIME TECHNOLOGY

China developed numerous seafaring innovations centuries ahead of the West. The Chinese were navigating long distances by the stars well before Europeans. The oldest Chinese star map dates to 2400 BC, and China's records are the only ones in history to document sightings of all four of the first known supernovae: in AD 1006, 1054, 1572, and 1604.

By the third century AD, the Chinese had developed paddlewheel boats, powered by men on treadmills. These were not seen in Europe for another 1000 years. By the fourth century AD, the Chinese had discovered that a magnetized iron needle floating in a bowl of water naturally aligned itself on a north–south axis—eight hundred years before Europeans used the compass.

By the ninth century, the Chinese understood the difference between magnetic north and true north. In building the giant treasure ships, the Chinese employed seven 1,500-foot-long dry docks, separated from the Yangtze River by high dams.

China had employed dry docks since the tenth century; the technology did not reach Europe until the end of the fifteenth. By the time of the treasure ships, the Chinese had developed watertight bulwark compartments for oceangoing ships, as well as balanced rudders that extended forward of the stern post as well as aft, making large ships easier to steer. This innovation was not known in Europe until the nineteenth century.

CHINESE EXPLORATION OF THE AMERICAS

Some present-day historians say there is strong evidence that Chinese voyagers made their way east across the Pacific to South and Central America sometime before the birth of Christ, and may have visited there as late as the ninth century AD. These historians claim that the Chinese sailed in virtually unsinkable balsa wood rafts which used an ingenious system of multiple rudders, and that some of these rafts could accommodate a hundred people or more. They also say the rafts were still in use when Spanish explorers reached South America in the sixteenth century.

What is the evidence for Chinese contact with the New World? In Peru, Chavin craftsmen suddenly, and seemingly without antecedent, produced bronze figurines of jaguars that bear an astonishing resemblance to Shang Dynasty tiger statuettes—the animals even have rings on their tails, which are not found on South American jaguars or pumas, only on Asian tigers. An isolated tribe in the Central Mexican highlands still

makes bark cloth precisely the way an ancient Chinese people did—in a very complicated pattern, with little variation, and using the same tools. Then there is the unmistakable resemblance between Chinese characters and Mayan glyphs, and between the complex Mayan and Chinese calendars.

More speculative is the theory put forth by Gavin Menzies and other writers that Zheng He—or at least, a detachment of his treasure fleet—rounded the Cape of Good Hope, reached America's east coast by 1421, and then were blown by prevailing winds around the Horn, across the Pacific, and ultimately back to China. No firm evidence of this has been found. But, in 2005, a map was discovered in a Beijing bookstore which dates to 1736, but is supposed to be a copy of a 1418 map. The map shows the Americas, Australia, and New Zealand, which were not known to Europeans at the time. The map does not mention Zheng He or his treasure ships, but is a tantalizing clue.

wanted to make sure that no one would attempt these voyages again. The only records that remained were three eyewitness accounts—two by officers on the treasure ships and one by a Muslim translator who had accompanied Zheng He on his later voyages.

An era was officially over. By the beginning of the sixteenth century, the art of building treasure ships was all but lost. Other countries stepped into the trading vacuum left by the Chinese, who were never able to regain their edge. In less than one hundred years, as European powers such as Portugal and Spain flexed their muscles in the New World, the Chinese navy disappeared. The country that had once launched the treasure ships had no way to defend itself, even from the despoiling Japanese pirates who now roamed its coastline.

It's tempting to imagine what could have been, especially when we remember that, at the peak of Chinese naval power, European countries had nothing to rival the treasure fleet or its technology. England did not even begin to develop a fleet until after 1500, and France, Spain, and Portugal had only the most rudimentary of navies. One can easily imagine the Chinese rounding Africa, heading north and into the Mediterranean and the English Channel. There would have been nothing to stop them from dominating all of Europe.

It was not to be. But there is one more tale to tell. In 1498, Vasco da Gama and his three tiny caravels rounded the Cape of Good Hope and landed in East Africa on their way to India. They were surprised that the Africans were indifferent to the

beads and bells the Portuguese offered them, and seemed not at all excited by the size of their ships. The Africans told the Portuguese about the huge ships that had visited their shores years before, bringing fine silks. The ships and the "white ghosts" who had sailed them had long since disappeared, to where the Africans did not know. But even the distant memory of them—now almost a myth—was more powerful than anything these ragged European wayfarers had to offer.

Although modern Chinese junks are nowhere near as large as those of Zheng He's fleet, methods of construction have changed very little over time.

THE SHOT THAT ECHOED THROUGH THE CENTURIES

THERE HANGS IN THE RIJKSMUSEUM IN AMSTERDAM A STRIKING PORTRAIT painted by the Flemish artist Adriaan Key, who lived from roughly 1544 to 1589. The subject of the portrait is a man in middle age wearing a leather skull cap, a ruffled collar, and a shirt embroidered with a gold design. The man is obviously a person of means and great rank, but what catches and holds the eye is not his dress but the extreme melancholy and weariness of his face. He has a short, fine brown beard and an expressionless mouth, and his eyes, in deep hollows, stare off to the side. The man appears haunted, or in shock.

The title of the painting is *William I, Prince of Orange, Called William the Silent*, and Key painted it in 1579. Five years later, his subject would get up from a table after lunch, reach out to greet a trusted retainer, and be blasted into oblivion by the first pistol shot ever to take the life of a head of state.

There would be more assassinations, of course, plenty more: King Gustav III of Sweden shot in the back at a costume ball in 1792; President Abraham Lincoln shot in the head while attending a play in 1865; Archduke Franz Ferdinand of Austro-Hungary murdered in his carriage in Sarajevo, Serbia, in 1914. All these and dozens of other handgun assassinations form a bloody trail, leading back to the melancholy man called Prince William the Silent.

HERO OR HERETIC? For most people living in the Low Countries, or Netherlands, in the mid-sixteenth century, William the Silent was a Dutch patriot fighting to free them from the cruel rule of King Philip II of Spain—today, in fact, William is known as the *Vader des vaderlands*, "Father of the fatherland," and the Dutch national anthem, the *Wilhemus*, is named for him. For most people living in Spain at the same time, however, William was a vile Protestant heretic who abjured the true church, fomented rebellion, and mocked the great king who had once befriended him—mocked him to the point where Philip had no other choice but to put a price of twenty-five thousand gold crowns on his head.

William was born in present-day Germany in 1533, the eldest son of Count William of Nassau. Despite the fact that Count William was also known as William the Rich, the family was not wealthy by royal standards of the day. But all that changed in 1544 when William's uncle, René of Châlon, who ruled the small principality of Orange in southern France, died. He had no direct heirs and he bequeathed Orange to his nephew, William, who was then eleven. Orange was a possession of the great Hapsburg Empire, which at the time controlled most of Europe and was divided between the Austrian Hapsburgs and the Spanish Hapsburgs, the latter ruling Spain, the Low Countries, and parts of France, Italy, and Portugal.

King Charles V was the reigning Spanish monarch in 1544 and William was sent to be educated at his court in Antwerp. By all accounts, he acquitted himself well, earning a reputation very early for being a judicious, soft-spoken, intelligent young man. One reason he needed to be all of the preceding was that he had been raised a Lutheran and now resided within a fiercely Roman Catholic royal society. Fortunately for William, his parents had not been fervent Protestants, and he himself did not see the need to make an issue of religion. While he was in Rome, as it were, he would do as the Romans did, which was to follow the Roman Catholic religion, if not fervently, than at least quietly and steadily.

In the mid-sixteenth century, the Spanish Netherlands encompassed the modern-day Netherlands, as well as most of what are now Belgium and Luxembourg.

William rose in the ranks, so much so that when Charles V, ill and aging, resigned in favor of his son, Philip, it was William of Orange's shoulder he quite literally leaned on while he gave his farewell address. When Philip became King Philip II, he made William a Knight of the Order of the Golden Fleece, an august brotherhood modeled on the English Order of the Garter, numbering only about fifty men. Interestingly, the Golden Fleece was a Catholic organization and membership was denied to "heretics," but no one questioned William's right to be in it.

RESTRAINT GIVES WAY TO REBELLION
So trusted was William of Orange by King Philip that in 1559 Philip made him stadtholder, or governor general, of the northern provinces of the Low Countries. This turned out to be, from Philip's point of view, a grave mistake. Now a member of the Raad van State (Council of State), the highest political advisory council in the Netherlands, William soon came under the influence of other members who

complained that the Spanish under Philip tried to centralize what was essentially a disparate, still somewhat medieval, array of independent duchies, counties, and seigneuries. Charles V had been far better at keeping a lid on the opposition in the Netherlands, in part because he lived there much of the time and spoke the language.

William steered a middle course, not yet directly confronting Philip, and it was around this time that he received the sobriquet *le taciturne*, "the tight-lipped one." Soon, though, it became hard to be quiet. Philip II reorganized the Catholic Church in the Netherlands—despite the Reformation, still a formidable presence—so that more money flowed directly to the church in Spain, and he appointed the hated Cardinal Granvelle to make sure this happened. As part of his duties, Granvelle began an inquisition against Dutch Protestant heretics.

This was too much for Dutch patriots, Catholic or Protestant. In 1562, the Dutch nobility who were members of the Council of State banded together to overthrow Granvelle, essentially going on strike until Philip removed him. This he did, in 1564, but it was too late to stem the growing tide of opposition against the Spanish presence, particularly in the northern principalities of Holland and Utrecht, where most of the unrest was brewing. William's own brother, Count John of Nassau, delivered a petition to Margaret of Parma, Philip's regent, demanding more religious freedom for the Dutch people. Philip appointed William to quell the unrest, still unaware of his knight's true feelings. William successfully negotiated with John and other radical Calvinist Protestants of Holland, earning them some small measure of religious freedom while avoiding further confrontation with Philip.

But the Calvinists, in particular, continued to fan the embers of rebellion. At large gatherings, itinerant Calvinist preachers harangued crowds, inveighing against Philip and the Catholic Church, then moved on quickly before the Spanish authorities could reach them—for capture meant death, usually by hanging or burning. At the instigation of these preachers, Calvinists rampaged through Catholic churches, destroying holy statues, which they considered false idols.

Had Philip II been the kind of diplomat Charles V was, it is possible he could have defused the situation, but instead he reacted even more repressively, by sending in the Duke of Alva to quell the riots that were beginning to break out in the Low Countries. William the Silent resigned his position on the Council of State and retired to his land holdings in Germany to ponder his options. Should he gather a force of rebels and invade the Low Countries? Should he seek an alliance with France? Or might the situation resolve itself? Philip, through Alva, responded by seizing William's lands in the Low Countries. At this point, William began to send financial aid to the Dutch rebels, who included his brother John.

Opposite: Portrait of William the Silent. Initially, William sought to avoid confrontation with Spain. But Philip II's seizure of his properties in the Low Countries forced William into opposition.

THE IRON DUKE
The Duke of Alva, or the Iron Duke, as he became known, acted ruthlessly from the moment he arrived in the Netherlands. He set up what he called the Council of Troubles—and the Dutch referred to as the Council of Blood—to judge anyone who had been caught fomenting rebellion against the king. Ten thousand people were summoned to appear at the council. William the Silent was

THE HOUSE OF ORANGE

In 1672, almost one hundred years after William the Silent was killed, the French, under Louis XIV, attacked the Netherlands, placing the country in its greatest crisis since the war against Spain. The stadtholdership had been allowed to remain vacant by the regents governing the country, but in response to the attack the twenty-two-year-old William III, William the Silent's great-grandson, took command of the Netherlands and achieved a great victory against the French. In 1677, William married Mary Stuart, daughter of King James II of England. James was a militant Catholic who had antagonized his predominantly Protestant Parliament and subjects. His opponents in England sought William's support in ousting the king, and in 1688 William landed with a Dutch army, beginning the so-called "Glorious Rebellion." William and Mary were offered the crowns of England and, soon after, Scotland, and went on to rule as King William III (1689–1702) and Queen Mary II (1689–1694). Naturally, the Catholics, especially in Ireland, were not happy with this development, and rallied to King James. But William defeated them decisively at the Battle of the Boyne in 1690—a victory celebrated to this day by militant Protestants in Northern Ireland and elsewhere, who also still wear orange in honor of William. The House of Orange came to an end after King William died childless in a riding accident in 1702, and Mary's sister Anne Stuart took over the English throne.

called, but to appear would have been suicidal—by now a thousand Dutchmen had been executed by Alva. So he refused. In revenge, Alva kidnapped William's eldest son from the university he was attending and sent him to Spain, where he was forced to accept the Catholic religion. William was never to see him again.

Initially, William may have felt that, even in rebellion, his nobility would keep him and his family safe, but Alva and Philip had by now determined that William was their mortal enemy—Philip in particular had realized that William was the one man behind whom the rebellious forces of the Low Countries might rally. Becoming aware of this, William finally resorted to armed conflict, invading the Low Countries from Germany, in 1568 and again in 1570, with forces of expatriate Dutch rebels, along with German mercenaries. Each time, he was badly defeated, his ragtag armies no match for the merciless Spanish war machine. However, during the course of these battles, one important thing happened: William managed to capture and keep key towns in Holland and Zeeland, two northern provinces on the North Sea. With them, he gained control of oceangoing traffic. This was of great interest to Queen Elizabeth I of England, who had, heretofore, stayed out of the war. Now, seeing that William's rebels could help protect England from a Spanish naval invasion, she began to funnel money secretly to William.

William then planned an invasion of the southern provinces of the Low Countries, hoping to destroy the Duke of Alva's army. He had expected help from the French Protestants, but the Catholic-inspired massacre of the Huguenots on August 23, 1572—St. Bartholomew's Day—meant that no reinforcements would be forthcoming. William invaded anyway, but, in September of that year, pushed back by Alva's forces, he retreated to Holland. The Iron Duke then swept north through the Low Countries, killing, pillaging, and burning. On December 2, 1572, at Naarden, in the northwest, as an example to the rest of the country, he ordered the death of every man, woman, and child in the town. Five hundred people were tied together, back to back, and thrown into an icy river to drown. Many were hanged upside down by their feet from gallows, where they died slowly over the course of days. Children were chopped up with axes or pierced with lances and held aloft by laughing soldiers. The mayor was nailed to the doorway of his house. A few gibbering survivors escaped by fleeing through the dark and snowy fields that surrounded the town.

After this atrocity, Alva advanced farther into Holland, but now there was no one who would surrender to him. The Iron Duke took the city of Haarlem, but only after its defenders had killed eight thousand of his men. In 1573, Alva attacked Alkmaar, twenty miles northwest of Amsterdam, with sixteen thousand troops. But, although defended by only two thousand men, Alkmaar held out. Dutch rebels opened the dikes and flooded Alva's troops, driving them back. A Spanish naval force came up the Zuider Zee to rescue them, but it was met and defeated by the "Sea Beggars," a ragtag group of Dutch exiles who had put together a navy.

In response, Philip recalled Alva to Spain and sent in a new regent, Don Juan of Austria, with instructions to make some sort of peace with William and his rebels—Spain was also waging a war against the Ottoman Empire and could ill afford fighting on two fronts. But William's demands included limited monarchy, independent legislative bodies, and freedom of worship. Philip balked at this. A stalemate ensued, broken by intermittent battling.

THE STRUGGLE FOR UNITY

By 1579, when Adriaan Key painted his portrait, William was exhausted from waging war. The painting shows a forty-seven-year-old man who appears far older than his years, worn down by the burden on his shoulders.

William's chief problem now was uniting the different rebel religious groups who were fighting as much amongst themselves as against the Spanish—Calvinists were even refusing Catholics the right to worship in Calvinist-controlled cities. Partly because of this, Catholic provinces in the southwest signed, at the beginning of 1579, the Treaty of Arras, in which they agreed to accept the new Spanish regent, the Duke of Parma. Shortly thereafter, the Protestants in the seven remaining northern provinces—Holland, Zeeland, Utrecht, Gelderland, Overijssel, Friesland, and Groningen—signed the Union of Utrecht, thereby forming the so-called United Provinces—to which William gave his support, albeit reluctantly, since it did not unify the whole country.

By 1580, William was having a hard time getting different groups within the United Provinces to agree on a ruler, and had also expended much of his personal fortune financing the revolt. Out of desperation, he came up with the idea of inviting the French Duke of Anjou, brother of King Henry III, to the country to become "prince and lord of the Netherlands." Having the force of the French on his side would give the Spanish pause, William felt, and he also hoped that the rebels might be willing to unite under a foreigner. This turned out to be a miscalculation. The petulant and unattractive duke did nothing to help his cause, insisting on observing his Catholic religion openly and seeming to care nothing for what the Dutch Protestants felt or thought.

And this was how matters stood when the King of Spain put a price on William's head. In 1580, Philip wrote:

> If there be found, either among our own subjects, or amongst strangers, so noble of courage, and desirous of our service … that knoweth any means how to … set us free from [William the Silent] delivering him unto us quick or dead, or at least taking his life from him, we will cause, to be given and provided for him and his heirs, in good land or ready money, choose him whether, immediately after the thing shall be accomplished, the sum of twenty-five thousand crowns of gold.

Immediately after the thing shall be accomplished. Even after many centuries, this is a chilling line, Shakespearean in its intensity. It was personal: not just one ruler calling for the defeat of another, but a man who had been betrayed wishing to snuff out the very life of his betrayer. Outraged, William responded with a passionate treatise, in which he attacked Spanish policies and called for ousting the Spanish once and for

THE CARNAGE OF A GUNSHOT

It took people some time to adapt to the horrifying effects of bullets fired at close range. William died very quickly, bleeding profusely from large entry wounds, and those who saw the damage done by the bullets could not believe their eyes. A year after William's death, Henry Percy, the Earl of Northumberland, had run afoul of Queen Elizabeth I and was imprisoned in the Tower of London. Growing despondent, he had a pistol smuggled into him, loaded it, and put it to his head. The subsequent carnage was so extreme that the authorities refused to believe that he had killed himself, and decided that he must have been shot by assassins who had broken into the Tower.

all from the Netherlands. By mid-1581, William had succeeded in getting agreement from the United Provinces to depose Philip. (This Oath of Abjuration, as it was called—seen by some as the model for the U.S. Declaration of Independence—was to lead to the formation of the Republic of the United Provinces, which became the modern-day Netherlands.) All of this further enraged the Spanish monarch.

On March 18, 1582, William went to a church service in the chapel of his palace in Antwerp, had lunch, and then got up to meet with a young man named Jean Jauregay, whom he thought had a petition for him. Instead, the eighteen-year-old Jauregay took a pistol from his pocket and fired it point-blank at the prince. But the gun exploded, taking off Jaureguy's thumb. Flames seared his face and singed the beard of William the Silent, who fell backwards, blood pouring from his mouth. Despite the explosion, one bullet had struck his face, injuring him gravely. William's guards leaped upon Jauregay and stabbed him to death.

Upon investigation, it was found out that Jauregay had been employed as a servant for a Spanish merchant, who had fled Antwerp before the assassination and thus could not be punished. A Jesuit who had absolved Jauregay in advance for his crime was taken into custody and executed. Jauregay, though already dead, was beheaded.

There was nothing new about assassinations, of course, but what was truly disturbing about this attempt was that it was carried out with a handgun. The scenario is sadly familiar to us now—images of mortally wounded leaders, such as J. F. and Bobby Kennedy and Martin Luther King, are seared onto our consciousness—but for people of that time it was something totally new and terrifying.

Guns had been around since the Chinese first employed them in the early twelfth century, but these were cannons. The first "hand gonne" was not developed until the fifteenth century. It was basically a small cannon with a touch hole for ignition of the powder that would send the bullet into flight. It was so heavy it needed to be propped up on a shooting stand and had to be lit with a long fuse that took nerve-wracking seconds to burn its way down.

A true hand gun required a more reliable ignition system, and the solution turned out to be the wheel-lock. Supposedly invented by gunmaker Johan Kiefuss in Nuremberg in 1517 (although some claim that Leonardo da Vinci designed the first one), the wheel-lock represented true innovation. Think of a modern lighter. When you spin the metal wheel with your finger, it strikes against a flint and the lighter ignites. The wheel-lock worked in more or less the same way. Now, you no longer had to wait for fuses to burn down, nor did you have to hide while lighting it, so as not to give away your position. In fact, should you desire—and many did— you could hide numerous cocked wheel-lock pistols on your person and have yourself quite a gunfight.

By the 1560s, wheel-locks were considered status symbols. German gunsmiths started adorning the wooden stocks with inlays of ivory and horn, and fire-blueing the barrels to give them extra strength and beauty. Noblemen in England carried small pistols as standard adornments, calling them "dags," in an abbreviation of the daggers that used to hang in the same place.

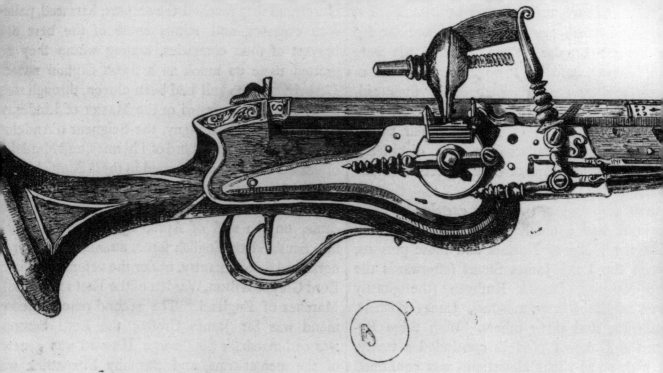

BREECH-LOADING WHEEL-LOCK PISTOL (ABOUT TIME OF HENRY VIII.). STOCK OF IVORY.

Thus far no one had used one to kill a head of state, but someone had to be first, of course, and Jauregay almost claimed that dubious distinction. Except that in his inexperience he made the mistake of overloading the gun with powder—even the best-made pistols at this time could stand no more than a quarter-charge of powder in the barrel. And so he died, and, amazingly, William the Silent survived.

DEATH IN DELFT With a hole the size of a large coin in his jaw, William the Silent was carried to his quarters. His fourteen-year-old son, Maurice, who had helped stab the assassin to death, made ready to take his father's place. But William would not die. Despite being unable to eat, he gradually made a recovery, possibly because the wound had been cauterized by the explosion of the pistol and thus infection did not set in. By May 5, he was able to appear in public. Unfortunately, the assassination attempt had weakened his position. Already harmed by his unpopular decision to back the Duke of Anjou, he was seen by many as being physically incapable of carrying out his duties. He found his power eroding.

Stringent security measures were put in place. The credentials of everyone who got close to William were thoroughly checked, and walls of bodyguards accompanied him everywhere, a burden to be borne by a man so essentially modest. This is a familiar sight to people these days, when even pop stars travel with a phalanx of security, but at the time it was unusual and disturbing—something had changed, now, people felt, forever. It was a little like the sensation felt by many on seeing Pope John Paul II riding behind the bulletproof glass of his "Popemobile" after the 1981 attempt on his life. But William's bodyguards had not yet realized the dangers posed by pistols. A man with a dagger or sword is visible as he lunges and can be stopped by a

A breech-loading wheel-lock pistol with an ivory handle, c. 1540. The introduction of the wheel-lock was a major advance in firearms technology.

Overleaf: This 1861 oil painting of the death of William I ably captures the chaos surrounding the assassination by the Catholic militant Balthazar Gérard.

determined effort. A man with a pistol can step out of the shadows and shoot before anyone else reacts. Another problem, at least in William's court, was the status level of pistols. Even after the first attempt on his life, the men around William still wore dags as part of their everyday attire—these pistols were, to use modern vernacular, cool, and every man wanted to show his off.

In the spring of 1583, William left Antwerp and took up residence at his palace, the Prisenhof, in Delft. This was something of a strategic retreat under pressure. The Duke of Anjou, frustrated by his lack of acceptance in the Netherlands, had sent his men rampaging through Antwerp in what became known as "the French Fury." The citizens of the town defended themselves ably, however, and finally Anjou, fed up with the whole affair, withdrew to France. But William's reputation had been tarnished by his association with Anjou, and he now became politically isolated.

It was at this point that Balthazar Gérard struck. French by birth, Gérard had been able to work his way into the employ of Prince William and rise to the level of trusted retainer—in fact, he had been ordered to spy on the troops of the Duke of Parma. However, he was not a double-agent, as some historians have said, merely a fanatical Catholic who, on the afternoon of July 10, 1584, waited for Prince William the Silent while the latter finished his lunch. William stopped to speak briefly with two English soldiers who had come to fight in his cause, then started to ascend a staircase, where Gérard waited with a number of other retainers. Gérard stepped forward and fired the wheel-lock pistol he had purchased just that morning from another (and unsuspecting) servant of William's. The gun was loaded with three bullets. All three hit William, who fell backward down the stairs. He is supposed to have cried: "Mon Dieu, mon dieu, ayez pitié de moi et de ton pauvre peuple!" ("My Lord, My Lord, have pity on me and on your poor people!"). But this was almost certainly a bit of propaganda put out later by the Dutch. For William seems to have died, as he was renowned to live, in silence.

To any student of assassination in the twenty-first century, Gérard will seem a familiar type: an utterly dedicated lone fanatic. He openly confessed that while he loved King Philip of Spain, he did not kill William for the reward, but because William was a heretic to the cause of Christ.

What happened to Gérard next is the very definition of overkill. He was executed over the course of several days. The first day he was subject to the strappado, which meant that his arms were tied behind his back and then the rope securing his wrists thrown over a high beam and pulled upward, causing him to hang in horrible pain. The next day, he was "whipped and salted" and his right hand cut off. On the third day, his other hand was chopped off, and his breasts were cut off and the exposed flesh sprinkled with salt. On the last day, Gérard was bound to a stake while torturers with hot pincers pulled out chunks of his flesh. He was then disemboweled alive, and his heart finally ripped out and thrown in his face. Astonishingly, or perhaps not, Gérard endured all this with great fortitude, praying like the Christian martyr he evidently considered himself to be.

Some time after Gérard's death, his family in France quietly received from the King of Spain cash and lands worth twenty-five thousand gold crowns.

AN OPERATIC ASSASSINATION

The next head of state to be murdered with a handgun after William the Silent was King Gustav III of Sweden, in 1792. Gustav was a fascinating and flamboyant character, a homosexual under whose guidance the royal court of Sweden rivaled the great courts of Versailles and Berlin. He fostered literary, artistic, and operatic talent—opera was a special love of his—but did not neglect palace intrigue, either. When his father, the rather meek and passive King Adolf Frederick died suddenly in 1771, Gustav, touring in France, let it be known that he would follow in the former king's footsteps, ruling merely as a figurehead. But, once back in Sweden, Gustav took control of all key fortresses, robbing the Swedish Riksdag, or legislative assembly, of power, and began to rule as an absolute monarch.

Gustav, indeed, was a study in contradictions. He believed in religious freedom for Catholics and Jews, but censored the press severely. Yet he also founded the Swedish Academies of Literature, Music, Language, and the Arts. On March 16, 1792, while attending a midnight masquerade at the Royal Opera in Stockholm, Gustav was shot in the back by a masked nobleman, acting alone, who had grown discontented with his reign. He died two weeks later. Fittingly enough, Gustav's assassination inspired Verdi to write *Un ballo in maschera* (*The Masked Ball*).

A CHANGED WORLD William's enemies rejoiced, but the full implications began to dawn on others, especially on political leaders. At the time of his death, despite his isolation, William was stadtholder of the northern Low Countries and still its official sovereign. He was a nobleman, well protected, in his own home, and yet some nobody had just waltzed up and snuffed out his life.

It was a different world now. After William's death, his royal court put out a copy of the interrogation of his killer, which begins with words that echo all the way down to our present day:

> Whoso considereth the state of Princes, although they are as God upon earth, being anointed by God, having their authority from God, and sitting in God's seat to rule the sword with the law, may perceive that they live in more care and greater danger than the simplest subject. Lamentable therefore is their late example of the Prince of Orange, slain (by a treacherous villain) in his own Court: his death and the manner thereof, may forewarn other Princes to be careful, whom they retain into the presence of their person …

It was realized, in retrospect, that having retainers, faithful or otherwise, wearing guns around rulers was not a good idea.

Queen Elizabeth I, of all Europe's rulers, was the most shocked by William's death, since she herself was also a mortal enemy of the King of Spain. She wrote to one of her agents in the Netherlands, William Herle, expressing sympathy for William's widow, the Princess of Orange, and expressing the hope that "the authors of this execrable act [will have reason to wish] that they had never been born." But she and her advisers continued to think that she herself must be a prime target for an assassin sent by the King of Spain. Within a week of William's death, one of her

The Tomb of William the Silent in the Nieuw Kerk in Delft, by Gérard Houckgeest, 1651. Even after his death, William was an inspiration for Dutch patriots.

advisers wrote another that "the same practice that hath been executed on the Prince of Orange" might be tried against the Queen: "There is no doubt that she is the chief mark they [will] shoot at."

The precautions then implemented around Elizabeth will be familiar to everyone who lives in our current age of terror. An order was issued banning anyone from discharging a handgun or even carrying one within two miles of a royal palace. People traveling from anywhere in Europe to London were singled out for excessive security at ports, their persons and luggage searched, and were sometimes followed by agents of the Crown. Descriptions were given out of suspected Spanish spies:

> Don Gaston … is a man reputed of action, of the age of thirty-three years, and hath but one eye, and [is] very resolute. His Father was a Genoese, his mother a Spaniard, and by his country [he is] a Sicilian, which is the worst commixture that ever was, and therefore for God's sake, let him be well observed.

Spanish "plots" were discovered everywhere, one of which, although not real, caused Elizabeth to finally sign a death order against her cousin, Mary Queen of Scots.

There were political ramifications, as well. With William gone, there was a very real possibility of Spain taking over the Netherlands and using it as a base to launch an attack on England, so Elizabeth ordered that the English fully involve themselves in the war against Spain, a war which would not end until the Spanish Armada was destroyed in 1588. The war between Spain and the United Provinces dragged on for another sixty years, until the Peace of Westphalia confirmed the Netherlands' independence in 1648.

For his pioneering part in the advance toward this independence, William of Orange is seen today as a Dutch patriot, and the man from whom every Dutch monarch is descended, including the present ruler, Queen Beatrix. He is also regarded as the father of the Protestant House of Orange, which eventually ruled England. He was not without flaws, however, chief among them being that he was too much the diplomat, too silent, in his way.

The shot that rang out to take his life has since rung out again and again, down through the centuries, sparking political upheaval and world war. Even with all the bodyguards in the world, all it takes is one shot, by a determined individual with a reliable firearm, who is not afraid to die.

THE SHIMABARA UPRISING AND THE DISAPPEARANCE OF JAPAN

EVEN AT THE BEGINNING OF THE TWENTY-FIRST CENTURY, JAPAN, WITH its distinctive culture and customs, appears remote and mysterious to many outsiders. There are numerous reasons for this, but it has much to do with the fact that, for a period of more than two hundred years, the nation cut itself off completely from the outside world, so that the Japan that suddenly began to display its territorial ambitions in the twentieth century was, in many ways, like a hermit returning to the world after a long time spent alone on a hilltop.

What brought this about was a tumultuous hundred years in the country's history, during which Christianity almost transformed Japan. It began in 1549, with a young man fleeing a crime, and ended with another young man being beheaded, after the bloody suppression of a widespread and violent uprising.

THE FUGITIVE The man on the run in the year 1549 was named Anjiro, although he would later style himself Paul of Japan. A member of a well-to-do family on the Japanese island of Kyushu, Anjiro got into a fight that resulted in the death of another youth. Fleeing justice, he found a sympathetic Portuguese ship's captain who offered to take him to Malacca. On the three-thousand mile journey south to the Malay Archipelago, Anjiro was wracked with guilt, so much so that he confessed his crime to the captain. The man responded that, if it was expiation Anjiro sought, he should talk to a "holy man," Francis Xavier, who was then in Malacca. When Anjiro encountered the famous priest, he poured out his story.

Born in Spain in 1506, Francis Xavier was one of the very first Jesuit missionaries to Asia. By the time Anjiro found him, Xavier had spent six years converting the poor of India, modern-day Indonesia, and the Malay Peninsula, and he was ready for a new challenge. He knew little about Japan—the Portuguese had only been trading there for five years or so—but decided immediately to return to the country with Anjiro, who had become his first Japanese convert. Once there, Xavier realized that Japan was like no place he had ever visited.

Most of the Japanese were Buddhists, which Xavier did not consider a true religion, since they did not believe in an afterlife and had no creation story. The Buddhist priests seemed to spend much of their time in meditation, a practice that the energetic, tall, and angular Xavier had little use for. The people worshipped idols, did not seem to frown upon homosexuality, and yet were remarkably moral—you could leave your valuables anywhere in Japan and they would be there undisturbed when you returned.

In the first year Xavier was there, he converted just one hundred or so Japanese to Christianity. He soon realized that the Jesuits' normal practice of targeting the poorest members of society was unlikely to effect lasting change in Japan, and that he needed to change his modus operandi. At the time of his visit and for some years afterwards, Japan was divided into about two hundred independent dukedoms, each controlled by a daimyo, or local overlord. The daimyos had long competed for control of the emperor, who was head of state in name only. The daimyo who controlled the emperor became the ruling overlord, or shogun, of the entire country and therefore the most powerful man in Japan.

Xavier decided to target these feudal rulers. He took to wearing fine robes. He visited the daimyo of the island of Honshu, presented him with Portuguese music boxes, eyeglasses, and clocks, and made a speech about his Christian God. He was received enthusiastically, because he appeared to be a person of power; the daimyo even gave Xavier the use of an abandoned Buddhist monastery as a church. By the time he left the country two years later, in 1552, to work in China, Xavier had made two thousand converts. What's more, it seemed to him that the Japanese took to Christianity better than any other people he had met. He wrote: "They are the best [people] we have yet discovered; and it seems to me that, among unbelieving nations, there will not be another to surpass the Japanese."

Japan in 1737, the year of the Shimabara Uprising. From this year on, the nation would retreat into mystery and isolation.

THE WORD SPREADS

While waiting on an island off the coast of China for permission to enter the country, Xavier fell ill and died. His successors in Japan were two Portuguese missionaries: a priest, Father Come de Torres, and a lay brother, Fernando. Anjiro at this point disappears from history. There are various stories of what happened to him: one that he was martyred in China preaching the Gospel in that country, another that he turned away from God, became a pirate, and died on a raid.

Amazingly, in the next thirty years, under de Torres and his successor, Father Francisco Cabral, one hundred thousand Japanese would convert to Christianity. A Japanese-language New Testament was created, Jesuits arrived to debate Buddhist monks on the merits of their religions, and even a few daimyo and samurai were converted.

In the early 1570s, a new shogun named Oda Nobunaga emerged, a nobleman who defeated rival warlords across the country to unify Japan into a military dictatorship. Nobunaga particularly hated the powerful and arrogant Buddhist monks, and destroyed their monasteries and murdered them during his conquest. The Buddhists' misfortune was a boon to the Jesuits, whom Nobunaga supported, or at least tolerated. Close relatives of the shoguns were baptized, and, although Nobunaga did not himself become a Christian, he opened up the Japanese city of Kyoto to the missionaries.

Then, in 1582, Nobunaga was murdered. His place was taken by a peasant warlord named Toyotomi Hideyoshi, a brilliant man who had risen to the top by eliminating everyone who stood in his way. At first it seemed as if it would be business as usual for the 120 Jesuits then in the country. After all, the new shogun's court was filled with Christians, and Hideyoshi even told the Jesuits that everything in their religion was fine with him, except their prohibition against having more than one wife. Five years of peace and stability went by. But in 1587, Hideyoshi suddenly and shockingly issued an edict that gave the Jesuits only a few weeks to leave the country or be executed. Oddly, however, he did not enforce this brutal edict immediately. Historians speculate that he couldn't decide whether evicting Europeans would prevent an invasion or prompt one. In any event, the Jesuits were put on notice that their status had changed.

In 1597, as a foretaste of the future, things turned bloody. A Spanish treasure galleon, heading for Mexico from the Philippines, was blown off course in a storm and ended up running aground near the Japanese island of Shikoku. A rumor reached Hideyoshi that the ship's pilot had not only threatened to kill any Japanese who approached, but had also warned that Spain was about to invade Japan. No pilot in his right mind would have threatened the Japanese in this way, nor was Spain planning to invade, but either Hideyoshi thought this was true or used it as a pretext. He rounded up twenty-four Roman Catholics—six Portuguese and Spanish Franciscans, three Japanese Jesuits, and fifteen Japanese Catholic lay people, and had them publicly crucified in Nagasaki. Cruciform shadows were cast for nine months as the martyrs' bodies were left hanging there.

The sentence of death made public by Hideyoshi said: "I have ordered these foreigners to be treated thus because they come from the Philippines to Japan, calling themselves ambassadors, when they are not; because they remain here for so long without my permission; because in defiance of my prohibition they have built churches, preached their religion, and caused disorders."

The very arbitrariness of this order—only certain Catholics, aside from the shipboard missionaries, were picked, others left alone—was cause for terror. No one knew what would happen next.

THE TOKUGAWA SHOGUNATE
In 1598, Hideyoshi died and civil war ensued. The ultimate victor, after the bloody battle of Sekigahara in 1600, was Tokugawa Ieyasu, who subsequently established the powerful Tokugawa Shogunate, which, with its capital at Edo, now Tokyo, would rule the country without interruption for the next 260 years.

Like Hideyoshi before him, Ieyasu was afraid that allowing the Christians to spread through the country might open the doors to foreign invasion. It is possible, too, that he was concerned about losing control of his people, who were becoming more and more enamored of the Jesuits and the religion they taught. One of the

This detail of a sixteenth-century Japanese folding screen depicts the arrival of Francis Xavier and his entourage in Japan, in 1550. Xavier targeted powerful feudal leaders for conversion.

An 1863 engraving of the "Testing of the Pit," a method of torture applied to Christians during the Tokugawa Shogunate. Victims were hung upside down with their heads in excrement.

first things Ieyasu did was to forbid any more of the daimyos to convert to Christianity—only one was baptized in the next fifteen years, and that occurred in complete secrecy. He also began to make public speeches against the Catholics, claiming that "the Christians have come to Japan longing to disseminate an evil law." Buddhists monks were instructed to make sure all Japanese were a part of one Buddhist sect or another.

When Ieyasu died in 1616 and his son Hidetada took over, the attacks on Chirstians became more direct and violent. The main reason for the viciousness of the persecution at this point seems to have been internal: the shogun feared the growing power of the Christian daimyos, who could threaten the ruling power of the shogun. One Christian daimyo was captured by Hidetada and ordered to commit hara-kiri; since he was a Christian, he refused and was beheaded. Other daimyos, particularly in Kyushu, where they were numerous, were so persecuted that they renounced their new faith to save their families. At this time, historians estimate that the Christian population of Japan had grown to close to three hundred thousand. Under Hidetada's orders, thousands were rounded up and killed. The persecution was so hideous that it surpasses what happened to Christians in the early church and in the first years of Communist China. In Nagasaki in 1622, twenty-three Japanese Christians were burned to death; after which their wives and children were beheaded. Some Christians were killed by a form of torture called *mino odori*, or "raincoat dancing," in which they were forced to wear a straw coat that was then set afire, while onlookers laughed at their grotesque death paroxysms. Another torture involved suspending a person upside down with the head in a pit of excrement, a slow torment so agonizing that it claimed its first European Jesuit apostate, Father Christopher Ferreira, who renounced his faith after six hours of such treatment.

During the reign of Hidetada and his son Iemitsu (1623–51), the third of the Tokugawa shoguns, the persecution of Christians got steadily worse. Ieyasu issued edicts against Christians, but did not kill them; Hidetada killed them, but did not torture them; and Iemitsu not only killed but tortured the Jesuits in an attempt to break men and women, body and soul.

ISOLATIONISM AND OPPRESSION

By the early 1630s, Iemitsu had begun to slowly close off Japan from the outside world, issuing one restrictive edict after another. Japanese people who had been living abroad for five years or more, unless unavoidably detained, were forbidden to come home. Japanese subjects were banned from leaving the country without a special permit. Any foreign ship arriving in Japan was immediately searched; if priests were found, they were taken off and executed. Mixed race children of Portuguese or Spanish and Japanese parentage were forbidden from remaining in Japan and no one was allowed to adopt them. The daimyos were banned from trading with any of the European powers. Iemitsu aimed to unify the country by returning it to its state prior to the arrival of foreigners, while consolidating his own position as undisputed leader of the country.

Catholics were not the only group mistreated during this period. Because there was little industry and almost no foreign trade, money to support the government had to be raised off the backs of peasant farmers. They made up eighty percent of the population of Japan, had few rights under their feudal lords, little say in their futures, and were generally treated like beasts of burden. Some of the worst mistreatment of peasants occurred on the Shimabara Peninsula on the island of Kyushu. The daimyo of most of Kyushu was Lord Matsukura Shigemasa, a tyrannical figure who charged the peasants, over and above their regular taxes, an incredible eighty percent of their crops and animals as tribute. The governor of nearby Nagasaki, Terewaza Hirotaka, forced peasants to build him a huge castle in the small town of Shimabara. His son Katakata, who succeeded him in 1633, even executed peasants

THE SILENCE OF GOD

The persecution of the Japanese Christians spawned a work of twentieth-century literature that Graham Greene called "one of the finest novels of our time." First published in 1980, *Silence* was written by Japanese novelist Shusaku Endo, who was born in Tokyo in 1923. It tells the story of a Jesuit priest, Father Rodriguez, on the run in seventeenth-century Japan, utterly isolated, pursued by the authorities as he tries to spread Christ's word.

The book is a moving treatise on the "silence" of God, his failure to respond to the screams of the devoted being tortured in his name. Father Rodriguez, captured at last by the Japanese, is told that if he renounces his faith, the Christians being tortured will be released. But to renounce his faith is, of course, to lose his soul. The novel has a taut, dark, suspenseful air to it—Martin Scorsese has said he would like to make a film of it—and is absolutely unrelenting in its portrayal of this desperate time.

for nonpayment of taxes. A large part of the population of the Shimabara Peninsula was Catholic, and so they were being doubly persecuted—for their religion and their estate in life. Finally, in October of 1637, they turned on their oppressors.

A JAPANESE MESSIAH

In 1637, a charismatic young man arose who would attempt to lead the peasants out of their bondage. There are many legends about Amakusa Shiro, as befits a figure whom some Japanese believed to be a messiah whose coming had been prophesied. Even his name and age varies. He was probably born in 1622, on the Amakusa Islands not far from the Shimabara Peninsula. He was almost certainly born Masuda Shiro, and only later took the name of his birthplace, Amakusa. After he became a Christian, he was known to some as Jerome. Shiro was the only surviving son of a ronin, a samurai without a master. He was a prodigy—when he was four, he amazed everyone by memorizing and reciting in public a long and difficult piece of Confucian literature; by the age of nine, he was appointed a page to a famous samurai warrior; and when he was twelve, he went to Nagasaki alone and studied to become a doctor. It was probably in Nagasaki that he was baptized a Christian.

By 1637, the young Shiro had returned home to a peasant population that could no longer bear the torments they were being subjected to. The rural population had been swelled by large numbers of Christians seeking to escape persecution in the larger cities. As has happened among many a tormented people, salvation myths began to spread. Villagers in both the Amakusa and Shimabara regions told each other that whoever believed in Christianity would be saved, while all others would be destroyed.

Rumors began to spread about Shiro: that he could heal the sick, or walk on water. It was said that a Jesuit who had been banished from the Amakusa Islands had left behind a book; in the book was a prophecy written in the last century by none other than Francis Xavier himself, which said that a child prodigy would appear to relieve the world from a tyrant, at a time when the eastern and western parts of the sky would be dyed red and the dead trees would be covered with blossoms. It was October, and it seemed to people that sunsets and sunrises were getting redder, and that the blossoms in the trees had never been fuller, despite the fact that it was autumn.

Shiro began wandering the countryside and preaching the Christian religion. It was recounted that, while talking in a church one morning, he reached out his hand and a dove appeared and laid an egg in it. Shiro touched the egg and out came a portrait of Jesus and a roll of holy writing. Another time, it was said, two Japanese officials came to arrest him, but one was struck dumb and the other lame, until they both apologized and became Christians. Many people at the time became convinced that Shiro was, at the very least, an apostle come to earth to liberate them, and they called him Prince Shiro. It is apparent that Shiro was a charismatic and revolutionary presence in his own way, akin to Joan of Arc or Wewoka, the prophet who inspired the Ghost Dancers among the late nineteenth-century American Plains Indians. When all hope is lost, some hope must be found, and these Japanese peasants found it in Shiro, who, in 1637, was all of fifteen years old.

SLAUGHTER AT HARA CASTLE

It is not clear how a rebellion was planned, only that, in October 1637, Shiro led an army consisting of peasants and ronins against the town of Shimabara. Shimabara was a medium-sized market town which depended on surrounding agriculture for its economy. The rebels were armed mainly with sticks, rakes, and rocks, and yet they managed to burn the town to the ground and kill some forty noblemen. During their rampage, they destroyed Buddhist symbols, at one point beheading statues of the bodhisattva Jizo (these statues can still be seen in Shimabara today).

The rebels probably numbered about twenty thousand. Some of the fighters were women. Although not all were Christian, many of them carried banners with Portuguese inscriptions that read "Praise be to the Holy Sacrament." When they charged into battle they shrieked "Jesus" and "Maria."

The Nagasaki governor, Terewaza Hirotaka, scornfully sent three thousand samurai against the peasant army. In a pitched battle on December 27, the rebels killed 2,800 of these men. Terezawa later claimed that he had been defeated by black magic spells cast on him by Shiro. In early January, two more samurai armies were sent by the authorities, and these managed to push Shiro and his rebels back to Hara Castle, an abandoned stronghold at the tip of the Shimabara Peninsula. There, behind three moats, the rebels waited, their numbers swelled to thirty-seven thousand, including men, women, and children.

The shogun Iemitsu now sent one hundred thousand Japanese samurai to do battle. Despite this, the rebels repulsed attack after attack. The wooden ramparts of the castle bristled with flags and wooden crosses and the defenders, now armed with muskets, fired volley after volley at the attacking samurai. They even counterattacked effectively by sortie, pushing the samurai back. Iemitsu, furious that this army of peasants could hold off his men for so long, prevailed upon the Dutch—who had by now gained most-favored-nation status over the Portuguese, mainly by virtue of the fact that they weren't Catholics—to bring up a warship to shell Hara Castle. They did, but to little effect. The rebels shouted praises to the sky, praying for deliverance.

By April, however, the defenders were nearly out of food, water, and ammunition. On April 12, a full-scale assault began on Hara. The forces, gathered by Iemitsu, now numbered about two hundred thousand and came from all of his loyal daimyos. It is said that Iemitsu even sent the best ninja master of the era, Yaguu Jubel, to make sure the rebellion was crushed.

With only empty muskets, rice bowls, sticks, and stones to defend themselves, the rebels were soon overwhelmed. The butchery that ensued was terrible even by Japanese standards of the day. The attackers set fire to Hara Castle. Six thousand rebels died in the flames, some throwing their children into the fire in order to spare them being tortured by the samurai. Those who remained after the castle fell were systematically beheaded over the course of two days.

Between thirty-five thousand and thirty-seven thousand rebels were killed in all—more than ten percent of the approximately three hundred thousand Catholics then in Japan. For days afterward, weeping relatives of the rebels and servants of

THE DUARTE CORREA MANUSCRIPT

The only contemporary Western account of the Shimabara rebellion comes from a Portuguese sea captain named Duarte Correa, who had been imprisoned in Omura Castle as a Jesuit sympathizer. Somehow, Correa managed to smuggle out a letter to the authorities in Macau, who sent it on to Lisbon, where it was published in 1643.

Entitled "Rising at Ximabara," the letter, obviously based on eyewitness accounts from the Japanese, describes the women rebel fighters, the shouts of "Jesus" and "Maria," and how the rebels taunted the government forces from their battlements. Later, as the killing begins, Correa tells us how the moat—measured by modern archeologists to be thirty-four feet wide and eighty feet deep—filled to overflowing with the dead and dying. "Not one [rebel] was left except those who were caught and put to death later on."

Correa also describes the panicked and paranoid response of the authorities to the rebellion, with cordons of armed guards being thrown around major cities, letters of passage being required for every traveler—a situation not unlike the United States in the aftermath of September 11, 2001. Correa was burned at the stake by the Japanese, probably not long after the events at Shimabara.

Terewaza Hirotaka, governor of Nagasaki, forced peasants to build him this castle at Shimabara as his local headquarters.

the ronins wandered Japan's roads. Amakusa Shiro, for all his magic and holiness, was soon captured by a vassal of a warlord and beheaded on the spot. His head was then taken to Nagasaki and placed on a pike.

UNDERGROUND CHRISTIANITY
After the massacre at Shimabara, Japan ended a century of trading with the Portuguese by expelling every single one of them from the country and forbidding them ever to appear on its shores again under penalty of death. The Portuguese could not accept this. In 1640, a trade mission was sent to Japan. The Japanese captured it and beheaded everyone who would not recant their faith—sixty-one crew members in all.

The Tokugawa shoguns had now, they believed, completely eradicated Christianity in Japan. But, unbeknownst to them, Japanese Christianity had merely gone underground and would, amazingly, last even longer than the Tokugawa dynasty. Indeed, in the mid-nineteenth century, when the shoguns died out, Japanese Christian cells came out into the open and revealed themselves to French priests entering the country. They had outwardly pretended to be Buddhists or Shintoists, but had secretly worshipped Christ, meeting in small groups, using ancient Portuguese prayer books, handing down the religion for generation upon generation. There are about one million Christians in Japan today; as many as half of them, according to one historian's estimate, are descended from the *kakure* (hidden) Catholics.

It is interesting to speculate on what might have happened had Christianity not been repressed by the shoguns. Today, less than one percent of the population of

Japan is Christian; the religion has little effect on daily life in a country where most people who are religious are Buddhists. Had Christianity fully taken hold in the country, the whole Japanese way of thinking might have changed. Christianity teaches belief in the importance of individual conscience, rather than blind adherence to superiors or to a group. At the very least, a Japan with more than one powerful religious force might not have followed so blindly the dictates of its twentieth-century military–industrial complex; in turn, this may have held in check the rampant Japanese aggression that extended World War II to Asia.

A WORLD APART

But what of Japan as a whole? In the years from 1640 on, after expelling everyone but the Dutch, who were confined to tiny Deshima Island in Nagasaki Bay, the Japanese had no contact with any European power. The Tokugawa era coincided with a lengthy period of peace in Japanese history—there were no major battles after Shimabara, and most samurai turned in their swords for pens, becoming clerks in the massive Tokugawa bureaucracy. Japanese culture flourished, as did Japanese national identity. On the plus side, that is why the Japanese have developed such an enduring sense of their national identity, and why their culture is so strong, so imprinted on each and every Japanese person.

On the other hand, Japan missed out on a great deal by withdrawing from the world when it did. The industrial revolution was late in coming to Japan—even during World War II, military supplies were often transported by beast of burden. When a militaristic Japan emerged in the late nineteenth century, with ambitions of dominating Asia, it was in a sense trying to play catch-up. But its inwardness and xenophobia led to fatal miscalculations. Having been bypassed by the intellectual revolutions of the eighteenth and nineteenth centuries, the philosophies of individual rights and social justice, Japan totally misjudged the strength of American democracy and the response that its attack on Pearl Harbor would provoke.

Would Japan have withdrawn from the world had Shiro and his fellow rebels not been slaughtered? It's hard to say, for Japan under the Tokugawa shoguns was tending towards isolation. But the presence of a vibrant Christian community would almost certainly have precluded total isolation. One thing is for certain: the violent deaths of Amakusa Shiro and his Christians on the battlements of Hara Castle at Shimabara changed Japan forever.

THE LAST PRIEST

The final foray of a European priest into Japan was made by an Italian abbot, John-Baptist Sidotti. He had been sent to Asia as part of a mission to China in 1708, but sneaked away and, with either incredible faith or incredible foolhardiness, somehow found passage to Japan, arriving in the dark of night.

Sidotti was completely alone—he could not even speak Japanese—and without friends, and was obviously planning on becoming a martyr. But the Japanese scholar who interrogated him after he had been found by a local peasant and turned in to the authorities was an unusual humanist and not one of those Japanese who blamed the Shimabara uprising on the Portuguese, as many in the ruling class still did. He advised the shogun not to kill Sidotti, but to imprison him so that Christianity would not spread again. Sidotti was placed in jail, where he died six years later.

ROGER WILLIAMS: FATHER OF AMERICAN CIVIL LIBERTIES

Oft have I heard these Indians say:
These English will deliver us
Of all that's ours, our lands and lives,
In the end, they will bereave us.
Roger Williams, *A Key into the Language of America*

SIXTEEN YEARS AFTER THE PILGRIMS TOUCHED DOWN ON PLYMOUTH ROCK and were busily doing whatever they could to steal land from the Indians and suppress religious freedom, one man had the courage to cry out in the wilderness against what he saw as the "unjust usurpation" of Indian lands. For this, Roger Williams, an English Puritan minister, was considered "erroneous and very dangerous" and driven out, literally, into the teeth of a howling snowstorm. How Roger Williams got through that snowstorm, and what he did in his exile, made him one of the preeminent spiritual men of his time—and ours.

There are no reliable representations of Roger Williams—no sketches, paintings, engravings, or sculptures—and few descriptions of him from his contemporaries. Twentieth-century artists tend to depict Williams in the "Christ-as-Anglo-Saxon-hippy" mode. The statue of Williams erected in 1939 in Providence, Rhode Island, the city he founded, has lank, flowing hair parted in the middle, a high brow, characterful nose, firm chin, and eyes that gaze outward in noble beseechment. For once, lack of imagination is a virtue. The artists who have endowed Williams with Christ-like attributes get pretty close to depicting the character of the man, if not the outside.

Interestingly enough, though he trained as a Puritan minister and founded the first Baptist Church in America, Williams was not a man who could stay in any organized religion for long. He was what was called in those days a "comer-outer," someone deeply religious who did not believe that any one church held all the answers, and who "came out" to find a different way. This is another reason why he seems so modern: he believed that above doctrine and liturgy, and all the trappings that go along with institutionalized religion, comes freedom of religious choice and expression.

BURNING FOR FREEDOM

Roger Williams was born in London, probably in 1603—there is uncertainty because St. Sepulchre's Church, where he was christened, was destroyed along with its parish records, in the Great Fire of London in 1666. He was the son of a prominent merchant and grew up in the Holborn district of London, near Smithfield Plain. Great boisterous fairs and festivals were held at Smithfield, as were public burnings of heretics. While Williams was growing up, the heretics would have been Puritans. There is no record of him having seen such an execution, but it is quite likely that he did; if not, he would have almost certainly smelled the odor of singed hair and melting flesh.

Williams was an excellent student who was educated at London's Charterhouse School and then at Pembroke College, Cambridge University, where he received a scholarship for his expertise in Greek, Latin, and Hebrew. Upon graduation, he was ordained a minister of the Church of England, and thereafter became private chaplain to a wealthy family.

In 1629, he married Mary Barnard, in Essex. By then twenty-six years old, Williams led a seemingly comfortable life. But the memories of those brutal executions must have preyed on his mind. For Williams was not just any Church of England minister, but a member of what was still one of the most controversial religious groups in the country, the Puritans.

The map shows the extent of English settlement in the mid-seventeenth century, in what would become New England.

In the sixteenth century, King Henry VIII had made his momentous split from the Catholic Church and, despite the attempts of Queen Mary I to bring the country back to Catholicism, England subsequently remained Protestant. Elizabeth I tried to alienate neither Catholics nor Anglicans, as members of the Protestant Church of England were called. But during her reign there arose a group of Protestants who believed that the Church of England had not separated itself enough from the Roman Church, that it had not, in fact, become Protestant to a sufficient degree. These Protestants became known as Puritans.

The Puritans felt that any traces of Catholicism, including ritual elements such as bowing at the name of Jesus and making the sign of the cross during the baptismal ceremony, should be done away with. They believed that every congregation should be independent, and that religion should be separate from politics.

A romanticized 1864 depiction of the Puritans at Plymouth Rock. The reality was more prosaic: the *Mayflower*'s sailors offloaded the Pilgrims at Plymouth because they had run out of beer and wanted to get back home.

After King James I of Scotland, a follower of the teachings of the Scottish reformist Protestant John Calvin, came to the throne upon Elizabeth's death, the Puritans made the mistake of thinking he would be sympathetic to their goals. He wasn't. In fact, he urged his government to monitor the Church of England more carefully, and even banned independent worship—all worshippers were to use *The Book of Common Prayer*, for instance. Puritan heretics—"Nonconformists"—were imprisoned or executed.

In 1620, a group of Puritans fled overseas, first to Holland and then to America—an extraordinary step—hoping to set up a community where they could not only worship in freedom, but could also provide an example for true believers back in England, who might subsequently join them.

The young Roger Williams was one of these true believers, and among the best and brightest of them. Certain that his truest expression of spirituality and faith in God could not be found in his home country, he and his wife, Mary, decided to set sail for Massachusetts in late 1630, ten years after the Pilgrims had landed in America at Plymouth Rock.

A SIN OF UNJUST USURPATION
After a rough, two-month sea voyage on the tiny bark *Lyon*, Williams and his wife landed in Boston in February. At first, all seemed to go well in the New World. Governor John Winthrop of the Massachusetts Bay Colony wrote of his happiness at the arrival of this "godly minister," and offered him the position of pastor of a new church in Boston.

But Williams's autonomous nature immediately began to assert itself. He thought that his new church was not sufficiently independent from the Church of England because it longed for reunion with it—in other words, these Puritans were simply not radical enough for the newly arrived minister. So Williams found another church in Salem, about fifteen miles north of Boston, which espoused more separatist beliefs. However, his appointment there was quashed by the religious authorities in Boston, who were miffed that Williams had turned down their offer.

Undeterred, he headed about forty miles south of the city to Plymouth, the Pilgrims' original landing place. The people there were the "ur-Puritans," the true radicals, and Williams may have thought he would be happy there, but within a year it was reported by a chronicler that Williams had begun to fall into some "strange opinions, and from opinion to practice."

For one thing, Williams was troubled by the fact that people appearing in civil courts were obliged to swear allegiance to the colony "so help me God." Well, what if they didn't believe in God, Williams asked. What then? Given that not believing in God was not an option in the land of the Puritans—and in some ways it is not an option in the present-day United States, either—people were shocked and outraged. They were also shocked when Williams asked what gave civil magistrates the right to force people to go to church and to prosecute them if, say, they took the name of the Lord in vain. Williams was thus one of the first voices in the United States that was heard to argue for what has since become a quintessentially American doctrine: the separation of church and state. This doctrine was spelled out a century and a half later in the U.S. Bill of Rights and Constitution, by American politicians including the likes of Thomas Jefferson and John Quincy Adams.

At this point, Williams was staking out territory for himself as a "comer-outer"— still at least nominally a Puritan, but following his own path. Chief among the strange beliefs espoused by Williams was one that aroused anger in the colony—his contention that the English were living unjustly on land that belonged to the Indians. King Charles I, who had succeeded King James, had granted the Pilgrims patent, or title, to the land around the Massachusetts Bay Colony. Roger Williams rejected the legitimacy of this land grant, claiming that a very unchristian "sin of usurpation upon others' possessions had occurred."

To Williams's contemporaries—his white contemporaries, of course—this statement was so far-fetched as to seem preposterous. In the minds of the settlers, the land was there for the taking. After all, only Indians—"savages" in contemporary parlance—lived on it. It lay "common," in other words. In any event, as preacher John Cotton said, the English made "improvements" on the land, while the Indians merely "burn[ed] it up for pastime."

WILLIAMS IN THE WILDERNESS

Although Roger Williams liked the Indians, he didn't want to live like them. Some American colonists "went native," abandoned their homes and families, moved to Indian villages, and, effectively, eradicated their previous identities. But not Williams. He rather disliked Indian food, called their lodges "smoky holes," and was always faithful to his wife, Mary. He preferred, whenever possible, the comfort of his own home and fire, and time spent with his six children, especially after his years on the run from the authorities in Massachusetts. He was an Englishman and a Puritan who would always love his home country; at the same time, he believed that this did not preclude freedom for others.

In fact, the tribes surrounding the Bay Colony were strong, vibrant, and numerous: the Nipmucs, Narragansets, Wampanoags, Mohegans, and Pequots. When the Pilgrims first arrived, Indians in the whole of New England, according to recent estimates, probably numbered around one hundred thousand, and the Pilgrims knew they had not come to a sparsely inhabited country. Although it does not match the rosy picture usually painted in American history books, the Pilgrims initially landed near a deserted Wampanoag settlement and in part survived their first harsh winter by robbing Indian graves for blankets and clothing and tearing apart huts to find hidden food. A smallpox epidemic brought by Europeans killed many in the 1620s, considerably weakening the tribes, but in Williams's time they were still strong, particularly the Narragansets, who had about four thousand men of warrior age. The local English were doing nothing at all to try to understand these "savage" neighbors. A bloody confrontation was likely, and soon.

Williams seems to have come to America in part to be with the Indians, for he immediately contacted and made friends with them. From 1661 to 1663, he learned the Algonquian language and mastered the dialects of the Narragansets and others. He came to appreciate that the Indians carefully divided up land and knew exactly where one person's property began and where another's ended. As Williams said, they were "very exact and punctuall" about property lines. If they were burning the land, it was to clear underbrush and enrich soil for sowing crops the next year. Williams also made important friendships. One was with Massoit, a sachem, or chief, of the Wampanoags, who was the father of Metacom, later called King Philip by the English. Another was Canonicus, an elderly but highly influential leader of the Narragansets, who would come to regard Williams almost as a son. It was because of his association with these men and their people that Williams began to see the European point of view, with regard to the Indians, as misguided. And it was to these men Williams appealed for help when his own people turned against him.

CAST INTO EXILE
There is something almost biblical about what happened next to Roger Williams, which is fitting, because this was truly a biblical dispute—one about the nature of God, spirit, and property—that he was entering into with his fellow Puritans.

By 1635, Williams was not only defending the rights of the Indians to their property, but also asserting that these "Natural men," as he called them, should not be forced to "the exercise of those holy Ordinances of Prayers, Oathes, &c." After all, Williams wrote, the world was "not a homogeneal … but an hetergeneal [sic] commixture or joining together of things most different in kinds and natures." This was too much for the Massachusetts Bay Colony authorities. Williams was claiming that the English were living on land that belonged to others *and* that these Indians should not be made beholden either to church or to state. In October of 1635, the General Court of the Colony convicted Williams of defying and defaming both clergy and magistrates. To control his "infections," they ordered that "the said Mr. Williams shall depart out of this jurisdiction within six weeks."

Roger and Mary Williams had a two-year-old child and a newborn. Where could they go? Not back to England, where the environment had become even worse for Puritans. Certainly not to any English-speaking settlement in the region, for no one would take Williams in and risk the anger of the Massachusetts Bay Colony.

But although his situation was precarious, Williams did not stop speaking his mind, and nor did he make any preparations to leave. By January 1636, the authorities decided to have him taken in chains to a ship leaving for England. Williams, however, heard about their plan, and realized that his only option was to become a fugitive. Leaving his wife and children behind, he fled, a few days ahead of the arresting officers.

Williams spent the next fourteen weeks in a "howling wilderness," as he wrote later. Heading southwest, he walked, alone, nearly forty miles, through a fierce snowstorm, to the village where Massoit lived near Mount Hope. Although he left no day-by-day record of his journey, it is certain that he suffered immensely: he later

After being banished from the Massachusetts Bay Colony, Roger Williams was welcomed by the Narraganset Indians, with whom he lived before founding his own settlement.

THOMAS MORTON: THE PAGAN PILGRIM

A short time before Roger Williams arrived in New England, another anti-Puritan founded his own colony—one with a far different tenor. Thomas Morton was an English lawyer and trader, who sailed to Massachusetts, accompanied by about thirty indentured servants, in 1624. He set up a trading post and soon befriended the local Indians; he also persuaded many of the indentured servants to throw off their harsh masters and help him start a colony just north of Plymouth.

The Pilgrims absolutely hated Thomas Morton. Not only did he consort with native women, but he also had the temerity to mock the Puritans and their pious pretensions. He made up sarcastic names for them: Miles Standish, the diminutive professional soldier hired by the Puritans as military adviser, was "Captain Shrimpe," and the strict Puritan John Endecott, magistrate and later governor of the Massachusetts Bay Colony, was "that great swelling fellow, Captain Littleworth." But Thomas Morton was most famous for the pagan May Day party he threw. Erecting an eighty-foot-high pine pole, Morton brewed "a barrel of excellent beer" and invited Indians and young indentured servants from all around to party down. The result was, as William Bradford wrote in his *History of the Plymouth Plantation*, "ye beastly practices of ye mad Bacchanalians."

Naturally, this would not do. Puritans under the command of Miles Standish attacked Morton's colony, now called "Merrymount," and conquered it without a shot being fired—mainly because the inhabitants were too drunk to lift their weapons. They put Morton in chains and had him sent back to England, where, however, he continued to write pamphlets attacking the Massachusetts Bay Colony. The Merrymount colony disappeared, but it was immortalized in Nathaniel Hawthorne's story "The May-Pole of Merrymount," which perfectly captures the tensions between pagan freedom, as embodied by Thomas Morton, and narrow fundamentalism, as personified by the Pilgrims.

wrote, "I bear to this day in my body the effects of that winter's exposure." After resting, Williams traveled another forty miles to the land of the Narraganset and his good friend Canonicus. There he recovered, and by the spring of 1636 he had begun to build a settlement. Soon his wife and children arrived, as did other European settlers sympathetic to his point of view—mainly dissatisfied Puritans from Salem and the Massachusetts Bay Colony, who greatly respected Williams and his principles.

Houses were built, crops began to grow, and something else flourished: an almost utopian community which housed both Indians and Europeans, without conflict. Much to the chagrin of his enemies in the Massachusetts Bay Colony, Williams became an indispensable mediator. If the Indians needed to contact the Puritans in Boston, or the Puritans the Indians, Williams was the man they went to first. He spent a good deal of time visiting Canonicus and Massoit at their villages in the forest, and the Narragansets sometimes held their council meetings at Williams's house.

Ironically, Williams soon found out that he had built his settlement on land that "belonged" not to the Narraganset tribe, but to the Plymouth colony. So he moved again, this time to a "sweet spring" at the head of Narragansett Bay, on land lent to him by Canonicus, who refused any payment but did accept gifts from Williams for the rest of his life. Williams called this place "Providence," as a symbol of his delivery from the wilderness.

Williams's colony was a magnet to freethinkers. Anne Hutchinson, midwife and theologian, was, like Williams, banished from the Massachusetts Bay Colony, in her case for claiming that she did not need the Bible nor the Puritan ministers because the Holy Spirit spoke directly to her, and to all who prayed for salvation. She and several dozen followers found their way to Providence and were welcomed by Williams, as was a former Puritan named John Clarke, who agreed with Hutchinson. Also welcomed from Massachusetts was Ezekiel Holliman, an Anabaptist or antipedobaptist—meaning a member of the sect, started in England, that did not believe that children should be baptized until they were old enough to make a free choice as to their religion. Holliman was influenced by Williams's belief in freedom of religious practice, and Williams in turn was influenced by Holliman. In 1638, he was baptized by Holliman and, along with eleven others, started the first Baptist congregation in America—a congregation that, deliberately, had no physical church, as followers held that the substance of the religion was its members, not its buildings. Typically, however, Williams remained a Baptist for only a few months before "coming out" again and restlessly seeking the truth elsewhere. However, he remained a supporter of the Baptist congregation, and the church endured and grew in America.

SLAUGHTER OF THE PEQUOT
In the summer of 1636, an English trader was killed by an Indian on Block Island. John Winthrop, governor of the Massachusetts Bay Colony, suspected the Narragansets were the offenders, but Williams was able to convince him that this was not the case. Winthrop then decided that the Pequots were responsible—and, in fact, they probably were—and made ready to go to war against them.

The danger here, well understood by the English in Boston, was that the Pequots were allied with the Narragansets; if there was war, the two tribes would fight together and almost certainly destroy the Massachusetts Bay Colony. Turning to Williams as their only hope, they pleaded with him in August of that summer "to use his utmost and speedy Endeavors" to keep Canonicus and his people out of the war. Williams responded quickly, leaping into "a poor Canow & ... cutting through a stormie Wind and with great seas, every minute in hazard of life." After going thirty miles, he arrived at the village of the Narragansets, a port town almost as big as Boston. There he convinced the sachem and other tribal leaders to sign a treaty with the English.

Williams also negotiated with the Pequots. But these were men who "reeked with the blood of my countrymen, murdered and massacred by them on the Connecticut River ... I could not but nightly look for their bloody knives at my throat also," and even Williams's equanimity seems to have faltered, for once.

In May of 1637, a force of English, Mohegans, and Narragansets attacked a Pequot village at Mystic, Connecticut. Six hundred men, women, and children were trapped in a burning building by the English, who slaughtered anyone who tried to escape. This was too much even for the most battle-hardened Puritan. As one wrote, "It was a fearfull sight to see them thus frying." The rest of the Pequots were hunted down and killed or sold into slavery. As a people, they simply ceased to exist.

Roger Williams was aggrieved and horrified. He had tried to stop the war, but had been unable to, and now the Pequots were destroyed. Afterward, however, a general peace existed in New England until 1675, and almost certainly Roger Williams's actions just before the Pequot War helped bring this about. He even heard rumors that the powers-that-be in Boston might, as payment for his services, "recall me from banishment," and also honor him "with some remark of favor." But he still had many enemies in the Massachusetts Bay Colony, and this did not occur.

A KEY TO AMERICA

After the Pequot War, casting about for a way to support his family and bring business to his fledgling colony at Providence, Williams hit upon the idea of a trading post. From about 1637 on, Williams ran one of the most successful trading posts in New England, on a site in a cove of Narragansett Bay, about twenty miles from Providence, picked out for him by Canonicus. Here he would receive goods shipped from English or American ports, as well as furs, animal skins, pottery, and other items brought by the Indians, who trusted Williams because of his honesty.

Around 1640, Williams began a series of epistolary debates with Puritan luminaries such as John Cotton; at the same time, he was working on an Indian grammar. Partly to find a publisher for these writings and partly to seek a charter for his fledgling colony, whose land was being eyed enviously by settlers, Dutch as well as English, Williams decided to make his first visit back to London in thirteen years. Arriving in England, Williams found himself in the middle of a bloody civil war, as the forces of Parliament and Oliver Cromwell joined to destroy King Charles I. It wasn't the best moment to seek a charter for his colony or a publisher, but Williams had some friends from his old days at Cambridge who were now in influential positions, and even so august a personage as John Milton lobbied for him. With their help, Williams found Gregory Dexter, a respected London printer, who helped prepare his work for publication.

Published in 1643 in London, *A Key into the Language of America* is one of the few truly seminal books to have come out of seventeenth-century America. Not only was it the first Indian grammar to be put into English, but it also included a healthy dose of useful advice regarding the natives of the New World. One of Williams's most important achievements was to show that the Indians were not savages, but human beings. His section in *A Key* on greetings, for example, revealed that, just like Europeans, Indians differed in character from person to person: some were friendly on first meeting, others shy. Like anyone, the Indians were "delighted with being greeted in their own language," and so, suggested Williams, it might behoove the Puritans to learn a word or two of Narraganset.

He pointed out how hospitable the Indians were, saying "it is a strange truth that a man can generally find more free entertainment and refreshing amongst these Barbarians than amongst the thousands that call themselves Christians." He described how there were no homeless beggars on the streets of Indian towns, and few, if any, aggressive acts of violence or murders. Indian society was in some ways more truly Christian than Christian society, so by what right did Europeans usurp Indian land?

In *A Key into the Language of America*, Williams also used the Indian way of life to describe what he wanted in his new colony of Providence: a place where "all men may walk as their consciences perswade them," where "all civil liberty is founded in the consent of the People." When the American Revolution started in the 1770s, these same principles were employed; later, they found their way overseas as revolution flamed through France.

Williams not only succeeded in having his work published, to some popular acclaim, but he also managed to obtain his charter—from Parliament, since there was no king. Returning to America, he was even allowed safe passage through Boston without arrest, and this time, walked the forty miles to Providence in comfort, and was met by cheering crowds. In November of 1643, Williams was named chief officer of the colony then called Providence Plantation and, later, Rhode Island.

ANIMAL AND HUMAN PREDATORS

Governing is very different from being a minister or even running a trading post, but Williams was a successful governor and put his own particular stamp on Rhode Island. One of his first jobs was a practical one. The place was overrun by wolves, which threatened livestock and people and needed to be culled. For this task, Williams employed a group of Narraganset hunters.

Williams was sympathetic to personal plights, as well. When hearing that a young parentless woman was going to marry a man solely for security, he asked that the colony act with "fatherly care, counsel, and direction" on behalf of the woman, to make sure her husband-to-be was an honorable man. He asked his community to do the same for people considered deranged in their senses, who normally would have been sent to a madhouse.

But more pressing issues threatened his new colony. There were human predators, too: men in Providence who would take advantage of Williams's humane approach to governing. He watched as fellow settlers set up land companies in order to hoard land for the future and sell it to the highest bidder. One man, William Coddington, claimed all of Aquidneck Island—then part of the province of Rhode Island—for his own, tried unsuccessfully to ally himself with the Plymouth colony, and even went so far as to go to London and finagle a charter for it, causing Williams no end of trouble. Finally, in late 1651, Williams sailed for England and was able to have Coddington's charter revoked, although it took him over two years to do so. Once back in Rhode Island, Williams served for two more years as chief officer, and then retired at the age of fifty-two, certain that he had set up a free colony where all could live and worship as they would.

But Williams's ideas scared a lot of people. He had continued to write, publishing another influential book, *The Bloudy Tenant of Persecution*, in which he made a powerful case against religious persecution, writing that "the forcing of conscience is soul-rape." His archrival, Puritan minister John Cotton, called him "the Prodigious Minister of Exorbitant Novelties." Another Puritan accused him of "seeking to take away all … instituted worship of God." The writings of Williams, it was said, would

THOUGHTS OF A POET

Not all of Roger Williams writings survive, but those that do indicate a writer of rare sensitivity, a man who is almost a metaphysical poet. In the introduction to *A Key into the Language of America*, Williams says:

I present you with a Key. This key respects the native languages [of America] and happily may unlock some rarities concerning the Natives themselves, not yet discovered.

With this key I have entered into the secrets of those countries, wherever the English dwell, about two hundred miles between the French and the Dutch plantations. For want of this key, I know what gross mistakes myself and others have run into.

A little Key may open a box, where lies a bunch of Keys.

A memorial statue of Roger Williams stands on a hilltop in the city of Providence, Rhode Island.

spark the Indians to rebellion. His books were burned publicly in Massachusetts and England. Yet Williams was not deterred. "God," he wrote, "requires not a uniformity of religion to be enacted and enforced in any civil state … [but that] Paganish, Jewish, Turkish, or Anti-Christian consciences and worships be granted to all men in all nations and countries." Words that would echo down through the next century and find their culmination in the American and French revolutions.

ONE LAST AND BLOODY WAR

Roger Williams was now getting old, complaining of "lameness, so th't sometimes I have not been able to rise, nor goe, nor stand," but his position in Providence and New England at large was a prominent one. He was much needed as a mediator because wave after wave of European colonists were arriving in New England and pushing against the Indians, who started to push back. His old friend Canonicus had by this time died, as had Massoit, the sachem of the Wampanoags. The new chief was Metacom, King Philip as the whites knew him, a twenty-five-year-old warrior who suspected the English had killed two of his brothers and who trusted almost no European. Metacom was incensed by the English, who stole land, scared away game, and got his people drunk with liquor, while Puritan officials stood back and let it happen. During his lifetime, he had watched the English population in New England double, while his people's lands dwindled to a small territory near Mount Hope. In 1675, when Roger Williams was seventy-two years old, the English decided they wanted that territory as well.

A series of killings took place on both sides, tensions heightened, and Williams was asked to mediate once again. He even allowed himself to be held hostage by the Wampanoags as surety for the safe return of Metacom, who had gone to negotiate with the Plymouth colony authorities. War was briefly averted, but broke out in late June, 1675. Shortly after this, Roger Williams encountered Metacom while the chief was riding in a canoe with his family. Williams warned him that warring with the English would almost certainly cause the extinction of his people, that the Wampanoag's situation was as precarious as that of a canoe on a stormy sea. To which Metacom, who had seen his people slowly dying over the years, replied: "My canoe is already overturned."

The war was vicious, and to the death. The Indians hung Englishmen by hooks inserted into their jaws; the English threw Indians to their savage hunting dogs, to be devoured. A war party of Indians appeared outside Providence and Williams went out to meet it. The Indians promised not to touch him, but they attacked Providence and burned it to the ground, including Williams's own house. He told the Wampanoag: "That house of mine now burning before mine eyes lodged kindly some thousands of you for these ten years."

In a final irony, Williams, the man of peace, was forced to become a military commander, rallying his people to fight off the Indians for the good of the colony. Yet, when one of his angry colonists caught an Indian and was going to torture the man to death, Williams intervened and had the Indian executed to spare him pain—a terrible decision for a man who loved peace and human life above all else.

King Philip's War marked the end of effective Indian resistance in New England. Metacom was captured and drawn and quartered. Every single Indian village was burned to the ground and any Indians remaining alive were sold into slavery. Over one thousand English colonists died.

THE DEATH AND LIFE OF ROGER WILLIAMS
Roger Williams, aged about eighty, died between January and March of 1683: it is fitting for this unknown man that the exact date of his death has been lost to history. In the years following his death, he became largely forgotten. His ideas, however, were not. What Williams thought and wrote was echoed in the writings of British philosopher John Locke, whose work in turn influenced libertarians from William Penn to Thomas Jefferson, and even the formation of the U.S. government. This truly radical man had, finally, set off a revolution.

While the image of Roger Williams as a seminal figure in America lived on, his actual works were not celebrated, after his death, until 1777, when a Baptist historian and minister named Isaac Backus published *A History of New England, with Particular Reference to the Denomination of Christians called Baptists*. Backus had researched Williams's life, and gathered many of his letters and writings that might otherwise have been lost, and traced his history, from his banishment from Massachusetts to his founding of Providence. Backus wrote that no one else who lived when Williams did "acted so consistently and so steadily upon right principles about government and liberty."

In 1834, in his *History of the United States*, historian George Bancroft called for the name of Roger Williams "to be preserved in universal history as one who advanced moral and political science" more than any of his fellows. Gradually, during the nineteenth and early twentieth centuries, Williams's writing was re-collected and reissued, and in 1953 Harvard's Perry Miller, in his influential book *Roger Williams: His Contribution to the American Tradition*, could write: "[Williams] was not a rationalist and a utilitarian who gave up the effort to maintain an orthodoxy because he had no concern about religious truth, but was the most passionately religious of men … His decision to leave denominations free to worship as they chose came as a consequence of his insight that freedom is a condition of the spirit."

Today, Williams's thoughts on American Indians are the thoughts of a majority of people in the world—it just took us 350 years or so to catch up with him. And, albeit belatedly, Roger Williams has received at least one bit of justice. In 1936, the State of Massachusetts passed a bill dictating that "the sentence of expulsion against Roger Williams by the General Court of the Massachusetts Bay Colony in the year 1635 be, and hereby is, revoked."

It was about time.

THE BATTLE OF POLTAVA AND THE FALL OF THE SWEDISH EMPIRE

AROUND THE TOWN OF POLTAVA, IN AN OBSCURE REGION OF THE UKRAINE, where the vast eastern steppes merge with the woods and marshes of the Vorskla River valley, local farmers regularly come across pieces of human bones buried deep in the soil—bones hacked to pieces by sabers and pierced by lances. These are the remains of one of the most important battles in history, which took place here on a steaming hot day in 1709. Aside from the farmers, few people outside the countries of Sweden and Russia, the two combatants, know much about the battle of Poltava. It was not a clash, like Waterloo or Gallipoli or Midway, that has captured the world's imagination; yet, had Poltava not happened, or had its outcome been different, Europe, and the world, would be a changed place today. For, in the chaotic collision of two proud armies, Poltava signaled the death of one great empire and the birth of another.

A GREAT BALTIC EMPIRE

Today, we tend to think of Sweden as a liberal but firmly neutral country, which seems to stand outside the swirl of geopolitics. It's a place where Nobel Prizes are handed out, and where peace conferences are held. But at one time, it was on its way to becoming an imperial power to rival Hapsburg Spain or France in the time of Napoleon.

At the end of the Middle Ages, as the Baltic region began to emerge from feudalism, the northern European states—Sweden, Denmark, Poland, and Russia—all scrambled for land bordering the Baltic Sea. By the late seventeenth century, Sweden had emerged as the preeminent power in the region. Its empire was centered on the Gulf of Bothnia, but it also extended into mainland Europe. In 1617, Sweden had defeated Russia and acquired the territories of Ingria and Kexholm, thus completely shutting Russia off from the sea. It had also bitten off large chunks of Germany during the Thirty Years War and later fought Denmark for the territory which became southern Sweden.

For most of the latter half of the seventeenth century, Sweden was ruled by a remarkable man: King Charles XI. Charles was an autocrat, but an enlightened one. Under his leadership, the vast territories of the aristocracy were reduced and more wealth and power placed in the hands of merchants and peasant farmers. Charles also reorganized the Swedish army in a truly original way. He divided the country up into tiny areas called *rota*, each consisting of roughly ten farmsteads. Every *rota* was responsible for, as it were, growing a soldier. A man was picked, educated, trained, fed, and clothed at the *rota*'s expense. In time of peace, he was supported; in time of war, he was sent off to do battle. If he died or was incapacitated, the *rota* picked and trained another man. Often, the soldiering profession was handed down from father to son.

By 1700, with the exception of certain elite cavalry units, the entire Swedish army was a product of the *rota* system (which continued to operate until 1901) and it had helped create an army that was one of the most feared fighting forces in Europe. Every man knew that he fought not just for king and country, but also for a small group of people from his hometown who had stood behind him almost since birth. The Swedes needed this kind of esprit and unit cohesiveness for simple arithmetical reasons: Sweden's population was no more than three million in 1700, while the population of Russia, its chief rival, was ten times that.

THE GREAT NORTHERN WAR

In 1697, when Charles XI succumbed to stomach cancer, Sweden had been at peace for over twenty years and its merchants had grown wealthy from Baltic trade. Its neighbors looked on enviously, particularly Russia, which had remained shut out of the Baltic and had suffered accordingly.

However, a brilliant and ambitious czar had taken control of Russia in 1686: Peter I, soon to be known as Peter the Great. Peter was an outsized figure—six feet, seven inches tall, with striking emerald-green eyes—and he had outsized ambitions. He wanted to Westernize Russia, to bring it out of its prolonged Dark Age and into contact with the rest of Europe. To achieve this, he introduced sweeping reforms, which ranged from forcing his courtiers to cut off their long beards to switching to the Julian calendar from the old Russian one. Peter also began to modernize the Russian army, hiring foreigners to become the heart of an officer corps and placing a huge emphasis on artillery firepower—a strategy that would bring striking results at Poltava.

In 1700, around the height of its glory, the Swedish Empire encompassed a large swathe of northern Europe.

Peter also wanted Russia to become a great sea power. To this end, he battled the Ottoman Turks, who controlled the Crimea, captured the Ottoman fortress of Azov, and started a small navy. But he knew he would be unable to defeat the mighty Ottoman Empire and so, in 1698, he turned his attention north, to the Baltic, a more natural sea outlet. Joining forces with Denmark, Norway, Saxony, and Poland, Peter declared war on Sweden and, in 1700, launched an offensive against the empire, thus beginning what is known as the Great Northern War.

The Swedish forces found themselves fighting almost continuously for the next nine years. They were greatly outnumbered, usually by two to one and very often by four to one. And yet they won a series of seemingly impossible victories. In the summer of 1700, they rapidly defeated Denmark, forcing her out of the war. In November of that year, they routed the Russians at Narva. Attacking through a snowstorm against entrenched forces numbering forty thousand, eight thousand Swedish soldiers devastated the Russian army, killing ten thousand and forcing the rest to flee. The following year, the Swedes defeated a Saxon army at Riga, chasing it into Poland.

How had the Swedes accomplished this? It was partly due to their cohesiveness and their innovative tactics—the favorite Swedish strategy was to aim small but formidable forces at a point in the enemy line, catching their opponents by surprise (as at Narva) and then routing them. The other reason was the country's extraordinary leader, King Charles XII, one of the finest soldier-kings of his era. He became King of Sweden at the age of fifteen, in 1697, when his father died—quite possibly his youth gave Peter I and his allies reason to think they could attack. But Charles XII was far from a pushover. Hard military training had helped him overcome a sickly childhood constitution, and by the time he was eighteen, when war broke out, he was ready to lead his armies.

Charles was not the kind of ruler who led from his nation's capital or the rear of his army. He was always in the thick of the battle. His coolness in combat was often remarked upon; and it wasn't just coolness, but a strange detachment, an almost otherworldly sense of disdain for his own survival. This may have derived, at least in part, from the fact that he was constantly surrounded by an elite bodyguard, the Drabants, an entire corps made up of men of officer rank, whose sole duty was to act as a human shield for the king. Of the 147 Drabants who went to war with the king in 1700, only 14 would survive.

THE PATH TO POLTAVA

In the winter of 1707, Charles XII and his army finally conquered Poland after years of fighting there. Charles then signed a treaty with Poland, which made sure that all Polish trade would go through the Swedish port of Riga, that Swedish merchants would be given highly favorable incentives to live in Poland, and that Russia would have no transit trade through to Europe. King Augustus the Strong of Poland was deposed and a Swedish puppet ruler placed upon the Polish throne. But the Swedish army, after years of campaigning the length and breadth of Saxony and Poland, was exhausted. It had been forced to live off Poland's limited resources, in turn provoking a violent guerilla

Opposite: Portrait of Charles XII, 1780. Charles's fierce, warrior-like attitude resulted in repeated military triumphs, but ultimately led him to overreach himself, in turn bringing down his empire.

war against the occupation. The Swedes responded with brutal reprisals, including the burning of entire towns and massacres of their inhabitants. Charles XII was unperturbed. He said that the Poles could suffer as much as they liked and his commanders were ordered to "extract and thrash and scrape together" whatever they needed in the way of foodstuffs. Moreover, the army was not going to return to Sweden; instead, it was to continue to push the Russian forces in Poland westward toward the Ukraine. There, the Swedes hoped to link up with an army of Cossacks under the hetman Ivan Mazepa, who had agreed to ally himself with the Swedes in return for the Ukraine's liberation from Russia. Together, the Swedes and Cossacks would invade Russia and destroy the czar once and for all.

In late December 1707, King Charles crossed the frozen Vistula with an army that was huge by Swedish standards—forty-four thousand men—and began to move after the Russians through Poland. So concerned was Peter the Great that he made several tentative peace offerings to Charles XII, but the twenty-six-year-old Swedish ruler brushed them aside, convinced of the invincibility of his army and the rightness of his cause. Others were convinced, too: so fearsome was the reputation of the Swedish army that Europeans living in Moscow at the time began to flee the city and the certain bloodbath they foresaw.

A SCORCHED-EARTH STRATEGY
The Russians applied the kind of tactics in 1708 that they would later employ with great success against Napoleon and Hitler. Refusing to give battle, they retreated just ahead of the advancing Swedish army, laying waste to the countryside as they went, burning villages and poisoning wells. The Swedes attempted to flank the Russians by moving north through the territory of Masovia, but found themselves embroiled in a bitter war as the Masovian peasantry resisted their incursion. In return, the Swedes destroyed villages and tortured farmers to find out where they had hidden food. One very effective tactic was to take the children of a village and pretend to hang them in front of their parents. Secret food caches would then emerge, as if by miracle.

By the summer of 1708, after months of hard campaigning, the Swedes finally caught up with the Russians near the Lithuanian village of Holowczyn. On July 4, they attacked and the Russians were driven back from their trenches, losing perhaps five thousand men. But something startled the Swedes. They had hitherto despised the Russians as fighting men, having beaten them handily and then watched them retreat for hundreds of miles at Narva and other battles. Indeed, it was the arrogant belief of all Swedish commanders that a small number of Swedes could always beat a much larger force of Russians. Yet, here at Holowczyn, the Russians had stood and fought skillfully for as long as they possibly could. In the years since Narva, while Charles XII had been busy conquering Saxony and Poland, Czar Peter had been busy as well—rebuilding and retraining his army. In fact, Peter was furious that his Russian troops had lost the battle at Holowczyn; he even had every man with a wound in his back executed, assuming that they must have been retreating when hurt. The Swedes began to suspect they had a real fight on their hands.

The path lay open to the Dnieper River and, beyond that, Moscow, but the Russians continued to lay waste to the country as they retreated and the Swedes were left to scramble for food. Although Charles XII's army was trailed by a massive baggage train of food, powder, ammunition, and artillery, as well as 12,500 reserves, all under the supervision of General Adam Ludwig Lewenhaupt, the army could not both pursue the enemy and remain close to its supply lines. Harried by Cossacks loyal to the czar, and with morale faltering, Charles XII decided to turn his army south to the Ukraine, where rich crops untouched by Russians, and the forces of Ivan Mazepa, awaited.

This, however, left the supply train exposed, and the Russians attacked it again and again; at one battle, they nearly destroyed the entire column and the Swedes were forced to retreat through the night—in a famous episode, about a thousand Swedish soldiers, drunk from breaking into liquor supplies during the battle, disappeared in the local woods and never returned, presumably having been killed by the Russians or local peasants. By the time Lewenhaupt caught up with Charles XII in the Ukraine, in October 1708, he had only six thousand men left. And very few of the supply wagons had made it through.

The newly aggressive Russians marched parallel to the Swedes as they headed south into the Ukraine, determined not to let them rest. In December, the Russians launched a surprise attack against the Swedish forces. Though they were beaten off, it was a sign that the war was taking a different turn.

The winter now turned horribly cold—not just in the Ukraine but all over Europe—becoming one of the worst winters in living memory. With little shelter available, soldiers on both sides died of the cold, forming white lumps in the snow all along the roads. Cavalrymen froze to death sitting on their horses, with their reins still held in their hands, like statues. Piles of amputated limbs showed up outside army surgeries, the results of frostbite.

In the spring of 1709, the Swedish army regrouped and counted heads. A little more than one-fifth of its total manpower was gone. The Russians had lost even more, but the Swedes were far from home, in enemy territory, and with no fresh troops or supplies available. For another commander, retreat might have seemed like the only option. But not Charles XII. He firmed up his alliance with the Ukrainian Cossacks, sent emissaries to the Ottoman Turks, hoping to convince them to join him against the czar, and then continued his offensive against the Russian forces. As spring turned into summer, it was evident that a decisive battle was near. Czar Peter joined his forces in the field and the two great armies circled each other near the town of Poltava.

A TREACHEROUS AND ANCIENT BATTLEGROUND
Poltava lies on an age-old route taken by armies since the time of Genghis Khan. Arriving from the east via the broad steppes, massed forces, once they reach Poltava, can either head south into the Crimea and Turkey, or move west through Poland and into Hungary and Western Europe. In 1399, Mongol forces under one of Tamerlane's generals destroyed an entire army of Lithuanians right where the Russian and Swedish armies now faced each other.

SPOILS OF WAR

In addition to national pride and a sense of duty to one's leaders, there was another reason why soldiers fought so hard in the eighteenth century: booty. Today, most modern armies frown upon doing anything more than rifling an enemy corpse for intelligence information and personal papers. If an American GI in Iraq came across a dead guerilla holding a suitcase full of Swiss francs, for example, he would be arrested if he tried to make off with the money. It was far different when the Swedes and the Russians went head-to-head.

Plunder was seen as a legitimate spoil of war—you had earned your booty with your blood, sweat, and tears. So much so that, in the Swedish army at least, loot was gathered and divided up in a highly systematic way: a wounded captain got booty to the value of eighty silver dalers (the Swedish currency of the time), an unwounded captain forty, all the way down to the lowly private who received one daler.

And plenty of loot was found on the battlefield as almost every soldier carried his money sewn into the lining of his clothes or on a spare horse, if he could afford one. For if you left your belongings back in camp, your friends would rob you before your enemies even got a chance.

SOLID SHOT

In this day and age of heavy explosives, uranium-coated armor piercing shells, and "daisy cutter" bombs that can destroy all life within a half-mile radius—and these are just the conventional weapons—we tend to think of the weapons of yesteryear as a bit quaint. That would be a mistake. Take solid shot, for instance, the round iron cannonballs used to such devastating effect by the Russians at Poltava. Unlike a modern artillery shell, a canonball could be seen by a soldier, rapidly turning from a small dot to a larger black ball before, whistling at unimaginable speed, it struck him, or his friends. A direct hit could pass through not just one man, but a column of ten men, eviscerating every one of them. Sometimes gunners would aim low so that the ball would ricochet up into a man's stomach. Even a glancing blow would knock off an arm. Such was a projectile's kinetic energy that, if you touched one still rolling a thousand yards away from where it had been shot, it could break your finger.

In 1709, Poltava was a small town the Russians had fortified only halfheartedly. East of it was the Vorskla, a tributary of the Dnieper. To the north was a large forest dissected by long corridor-like clearings; beyond the forest was what was known as the Great Ouvrage, a gully leading down to a small river with marshy banks.

The Swedish siege of Poltava had begun in May. The Swedes lacked siege engines, and were reluctant to risk a frontal attack, so their investment was as halfhearted as the Russian fortification. But gradually the Russians were running out of food and even ammunition. At one point, a defender threw a dead cat from the fortress, hitting the visiting King Charles on the shoulder, a grievous insult answered with a barrage of Swedish fire. Observers noted that the fact that the Russians hadn't had to *eat* the cat was a sign that they were still doing fairly well.

The real battle would not take place at the town of Poltava, but slightly to the north, where Peter I had placed his main army in formation. There, in one of the long open corridors through the woods, the Russians built a series of log redoubts (small, temporary forts) in the shape of a wide *T*—four of them as the stem of the *T*, six as the top. The redoubts were about 150 yards apart, bristling with infantry behind protected positions on parapets, and backed up by artillery positioned at the top of the *T*. Soldiers in the redoubts could fire in all four directions; thus, even if bypassed, they could shoot the enemy from the rear and flanks.

It was a brilliant idea. To reach the main army, stationed behind the top line of forts, not only would the Swedes have to charge up the corridor, blocked by deep woods on both sides, but they would also have to survive the murderous fire of these small palisaded emplacements.

A FATEFUL DECISION

The Russians had approximately 30,000 infantry, 9,000 cavalry, 3,000 Cossacks and over 100 cannons. The Swedes had about 9,500 infantry, nearly 13,000 cavalry, a force of 5,000 Cossacks under Ivan Mazepa, and 32 cannons. For a few days, both sides made feints and harrying attacks, each waiting for the other to make a move. In one of these brief actions, Charles XII was wounded by a shot to the foot; this kept him from being able to stirrup his horse and meant that he had to be carried everywhere on a litter slung between two horses.

On the afternoon of June 27, Charles XII convened a meeting of his senior staff. His two closest advisers, Field Marshall Count Carl Gunter Rehnskold and General Adam Lewenhaupt, warned that the Swedish forces were in deep trouble. Not only were they thousands of miles from home, with inadequate supplies of food and fodder, they were desperately short of ammunition—in fact, the Swedish army only had enough for one more major battle.

Morale among the troops was also low, too. The Swedish soldiers longed for home, and the Cossacks, sensing they might have chosen the losing side, had begun to desert. Wasn't it time, the generals suggested, to retreat to Poland, or perhaps cross the Dnieper in the south and find their way to the Crimea and the support of the sympathetic Ottoman Turks?

The answer, according to the king, was no; their only option was to attack. This decision on the part of Charles XII has struck some historians as incomprehensible, but, in fact, it was probably the only decision he could come to, given the situation. For a start, retreating in the face of a numerically superior enemy is one of the trickiest maneuvers in all warfare and could have resulted in a slaughter of the Swedes by the pursuing Russians. There was also the fact that Charles and his commanders still believed in the inferiority of the Russan soldiers, that they could be beaten with a concerted attack by a committed Swedish army.

Once the decision had been made, the plan came together. In typical Swedish fashion, it hinged on surprise and shock: during the following night, the Swedish infantry would charge through the redoubts, not attacking them but bypassing them as quickly as possible, to smash the main line of Russian forces waiting beyond. As this was happening, Swedish cavalry would swing wide around the flanks of the enemy lines, around the forest, and attack from the rear. It was an extremely risky plan—hindsight might call it a desperate one—but, if it worked, the Swedish army could still pull out a victory.

Generals Lewenhaupt and Rehnskold divided their troops into four columns and marched through the night as quietly as possible, to a point about six hundred yards from the first Russian redoubt. Then the Swedish advance infantry, eight thousand strong, lay quietly down in the warm summer grass. It was about 2 a.m, on June 28.

The men could see the stars above, which seemed distant echoes of the campfires of the Russians. Hammering could be heard as work continued on the redoubts. More than likely, most of the waiting soldiers whispered a prayer. The Swedes were Lutherans who believed in predestination: whatever happened in battle, it was because God had willed it. King Charles joined the army shortly after two o'clock, with his entourage of Drabants and his commanders, Lewenhaupt and Rehnskold. When the cavalry came up behind them, ready for its flanking movement, the infantry would attack.

Finally, at about 3:30 a.m., the horsemen, having gotten lost and wandered for miles in the dark, showed up. The grey light of dawn was seeping across the steppes and now the Swedes could plainly see Russian troops working on the embattlements of the nearest redoubt. So far, miraculously, the Swedes hadn't been spotted. But it would just take one Russian, looking up, squinting off into the distance …

Quickly, the Swedes drew up in battle order. Then a shot rang out. The Russians had seen them. Fevered shouts arose from the Russian front as men scurried back and forth. There was nothing for the Swedes to do but attack. The line surged forward, cavalry ranging out to the flanks. Almost immediately, Russian artillery opened up with solid shot, and cannon balls began to rend apart the Swedish lines.

When the Swedes got close to the Russian redoubts, enemy gunners opened up with canister shot—wood or metal containers packed with metal fragments—that decimated the attacking Swedes. Still they kept on coming, through enemy musket fire, and made it to the first redoubt, which had not been fully fortified. Once inside, they cut down the Russians, giving no quarter, executing even those who surrendered.

Overleaf: *The Battle of Poltava*, by Jean-Marc Nattier, 1717. The painting shows the slaughter of the Swedes by the victorious Russian troops.

Heartened by their initial triumph, the Swedes moved on to the next redoubt, also incompletely fortified, and took that, too. Meanwhile, the cavalry, especially on the left flank, was driving the Russian cavalry back toward the Great Ouvrage. These successes seemed to bode well for the Swedes. But things were about to go horribly wrong. For somehow, it had not been properly communicated to commanders that the point was to head straight for the main Russian forces and *bypass* the redoubts, not attack them.

By around five in the morning, General Rehnskold had led the Swedish troops to within a mile of the main Russian formations near the top of the *T*. In order to have any chance at all of overcoming the superior enemy forces, he had to attack without delay. But all of his forces were not with him. About 2,600 men commanded by Major General Carl Gustaf Roos had stopped to attack the third redoubt. Roos was under the mistaken impression that each redoubt needed to be captured. No one has yet discovered where this confusion came from, but it was probably the result of the attack plan being implemented so quickly and in darkness.

Roos led his infantry against the redoubt time and time again. But the third redoubt was fully fortified, larger than the first two, and fully able to defend itself. And Roos did not have any artillery support. Charles and his commanders tended to underplay the importance of the big guns, considering them a hindrance to an army whose most vital weapons were speed and surprise—Charles even called his head artillerist, the very able Count Rudolf von Bunow, "Grandad." And no one seems to have thought of turning the guns of the captured redoubts against the enemy.

Roos retreated into the woods along the right flank, having lost one thousand men in his futile attacks. The Russians then counterattacked, driving Roos back to the town of Poltava, where he was forced to negotiate surrender terms at about nine thirty in the morning. The czar now sent twenty-two thousand infantry, flanked by dragoons, against the remaining forces of Rehnskold and Lewenhaupt. Though vastly outnumbered, the Swedes attacked and managed to burst through. But the mass of Russians closed in on the smaller number of Swedish troops, and then the slaughter began.

Eyewitness survivors describe the Swedes clustered together in small groups as the Russians hacked away at them with pike and bayonet. Those who broke away were hunted down by Russian cavalry and speared with long lances. King Charles XII, knocked numerous times from his litter, his loyal Drabants falling around him, finally fled south to the village of Perevolochna on the Dnieper. He and his retinue managed to make it across the river, but left thousands of Swedes to surrender to the Russians, including Generals Lewenhaupt and Rehnskold.

None of the Cossacks under Ivan Mazepa were allowed to survive. They were either broken on the wheel—tied spreadeagled to wagon wheels, after which their arms and legs were cut off—or strung up on makeshift gallows. The Swedish prisoners were stripped naked and led into captivity in Russia, where they would help build Czar Peter's new grand city, St. Petersburg. Twenty thousand Swedes entered captivity that day; at most, four thousand returned home. Meanwhile, Peter the Great wrote to his mistress Catherine: "Little Mother, good day. I wish to tell you that God today in his great mercy has granted us a matchless victory."

BIRTHPLACE OF A SUPERPOWER

The two men who faced each other across the battlefield of Poltava remained rivals until the very end. After escaping to the Ottoman Empire, Charles tried to foment a war between the Turkish sultan and the Russians. He was aided in this by Peter, who foolishly decided to attack the Ottomans in 1711, and was badly beaten and forced to return Black Sea lands he had seized in an earlier war. However, as part of the peace treaty, Sultan Ahmed III, who was tired of Charles's constant scheming, agreed to expel Charles.

By this time, 1714, Russia had replaced the rightful king on the throne of Poland, seized the Swedish province of Livonia, occupied Finland, and menaced Sweden itself with its now powerful navy. Back home, Charles XII led an increasingly unpopular resistance to the Russians, refusing to sign a peace treaty. But in 1718, he was killed in combat during a Swedish siege of the fortress of Frederikshald, having become so unpopular that some still say that it was a Swedish bullet that killed him. After this, all Swedish forces retreated into Swedish territory and all effective Swedish resistance against its enemies ended.

In 1721, Sweden and Russia signed the Treaty of Nystad, ending the Great Northern War. Russia now had permanent access to the Baltic Sea and Western Europe.

Of course, had things gone differently at Poltava, had Sweden and King Charles won, Europe might have been a very different place. It's highly unlikely that the Swedes could have destroyed the Russian army, and retreating Russians would no doubt have continued their scorched earth policy, thwarting the weakened Swedes' advance. But a victory would have at the very least allowed Sweden to hang on to Poland, Finland, and much of northern Germany, continue to deny access to the Baltic to Peter the Great—who might, as a result, have become Peter the Sort-of-Mediocre—and successfully conspire with the Ottoman Empire to attack Russia, or at least keep her contained.

Had this continued, Sweden could, feasibly, have retained control of most of northern Europe, and the power of the czars might have diminished accordingly. Ultimately, Sweden might have taken over Russia, instituting a more humane form of government that might even have obviated the need for the Russian Revolution.

But this, of course, is the height of speculation. Sweden did not win. The Treaty of Nystad brought her peace at last, but at a price. She was never to regain her position as regional power, while Russia went on to become a superpower. At the same time, while Russia has fought and bled in numerous wars, Sweden has remained resolutely neutral, and her culture has become a welcoming beacon to those who value peace in the world. An unintended consequence, and possibly one of which Charles XII would not approve, but ultimately not a bad outcome.

CHARLES AND THE RIGHT

The Swedes are a little tough on Charles XII these days. After the debacle of the Great Northern War, the good things he did were forgotten. They included scientific expeditions he supported, architectural projects he funded, and even the introduction of right-hand traffic on Sweden's roads to keep pace with other European nations who, with the exception of Great Britain, were then taking up this practice.

Charles is now remembered as a warmonger, as the man who lost Sweden her empire. Left-hand traffic was even restored by ensuing Swedish leaders, possibly to spite the right-hand-driving Russians, though the country was finally brought into line with its neighbors, at great expense, in 1967. In a final irony, Charles has of late been adopted by Swedish skinheads and ultra right-wingers as a brave symbol of Swedish nationalism.

An unfortunate fate for a daring young king.

VITUS BERING AND THE RUSSIAN DISCOVERY OF ALASKA

HIS NAME REMAINS FAMILIAR, HAVING BEEN GIVEN TO THAT FRIGID passage of water that separates the northernmost reaches of Asia and North America, the Bering Strait, as well as the Bering Sea to the south. Yet few people today know anything about Vitus Bering or about the impact of his discoveries on the modern world. Those who have heard of him tend to assume he was Russian. But although he lived in Russia most of his life and labored loyally in the service of the xenophobic Russian royal court of the eighteenth century, he was in fact born in Denmark. His foreign status would eventually curtail his discoveries and, finally, contribute to his death; but without the employment the Russians provided Bering never would have made his way to the *Bolshaya Zemlia*, the "Big Land," as it was identified on early Russian maps, that mountainous vastness that could be glimpsed on clear days across the strait that was to bear his name.

This is the story of a proud man trapped in the web of an unforgiving bureaucracy who, somehow, still managed to pioneer discoveries that changed the future of the largest nation on earth. Bering was an explorer on a grand scale. He led enormous expeditions that included hundreds of people and covered thousands of miles, expeditions that were among the first to include scientists. In turn, these expeditions expanded Russia's empire into Siberia and North America and helped open California and the Pacific Northwest to European settlers, who rushed to America's west coast, fearing that Russia would win the race for that side of the continent. Despite all of this, Vitus Bering has not been celebrated in the way that legendary explorers such as Ferdinand Magellan and James Cook have been, in part because, for decades after his death, the Russian government sought to keep all records of his adventures secret.

AN OUTSTANDING RECRUIT

Czar Peter the Great became ruler of Russia in 1689 and went to war, with the Ottomans and the Swedes, in part to make sure his vast country did not remain landlocked. Peter loved the sea and desperately wanted a Russian navy. He grew up with a passion for sailing and spent part of his youth in the Netherlands, disguising himself as an apprentice carpenter in a shipbuilding yard and then traveling about the country learning as much as he could about ship architecture. After Russia defeated Sweden in the Great Northern War, the Russian Imperial Navy expanded rapidly, with Peter—one of history's great micromanagers—guiding it step by step.

Because there were not enough Russians with oceangoing experience, Peter had to seek help overseas, in countries that had proud seafaring traditions, such as England, the Netherlands, and Denmark. In this, he had two options: he could send Russians abroad for training or he could import foreigners to run his navy. The first would take years, and Peter wanted to expand his fleet much faster than that, so he chose the latter option, importing experienced seamen from among the English, Dutch, and Danes. This provided a ready-made team of experts, but it was also to create a xenophobic backlash that would seriously affect subsequent expeditions.

One of the earliest and most able of the foreign officers who peopled the Russian Navy was a young man named Vitus Bering. He was born in Denmark in 1681, into an unremarkable family, and raised in the small Baltic port of Horsens, from which he couldn't wait to escape. In 1696, at the age of fifteen, Bering shipped out as a cabin boy and spent eight years sailing to India, the Dutch East Indies, and probably the West Indies and North America, as well. While completing officer training in an Amsterdam school, he came to the eye of an admiral in the Russian Navy named Cornelius Ivanovitch Cruys. Norwegian by birth, Cruys was seeking likely foreigners for Peter's fleet and he recruited Bering.

Prior to Bering's first expedition in 1725, Russian geographers had little knowledge of the seas and lands that lay beyond the eastern edge of their vast country.

During the Great Northern War between Russia and Sweden, Bering spent much of his time transporting ships and goods from one port to another. But in 1711, an opportunity came along that was to change his career forever. After destroying the Swedes at the battle of Poltava in 1709, Peter had pushed his luck a little too far and foolishly made war on the Ottoman Turks, who defeated him handily. One of Peter's beloved ships, the *Munker*, remained trapped in the Sea of Azov, and Bering bravely rescued it by running it through the Black Sea, right under the Turkish guns at Constantinople, and back to the Baltic. This and his steady performance as a navigator and seaman brought Bering to the attention of Peter the Great, who subsequently offered him a once-in-a-lifetime opportunity: a chance to explore the barely touched, far northwestern regions of Russia: Siberia, Kamchatka, the shore of the so-called Icy Sea, or Arctic Ocean, and, to the east, the Big Land.

During the sixteenth century, the collapse of the Mongol Empire and the rise of the czars had helped extend Russia's territory all the way to the Pacific Ocean in the east and the Arctic Ocean in the north. Despite nominal Russian possession, eastern regions such as Siberia and Kamchatka were little settled, though Cossacks had moved into the area in the seventeenth century, bloodily subjugating some of the natives. However, Peter and his advisers knew how valuable these territories were, even beyond their rich natural resources. Foreign nations such as England, Holland, and France still hungered to discover a northern ocean passage from the Atlantic to the Pacific to facilitate their trading, and were already sending ships into the northern Pacific. If there was a northern passage, the Russians wanted to be the ones to discover it first. They also wanted to find out, once and for all, if there was a land bridge between the Asian continent and America. At this time, the distance between these continents was little understood by geographers; estimates of the breadth of the sea there varied from a small strait to a large ocean.

Peter had been distracted from these matters by the Great Northern War, but the discovery, in 1724, that he was gravely ill focused his attention. He immediately began to plan the undertaking that would become known as the First Kamchatka Expedition, and appointed Bering to lead it. As well as being a promising career move, the offer appealed to the Dane's appetite for adventure, still strong even after the many journeys he had already made overseas.

OVERLAND TO KAMCHATKA
In 1725, Vitus Bering was thirty-four years old. Descriptions of him vary. He appears to have been handsome, with dark hair and eyes, and is variously described as "stout" or even "corpulent." He was happily married to Anna Pulse, a Swede, and they lived in an expatriate colony centered on the new Russian capital city of St. Petersburg.

With only about a month to live, Czar Peter firmed up the details of the expedition, selecting two lieutenants—another Dane named Martin Spangberg and a Russian named Aleksey Chirikov—and defining its goals. Bering and his men were to map an overland route all the way from St. Petersburg, across the Ural Mountains and through Siberia, to the east coast of the Kamchatka Peninsula. There, they would construct a fleet of ships so that they could travel northeast, map the coastline of Siberia, and search for a land bridge to the fabled Big Land, which, as far as anyone knew at the time, might be America or another landmass in-between. Bering and his men were also instructed to seek an island that Russian court cartographers called Gamaland, which supposedly lay off Kamchatka (but, in fact, did not exist). The entire expedition was to take three years.

As it turned out, it took Bering three years just to get to Kamchatka. This in itself was an incredible journey, probably the longest overland expedition taken by anyone to that date, covering six thousand miles, more than a third of the distance around the Northern Hemisphere. Bering started out with thirty-four men, but picked up hundreds more along the way to help him carry supplies and fell trees to build ships. Once the expedition crossed the Ural Mountains and began traversing

Siberia, the trip became a nightmare. The explorers passed through huge bogs that sucked at horses and people, forded winding rivers as many as half a dozen times a day, wandered through bleak forests, and fought off fiercely biting flies and mosquitoes. Numerous men deserted, never to be seen again.

The Siberian natives, according to Bering, canoed across the rivers in birch-bark canoes, worshipped "the sun, moon, and certain birds like swans, eagles, and ravens," and were led by "sorcerers." "Evil" practices abounded: twins were considered to be bad luck, and one was always killed at birth; the dead were not buried, merely thrown into forests to be devoured by wild animals.

Once in Kamchatka, Bering's men constructed a sturdy ship, sixty by twenty feet long, with three cannons. It was named the *Archangel Gabriel*, and in mid-July, 1728, it was launched on its voyage of exploration. Bering and his crew sailed north, hugging the coastline, which curved to the northeast. Beyond sixty-five degrees north, they entered what, half a century later, Captain James Cook, who confirmed so much of what Bering discovered, would name the Bering Strait.

Although an adventurous Russian merchant had traveled this way about seventy-five years before, no other Europeans had been here. Bering and his men made contact with eight natives in a skin boat, who were probably Sirenikski Eskimos, but because of the language barrier he learned little from them. However, the land they were rounding turned decisively to the west. By Bering's way of thinking, they were now in the Icy Sea, and, if they sailed westward, they would reach the top of Siberia. Therefore, he had proved to his own satisfaction that there was no land bridge between Russia and America.

By this time it was mid-August. With the short Arctic summer season closing, it was time to turn back. Bering was deeply concerned about getting caught in the ice or being forced to winter in eastern Siberia, among the reputedly vicious Chukchi natives. And so he turned the *Archangel Gabriel* around. On his return, he discovered Big Diomede Island, sailing past it in fog so thick that he was unable to see America, which at this point was only fifty-three miles away—the closest he got on this trip. Despite getting caught in a violent storm, he brought his ship safely back to its Kamchatkan port in September. From there he returned west overland and by 1730 had arrived back in St. Petersburg—but not to the acclaim he had expected.

BERING'S SECOND EXPEDITION
The atmosphere at the Russian court had changed greatly since Bering's departure five years earlier. Peter the Great and Catherine I had both died; Peter II, Peter's son, had been named ruler in 1727, but had died of smallpox at the age of fourteen in early 1730, just before Bering's return. The new empress was Anna Ivanovna, Peter the Great's niece, but it took a while for Bering to gain an audience with her. In the meantime, he found himself the subject of criticism, particularly from the native-born Russians of the court and Admiralty. Had he really sailed far enough? Was he sure that there was no land bridge to America? And what about Gamaland—why hadn't he found it?

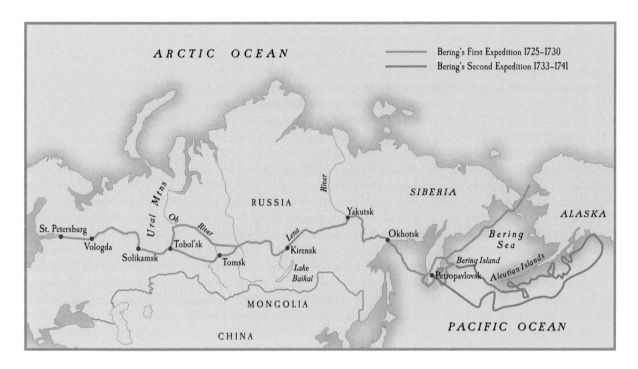

Bering's modest renown derives from his exploration of the waters that separate Asia from North America, but, as this map shows, his expeditions also spanned the entire Russian landmass.

Despite the fact that he had been away from home for five years and deeply missed his wife and family—he already had two sons and would soon have another boy, then a daughter—Bering decided to chart an ambitious plan for a second expedition that would silence his doubters once and for all. At last given a chance to present his idea to the Empress Anna, he outlined three main objectives for the expedition: first, to sail to North America, chart the coastline there, and establish trade relations, if possible, with the natives; second, to send a party to Japan, to open up trade relations with that relatively unknown country; and, finally, to send a contingent north, by way of the Lena River, to chart the Arctic coast of Siberia and possibly find a passage to the Pacific.

The plan was accepted, but the bureaucrats in the Admiralty foisted on Bering further, almost unachievable objectives. In addition to the aims he had outlined, Bering was also asked to develop Siberia—by building iron foundries (to make cannons) and shipyards, establishing nautical schools, introducing cattle raising, and even setting up a postal system between Kamchatka and St. Petersburg!

Worse was to come. As with his first expedition, Bering was to be accompanied by Aleksey Chirikov and a host of lesser Russian staff officers. But now, the xeno-phobes in the Admiralty agreed, Bering, as a foreigner, would be forced to submit all important decisions to a "sea council" made up of his subordinate officers. If they disagreed with him, they could overrule his orders. Not only that, but Chirikov was given the power of veto over everything. And there was one more thing. Bering was to have *no authority whatsoever* over the numerous scientists who would accompany the expedition. He was simply to make sure they got what they needed to eat, were given a place to sleep, and allowed to make their studies of the local flora and fauna. Never has the commander of such an important expedition been so hamstrung before he even set off, and yet such was Bering's profound desire to prove himself, that he accepted all these conditions and, in March of 1733, set off with a party of six hundred soldiers, sailors, cartographers, scientists, blacksmiths, and ironworkers, as well as his wife and two of his children.

FOUR YEARS IN SIBERIA
Going once again eastward across Russia, Bering made his way to Yakutsk on the Lena River, reportedly the coldest town in Siberia, which had been established as a base camp of sorts—although nothing that Bering had ordered had been set up as he commanded. There he directed one of his lieutenants to build a small ship, and sail it up the Lena to explore the Arctic coast. The unfortunate lieutenant died of scurvy during this voyage and although the rest of the crew made it to the Icy Sea, they were unable to find any passage to the northeast (in fact, the pack ice present for most of the year made sailing this coastline difficult and unprofitable).

In the meantime, Bering threw himself into furious activity, and, by the late summer of 1736, had built a foundry and a shipyard, and sent another expedition to explore the Arctic coast, which had as little luck as the first. In September, Chirikov arrived with supplies and the main body of scientists, so that this desolate place now held over two thousand people. Like a small-town mayor, Bering became bogged down in the details of administration. The scientists were particularly troublesome. Their baggage included nine cartloads of scientific instruments—telescopes, barometers, drafting tables—as well as, in some cases, personal servants and even wine cellars. The scientists held Bering responsible for everything and complained to him constantly about such matters as food and lodging.

Four years went by in Yakutsk while Bering tried to deal with all of this—four years in which the cost of his expedition, which had not yet even reached the Kamchatka coast, rose to three hundred thousand rubles—the equivalent of perhaps two million modern dollars. At one point, Empress Anna almost pulled the plug on the expedition, only allowing it to continue after putting Bering on half-wages to save money!

Bering finally arrived in Kamchatka in 1739. Martin Spangberg, his Danish lieutenant from the First Kamchatka Expedition, was already there and had built a ship; Bering happily sent him off to explore the Japanese islands during the summer of that year. Then Bering had his men build two vessels, each ninety feet long and twenty-three feet wide. He christened them the *St. Peter* and the *St. Paul*. They carried fourteen cannons and provisions for seventy-six men for six months. On May 29, 1741, Bering set sail. He commanded the *St. Peter*, while Chirikov was in charge of the *St. Paul*. Bering's trusted second-in-command on the *St. Peter* would be a Swede named Sven Waxell. Fortunately, he had been able to leave all the troublesome scientists behind. All except one, a young man named Georg Steller, who joined the expedition at the very last minute, yet would have a momentous impact on it.

SCOURGE OF THE SEAS

The sad thing about the disease of scurvy, which killed hundreds of thousands of sailors, is not only how easily it is cured—by the consumption of plants or fruits that replace ascorbic acid, or vitamin C—but also how many times in history the cure was found, then forgotten.

Scurvy was first described for medical literature by a Dutch physician working in Cologne, Germany, in 1541, although he identified the disease as infectious, which it is not. A year earlier, the French explorer Jacques Cartier had learned from North American Indians how to cure the ailment using vitamin C from the needles of certain pine trees. In 1617, an English ship's physician named John Woodall described scurvy and listed lemon juice as a cure—and told the East India Company. His advice was ignored and forgotten. In 1747, James Lind, a British Royal Navy officer, lobbied the Navy to give its sailors ample amounts of lime juice (hence the name "Limeys"), but it took the slow-moving British Admiralty forty-one years to act on this.

Again and again, the cure was discovered then lost. Perhaps a simple herb or piece of fresh fruit seemed too simple a cure for such a dreaded and deadly condition.

STELLER SHARES HIS THOUGHTS
Steller was born in Germany, near Nuremberg, in 1709, and raised in a Pietist Lutheran family, which engendered in him a strong obligation to the poor and the prevention of social injustice. He trained in St. Petersburg as a scientist—primarily a naturalist, but also an ethnographer—and then took himself east to study the Itelmen people of Kamchatka. He grew to respect and love them and was horrified at how they were treated by the Russians, especially the Cossacks.

As a natural scientist, Steller was extremely observant. The expedition Bering had sent to the Icy Sea had been plagued by scurvy, and it made him wonder why the Itelmen never got this dread disease. After much study, he decided the answer was their diet: the Itelmen ate plants with antiscorbutic properties—in other words, the plants prevented them getting scurvy—while the Russians did not.

Steller was introduced to Bering just before the expedition set sail, by a mutual acquaintance. Bering took a liking to Steller, who seemed not at all like the pompous scientists he had dealt with in Siberia; as well, Steller had some training as a physician, and Bering needed a ship's doctor. So when the *St. Peter* and *St. Paul* sailed, he took Steller along.

But, for all his admirable qualities, Steller simply could not keep his mouth shut, often butting into conversations between Bering and his officers, advising them on matters that were simply none of his business. For instance, there was the little matter of how close America was.

In conversations with Cossacks and Chukchi natives, Steller had learned that there was a large landmass just across what was to become known as the Bering Strait. It could be seen on clear days, trees drifted across from it, and, sometimes, natives came from there to trade. When he excitedly reported this information to Bering, the captain replied, "People talk a lot. Who believes Cossacks?" (This and other conversations were recorded in Steller's journal, which is obviously subjective, but more than likely accurate, as one of Steller's faults was an almost total absence of dissembling.)

Steller was convinced—rightly, it turns out—that the expedition should go to the northeast, but Bering was not. Nor were the other officers. At a sea council just before the ships sailed—to which Steller was, naturally, not invited—the decision was made to go to the southeast to find America and, then turning north, to follow the North American coastline back to about longitude sixty-four degrees north, and from there sail back to Kamchatka—Bering's rigid instructions from the Admiralty mandated him to find America in one sailing season, so the ships could not winter there.

This was a highly flawed decision, based partly on the need to convince the Admiralty that Gamaland did not exist, by extending the voyage across a wider arc. Moreover, Bering, and Chirikov, greatly underestimated the distances they would have to cover by sailing to the southeast—at least four hundred nautical miles to Alaska (indeed, had they turned just slightly more to the south, they would not have made landfall until the Hawaiian Islands).

CROSSING THE PACIFIC
As the ships headed across the Pacific, Steller vented in his journal. He claimed that the officers mocked "whatever was said by any person not a seaman"—that person obviously being Steller. Bering himself continued to meet the "advice" Steller was giving him with general mockery and sarcasm. It is difficult to see what kept Steller going, aside from his unassailable self-confidence: even when Steller was wrong, he was absolutely convinced he was right.

On June 20, after about eight days, Bering and Chirikov hove their ships to for a conference via speaking trumpets between the pitching decks of their vessels. They had sailed all the way to forty-five degrees north finding no trace of Gamaland; it was now time to head northeast. But almost as soon as the decision had been made a storm blew the *St. Peter* and *St. Paul* apart. It was the last time they were to see each other, though Chirikov eventually returned safely to Kamchatka.

Separated from her sister ship and now wandering in a thick fog, the *St. Peter* made her way east-northeast, Bering becoming extremely concerned about the low level of fresh water remaining onboard. All of a sudden, on the afternoon of July 16, a dazzling sun dispelled the fog and, almost as if in a Christian Orthodox miracle, a beautiful snowcapped mountain loomed ahead of them on the horizon. It was Alaska's eighteen-thousand-foot-high Mount St. Elias. Below the mountain, extending to the shore, were dark primeval forests. They had found the Big Land.

Officers ran below to rouse Bering, who came on deck, looked at the mountain, and then, to the bewilderment of the crew, shrugged and went back below. "He received [the sight of land] very indifferently," Steller wrote in some puzzlement, although with hindsight it became clear to him that Bering was suffering the initial effects of scurvy.

The *St. Paul* anchored off present-day Kayak Island, and Bering sent a party ashore to gather fresh water. Steller, wildly excited about having the chance to explore the natural life of this new land, asked for permission to go along. Permission denied, said Bering, who, one suspects, took a perverse pleasure in annoying Steller. What if there were hostile savages on the island?

Steller could not believe his ears and, to everyone's surprise, began screaming at Bering at the top of his lungs. What was the purpose of their journey, he asked Bering with cutting sarcasm: "to carry American water to Asia?" He wasn't afraid of a few savages. Since when did he, Steller, "act like a woman" in the face of danger. If Bering did not let him make a scientific study of this new land, he, Steller, would report him!

Bering, who probably did not want to stay long because he was uncertain of his anchorage in the event of a storm and was running out of time to get back to Kamchatka before winter, listened in silence, and finally agreed to let Steller go on the condition that he return as soon as the ship was ready to leave. But as Steller boarded the boat to row to shore, Bering summoned the ship's trumpeters to play the scientist a fanfare normally used to greet royal personages. It was a classic Bering vs. Steller moment.

HISTORY MAKERS
Martin Spangberg and Aleksey Chirikov were the other two ship commanders on the Second Kamchatka Expedition. Each, in his own way, made history.

Sent by Bering in search of a trade route to Japan in the summer of 1739, Spangberg sighted the island of Honshu in June, traded with the Japanese, and then sailed away when numerous Japanese vessels began to appear around him. He recorded in his ship's log a fascinating glimpse of the Japanese who boarded his ship—men with embroidered capes, who bowed deeply before him and called their nation Nippon. Upon Spangberg's return, however, an incompetent Admiralty functionary stationed in Siberia insisted that Spangberg had in fact visited Korea, not Japan. An enraged Spangberg was ordered to repeat the voyage. Before he could do this, news of Bering's death came and the expedition was called off.

Though Chirikov, on board the *St. Paul*, was separated from Bering's ship by the storm of June 20, 1741, and never saw it again, for the next months he remained close by. Indeed, he actually spotted Alaska before Bering did and sent fifteen men in two boats to explore the shore. The boats never returned and the men were lost, presumably in riptides or to hostile natives. The *St. Paul* made it back to Kamchatka safely, in September, although many of its crew died of scurvy.

RETURN FROM KAYAK ISLAND

When Steller's boat touched down on Kayak Island, it was the first time a European had landed on America's northwest shore and lived to tell the tale. Steller spent his time identifying strange plants and birds—Steller's jay is still named after him—thus becoming the first European naturalist to make identifications in the American northwest. He also found signs of native habitation, including still-warm cooking stones, and stored jars of deliciously smoked salmon. As the day drew to a close, Steller sent a message back to Bering on the boat ferrying water barrels to the *St. Peter*: he needed to stay longer to investigate these signs of human habitation. In his journal, Steller wrote down Bering's "patriotic and gracious reply": he was to "get his butt on board" the *St. Peter*, or he would be left behind. On board he went, and the *St. Peter* dropped anchor and headed back to sea.

Continuing now southwest, roughly parallel to the Aleutian Islands, the *St. Peter* began to be plagued by scurvy. First one seaman was afflicted with it in early August, then another and another. Bering himself had probably had the disease since mid-July. The *St. Peter* stopped at bleak Nagai Island to take on water that unfortunately turned out to be brackish. There, a crewman died, a man named Shumagin, who thus gained the unfortunate distinction of being the first European to be buried on northwestern American soil—the island is now named after him. On Nagai Island, Steller gathered the antiscorbutic herbs he had identified while working with the Itelmen, but the crew, who were fed up with him, refused to take them. He kept them for himself and for Bering, who was now, at least in this matter, listening to Steller. The herbs allowed Bering, almost bedridden, to begin to stand up and take a few steps.

It was here, on Nagai, that the Russians met their first Americans, Aleuts who rowed out in skin boats to trade with them. But the *St. Peter* could not stay. It was now nearly September. Weighing anchor, the ship headed west, abandoning all pretense of exploring, in a race against time to reach Kamchatka. But at the end of the month, they were hit with a wild, almost apocalyptic storm, with walls of freezing water splashing over the ship, and St. Elmo's fire crackling among the mast tops. The ship

survived the storm, but was considerably weakened. More men died of scurvy and those who remained were almost too far gone to climb the rigging and set the sails. The *St. Peter* was at the mercy of gales howling down from the Arctic. Steller's herbs had run out and Bering was once again bedridden. First mate Sven Waxell performed a heroic task just keeping the ship afloat. At last, in November, with the rigging nearly collapsing, the *St. Peter* was blown into the bleak Commander Islands, some 110 miles off the Kamchatkan shore. The ship made landfall, and her weakened captain, officers, and crew staggered ashore.

The men found themselves on a desolate spot. There was no wood, except for a few pieces of driftwood, and little shelter from the relentless winds. There was fresh water, though, and food in the form of tame sea otters, seals, and ptarmigans. Steller set about gathering antiscorbutic herbs while the others stretched sailcloths over crevices in the frozen sand, to make lean-tos that afforded at least some protection from the elements. Bering, now on a stretcher, was placed in one of these makeshift shelters.

Sven Waxell wrote in his journal: "Men were continually dying. Our plight was so wretched that the dead had to lie for a considerable time among the living, for there was none able to drag the corpses away." And into this horrendous situation came the foxes: little red and silver arctic foxes who plagued the men continually, sneaking up to snap off the fingers and toes of the dead and attack the living. These "wicked foxes" were almost more than the men could bear, getting into their poor dwellings, making off with boots and clothes, even—or so it seemed to the crew—warning off the otters the men were trying to hunt. Those men strong enough would engage in wholesale slaughters of the foxes, yet still the animals came—some of them with eyes gouged out, some with limbs missing—to harry the Russian sailors.

The only glimpse of light in this nightmarish situation was Georg Steller, who was transformed, in the ailing sailors' eyes, from despised scientist into lifesaving doctor. Steller worked tirelessly to feed the men herbs, help them build their shelters, and keep their spirits up. His special patient was Vitus Bering. The two of them now, in these desperate straits, became close. Bering told Steller much about his life, including that he was grateful for the "good fortune" that had lasted all his life, until now. Bering's mental faculties remained intact and he continued to issue orders, sending groups of the strongest men out to explore the large island.

But by December, Bering had grown quiet and reflective. When some of the sand around him in his crevice caved in, Steller offered to shore up the walls, but Bering replied: "The deeper in the ground I lie, the warmer I am." On December 8, Bering died, not so much from scurvy, although that was a contributing factor, but from "hunger, cold, thirst, vermin, and grief." Or so wrote Steller, grieving himself.

Bering had traveled a long way from his small Danish village, had explored vast tracts of the earth, and had come within 110 miles of making it back to his adopted country and his beloved wife and family. The men fashioned a makeshift coffin—Bering was the only man on the island afforded one—and buried him on a ridge, not far from their shelters. With the help of Steller, the remaining crew spent the

A PIONEERING NATURALIST

After returning to Kamchatka from Bering Island, Georg Steller decided to stay and write a treatise about the native peoples, and he later opened a bicultural school for Russians and natives. He sent his journals of the Bering voyage to the Admiralty offices in St. Petersburg; they went unacknowledged and vanished into the archives. In 1746, Steller was accused of being a traitor because he had helped some natives maltreated by the Russians. As self-confident as ever, he hurried to St. Petersburg to defend himself, but died of fever along the way.

Steller's observations of flora and fauna contributed significantly to scientific knowledge of the Pacific Rim and he is now seen as a pioneering naturalist. A jay, an eagle, and a sea lion are named after him—as well as the Steller's sea cow. Remarkably, during the horrible period on the Isle of the Foxes, Steller managed to make natural observations. He was amazed to see a huge animal, between twenty-eight and thirty-five feet long, frolicking at the water's edge. In typical Steller fashion, he created a blind and observed the creature for days at a time. He wrote that it was an animal above the waist and a fish below, and weighed, he estimated, eight thousand pounds. It was, in fact, a northern manatee or sea cow, and it was named in the scientist's honor. Sadly, it is now extinct and Steller's description of it is the only scientific record of its existence.

winter on the island and then built a new ship from the remains of the *St. Peter* that lay wrecked upon the shore. This they sailed to Kamchatka, arriving on August 27, 1742. There were forty-six men left out of seventy-five. They were assumed by the Russian authorities to be long dead, and arrived to find that all their possessions had been sold.

A forensic examination of Bering's remains, following their rediscovery in 1991, allowed scientists to create this bust of the Danish explorer.

REBURIED WITH HONOR

It was Bering's fate to be a man without honor in his adopted country. A combination of factors may have brought this about. By the time the remnants of the expedition straggled back to St. Petersburg, the country was being ruled by the Empress Elizabeth, under whose rule hatred of foreigners reached an all-time high. The Russian government decided to keep the expedition's discoveries quiet, perhaps because they were scared that some other country might attempt to capitalize on them, or simply because they didn't realize their significance. Possibly because of his lack of noble gestures, of his inbred seaman's caution, Bering was widely portrayed as a functionary, some kind of sea-going bureaucrat. Almost from the time of his return, his achievements were called into doubt by many writers, notably in France and England. It was suggested that he did not actually make it to North America, and that Chirikov had been the real commander of the expedition and Bering his subordinate. As a result, the full account of the expedition quickly disappeared into the Russian government archives, where it would remain for decades. Even Captain James Cook's confirmation, fifty years later, of the accuracy of Bering's maps did little to revive the Dane's reputation.

It was a grave injustice, for Bering's achievements were significant and lasting. He had opened up and charted Russia's Pacific coast, not to mention the vast interior of Siberia, paving the way for evergrowing numbers of Russian traders to travel to America, first to the Aleutian Islands, then farther and farther south. This in turn allowed Russia to lay claim to North America as far south as fifty-five degrees north. By 1799, the Russian–American Trading Company held a monopoly on Alaska that was only relinquished when the United States purchased the territory from the company in 1867.

The story of Bering's voyage spread overseas, too. Fearing Russian competition, Spain extended its missions from San Diego to San Francisco. Columbus had started off a rush of European exploration of eastern America, and Bering now prompted a slower procession of Europeans to the West—the Hudson's Bay Company pushed into the Pacific Northwest partly because it feared the Russians would claim the territory.

Despite this, Bering's reputation continued to take a beating well into the twentieth century, when he was still portrayed as an indecisive leader who did not know his own mind. In the 1980s, however, the release of documents relating to Bering's voyages from the Russian archives, as well as the publication of a revisionist biography in America, led to a resurgence of interest in the explorer. His birthplace in Denmark created a small museum in his honor.

In 1991, a team of Danish and Russian forensic scientists arrived on Bering Island, formerly known as the Isle of the Foxes. Having read Georg Steller's journals, as well as those belonging to Sven Waxell, the team members knew exactly where to dig, and within a short period of time had found the bones of Vitus Bering. Their forensic examination, which took place in a laboratory in Kamchatka, brought interesting results. Far from being obese, as he had been depicted in numerous unflattering portraits, Bering, even at the age of sixty when he died, had the build of a weightlifter. Weighing 168 pounds, he would have been, according to the scientists, physically strong. Also, his teeth were intact, backing up Georg Steller's observation that it was not scurvy, directly, that killed Bering, since scurvy loosens the teeth of its victims.

A year later, in September of 1992, Bering's remains, along with those of the crewmen buried with him, were reinterred on Bering Island, with great honors from both the Danes and the Russians. An existing statue of Bering on the island, which showed him as heavyset and mustachioed, like a well-fed bureaucrat, was replaced by another, newly commissioned, that captured the face of a strong man in his prime. Looking at it, one has the feeling that it is the real Vitus Bering.

A LEGEND OF FREEDOM: FRANCISCO DAGOHOY AND THE REBELS OF BOHOL

THE ISLAND PROVINCE OF BOHOL LIES IN THE CENTRAL PART OF THE Philippine archipelago, in the Visayan Island grouping that includes Negros, Cebu, and Leyte. Modern guidebooks speak of Bohol as a tropical gem, a place of natural beauty, its 160-mile shoreline dotted with gentle coves and white sandy beaches. When tourists come, they come to swim or dive, to visit the Jesuit Baroque mission churches that dot the landscape, or to search for the endangered Tasier monkey, the smallest primate in the world, a nocturnal creature measuring only four to five inches, with a tail longer than its body.

Not everything in the region is so peaceful, however. Just to the south, the island of Mindanao is the site of long-running insurgencies in which 120,000 people have died in three decades. The New People's Army (NPA), a Communist group, has been fighting in Mindanao and on Bohol for thirty-one years. The Moro National Liberation Front (MNLF) is also active in southern Mindanao. The Moros are known as fierce fighters, but just as dangerous are the Islamic terrorists now operating in the region, the Jemaah Islamiya (JI) and the Abu Sayaaf Group (ASG), both of which have links to al-Qaeda and have kidnapped and killed Western tourists.

In a way, all of these rebellions began on Bohol, in 1744, when a man who would come to be called Dagohoy took three thousand followers, went into the island's rugged mountains, and established a separate republic. Twenty Spanish governors-general could not oust these rebels for eighty-five years, making this one of the longest insurgencies in the history of the world.

Inspired by Dagohoy's example, the Philippines became free from the domination of imperial Spain and, later, the imperial United States; and throughout the twentieth century, Dagohoy's name has been used as a model and rallying point for

Filipino rebels. Yet it's unlikely that the ideologues of the NPA, MNLF, JI, and ASG would have much in common with him. Ironically, the current crop of guerillas are fighting against the children of Francisco Dagohoy.

SLAVES BECOME MASTERS

The islanders of Bohol are thought to be descended from the last people to arrive in the Philippines before the Spanish, who were called the Pintados, or "tattooed ones." There is some archeological evidence to indicate that by the 1200s Bohol was a trading center. Designs associated with the Ming dynasty have been found on pottery shards and other artifacts around Bohol, indicating that contact with the outside world may have been widespread.

Bohol emerges into the glare of Western history with the arrival of Magellan in 1521. Magellan and his crew were the first Europeans to reach the Philippines, and Magellan would die there, killed on Cebu after a dispute with a local *datu*, or chief. It's likely that the Magellan expedition either landed on or sailed past Bohol; in any event, the island comes more firmly into focus with the arrival, in 1526, of the expedition led by García Jofre de Loasia, which had been sent out to capitalize on Magellan's discoveries. This expedition was struck by a hurricane and its vessels scattered. One of the ships, the *Santa Maria del Parral*, ran aground on the northern shores of Mindanao and its surviving crew were enslaved. One of the slaves was then sold to a Boholano chief named Sikatuna, and this became the first recorded contact between the Boholano people and the Spaniards. It would not take long for the master–slave relationship to be reversed.

In 1565, sailing westward from Mexico, Captain Miguel López de Legazpi brought a convoy of four ships and four hundred men to begin a Spanish settlement in the Philippines. With Legazpi were a Roman Catholic missionary named Andrés de Urdaneta, four Augustinian priests, and a lay brother. Urdaneta was an interesting man, a former military commander and expedition leader who had survived Spain's abortive visit to the Philippines in 1526, then become tired of fighting and entered a monastery. When Legazpi asked him to pilot the 1565 expedition, he agreed, but only on condition that he was given the title of "protector of the Indians," for he intended to start a mission and begin baptizing the people as soon as possible.

In 1740, the Philippines were ruled with an iron hand by Spain. But the island of Bohol was about to become the site of a fierce, enduring, and influential rebellion.

Legazpi and Urdaneta found themselves in difficulties right from the start. They were met with a hostile reception in Cebu, the place where Magellan had been killed, and so diverted to Bohol. There the Spaniards were nearly killed before they found out, using their Malay guide as an interpreter, that Portuguese raiders, coming from the Moluccas, had in 1563 attacked Bohol and surrounding islands, and carried off or killed as many as a thousand people.

MODERN REBELLIONS

The Communist New People's Army (NPA) is the most active rebel group on Bohol. In the late 1980s, an NPA ambush cost the lives of ten government soldiers, and insurgents since then have continued to ambush the army, although in smaller numbers than on Mindanao. The army, based, ironically, at Camp Dagohoy, makes regular patrols deep into the countryside. An article from the *Bohol Chronicle*, the island's newspaper, tells of a typical encounter, wherein an army patrol stumbled across twenty armed rebels. After a forty-five-minute firefight, the rebels withdrew, leaving the bullet-ridden body of one man, "a cadaver described as thirty-five to forty years old, five feet four inches in height, and sporting short hair and a mustache." The dead rebel, identified by his sister, turned out to be a local man who had left his home two years earlier, supposedly to seek a job. Two more rebels, wounded, were seen escaping into the mountains.

At this point, Legazpi explained that he was not Portuguese and that he came in peace. Meeting with the *datu* on March 16, he and the native king performed a blood ceremony, the two men cutting their arms and mixing their blood together so that, forever, the two nations would remain friends. The event is still commemorated on Bohol, by a statue and an annual "One Blood" ceremony.

TAMBLOT'S CHALLENGE

During the next one hundred years, Spanish control spread across the azure waters and green islands of the Philippines. It seemed to the Spanish, as it seemed to the Portuguese in Japan, that the native population was innately and profoundly religious, possessing a passion, fervor, and devotion rarely seen in Europe. By the early 1600s, four missionary orders vied for spiritual control of the people: the Augustinians, the Franciscans, the Dominicans, and the Jesuits—a total of about 130 missionaries in all, for perhaps seven hundred thousand people, of whom half, according to a missionary count, had been converted by 1600 or so.

To keep the missionaries from competing against each other, the islands were divided. The Jesuits were given Bohol, among other islands. But in the 1600s, the initial religious fervor of the native people began to die down, and was replaced by a fervor for rebellion. The Filipinos had traditionally lived in small units called *barangays*, communities of two hundred or so people with a small amount of territory, led by a local *datu*. But now, the Spanish built *reducciones*, small villages with churches and central plazas, around which they began to force people to live. Filipinos who had once been free now saw that the Spanish and the missionary orders were not friends or protectors, but enslaving conquerors who sought nothing less than the destruction of the traditional fabric of island life.

On Bohol in 1622, a native spiritualist, or *babaylan*, named Tamblot decided that he would not live where the Spanish authorities wanted him to live or worship the god that the Jesuits wanted him to worship, and that he would return the people to their former gods and oust the Spanish. When the Jesuit priests were absent, having gone to Cebu for a ceremony for the beatification of Francis Xavier, the revered Jesuit missionary (see p. 94), Tamblot led two thousand natives in a revolt. When the Spanish on Cebu heard about it, they sent troops to Bohol, but in a battle fought during an apocalyptic thunderstorm, Tamblot and his rebels forced the Spanish and their Filipino allies to retreat.

About six months later, the rebels won a second battle, but in its aftermath a party of armed men—Boholano tradition suggests they were Spanish priests—came into Tamblot's camp and assassinated him.

Without its leader, the revolution soon collapsed. Despite this, revolts continued. In 1663, a mystic named Tapar created a new religion combining eucharistic rites with native religious practices. Tapar, who wore women's clothing, declared that he was "God Almighty" and that two of his fellow rebels were Christ and the Holy Spirit; a female friend became the Blessed Virgin Mary. Tapar and his followers murdered a missionary with spears and then carried out hit-and-run attacks on

the *reducciones*, but the revolt was decisively quashed, within the year, by the Spanish authorities. They fed the Holy Trinity live to the crocodiles, and they beheaded the Blessed Virgin.

THE DEATH OF SAGARINO SENDRIJAS
By the mid-eighteenth century, the Spanish were firmly established all over the Philippines. In Bohol they had six *reducciones*, each with its own stone church. Having been forced to abandon their *barangays*, Boholanos were now also heavily taxed by the Spanish authorities.

In one of these *reducciones*, a town called Inabanga, there lived a young man named Francisco Sendrijas and his brother, Sagarino. There are no available birth records for these men, no stories of their families prior to 1744. They come to us fully born, as it were, men who would soon become as symbolic as they were human.

Sagarino was a constable in Inabanga, which was under the effective rule of a Jesuit priest, Gaspar Morales—the line between church and state in the Spanish colonial world at this time was crossed frequently. Morales sent Sagarino into the mountains of Bohol to catch a local Indian who had absconded from the farm he worked on; some say the Indian was a thief, others that he was simply escaping harsh labor conditions under a Spanish overseer.

Sagarino did as he was told and managed to track down the escapee, but, in a fight with the Indian, Sagarino was killed. When Francisco heard the news, he left Inabanga and went up into the mountains to retrieve his brother's body. But when he brought it back to Inabanga and asked the priest to bury it, Morales refused to allow it. He said that because Sagarino had been killed in a duel, which was forbidden by the church, and had thus died in a state of mortal sin, he could not allow him to be buried in consecrated ground.

There is another story of how this happened, in which Sagarino is actually the fugitive—a renegade who had given up Christianity—and Morales sends a constable to arrest him. In this version, Sagarino kills the constable before being killed himself. If this second story is not true, and most sources do not cite it, then Morales' refusal to bury the man he had sent out to his death was breathtaking in its stupidity and arrogance.

Francisco left his brother's body lying for three full days in front of the church, but Morales's refused to budge, and eventually Francisco buried him himself. After that, seething, he stopped paying taxes to the Spanish, and began to talk among his friends and relatives about rebellion. In about six month's time, in mid-1744, having gathered almost three thousand men and women, he headed up into the rugged mountains near the island's northeast coast.

A GENTLE WIND
Francisco's rebellion was, at first, a sort of withdrawal. He and his compatriots were declaring independence simply by leaving. They would not pay taxes and they would not be obedient to the priests. Under Francisco's supervision, the Boholanos dug huge trenches and topped them with rocks, as embattlements. They built houses for their families and cleared forests to plant subsistence crops.

But Francisco was still yearning for revenge. So, in January of 1745, he and his men attacked a *reduccione* and killed an Italian Jesuit priest, Father Giuseppe Lamberti. Then they struck at Inabanga and killed Father Morales. They also raided a Jesuit estate at San Xavier and made off with livestock as well as food and silver.

Elegant Spanish churches dating back to the eighteenth century are still a feature of many of the villages on the island of Bohol.

Finally, the Spanish authorities reacted. In 1747, they sent an expedition into the mountains against Francisco and his men, only to have it quickly repulsed. The Spanish commander, Don Pedro Lechuga, then sent a smaller unit of elite soldiers to try to kill Francisco, but this, too, failed and the Spanish were forced to retreat.

In part because of this victory, and in part because of his continuing raids against Spanish settlements, Francisco began to be called "Dagohoy," a combination of Tagalog and Cebuan words which mean "talisman" and "gentle wind," respectively. Francisco was perceived as the embodiment of the wind, one who could flow from one hillside to another, who could even turn invisible if he needed to. He was also reputed to be able to see in the darkness.

Like many another successful revolutionary, Francisco passed into myth, but some deep strength of character must have attracted people to him and his cause, despite the hardship of leaving their homes and joining him. Soon, more and more people poured into the mountains to join him and his rebellion.

Successive Spanish governors sent expedition after expedition against Dagohoy, and he defeated them all. Interestingly, his was not a revolution—like the French, Chinese, or American revolts—that sought to take over an entire country. Although he continued to make raids, Dagohoy's main intention was to stay in the hills and to live in freedom. Once Dagohoy's initial desire for revenge had been satisfied, this was a revolt that simply aimed to establish distance and breathing space. This was a fight for freedom, and freedom alone.

One historian of the revolt, Renato Constantino, points out that "the best indication of the importance and success of the rebellion may be seen in the persistent efforts exerted by both the state and the church to negotiate with Dagohoy." Unable to beat him, the Spanish persistently attempted to talk to him, offering him and his people amnesty. Bishop Line de Espeleta, the Archbishop of Cebu, met with Dagohoy to offer an unheard-of compromise, promising he would replace all Jesuits on Bohol with secular priests; yet still Dagohoy would not come down from the mountains. When the Jesuits were recalled to Spain at the end of the eighteenth century, their place was taken by the Augustinian Recollect order, which sent a representative into the mountains to interview Dagohoy. The leader met with him politely, but told him that his people were living a good life and a free life. There was no reason for them to leave what had become their homes.

At some point after this, almost certainly by the early 1800s, Francisco Dagohoy died and was buried in ground he had consecrated through his rebellion.

By the mid-1820s, the rebels in their mountain stronghold had swollen to about thirty thousand men, women, and children. Spain could no longer afford to allow them to continue to hold out. By now, the American and French revolutions had taken place and, in 1810, the Mexicans had revolted against Spanish rule.

The Spanish decided to make an all-out attempt to regain control of Bohol. With a combined Spanish–Filipino army, a new governor-general, Mariano Ricafort, launched an assault against the island. After a year's fierce fighting, with casualties on both sides numbering in the hundreds, the Spanish had moved into the mountains and surrounded the remains of Dagohoy's followers, who were exhausted from constant combat and dying of hunger and thirst. Assaulting with artillery, the Spanish drove the Boholano rebels into a mountain cave. Those who would not surrender were killed. A marker now commemorates this last battle, and the skeletons of the rebels remain sealed in the cave.

According to Spanish authorities, who treated those who surrendered with unusual kindness—perhaps out of respect, or out of fear—some nineteen thousand men, women, and children were then resettled on Bohol and surrounding islands.

DAGOHOY'S SUCCESSORS

But the Boholanos and the rest of the Filipinos did not stop fighting. Several rebellions were launched during the course of the nineteenth century. An uprising in Cavite led by three Filipino priests in 1872 was put down bloodily by the Spanish, but inspired a revolution led by Dr. Jose Rizal against the abuses of the Spanish government and its friars, who had blocked Filipino clergy from positions of power in the church, controlled parishes as petty fiefdoms, and even engaged in sexual abuses of children. In 1896, Rizal was executed. But by this time the Philippines were on fire.

THE POWER OF THE PROPHETS

Francisco Dagohoy was a rebel fighting for freedom, but not a messianic figure like Tamblot or Tapar, both of whom combined the Christian religion with native beliefs. The Spanish clergy were frightened of such cults, and with good reason, for cultists tended to be the most irrational and strangest of rebels.

In 1841, a formerly devout Catholic clerk in Manila named Apolinaro de la Cruz launched a rebellion against Spanish authorities on Luzon. He claimed that God was telling him to deliver his people from slavery. Accompanied by a frightening army of four hundred men armed with muskets and bolo knifes—and a close associate he had named Purgatorio—de la Cruz cut a swathe of destruction through several Luzon towns, beating off an attack by the provincial governor and killing the man in the process. It took an army of a thousand Spanish–Filipino troops to defeat de la Cruz.

The messianic rebel and two hundred of his followers were executed, but remnants of the group took to the mountains and continued to fight, developing into an organization called the Colorums (from the Latin phrase *Saecula saeculorum*, meaning "for all eternity" or "without end"), which joined with the rebels who fought both the Spanish and the United States at the end of the century.

THE MORO REBELLION

The Catholics were not the only ones in the Philippines fighting for their freedom: the Muslim Moro population has been at war ever since the Spanish conquest. The word *moro* has a couple of different derivations. It is a Tagalog term for a Muslim inhabitant of Mindanao or the Sulu Archipelago, but according to some linguists it derives from a derogatory usage employed by the early Spanish, being short for "Moroccan," or "Arab".

There were numerous Moro revolts in the three hundred plus years of Spanish rule, each one put down in bloody fashion. The Americans also fought the Moros after taking over the country, and the battles between the Moros and the U.S. Marines remain legendary. One reason why the 1911 Colt .45 pistol was developed is that the Americans were unable to stop the ferocious Moro warriors with a bullet of ordinary velocity. The American–Moro War went on until 1913, when the Americans captured the Sultan of Sulu and forced him to sign a treaty relinquishing his authority. In modern times, the Moros have continued to fight against the Christian population of the Philippines, although the guerilla war now has a jihadist bent.

The Spanish, defeated in the war of 1898 against the United States, ceded the Philippines to America. By then, Filipino revolutionaries had taken over all of the country except for the capital city of Manila. At first the Filipinos welcomed the Americans, but they quickly realized that the Americans were there to reconquer and control the country. At a constitutional convention held against the wishes of the American occupying forces, the Filipinos declared General Emilio Aquinaldo, a rebel who had fought with the Americans against the Spanish, as their president. He was declared an "outlaw bandit" by the McKinley administration, and a rebellion that would last a decade then began. In Bohol, in 1900, rebels organized a resistance against American troops commanded by Major Henry Hale. There ensued a bloody struggle that saw the Boholano insurgents inhabiting the same mountain strongholds that Dagohoy and his followers had used. The Americans burned twenty Boholano towns and killed hundreds of people before forcing the rebels to submit—a pattern repeated all over the Philippines.

After the country gained its independence following World War II, the island of Bohol did not develop as rapidly as the rest of the Philippines. One reason for that is that the Boholanos have a history of being fiercely independent and dislike large landowners and businessmen—or just anyone who appears to be getting too powerful.

In Bohol today, the town of Inabanga is the site of the Francisco Dagohoy Municipal Hospital, and the Philippine Historical Commission has placed a historical marker in the town of Magtangtang, near the site of the cave where the rebellion ended. All over the Philippines, in the two centuries since his death, Dagohoy has been seen as that talismanic wind of freedom, an emblem of one man standing against oppression. On the island of Corregidor, at the Filipino Heroes Memorial, which celebrates other island battles against overwhelming odds, including American resistance to the Japanese during the World War II, there is a mural that depicts Francisco Dagohoy. He is shown with his fist upraised, leading his rebels into the fight.

Opposite: American soldiers guard Filipino insurrectionists in the early twentieth century.

PIONEERING PEACEFUL PROTEST: THE BRITISH ABOLITION MOVEMENT

LET'S SAY TRUCKS FROM THE ACME BREAD FACTORY ARE SPEEDING BY TOO fast on the streets of your residential neighborhood, endangering the children who play there. You complain to the company, which shuttles you off to a PR person, who treats you like a crank. You then go to the police, but they're pretty busy, and, anyway, the chief is married to the secretary of Acme's CEO.

What's your next step? Well, you might get your neighbors to sign a petition to take down to City Hall. You could begin a letter-writing campaign to your council representative. Even better, you could start a boycott of the company's bread ("Acme Bread Endangers Our Children"). You'd call the local newspaper, of course. And, if you were the more radical sort, you might even indulge in a bit of guerilla theater: tossing dolls in front of the speeding trucks, for instance, or splashing Acme Bread with red paint.

If someone asked you where these protest techniques came from, you would probably, and correctly, answer that they were the same ones employed by the civil rights movement, by consumer boycotters, by women's and gay liberation groups, by antiwar protesters, by environmental crusaders. But these time-honored methods of civil disobedience did not begin in the fractious and disorder-loving late twentieth century, but two hundred years earlier, when a dozen men gathered in a print shop in London, England, with the single-minded purpose of ending the cruel slavery that sustained an empire.

THE DEADLY TRIANGLE ROUTE
Enslaving black people had been a way of life for the English since the mid-sixteenth century, when English mariner John Hawkins sailed back from West Africa with a cargo of human beings. For the next two hundred years, English slavers supplied as

many as forty thousand chained Africans a year to French, Spanish, Dutch, and Portuguese colonies. But by the 1700s, the main British market for slaves was the nation's own colonies in the West Indies, where the production of sugar generated huge profits. Slave captains sailed their ships on the so-called "Triangle Route"—Britain to Africa to the Caribbean and back—carrying slaves that had been captured for them by African and Arab slavers in countries that stretched along the west coast of Africa from modern-day Senegal to Nigeria.

Carrying human cargo was a brutal business. The slaves were packed like sardines below decks, into spaces just over two feet high. The suffocating hold was so unsanitary that it was said that other ships could smell a slave ship a mile downwind. On the "middle passage," the second leg of the triangle from Africa to America, slaves tried to commit suicide whenever they could—one reason why sharks were said to follow these ships. Africans who failed in their attempts to kill themselves were savagely flogged.

Things did not get better once the slaves reached the sugar plantations of Barbados, Jamaica, and other Caribbean islands. In the mid-1700s, Britain imported approximately one hundred thousand casks of sugar a year. Such was the impact of sugar on the British and European economies that some modern historians have called it the oil of its time. If sugar was a master, it was a cruel one. Since Europeans (and European diseases) had long since killed off the Indians of the West Indies, the demand for human labor on the plantations, with their sugar-processing refineries, was insatiable.

Slaves labored twelve hours a day, sometimes more, and died young. Horrible stories abound. One master, when his slaves became too old or infirm to work, simply tossed them alive over a precipice. Rival planters would often shoot each other's slaves, out of spite. Bone-weary slaves fell asleep in the refineries and tumbled into boiling vats of processed sugarcane. If slaves tried to escape, they were burned at the stake—a form of execution that had not been used in Britain since medieval times. Roughly one-third of all slaves died soon after reaching the West Indies.

Slavery in the continental United States was not pretty, by any means, but compared to what happened to British slaves in the Caribbean, it was a walk in the park. American slaves lived longer and their population increased. When the Emancipation Proclamation put a halt to slavery in the United States, the slave

In the late eighteenth century, many of Britain's major ports were dependent on the slave trade or slave-produced imports.

A slave girl being tortured by a British slave-ship captain, as illustrated by Isaac Cruikshank. Images like this one helped turn the British public against slavery.

population was ten times that of the four hundred thousand slaves originally imported. When slavery ended in the British West Indies, there were only 670,000 slaves left from imports of over two million.

THE STORY OF THE *ZONG*

How did a people with a centuries-old system of law and at least a nominal belief in justice live with such horrors? Well, for one thing, they did not. There were few blacks in Britain, and most British people simply did not have firsthand knowledge of the slave world. Moreover, like any profitable modern-day venture, slavery had powerful supporters in business and government. Finally, the times were different in the late eighteenth century: it has been estimated that perhaps three-quarters of the entire population of the world was then enslaved in some fashion, whether they were working on a sugar plantation in the Caribbean, rowing a galley for the Ottoman Empire, a captive of an American Indian tribe, or serving under duress in the Royal Navy after being kidnapped by a press gang—a form of slavery all too prevalent in Britain. And it had been ever thus, all the way back to the days of the Greek and Roman empires, and before.

But the times were about to change, and the seeds for change were sown by one particularly horrific incident that occurred aboard a British slave ship in 1782. In January of that year, a vessel called the *Zong*, captained by Luke Collingwood, set sail from Africa, heading to Jamaica, with a cargo of four hundred slaves. Collingwood, an inexperienced master on his first voyage, had packed too many slaves into his hold, and they began to sicken and die rapidly. The good captain was in a quandary: his payment depended on the number of slaves he delivered, and each dead slave meant less money in his pocket and the pockets of the ship's owners.

But then he thought he had hit on a way out. The slaves, he remembered, were insured for thirty pounds apiece—more than four thousand dollars in modern currency. Collingwood decided that he would throw any sick slaves overboard, making up the excuse that the ship had been running short of water, and "property" thus had to be jettisoned in order to lighten the load and get the *Zong* to port sooner. So he ordered his officers to throw 133 slaves over the side of the ship in mid-ocean.

When Collingwood got back to England, the *Zong*'s owners put in an insurance claim for the dead slaves. But the insurance company balked at paying it, particularly when the first mate of the ship testified that, in fact, the vessel had had plenty of water. Still a court found in favor of the *Zong*. No one involved in the court case was concerned about the atrocity that had taken place: Collingwood was not on trial for murder, nor were his employers. This was merely a dispute over property that was wending its way through the English civil court system.

However, a newspaper article about the case came to the attention of Olaudah Equiano, a freed slave living in London. Equiano, by 1783, had led an extraordinary life. He was born, probably in present-day Nigeria, sometime in the 1740s. Kidnapped as a boy, he was sold to British slavers and taken in captivity to Barbados. He might have died on the sugar plantations, but for the fact that his owner sold him to a Royal Navy captain, who took him to sea. For the next six years, he fought in naval battles against the French, survived smallpox, and visited Spain, Nova Scotia, and London. In London, some of his master's relatives helped him to learn to read and write; he was then promoted to able seaman in the Royal Navy.

But Equiano's master sold him to another slaver, who took him back to the Caribbean. Here, his learning stood him in good stead: working as a clerk and doing business deals on the side, he bought his freedom in 1766. For the next two decades, he took jobs on ships sailing all over the world. He was shipwrecked in the Bahamas, joined a Royal Navy expedition that made it to within six hundred miles of the North Pole, and traveled to Turkey and Central America. Everywhere he went, he would later write in his autobiography, he saw slavery and despaired that it would ever end.

At the time of the *Zong* story, he was living in London and working as a house servant. When he saw the newspaper article, he knew just what to do. He brought it to the attention of a man named Granville Sharp. Born in 1733, Sharp was one of eight children of an Anglican minister. His brother, William Sharp, was Surgeon to the King, but the Sharp siblings' main claim to fame was as a sort of floating Partridge Family. They gathered periodically on a barge belonging to William, musical instruments in hand—Granville's preferred instruments were clarinet, oboe, and kettle-drums. Then, towed by horses, they moved up and down rivers and canals, giving concerts. People flocked from all over to hear them.

LIBERTY TO SLAVES

It is a little-known fact that the British government was responsible for freeing American slaves during the Revolutionary War. In I775, as the colonies were starting to rebel, the British hit upon an ingenious recruiting device for the military: they promised freedom to any male slaves who would join the British Army. Three hundred blacks immediately deserted their owners. They were formed into the Royal Ethiopian Regiment, and issued uniforms bearing the words "Liberty to Slaves." Later, expanding on the success of this program, the British promised freedom to any slave—man, woman, or child—who would desert his or her rebel master. Thousands did just that, fleeing to New York, a British stronghold throughout the war. After the war, three thousand ex-slaves remained on the island of Manhattan. In one of history's ironic footnotes, George Washington met with his British counterpart, Sir Guy Carleton, in New York to arrange to return the slaves to their owners. Washington had earlier written a representative in New York: "Some of my own slaves ... may probably be in N York ... I will be much obliged by your securing them." But Carleton refused to return the slaves. Instead, he took them with the departing British fleet to Nova Scotia, where they formed what was, at the time, the largest group of free blacks in British North America.

One day in 1765, Granville was visiting the offices of his brother when a young black slave who had been badly beaten and abandoned by his master was brought in. "The boy seemed ready to die," Sharp later wrote. After William had patched up the young man, whose name was Jonathan Strong, Granville helped get him a job as a footman. But, after two years, Strong was spotted by his former owner, who kidnapped him and arranged to sell him. Sharp, a self-taught lawyer, intervened. He went to court to free Strong, and won the case. After this, he became known as the country's chief defender of slaves, which is why Equiano came to him with the *Zong* case.

Always seeking a way to put British slave owners on trial and continue his social protest, Sharp attempted to bring murder charges against the *Zong*'s owners and captain. He was unsuccessful in this, but garnered enough publicity that an Anglican vicar, Dr. Peter Peckard, heard about the case. It made an indelible impression on Peckard, who was already disturbed by the slave trade. When he became vice-chancellor of Cambridge University in 1785, he selected as the topic for the school's famous Latin essay contest the question, *Anne liceat invitos in servitutem dare?*, or "Is it lawful to make slaves of others against their will?"

The third link in the chain of causality that set off Britain's abolition movement was forged when young Thomas Clarkson, a minister's son studying to be a minister, entered the essay contest. Not a lot is known about Clarkson's early life, except that his father, who died when Clarkson was a boy, sought to help the sick and poor. Perhaps inspired by the elder Clarkson's memory, Thomas spent two months researching the topic of slavery, interviewing people like his brother John, a Royal Navy officer, who had firsthand knowledge of the trade. His impassioned antislavery essay won him first prize, and he read it aloud to an admiring audience at Cambridge's Senate House. Then he mounted his horse and set off for London, where he was about to begin what was now likely to be a successful career in the Anglican Church.

But then … he stopped, literally: he dismounted his horse halfway through his journey and sat down by the side of the road. It wasn't enough to write essays about slavery, he had suddenly realized. As he wrote later: "A thought came into my mind that if the contents of the Essay were true, it was time some person should see these calamities to an end."

CLARKSON AND THE QUAKERS
When Clarkson got to London, he decided to publish his prize-winning essay. There was no shortage of interested printers (the Latin Essay prize from Cambridge, in its day, was as famous as a Rhodes scholarship is now). But Clarkson sought a printer who understood that what he, Clarkson, wanted was not just the prestige of publishing his work, but to reach like-minded people who would join him in attempting to outlaw slavery.

He found such a man in James Phillips, a Quaker who owned a London bookstore and print shop, and who not only helped him edit his essay but also introduced him to fellow Quakers, a religious group that had been struggling against slavery, both in England and in America. As Clarkson later recounted in his history of the abolition

Thomas Clarkson, in a portrait made around 1800. Passionate and selfless, Clarkson was the driving force behind the British abolitionist movement.

movement, "from the time they had first heard of the Prize Essay, [the Quakers] had had their eyes on me." Through Phillips and the Quakers, Clarkson met Olaudah Equiano and Granville Sharp, for whom Clarkson—at twenty-five, twenty years younger than Sharp—developed an immediate affinity.

It was decided that an organization needed to be formed to combat slavery, and thus the Society for the Abolition of the Slave Trade, also known as the Slave Committee, was born. On May 22, 1787, twelve men gathered in the back of Phillips's print shop: nine Quakers and three Anglicans, including Clarkson and Sharp.

BENJAMIN LAY'S GUERILLA THEATER

Before Thomas Clarkson, Granville Sharp, Olaudah Equiano, and William Wilberforce came the American Quaker Benjamin Lay, a man far ahead of his time in employing guerilla theater techniques to campaign for reform. Lay was born in England in 1682, but, as a result of some "extravagances in conduct and language," was exiled to the West Indies in 1730, where he became personally acquainted with the plight of slaves in the sugar fields. When he moved to Philadelphia in 1731, Lay—a curiously troll-like figure, only four and a half feet high, hunchbacked, his face encircled by unruly white hair and beard—became a goad to the local Quakers, many of whom still owned slaves. Because slavery was still permitted in the city of Philadelphia, Lay refused to live there, instead inhabiting a cave in the woods, and rejected any food or clothing produced by the labor of slaves.

Lay liked to haunt Quaker worship meetings and put on displays of guerilla theater that prefigured methods used by Vietnam War protestors in the 1960s. One time he barged into a New Jersey Friends meeting and strode down the aisle brandishing a sword and a large Bible. "In the sight of God," he cried, "you are as guilty as if you stabbed your slaves in the heart, as I do this book." He then stabbed the Bible, piercing a small bladder of juice that he had hidden between the covers, so that bloodlike liquid sprayed over worshippers in the front rows.

Lay also once stood for hours outside a Quaker meeting house, his bare legs deep in snow, to demonstrate the plight of slaves not given adequate shelter. You invited him to your house at your peril, for whenever he found a teacup in which slave-grown sugar had been consumed, he smashed it. It is also said, though this may be apocryphal, that he once kidnapped a slave owner's child for a few hours, to show his parents what it felt like to have their child taken into captivity.

Partly as a result of Lay's radical tactics, Quakers in Philadelphia passed a resolution against the slave trade in 1758. A year later, Lay died.

Clarkson took notes for the meeting, where it was resolved "that the [Slave] Trade was both impolitick and unjust." At a subsequent meeting they debated whether they should campaign for only the abolition of slavery, or for freedom for all slaves— in other words, emancipation throughout the British Empire. They finally decided that, for the time being, they would call only for the abolition of the slave trade, which seemed a more attainable goal. Even this desire was bold in the extreme: the slave trade was entrenched in Britain and many people's livelihoods depended upon it, especially in the port cities.

But the Quakers were not afraid of a challenge. As a minority religious group in a country dominated by a government-sanctioned religion, they had learned how to organize, how to get around stonewalling by bureaucrats, which important people to contact, and how to raise needed funds. The Quakers were a perfect backbone for the movement, and Thomas Clarkson just the activist and spokesperson the abolitionists needed. Over six feet tall, with flaming red hair, he had boundless energy—his friend Samuel Taylor Coleridge called him "a moral Steam Engine."

In the summer of 1787, Clarkson got on his horse and rode, first to Bristol, then to Liverpool, the port cities that were the centers of the British slave trade. It was akin to a civil rights activist in the 1960s heading for the American Deep South. Clarkson was on a fact-finding mission. He finagled his way aboard a slave ship in Bristol and was able to measure exactly how much space the slaves had below decks: two feet eight inches in height. He persuaded a slave ship's doctor to keep a log of all he saw on his next voyage. He copied a ship's rolls, seeing that even the crews of slave ships died in high numbers, often from brutal treatment by their captains: he interviewed one poor sailor who had been chained to a deck for days on end, another who had tried to commit suicide.

Word began to get around about his mission and in Liverpool he was attacked and narrowly escaped being killed by a group led by a slave ship's officer. In the window of a ship chandler's shop, he found the instruments of the slaver's trade: handcuffs, leg shackles, thumbscrews, and a surgical instrument used to pry open the mouths of slaves who tried to starve themselves to death. He bought examples of all these instruments and headed back to London with them.

On the way, he stopped in the manufacturing town of Manchester. Predominantly a textile-manufacturing town, Manchester produced millions of pounds' worth of cotton every year that was traded for slaves; however, perhaps because the connection to the slave trade was less direct than in Liverpool, Clarkson found that the citizens welcomed the idea of abolition. For the first time in his life, Clarkson preached an antislavery sermon. It was attended by an overflowing crowd, which included forty or fifty blacks. Clarkson started a petition to send to Parliament, and in a few weeks it had over ten thousand signatures—one out of every five people in the city. It was the first sign of change.

SPREADING THE WORD

At this point, the campaign to end the slave trade began to employ all the stratagems that are now common among protest groups. The Slave Committee periodically printed a "Letter to our Friends in the Country," to keep supporters informed. Today, most organizations use newsletters as a matter of course. It issued a fund-raising plea, signed by Granville Sharp, and had it hand-delivered to potential donors who lived in London—probably the first direct-mail, fund-raising solicitation.

Josiah Wedgwood, the well-known pottery maker and new committee member, had his workers design a special seal for stamping these letters. It showed a slave in chains holding up his hands, and read: "Am I Not a Man and a Brother?" This image was soon ubiquitous all over Britain—embossed on snuffboxes, engraved on cufflinks, worn as a medallion, and attached to ladies' bracelets. The modern equivalents of these items include the lapel pin, badge, and T-shirt.

All of this had an effect. In public debates, which were presented by impresarios in theaters as a form of entertainment, the slave trade became a hotly contested topic, as it did in the "Letters" columns of newspapers. By 1788, this "ferment of the public mind," as Clarkson called it, was being expressed in the form of petitions to Parliament, including one bearing about one hundred thousand signatures. Of course, petitions can raise the pressure on lawmakers, but won't necessarily make them change the law. To achieve their goals, the abolitionists needed a politician on their side, and they found their man in William Wilberforce.

A young Member of Parliament, Wilberforce was politically independent and had read Thomas Clarkson's essay on slavery. He was frail and somewhat eccentric, but he was known for the force of his personality and the magnificence of his speaking voice, which contemporaries described as mesmerizing. After Clarkson met and spoke with him, beginning a lifelong friendship, Wilberforce agreed that he would introduce a bill in Parliament to abolish the slave trade.

By 1789, the abolitionist forces were poised for victory, but circumstances conspired to thwart their success, at least temporarily. To begin with, King George III went mad. Suffering from what was possibly porphyria, a blood disease that can sometimes cause temporary symptoms of mental illness, the king grabbed the Prince of Wales and smashed his head against a wall. He thought he could see Germany through a telescope. He began to talk to dead people and howl like a dog. For almost a year, the government was entirely preoccupied with the king's condition (thereafter he quickly recovered, though the illness would recur later in life). When Wilberforce finally managed to present the abolitionists' bill, he found himself out-maneuvered in Parliament by the proslavery forces. The delay had given them a chance to regroup and organize, and they were able to tie up the bill in committee hearings for almost two years.

In the meantime, the outbreak of the French Revolution absorbed everyone's attention. Clarkson went to France in the summer of 1789 and was intoxicated, like many in Europe at the time, by this manifestation of the ideals of equality. However, he was soon to be disillusioned. Despite its change of government, France retained almost seven hundred thousand slaves in the West Indies, and sugar plantations that outstripped those of the British in production; furthermore, the French planter lobby remained powerful. Clarkson, who began to receive anonymous death threats while in France, soon realized that the ideal of *"liberté, égalité, fraternité"* did not apply to black people.

Back home, despite the fact that the abolitionists' bill was still being debated in committee, the fight went on. Olaudah Equiano wrote a two-volume autobiography, *The Interesting Narrative of Olaudah Equiano*, which graphically depicted the evils of slavery. It became a bestseller, even at a cost of seven shillings—forty-eight dollars in modern currency!—and was translated into Russian, Dutch, and German. Equiano embarked on probably the first political book tour, traveling all over Britain, making speeches and selling copies of his book wherever he went. A smart businessman, he gave discounts to people who bought six or more copies, and also offered a luxury edition on fine paper.

Thanks to Equiano's book, many thousands of British people discovered the horrifying human cost of slavery and learned to personalize rather than generalize this great evil. And though the book was forgotten after Equiano's death, it was rediscovered and republished to the admiration of a new generation of readers in the mid-twentieth century.

Designed by the well-known potter Josiah Wedgwood, the image on this medallion was as ubiquitous in its time as the peace symbol is in ours.

However, the proslavery lobby was led by powerful men, including Banastre Tarleton, the dashing and brutal British general known as "Bloody Tarleton" to the Americans who fought against him in the Revolutionary War, and the Duke of Clarence, the licentious third son of the king. In 1791, despite the eloquence of William Wilberforce, the abolitionists' bill was finally defeated. Business interests had prevailed. As Horace Walpole wrote: "Commerce clinked its purse."

The committee was discouraged. But then something marvelous sprang up, something that occurred independently of the efforts of Thomas Clarkson and his friends: a boycott. Shortly after the failure of the bill in Parliament, and spurred on by popular abolitionist broadsides making explicit the connection between slavery and sugar, thousands of people in the British Isles stopped using sugar grown by slaves. Modern scholars have put the number of people involved as high as four hundred thousand. In some areas of the country, sales dropped to half of what they had been, while sugar imports from India increased dramatically. This probably wasn't the world's first consumer boycott, but it was remarkable for its size and for the fact that it was led by women, the people who, for the most part, shopped for the sugar and put it on their families' tables.

The fact that the committee did not start this boycott was a positive sign, as it indicated that public consciousness was changing. Unfortunately, in 1793 King Louis XVI was executed in France, and shortly thereafter, war between Britain and France broke out. When war breaks out, civil liberties tend to be eroded and jingoistic patriotism takes over. Try as they did, the abolitionists were unable to rekindle their antislavery bill. Their efforts were seen as treasonous, as giving support to the enemy—Britain's withdrawal from the slave trade, it was argued, would benefit France and leave Britain short of manpower. The abolitionists' years of endless labor seemed to have come to nothing.

It even appeared that the situation was getting worse. When the British Navy in the Caribbean captured ships with free blacks in their crews, they immediately sold them into slavery. And, if the British campaign to seize French islands in the West Indies succeeded, they would more than double the number of the empire's African slaves.

On the verge of a breakdown from overwork, Clarkson retired to the country, married, and started a family. Equiano died in 1797, after a short illness, a powerful voice lost to the movement. It was a time for abolitionists to keep their heads down, to say as little as possible, and to keep their eyes on a distant and brighter horizon.

REBELLION AND VICTORY
The campaign was revived by events that followed a particularly brutal slave revolt on the French island of St. Domingue (now Haiti) in 1791. After a series of clandestine meetings, the slaves rose up with a vengeance against their owners, setting fire to sugar plantations and refineries, and raping, murdering, and pillaging. The French army responded with equal viciousness, and the subsequent conflict was marked by extreme cruelty and violence. Slaves murdered white men by sawing them in half, or

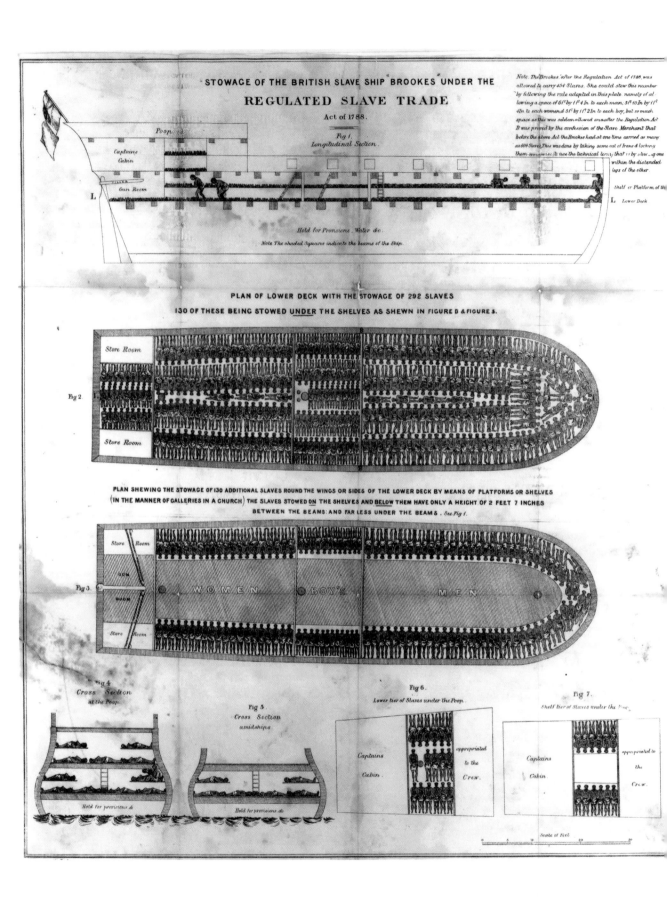

STOWAGE OF THE BRITISH SLAVE SHIP "BROOKES" UNDER THE

REGULATED SLAVE TRADE

Act of 1788.

Fig 1
Longitudinal Section.

Note. The Brookes' after the Regulation Act of 1788, was allowed to carry 454 Slaves. She could stow this number by following the rule adopted in this plate: namely of allowing a space of 6ft by 1ft 4 In. to each man, 5ft 10 In by 1ft 4In. to each woman & 5ft by 1ft 2In. to each boy, but so much space as this was seldom allowed even after the Regulation Act. It was proved by the confession of the Slave Merchant that before the above Act the Brookes had at one time carried as many as 609 Slaves. This was done by taking some out of Irons & locking them spoonwise, to use the technical term, that is by stowing one within the distended legs of the other.

Poop
Captains Cabin
Gun Room
Tiller

Hold for Provisions, Water &c.

Note The shaded Squares indicate the beams of the Ship.

Shelf or Platform of the Lower Deck

PLAN OF LOWER DECK WITH THE STOWAGE OF 292 SLAVES

130 OF THESE BEING STOWED UNDER THE SHELVES AS SHEWN IN FIGURE D & FIGURE S.

Fig 2

Store Room

Store Room

PLAN SHEWING THE STOWAGE OF 130 ADDITIONAL SLAVES ROUND THE WINGS OR SIDES OF THE LOWER DECK BY MEANS OF PLATFORMS OR SHELVES (IN THE MANNER OF GALLERIES IN A CHURCH) THE SLAVES STOWED ON THE SHELVES AND BELOW THEM HAVE ONLY A HEIGHT OF 2 FEET 7 INCHES BETWEEN THE BEAMS; AND FAR LESS UNDER THE BEAMS. See Fig 1.

Fig 3

Store Room

Store Room

W O M E N   B O Y S   M E N

Fig 4
Cross Section
at the Poop.

Hold for provisions &c

Fig 5
Cross Section
amidships

Hold for provisions &c

Fig 6.
Lower tier of Slaves under the Poop.

Captains Cabin

appropriated to the Crew.

Fig 7.
Shelf tier of Slaves under the Poop

Captains Cabin

appropriated to the Crew.

Scale of Feet

THE BROOKES DIAGRAM

In the early eighteenth century, the *Brookes* diagram could be found hanging in homes, pubs, and coffee-houses all over Britain, mainland Europe, and the United States. Distributed by abolitionists, this plan and cross-section of a slave ship became as iconic to the British abolitionist campaign as any image we can imagine from our times: the body of a lynched black man hanging from a tree, the sight of the Berlin Wall crumbling, a poster of Che Guevara. Provided to Thomas Clarkson by an abolitionist in the port of Plymouth, the diagram shows the top, side, bow, and stern views of the *Brookes*, which regularly transported slaves from Africa to Jamaica. There are over 480 closely packed bodies in the diagram. Legally, the ship could carry only 450 slaves, but on other voyages it apparently transported as many as 750. Anyone looking at the diagram could see how tightly packed the slaves were, how inhuman was their allotment of space. Not surprisingly, Thomas Clarkson immediately printed up nearly nine thousand copies.

nailing them to boards and cutting off their limbs. The French retaliated by butchering thousands of slaves; when they caught one rebel lieutenant, they nailed his epaulettes to his shoulder, then killed his wife and children in front of him.

Ultimately led by Toussaint L'Ouverture, the slaves overcame the French, and then fought to a standstill the British forces that came to attack the island. Just as the revolution had done in Europe following events in France, slave revolts spread like wildfire, through the Caribbean, to Jamaica and other islands. These revolts, brutal as they were, gave the abolitionists heart to make one final push to end the slave trade. And they got smart this time. They employed a lawyer, James Stevenson, who cleverly helped William Wilberforce draft a bill that made it a crime for any British subject to participate in the slave trade with France or her allies. The bill was passed. It was a brilliant stroke: under the guise of patriotism, the Foreign Slave Trade Act effectively crippled the British slave-trading industry. With this success under their belts, the abolitionists proposed a bill abolishing the entire slave trade. It was passed by both houses of Parliament and signed into law by George III on March 25, 1807.

It had taken twenty years, and the job was not yet complete. Although the bill made it a felony for any Briton to engage in the slave trade, half a million captive slaves still worked under inhumane conditions in the plantations of the West Indies. Not until August 1, 1838, did the British parliament grant full emancipation to the empire's slaves. In one church in Jamaica, abolitionists watched the clock strike off the hour of midnight on July 31 of that year, then let out an exuberant cry: "The Monster is dead."

Of the men who had met on that spring day of 1787 in James Phillips's print shop, Thomas Clarkson was the only one still alive. Granville Sharp, William Wilberforce, and all the others had passed away years before. (July 30, 1833, the date of Wilberforce's death, is still commemorated by the Church of England.) Clarkson lived on until 1846; that year, shortly before his death, he received two visitors from the United States: William Lloyd Garrison and Frederick Douglass, part of a new generation of abolitionists. Waging their own war against slavery, they came to learn all they could about how to fight the Monster to its grave.

Opposite: The so-called *Brookes* diagram, which graphically depicted the atrocious conditions in which slaves were shipped and became a persuasive piece of propaganda for abolitionists.

DAVID THOMPSON: NORTH AMERICA'S GREATEST GEOGRAPHER

N THE EARLY NINETEENTH CENTURY, TWO COMPANIES VIED FOR CONTROL OF Canada's lucrative fur trade: the Hudson's Bay Company and its upstart rival, the North West Company. Both set up palatial trading headquarters in the wilderness—if a palace can be made of logs. At the North West Company headquarters at Fort William, on Lake Superior, in the aptly named Great Hall, hung an extraordinary map. Measuring six and a half feet by ten feet, it represented 1.5 million square miles of northwestern North America, and it was as accurate as it was massive. Its gargantuan size matched both the outsized territory to the west of Superior and the outsized ambitions of the company that chose to hang it on its wall.

The map was the work of a single man: David Thompson.

David Thompson was an explorer, surveyor, and humanist who roamed the Canadian wilderness from 1784 to 1812. He walked, canoed, and rode a horse for fifty thousand miles, was the first European to traverse the entire length of the Columbia River, and filled seventy-seven notebooks with astute observations of life on the North American continent. And yet, like the gigantic map that hung on the wall of the North West Company, Thompson was to disappear from public view, so that today, a man who should be mentioned in the same breath as Lewis and Clark and Canadian explorer Alexander Mackenzie is close to forgotten by the world at large.

Yet if you have driven a road in northwestern North America, chances are you've driven along something that was first a squiggle on David Thompson's Fort William map. And if you've read about woodland Indians at the dawn of European contact, in works such as Charles C. Mann's bestselling *1491*, you've read stories from the portion of David Thompson's journals dealing with his friendship with the Piegan Indians, especially an elder named Saukamappee and a young warrior, Kootanae Appee.

It's hard to know why David Thompson has been forgotten. It may be because he was a solid and unflamboyant Englishman with little sense of self-aggrandizement, who stayed married to the same woman for fifty years. Undoubtedly, it had much to do with his eventual feud with the powerful Hudson's Bay Company. In the end, though, what counts is that he was a man whose work shaped a large part of the world North Americans live in today.

FROM GREY COAT TO THE WILDERNESS

David Thompson was born to a Welsh couple on the outskirts of London on April 30, 1770. The family, which included his brother John, was poor and became even poorer when his father died when David was only two. However, as would often be the case with Thompson, the misfortune brought benefits. In this case, the sad event of his father's passing led to his admittance to the Grey Coat School, a charity school supported by private endowments, which was housed in a handsome brick building in the shadow of Westminster Abbey. Instead of being apprenticed young after a rudimentary education or none at all, he was sent to Grey Coat at the age of seven and spent seven years there, showing himself to be a bright student, particularly at mathematics. Going to a charity school carried no stigma for Thompson, who loved Grey Coat's location, so near Westminster. "I was free in Westminster Abbey," he would later write. "Its venerable cloisters were my playground."

The Hudson's Bay Company, the largest fur trading company in North America, sometimes drew its clerk apprentices from Grey Coat, and, because of his aptitude for numbers, David was chosen, at the age of fourteen, along with another boy. So horrifying was the prospect of being shipped to the wilds of Canada that the other child ran away, never to be heard of again. But Thompson considered it a great adventure and, in May of 1784, signed his indenture papers and boarded a ship bound for Hudson Bay, Canada. After two months, the ship raised Resolution Island, then took another month to make its painstaking way through the ice-clogged, fog-enshrouded Hudson Strait and into vast Hudson Bay. It arrived at Churchill Factory, where the Churchill River disgorged into southwestern Hudson Bay, on September 1.

The Churchill Factory was a Hudson's Bay Company outpost—in company lingo, outposts were "factories," the trading agents "factors," or "merchants"—that was the hub of the company's vast network of trading posts. From Hudson Bay, men with canoes could reach the Arctic and the Gulf of St. Lawrence, even find their way to the Mississippi and the Gulf of Mexico, bringing back a harvest of furs from all over the

In 1791, northern North America was still a vast wilderness where European powers vied for control of the lucrative fur trade and Indians attempted to play one country off against the other.

153

ALEXANDER MACKENZIE

Roughly contemporaneous with David Thompson was Alexander Mackenzie, a Canadian explorer born in Scotland in 1764, who had a much more illustrious career. Mackenzie's family arrived in Montreal when he was ten. As an adventurous fifteen-year-old, he obtained a job with the newly formed North West Company in 1779. Seeking a route to the Pacific, Mackenzie followed the river later named after him out of Great Slave Lake in northwest Canada and ended up at the Arctic Ocean, having covered a distance of more than six thousand miles. He and his partners at North West considered this a setback rather than an achievement, and in 1793 he set off once again to try to find a route to the Pacific. He then became the first European to cross the Great Divide and the Rocky Mountains, reaching the Pacific coast in July of that year. He was knighted in 1802 for his accomplishments. Although he received far more acclaim for his journeys than did David Thompson, the two remained mutual admirers until Mackenzie's death in 1820.

continent. In late summer, ships arrived at Churchill Factory from England, bringing trade goods and supplies—bales of tobacco, rum, firearms and gunpowder, salt, and Bibles—then loaded up with the year's furs and returned across the Atlantic.

David Thompson watched his ship set off again with a sense of sadness, for "while the Ship remained at anchor, my parent and friends appeared only a few weeks distant, but when the ship sailed, and from the top of the rocks I lost sight of her, the distance became unmeasurable." In fact, Thompson was never to return to the land of his birth.

Despite his homesickness, Thompson learned his job as best he could, although counting bales of fur and sacks of salt was not exactly, as he later wrote sarcastically, a challenge for "a scholar who had a mathematical education." He lived in a tiny room and became acquainted with the vagaries of North American weather. "In the winter, the cold was so intense that all our movements were more or less for self-preservation … Summer, such as it is, comes at once and with it myriads of tormenting Muskitoes; the air is thick with them, there is no cessation day or night suffering from them."

Even as well-balanced an individual as Thompson was affected by the isolation. He describes sitting idly down to a checkerboard by himself one winter's day only to have the devil take the seat across from him. "We played several games and he lost every game, kept his temper but looked more grave; at length he got up or rather disappeared. My eyes were open and it was broad daylight. I looked around, all was silence and solitude; was it a dream or was it reality?" Whatever it was that he had seen, Thompson took it as a signal: he became a staunch Christian, and remained so until his death.

TO THE ROCKIES
Along with the mosquitoes in summer came flotillas of canoes from the interior, carrying European trappers and Indian hunters and vast numbers of pelts for trade—seven pelts were worth one blanket; a gun cost fourteen. Thompson enjoyed these rough men and loved to hear their stories of adventure. After two years of clerking at Churchill, he leapt at the chance of an "inland posting"—an opportunity to travel west with a group of Hudson's Bay factors to establish a network of trading posts in the foothills of the Rocky Mountains.

In the summer of 1786, paddling birch-bark canoes, the seventeen-year-old Thompson and his party headed south and west on the Hayes River, portaged around the northern end of Lake Winnipeg, and then ascended the Saskatchewan River, through massive herds of buffalo and grass fires set by Indians, to the foothills of the Rocky Mountains.

Thompson would spend the next twenty-five years roaming the Rockies, and he never forgot his first view of them: "At length the Rocky Mountains came in sight, like shining white clouds on the horizon. As we proceeded, they rose in height, their immense masses of snow appeared above the clouds and formed an impassable barrier, even to the eagles." In the foothills of the Rockies, Thompson and his cohorts found themselves in direct competition with a coalition of Quebecois traders—Hudson's

Bay Company managers referred to them as "peddlers from Quebec"—who were also trading with the Indians for furs. These independent traders had just formed a company called the North West Company to compete against the Hudson's Bay Company. Both companies knew that a fruitful and largely untouched area for trappers lay to the west, across the formidable Rockies.

David Thompson was first introduced to Indian life in the foothills of the Rockies, where a large, temporary tent city of a thousand Piegan, Cree, and Assiniboin Indians camped for their summer buffalo hunt. In his dealings with them, he was able to learn the rudiments of the Cree language. In the fall of 1787, Thompson and a few other men were sent on a trading mission to the Piegan Blackfeet Indians, a month's ride south and west on the Bow River. Thompson wintered there and was taken under the wing of an elderly Indian named Saukamappee, whose name meant "young man." He also met a renowned young warrior named Kootanae Appee, who would become an influential chief and have a significant impact on Thompson's career.

The Cree Indians were among the most populous tribes of western North America. David Thompson learned their language and befriended many of their number.

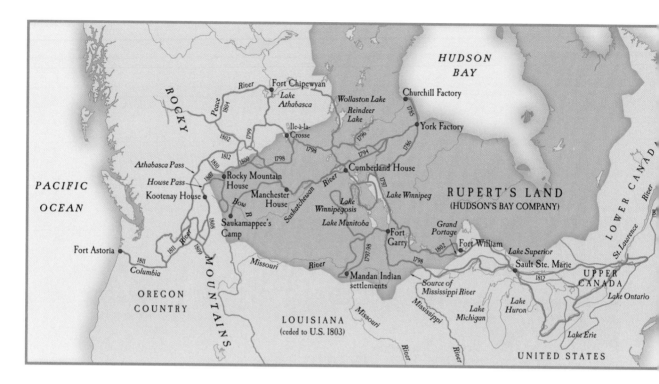

Between 1784 and 1811, David Thompson mapped 1.5 million square miles of North America, from Hudson Bay to the Great Lakes and from the St. Lawrence River to the Pacific Ocean.

Saukamappee had been born a Cree, probably about 1700, and he and Thompson discovered they could converse in that language. Thompson spent four winter months with Saukamappee, seeing Indian life firsthand: how modern utensils like pans made their daily work easier; how rifles allowed the Cree to conquer other tribes; but also how cohesive the tribes were and how they valued family and friendship.

Saukamappee told Thompson of the Blackfeet's first encounter with horses, in the form of a dead animal that had been killed in battle along with its Snake Indian owner. The Blackfeet were afraid to approach the animal, even though it was dead. They called it "Big Dog," because it carried the Snake Indian and his possessions, but soon changed its name to "Elk Dog," because of its size. Saukamappee also described a long-ago raid by his band of Blackfeet—who had not yet encountered a white man— against a strangely deserted Shoshone village, a scene that stands as a microcosm of the tragedy that was to befall the North American Indian: "With our sharp, flat daggers and knives, we cut through the tents and entered for the fight. But our war whoop instantly stopped, our eyes were appalled with terror. There was no one to fight with but dead and dying, each a mass of corruption." The Shoshone were all dead of smallpox. Having no understanding of infectious disease, the Blackfeet stripped the clothing from the dead and carried it back to their village. A third of Saukamappee's people then died of smallpox, the disease that, far more than European weapons, destroyed the native population of North America.

A LUCKY BREAK In the spring of 1788, just as he turned eighteen, Thompson left the Piegans and returned to the Hudson's Bay Company's Saskatchewan River site, where a large trading outpost, Manchester House, had now been built. One day near Christmas, while he was bringing back a load of meat on a sled, he tripped and fell down an icy riverbank, seriously breaking his leg. The bone was splintered and badly set; he spent months in bed and by spring was still unable to walk. So he was shipped by canoe down the Saskatchewan to Cumberland House, a trading outpost farther to the east, where, disinclined to eat the rich sturgeon that was the only food available, he nearly starved, until native women took pity on him and brought him wild berries.

He was up on crutches by the fall, but still hobbling, when a man named Philip Turnor arrived, and changed his life. The Hudson's Bay Company's surveyor, map-maker, and astronomer, Turnor was wintering at Cumberland House while planning a spring expedition to the west to make maps to be given to all the Hudson's Bay traders. Turnor taught Thompson how to use a sextant to take readings of the sun, moon, and stars, and how to use trigonometry to calculate latitude and longitude.

Thompson worked so hard that he lost the vision in his right eye, possibly from staring into the sun while taking sextant readings. But he was one of the most able students Turnor had ever met and Turnor commended him to his superiors at the Hudson's Bay Company office in London. Thompson, now permanently lame, was offered a position as a mapmaker and surveyor, based near York Factory, not far from Cumberland. In 1791, when his initial seven-year apprenticeship with the company was up, he signed on for another three years, and a pleased Hudson's Bay Company sent him his own set of instruments, including a brand-new sextant, compass, and magnifying glass, and relieved him of his clerking duties. He was now, officially, a "writer"—a mapmaker—and his career was launched.

Between 1792 and 1796, Thompson honed his skills—and earned a growing reputation as a mapmaker and surveyor—by traveling between Hudson Bay and Lake Athabasca to the west, setting up new trading posts, and fostering good relations with local tribes. He was paid well enough by the Hudson's Bay Company to be able to send home a portion of his wages to his mother, but soon became frustrated with the company's heavy-handed bureaucracy and by its insistence that he focus solely on mapping the known fur-trading routes. Thompson wanted more opportunity, wanted to be able to explore, like Alexander Mackenzie, who worked for the North West Company.

In 1797, at the age of twenty-six, he wrote Hudson's Bay a letter of resignation, walked eighty miles through the snow to the North West Company headquarters at Grand Portage, Lake Superior, and never once looked back.

Thompson's decision to leave the Hudson's Bay Company to join North West was the cause of bitter feelings at his former employer, which would exact its revenge in the future. But, for now, Thompson was elated. Sounding very much like a twenty-first-century employee who has switched corporations, he wrote: "How very different the liberal and public spirit of this North West Co. of merchants of Canada from the mean, selfish policy of the Hudson's Bay Co."

Overleaf: York Factory, in present-day northeastern Manitoba, was one of the Hudson's Bay Company's main trading posts and for several years David Thompson's base.

One of Thompson's first assignments with North West was to map, exactly, the boundary drawn between Canada and the United States after the end of the American Revolution. The boundary as fixed after the 1783 Treaty of Paris was notoriously inexact: for one thing, the headwaters of the Mississippi River had been located much farther to the north than fur trappers in the area knew them to be. In November of 1797, Thompson headed west, mapping the location of parts of the upper Missouri, including the Mandan Indian villages he found there. Then he turned east. He and his party of nine men, towing their canoe on a sled across the frozen ground, traveled to Turtle Lake, in present-day Minnesota, which Thompson declared "the very head of the Missippe." Latter-day observations would reveal that the headwaters were at a small lake a few miles away, but he got quite close. Thompson then went on to survey the southern shore of Lake Superior all the way to Sault Ste. Marie. By the time he found his way back to Grand Portage, ten months had elapsed and he had mapped close to four thousand miles of the border. Based on his observations, the North West Company headquarters at Grand Portage was actually located in American territory; the company soon moved inland to Fort William, on Thunder Bay, Ontario.

In an early indication of the value and significance of Thompson's work, parts of his map showing the Great Bend of the Missouri and the Mandan villages were used by the Lewis and Clark expedition in 1804. There is in the Library of Congress in Washington, D.C., a tracing of the map, with the notation, in President Thomas Jefferson's handwriting, "Bend of the Missouri ... by Mr. Thomson [sic], astronomer to the N. W. Company." It is ironic that Thompson is nowhere near as well known as Lewis and Clark, yet they used his map during their expedition and he explored a much wider expanse of North America.

MARRIAGE AND A NEW CHALLENGE
In the spring of 1799, Thompson, on another surveying journey, arrived at the Île-à-la-Crosse trading post in present-day Saskatchewan. There he encountered a thirteen-year old part-Cree, part-white girl named Charlotte Small. It was love at first sight, for both of them, and they married in June. Many years later, Charlotte was to write movingly:

> When David came to Île-à-la-Crosse it was in the spring ... You cannot know how beautiful it is when the grass is new and soft ... He was not very tall but his eyes were dark like ours and his hair was dark, too, and fine. And I liked him from the first day he asked me, Charlotte Small, to marry him with the permission of my brothers. I was ... so proud to be the wife of a man how knew the ways of my people and would never disgrace me before them.

In one of the great love stories of nineteenth-century Canada, Thompson and Charlotte would be married for over fifty years, have thirteen children together, and die within three months of each other. Right after they were first married, they moved to the North West Company's Rocky Mountain House in the foothills of the Rockies on the Saskatchewan River, where Thompson began to prepare for the company's next grand move: over the Rockies, to the Columbia River, where a new and rich source of furs lay.

By 1806, the North West Company was ready to cross the Great Divide. It had already been traversed by Alexander Mackenzie in 1793, but Mackenzie's route was too far north; the North West Company wanted a more southerly route that would connect with their trading posts on the eastern flank of the Rockies. The politics of the matter were tricky. Not only would Thompson be competing with the Hudson's Bay traders and the roving Yankee fur trappers moving into the area, but he would also have to deal with the Piegan Indians, who controlled the routes through the mountains. While they did not trap beaver themselves, they supplied the white traders with dried meat and other goods, and, in return, were provided with the guns that had helped them become the preeminent tribe in the region. If the tribes west of the Rockies were to trade with the whites, they, too, would receive guns, and the balance of power would be upset. Fortunately, Thompson's old Piegan friend Kootanae Appee appeared and with his help—and the liberal provision of trade goods—Thompson was able to make peace. In the summer of 1807, he made ready to cross the Rockies.

ACROSS THE GREAT DIVIDE

On May 10, 1807, Thompson took Charlotte, their three small children—one of the most touching artifacts left from this era is the scribbling of Thompson's five-year-old son over his journal pages—and a group of eight men to the Kootenay Plains, just east of the Rockies. Leaving Charlotte behind for the moment, Thompson and his men sought a pass they had heard about from the Indians. Following landmarks—a black cliff, a large split rock—they arrived within days at the place where "the Springs send their Rills to the Pacific Ocean," as Thompson wrote, or the Continental Divide.

They had crossed what would come to be known as Howse Pass, although not easily. Thompson and his men were starving and attempted to shoot a mountain goat, only to discover that these creatures were wily adversaries: "the Natives relate that they are wicked, kicking down stones on them." And when the party began to descend to the other side of the mountains, following the roaring Blaeberry River, they nearly drowned numerous times at crossings.

On June 30, Thompson and his men found themselves on the west side of the Rockies, on a broad plain through which a large river ran. It was actually the Columbia River, but, because it was flowing northward and the Columbia was then known only as a southward-flowing river, Thompson called it the Kootenay, after the tribe who lived along its banks. Thompson and his men immediately built a trading post, Kootenay House, and set about contacting the local Indians. But they discovered an unexpected problem: this low, flat plain through which the river ran contained little game. The men nearly starved. One was so hungry he ate a porcupine, including, unfortunately, one of its sharp-tipped quills, which Thompson found protruding from the man's stomach and pulled out with pliers. Eventually, however, the North West men learned to spear and trap fish for their sustenance.

MAPPING THE WORLD

We take that wrinkled map we keep in the sun visor of our car for granted, but early peoples would have killed for such an exact representation.

Maps have been around as long as people have had the urge to discover where they stand in the world. Pre-Columbian maps in Mexico used footprint symbols to represent roads, while Eskimos carved coastal maps in ivory walrus tusks. Probably the earliest map we might recognize today came from ancient Babylonia, where features were inscribed on flat, circular, clay disks. In the seventeenth and eighteenth centuries, mapping became far more accurate as a result of the discovery of a way to measure longitude using a series of complex calculations, plus the implementation of the metric system, which introduced a simpler and more universal language for map scale.

Today, aerial photographs, computers, inertial navigation systems, remote sensing, and space science combine to create maps that are just about as accurate as they can get. Go on the Internet and with a few clicks you can create and print out the kind of map that David Thompson would take six months to make. But it won't be anywhere near as beautiful.

THE BEGINNING OF BIG FOOT

In 1811, while making his desperate crossing of the Athabasca Pass, David Thompson found some massive animal tracks that some of his party claimed to belong to a mammoth—at this time, there was some belief, possibly fueled by the discovery of dinosaur bones by earlier explorers, that the mammoth still roamed the unexplored wilds of North America. Thomas Jefferson even reported the mammoth theory, writing down a Delaware Indian legend to that effect in journals. Thompson, to the end of his life, remained convinced that the tracks he saw in the Rockies that day belonged to an unusually large grizzly; but to this day, believers in Big Foot, or the Sasquatch, cite this as one of the first near-encounters with the legendary creature of the Pacific Northwest by a European.

Another problem was the Indians. Despite Thompson's uneasy peace with the Piegans, they visited his post in a vaguely menacing way, hanging around to spy on him, and stole the horses of the friendlier Kootenay Indians, with whom Thompson hoped to trade. Thompson also began receiving threats from another source: letters from a U.S. Army officer, who variously signed himself as "Jeremy Pinch" or "Zachery Perch," suggesting that Thompson was in American territory and should decamp. Interestingly enough, there is no record of any such name in the U.S. Army rolls at the time. One of Thompson's biographers, Jack Nisbet, suggests that the letters were sent by American trappers seeking to scare Thompson, and the North West Company, away.

But there was no frightening Thompson out. The next spring he brought Charlotte and the children to Kootenay House and spent the next few years exploring, moving as far south as modern-day Thompson Falls, Montana, trading with Indians, and adding to the notes for the great map he was envisioning.

A LAST HARD JOURNEY

By the spring of 1811, David Thompson had covered thousands of square miles of territory on the western side of the Rockies, setting up trading posts, and befriending local tribes in what is now British Columbia. He was the first to record the Salish Indian vocabulary; watching him with his sextant and telescope, the Salish called him *Koo-Koo-Sint*, or, roughly, "the man who looks at the stars."

The celestial man was getting tired. He was forty-one years old, had put in some hard traveling, and longed to spend more time with his burgeoning family. But he had one more journey to undertake for the North West Company. Although its fur-trading posts in British Columbia were productive, they were a significant distance from the Pacific Ocean, and trade with coastal tribes was sparse. The company wanted Thompson to find a more convenient route to the ocean, one that might even open up trade with China.

The competition was even fiercer than it had been before: new rivals included John Jacob Astor's Pacific Fur Company, which, even as Thompson began his last journey, had a ship sailing through the Pacific, en route to build a trading post at the mouth of the Columbia. Thompson wrote in his journal: "The critical situation of our affairs in the Columbia obliged me to return. I am getting tired of such constant hard journeys. For the last twenty months I have spent only [a] bare two months under the shelter of a hut." But he would persevere one last time, to establish a North West Company presence along the Columbia and west to the ocean.

Attempting to cross the Rockies, Thompson and his party were ambushed by Piegan Indians, who were no longer controlled by Thompson's old friend Kootanae Appee. Angry that he had traded guns to their enemies, they chased him and eventually blocked Howse Pass, forcing him to detour six hundred miles to the north to cross the mountains via the Athabasca Pass. It was a treacherous crossing, in midwinter, "some very bad hauling," as Thompson wrote, "snow seven feet deep. The Courage of part of my men … is sinking fast."

They finally made it over the Rockies, but all but three of his fellow travelers deserted Thompson and he was forced to winter where he was. In the spring, using canoes he had made out of overlapping cedar planks, and surveying as he went, he descended the upper Columbia River all the way to the Pacific Ocean, becoming the first European to do so. He had with him seven other people, three Europeans who had crossed with him at Athabasca, and four Indians. For four hundred miles, he met tribes who had never seen a white man: the Sanpoil, Nespelim, Methow, and Wenatchee Indians. He passed from forest to the arid plains of the central Columbia Plateau, where desert and steep rocks bordered the river. Typically, he noted minute aspects of Indian life: how they ate "sweet, wholesome, and nutritious berries," but also "small dried fat Animals," which Thompson took to be marmots, and which he found disgusting. He described the Indian dances—"They all both [sic] Men, Women, & Children formed a Line in an Ellipsis; they danced with the sun in a mingled manner"—and depicted a huge salmon run on the Yakima River that brought large groups of Indians out to fish.

After two weeks of canoeing, Thompson and his men made it to the sea, only to find that the men of John Jacob Astor's Pacific Fur Company had arrived there first—actually three months earlier—and had already completed their trading post, Fort Astor, now the town of Astoria. One of the Astorians made this dryly humorous note: "On the 15 of July ... Mr. Thompson, northwest-like, came dashing down the Columbia in a light canoe, with eight Iroquois and an interpreter."

THE GREAT MAP
Although Thompson had been unable to open up a route from the sea, he was able to claim much of present-day British Columbia for the North West Company. But he had had enough of wandering. In August of 1812, he retired with a good deal of North West Company stock and headed east to Montreal, where Charlotte had relatives. His life's work was far from over, however. Working at a large writing desk, he turned to his epic mapmaking project, beginning in the Far West with his charting of the Columbia River. Going over page after page of his journal, which he had filled with tabulations and coordinates of longitude and latitude, he gradually sketched out the big map. The work took him years, as children were born and, sadly, died—five-year-old John and seven-year-old Emma passed away of illness within a few weeks of each other—and his life proceeded. A typical journal entry from this period reads: "July 14 ... Calculated a little & finished all the Columbia courses &c. In the afternoon, cut hay."

By 1814, his *Great Map of the North West Territory of the Province of Canada* hung in the Great Hall of the North West Company at Fort William, with the notation by Thompson: "This Map made for the North West Company in 1813 and 1814 ... comprising the Surveys and Discoveries of Twenty Years."

Unfortunately, David Thompson's life was thereafter plagued by ill fortune. He made some bad investments and lost a good deal of the money he had retired with, and was then unable to make a living selling his maps and charts. The British government turned him down for a pension. He even put together a version of his journals as a

memoir, *Travels*, hoping to sell it to a publisher, but the only offer he had was from the American popular writer Washington Irving, author of "The Legend of Sleepy Hollow," who wanted to buy the material outright and turn it into fiction. Thompson refused.

Perhaps the unkindest cut of all took place in 1821, when the North West Company was acquired by the Hudson's Bay Company, Thompson's old employers. Governor George Simpson, head of the Hudson's Bay Company, sent Thompson's "Great Map" to London mapmaker Aaron Arrowsmith, along with numerous Thompson charts and notebooks that had been the property of the North West Company. Arrowsmith then incorporated this information to correct his existing maps and make new ones. David Thompson was never credited.

It was the beginning of Thompson's gradual eradication. As he grew older, his eyesight deteriorated and he was unable to work. Finally, on the verge of penury, he and Charlotte moved in with one of their daughters in Montreal. At the very end of his life, Thompson, now completely blind, sat outside, staring up at the stars, night after night. He died on February 10, 1857; Charlotte died three months later.

Although it took many years, Thompson's reputation was gradually resurrected in Canada. In the 1880s, a Canadian geologist, Dr. Joseph Tyrrell, was working in the West as a member of the Geological Survey of Canada. The old government maps Tyrrell was using were so accurate and precisely detailed he began to wonder where they came from. Out of idle curiosity he visited the archival file of the Crown Lands Department in Toronto, Ontario, and discovered a treasure trove: numerous journals and notebooks of David Thompson, as well as a huge map of western Canada—either the one that hung on the wall of the North West Company headquarters at Fort William, or another one Thompson had created in retirement. Tyrtell's further studies—he eventually became the editor of the first published edition of Thompson's journals—showed that all subsequent maps of western Canada were based on the Great Map.

In 1927, the Champlain Society published Thompson's memoirs and erected a monument over the geographer's grave in Montreal's Mount Royal Cemetery; the Canadian government issued a David Thompson postage stamp in 1957, on the centenary of his death. And the Great Map is now on permanent display in the Archives of Toronto. Today it is clear that Thompson's legacy of mapping and, even more, his approach to exploring—his respect for what he found in front of him, from the unknown Indian tribes to the pristine Rocky Mountain landscape—make him almost as much a man of the twenty-first century as of the nineteenth.

Opposite: Part of Thompson's *Great Map of the North West Territory of the Province of Canada*, which measures six and a half by ten feet, and hung for many years in the headquarters of the North West Company.

GEORGE AUGUSTUS ROBINSON: THE GREAT CONCILIATOR OF VAN DIEMEN'S LAND

T'S A COMMONPLACE OF THE AGE OF EXPLORATION THAT EXPLORERS FOUND what they were not looking for. Columbus sought the Indies and came upon America. Spanish explorers questing for a city of gold discovered the mighty Amazon River. And Dutch trader Abel Tasman, seeking Australia in 1642, sailed past it and discovered an island he called Van Diemen's Land, after his patron in the Dutch East India Company. The island seemed wild and remote to the eyes of a trader and although the Dutch sailors noticed notches cut into trees, watched fires burn in the woods, and heard "certain human sounds," they saw no one. They did, however, conclude that "there must be men here of extraordinary stature."

The Aboriginal inhabitants of Van Diemen's Land, or Tasmania as it was renamed in 1856, had for ten thousand years been isolated from the rest of the world—the longest period of isolation in human history. But within two hundred years of Tasman's arrival, they would receive a lethal dose of Western "civilization." The wonder is not that they died out—for contrary to a view held widely until the late twentieth century, they did not—but that any of them survived at all.

At the heart of the Tasmanian story in the century of their reckoning with white culture is a man named George Augustus Robinson, who, in a series of journeys through Tasmania, beginning in 1829, rounded up the island's remaining Aboriginal people, and brought them to a supposed place of safety, an island called Flinders. Robinson is sometimes called the "Great Conciliator," which is probably accurate. To conciliate, after all, is to stop someone from being angry, to placate or pacify, to mediate. However, it does not mean to make peace, for to be a genuine peacemaker you must hold truth in your heart. And what really lay in George Augustus Robinson's heart is the object of some debate.

THE ORIGINAL TASMANIANS

Tasmania lies about 125 miles south of Australia, separated by the shallow, turbulent Bass Strait. Thirty-five thousand years ago, however, there was no water, and the first inhabitants of what would become Tasmania simply walked across from present-day Australia. About ten thousand years ago, the sea rose, separating Tasmania from the mainland and thus isolating the island's inhabitants—until Abel Tasman sailed by in 1642.

Developing on their own in their mountainous country (roughly the size of England, with a similar climate) the Tasmanian Aboriginals formed into nine or so major groups, which were divided into about fifty small family-based clans; at the time of European contact the total population was probably between five and eight thousand, although some estimates place it as low as two to four thousand. The Tasmanians were hunter-gatherers, who used simple bone and stone tools but no bows and arrows, boomerangs, edged axes, agriculture, livestock, or pottery. They carried firesticks, pieces of smoldering wood, but may not have been able to make fire. Some anthropologists say that because of their isolation they went into "cultural decline," others that they successfully did what they needed to do to adapt to their environment.

The Tasmanians left no written records from pre-Western contact, but we have learned a few things: that each band had its totem animal—a seal, or kangaroo, or wallaby—and that there was a good spirit that ruled the day and a bad one that governed the night. They wore amulets made from the bones of dead loved ones to ward off evil spirits—one reason why they protested bitterly when the European custom of burial was foisted upon them. They believed in an afterlife, believed that their souls emerged from their bodies and went to live in other, earthly locales. The Aboriginal peoples of northern Tasmania, for instance, understood that after death their spirits inhabited the islands of Bass Strait, which included Flinders.

Up until quite recently, there has been a tendency among historians to view indigenous cultures at the moment of first contact with Europeans as in stasis. This is part of the noble savage myth, which is, at heart, racist. Western culture might evolve, but the woodland Indians of North America or the Aboriginal peoples of Tasmania were ever thus, always frozen at that moment when they looked up to see the huge wooden houses with sails on their horizons. In fact, the indigenous Tasmanians were probably evolving, albeit more slowly than a culture with more contact with other peoples. There is evidence that in the last thousand years before the Europeans came they had opened up tracts of land for agriculture and developed sealskin boats with which they made short voyages. Given more time, they might have reversed their primal journey and sailed back to Australia. But after Tasman sighted the island, the Aboriginals had only about 130 years of solitude left.

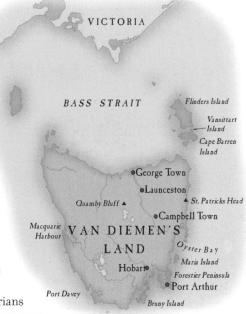

Van Diemen's Land, as Tasmania was known to the first European settlers, in 1830. Robinson's treks took him through the wild western part of the island.

THE BRITISH COME TO STAY

A French expedition sailed into Tasmania in 1772, skirmished with local Aboriginals—who heard their first musket fire, though not their last—and left. James Cook arrived four years later and stayed a few days. He decided, based on his brief observation of the country and its inhabitants, that it was "practically unoccupied" and, with a climate so like England's, perfect for settlement.

The French made a few more forays into the area, which upset the British, who had already formed a colony called New South Wales in present-day eastern Australia. British sealers discovered rich sealing grounds on Cape Barren Island in Bass Strait, and on the northeast coast of Tasmania. British ships would drop off sealers at the beginning of the season, in November, and pick them up in May. The local Aboriginal people began to provide women to the sealers as wives and workers, then found the sealers were kidnapping their women without their consent.

Beginning in 1803, however, the British found a use for Tasmania which brought in far more people than sealing did: as a huge prison camp. They had already turned New South Wales into a place in which to confine the thieves, pickpockets, and prostitutes of Britain and they now opened several penal colonies in Tasmania. The first settlement was at Risdon Cove on the southeast coast of the island, followed by one nearby that would become known as Hobarttown, or Hobart, and end up as the capital city of modern Tasmania. The early settlers here were rough men, convicts and their guards, who surveyed the sites of future farms, hunted kangaroos, and collected oysters from the banks of the Derwent River.

In May of 1804, a large group of Aboriginals surrounded the hut of a former convict, outside of Risdon Cove. Although the ex-convict later told an inquiry that the Aboriginals appeared to be hunting, and were armed with nothing but clubs, the Risdon Cove commander sent soldiers to disperse them. The soldiers opened fire and three of the Aboriginals were killed.

It was the first blood drawn between the British and the indigenous Tasmanians and the subject of much later dispute. Although a strong oral tradition insisted that a massacre of perhaps fifty Aboriginals took place that day, most histories, which relied on government records, did not report it as such. In the 1970s, however, revisionist historians, including Henry Reynolds and others, started to question the official, patriotic version of Australian history, citing a much wider range of sources, including oral histories.

In the case of Risdon Cove, this led some of these historians to repeat the line that a massacre had occurred, with as many as fifty Aboriginals killed. Based on this premise, the Tasmanian government gave back land at Risdon Cove to the Aboriginal community in 1995, as a gesture of reconciliation. But the latest historical research indicates that the massacre may not have happened.

Even so, three dead Aboriginals set a pattern for violence that continued as increasing numbers of white settlers arrived in Tasmania. More penal colonies opened up, most notably Macquarie Harbour on the country's wild west coast, which was so dreaded by convicts that they were known to commit murders just to

Opposite: George Augustus Robinson, in a portrait painted by Bernardino Giani in 1853, two years after Robinson returned to England.

A view of the thriving colonial town of Hobart, Tasmania, painted by John Glover in 1832. Robinson occupied a house in the town when not on his travels.

be hanged in Hobart, and so escape the prison for the last few days of their lives. Settlers began to hunt kangaroos because of a shortage of salt meat, and in doing so clashed with local Aboriginals over hunting land. Further clashes occurred when escaped convicts, military deserters, and other assorted ne'er-do-wells went into the bush to carve out a life for themselves. Some of these bushrangers, as they were called, murdered Aboriginals and stole their women.

In 1807, when seven hundred settlers arrived from Norfolk Island to begin farming the land, the die was truly cast. The Aboriginals did not take kindly to the increased presence of farmers. They began a campaign of harassment, attacking settlers who had wandered off on their own, driving off groups gathering water from local water-holes, and setting fire to crops. But the farmers kept coming, and, after them, the sheep-ranchers, or graziers as they are known in Australia.

CULTURES COLLIDE
In 1817, the European population of Tasmania was approximately 2,000, including free settlers and convicts. In 1823, it was 12,640. By 1830, it was 23,500, of whom 6,000 were free settlers. Many of the settlers were retired army officers or the sons of landed gentry, who came with recommendations from the Colonial Office in London that they be given large grants of land. These were the graziers. By 1830, there were one million sheep in Tasmania, pushing out from the rivers onto the plains, which were the Aboriginals' chief hunting areas. In the same pattern that had by then been occurring for two centuries in North America, whites and indigenous populations were on a collision course.

In 1824, there arrived in Hobart a new lieutenant-governor, Colonel George Arthur, an ex-army officer who had seen service against Napoleon and had worked as a commandant in British Honduras. Arthur was about forty when he arrived in Tasmania, and had a reputation as something of a reformer for his work in protecting the enslaved Mosquito Indians of Honduras. But he was also an evangelical Christian who believed that human beings had been put on the earth to be saved from their natural wickedness. He didn't like dancing, promoted abstinence from alcohol—a tough sell in this rough and ready colony—and often included prayer in his social gatherings at the governor's house.

Unlike previous administrators, Arthur insisted on having comprehensive powers to change things in the colony as he liked, without having to ask the administration in Sydney. Sydney did him one better, by making Tasmania a separate colony from New South Wales in 1825.

Despite the number of free settlers, Arthur knew that, above all, he was the head of what was essentially a convict state. Arthur ran the island like a precinct captain with a mania for organization. He categorized and counted the convicts, found out what they were there for (some weren't even listed in official records), and instituted a program by which they could shorten their sentences through rigidly prescribed rules of good behavior. It was later claimed that he was a sadist, but more likely he was simply a prig and a religious zealot. In his own way, he treated people fairly.

By the late 1820s, Arthur had managed to organize the colony to his liking, but there remained the problem of the Aboriginals. It was hard to tell how many of them there were left in the country, since in the thirty or so years since their first encounters with white sealers so many of them had died after violent encounters with settlers and bushrangers, or as a result of diseases such as influenza and tuberculosis, which moved well ahead of the white population. Numbers had also been reduced through the sale of numerous women of reproductive age to the sealers in the north.

However, the Aboriginals who were left had begun to fight a sporadic war against the graziers who had pushed them off their land. They crept up on herds and killed sheep, leaving them there, uneaten, to show their contempt. They raided and burned remote homesteads. One farmer wrote to Arthur: "I can assure you we all feel so fearful of their being near us, that we never move without a gun … [My wife] is uneasy if I even go so far as the Barn, and even to that short distance I always carry a gun. The trouble and loss they cause and still will cause us is quite paralyzing."

By 1829, it appeared to Arthur and the settlers that the Aboriginals' attacks were part of a common strategy, "a systematic plan of attacking the settlers and their possessions." The Aboriginals no longer seemed to dread firearms; they seemed to be watching the settlers, and often waited in ambush for them. Between 1824 and 1830, according to official reports, sixty Europeans were killed in attacks by Aboriginals. In the first three months of 1830 alone, eight whites were murdered.

How many Aboriginals died is still the subject, once again, of historical speculation. A revisionist historian, Lyndall Ryan, claimed that the Big River people, who were closest to white civilization and doing most of the fighting, lost possibly two-thirds of their total population in the period between 1823 and 1831. The official figures, written down by European record-keepers, were much lower, probably because many of the Aboriginals killed did not get counted. The discrepancies in these and other figures led some historians, including Ryan, to claim that the colonial Tasmanian government had waged a deliberate campaign of attempted extermination against the Aboriginals. In recent years, however, other historians have challenged this, claiming that many of the figures gleaned from oral histories and other non-governmental sources are also likely to be inaccurate. This has sparked a fierce debate over the validity of historical sources—government records versus folk history, the parson's journal against the elders' oral traditions—that raises vital issues for historians not only in Australia, but around the globe.

THE BLACK LINE When it comes to George Arthur, the evidence seems to support the fact that, while he certainly wanted the Aboriginals to stop fighting with the settlers, he did not issue orders to exterminate them. Instead, his strategy was one of segregation and distance. He needed, he decided, "to restrict the intercourse" between blacks and whites and so, in 1829, he declared martial law, indicating that Aboriginals must not enter into the settled districts of the country, but could move freely about the rest. Naturally, the Aboriginals did not take kindly to being told where they could go in their own country. And whites took martial law as an excuse to shoot Aboriginals wherever they found them.

The failure of martial law led Arthur to seek opinions on what should be done. Some settlers cried that a force of convicts should be mustered to hunt down the Aboriginals in the bush—with parole granted if a man shot three blacks. Others wanted to set up decoy caches consisting of poisoned sacks of sugar and flour for the Aboriginals to discover and ingest. Still others claimed that dogs should be imported to hunt the Aboriginals—"Spanish bloodhounds from Manila" would do quite nicely, they said.

Arthur blamed the whites for causing many of their own problems. The Committee on Aboriginal Affairs, which he had set up, wrote that the Aboriginals had been "cruelly wronged" by the colonial Tasmanian version of white trash—escaped convicts and the like. However, now the Aboriginals were taking their revenge on innocent settlers, and it had to stop, and in response Arthur came up with the idea of the Black Line.

The strategy was akin to herding livestock, except that the livestock in this case were humans—the island's entire Aboriginal population. What Arthur wanted to do was force the Aboriginals out of the eastern, more settled areas of the island and confine them to the Forestier Peninsula in the far southeast. On October 7, 1830, the army, almost every able-bodied free settler (settlers joined in enthusiastically, seeing a chance to gain more land), and numerous convicts—about 2,200 men in all—carrying a thousand muskets and three hundred pairs of handcuffs, formed a line stretching across the eastern half of the island, from St. Patricks Head on the east coast through Campbell Town in the Midlands to Quamby Bluff in the Western Tiers. This line was supported by two smaller forces on the flanks.

The men then marched south in line, sometimes a few feet apart, at other times separated by yards of heavy underbrush. They yelled, cursed, and shot their muskets in the air. At night they made defensive encampments and stood lookout.

HISTORY WARS

The contention of some revisionist historians that the colonial government of Tasmania had deliberately murdered thousands—perhaps as many as five thousand—Tasmanians before letting George Robinson lead the remaining, starving three hundred to Flinders Island was queried in 2002, when Keith Windschuttle published his book *The Fabrication of Aboriginal History, Volume I: Van Diemen's Land 1803–1847*.

The book is really a revision of the work of the revisionist historians and as such is open to question: Windschuttle is an avowed conservative, while the majority of the revisionists, including Lyndall Ryan and Henry Reynolds, are political liberals. But some of Windschuttle's arguments are hard to ignore. He convincingly debunks the idea of a Risdon Cove massacre, since the records cited by some historians for it do not even exist. He cites another case, where after listing numerous deaths of blacks in 1828, a historian cites the words "more killed" from a handwritten police record. Windschuttle looked up the record and found that it said "mare killed"—in other words, a horse had died. Windschuttle also goes back to the record to find out that Governor Arthur of Tasmania had written that he fervently hoped that by careful measures he could "prevent the eventual extirpation of the aboriginal race itself." Somehow, a revisionist historian had turned these words around to have the governor say that what he feared was: "the eventual extirpation of the Colony."

Windschuttle himself has been criticized for sticking steadfastly to official casualty records, which are almost certainly not accurate when it comes to black deaths. But he has succeeded at least in raising the temperature of the debate on Aboriginal history in Australia more than a few degrees.

In the morning, they got up and did it all over again. Finally, seven weeks later, they closed their circle at the Forestier Peninsula. And when the trap closed they had succeeded in trapping a grand total of ... two Aboriginals—a man and a boy. The rest had escaped.

The soldiers and settlers returned, empty-handed and discouraged. But although the Black Line was seen at the time as a failure, even by Arthur, it had the effect of driving the Aboriginals farther away from civilization and convincing Arthur that there were not as many of them as he had previously thought—in fact, there may have been as few as three hundred or so Aboriginals remaining on the island at this point.

PATRON AND PROTECTOR
Arthur had been toying with the idea, before the Black Line, of rounding up the Aboriginals through the use of a "conciliator." In 1829, he had set up a small mission for Aboriginals on Bruny Island, off the colony's southeastern coast, and sought someone to run it for him. That man turned out to be an English house-builder named George Augustus Robinson, married with five children, who arrived in Hobart in 1824. He, too, was an evangelical Christian who had been thinking about the plight of the Aboriginals for some time, and was concerned that no real attempt was being made to bring them to the knowledge of God or to protect them. "There is scarcely one among them," he wrote in his journals, "but what has some monstrous cruelty to relate which had been committed upon their kindred or nation or people." When

Robinson arrived on Bruny Island in March of 1829, he found only nineteen Aboriginals there, including a tribal chief named Woorrady and an eighteen-year-old girl named Truganini.

Robinson was an idealist who was, in a very real sense, attempting to set up a Christian utopia for the Aboriginals on Bruny—an "Aboriginal village," as he called it, with fertile soil, plenty of fresh water, and church services galore. But like a lot of do-gooders, his best intentions may have caused harm. He separated Aboriginal children from their parents to educate them in the European fashion, and introduced a European diet of bread, potatoes, salt pork, and tobacco, which was far lower in protein than the diet the Aboriginals were used to.

He became surprised and hurt—for one of Robinson's flaws was that he took these things personally—when many of the Aboriginals became ill then deserted the settlement, even though they explained to Robinson that they never stayed in a place where illness had struck. But resilience was one of Robinson's strong points—he had the qualities of an entrepreneur, always seeing new ways to attain his goals. In December of 1829, faced with the failure of his Aboriginal village, he hit on another idea: going around the country with his Bruny Island Aboriginals to try to round up *all* the remaining Tasmanians and bring them into a single large settlement. His first trip, he decided, would be through Tasmania's southwest to Port Davies on the west coast, a journey no white man had yet undertaken.

Given the rough country, the distances he would have to travel, and the unknown dangers, it was an audacious proposition. Robinson approached Arthur for government backing. Arthur was then developing the idea of the Black Line; but since, even if successful, it would resolve the Aboriginal issue only in the settled eastern areas of the country, Arthur gave Robinson permission to make his journey "for the purpose of endeavoring to effect an amicable understanding with the aborigines in that quarter, and through them, to the tribes in the interior."

Having obtained Arthur's permission, Robinson set off to the southwest, taking with him a few convict servants and a party of Aboriginals that included Woorrady and Truganini. Only about four feet three inches high and of very slight build, Truganini had a background that made her, potentially, a symbol of white oppression. Her mother had been stabbed to death by a white sealer. Her stepmother had been abducted by convicts and never seen again. She herself had been raped by sealers.

And yet she still spent the next four years as a guide and aide (and sexual companion) to George Augustus Robinson, helping him to bring Aboriginals in from the wild. Truganini has been called a traitor to her race, a woman out to betray her own for personal gain. (The same revisionist fate has been visited upon Sacagawea, the Shoshone Indian who guided the Lewis and Clark expedition, which helped open up the American West to settlement, and the Aztec woman Malinche, who was Hernando Cortez's guide, interpreter, and mistress.) But that is to ignore the immensely complex relationship she and other Aboriginals had at the time with the whites. It also credits her with too much hindsight and historical perspective; as if she could know that her journeys with Robinson would end in the near-disappearance of her people.

Proclamation boards like this one were posted on trees in Van Dieman's Land in an attempt to show Aboriginals that they and Europeans were equal under the colony's martial law.

On that first journey through the southwest, Robinson made contact with Aboriginals who had had little direct contact with the whites, although they were aware of the European presence. Whenever he became aware that Aboriginals were nearby, by, for example, finding empty huts or seeing smoke rising from a forest, he would send Woorrady and Truganini and others to contact them while he waited anxiously in camp. When they returned with local people, he would try to convince them that he had not come to do them harm. He gave them food and cheap trade goods and sought to persuade them to surrender to him when he came by again, so that he could take them out of the danger that would soon present itself from white settlers.

Robinson extended his journey up the west coast to Macquarie Harbour and then around the northwest tip of the island to Launceston. He finally returned to Hobart in the fall of 1830, as the Black Line operation was taking place. The trip had taken him eight months in all, and was a journey that would be daunting even today. He had contact with a wide range of Aboriginal groups. Many of them still preferred the uncertainties of life in the bush to the "civilized" reserve he was offering them—and one group had even stalked him, with the apparent intention of killing him—but Robinson had learned a lot about the art of conciliation. He learned not to carry guns—on his first trip, he carried three pistols with him, which caused the Aboriginals to distrust him—and to offer tea and food before anything else. He understood that he needed to travel lightly and swiftly: when he went too slowly the Aboriginals with him would grow impatient and simply melt away into the bush. And he had decided, next time, not to take any Europeans with him, for none of them shared the same evangelizing sense of mission that he felt.

A NEW ISLAND HOME
Robinson finished his first expedition convinced that Aboriginals needed to be taken out of the gradually encroaching path of the settlers and resettled in a sanctuary, where they could be "civilized" and Christianized. Arthur was impressed by his journey and, as the Black Line was occurring, immediately sent Robinson to the northeast—beyond the starting point of the Black Line—to find any Aboriginals in settled districts there.

Once again, Robinson, with the help of Truganini and Woorrady, talked to the Aboriginals, made tea for them, and told them they needed to come with him, lest the settlers' guns get them; a number agreed to go with him at once. He even went to islands on Bass Strait and rescued three women held captive by sealers, which raised his status in the eyes of other Aboriginals. By January of 1831, Robinson had gathered a group of forty Aboriginals together, whom he placed temporarily on Swan Island, just off the northeast coast, with the approval of George Arthur and the Committee on Aboriginal Affairs, which was now dealing with the issue of placement. An island was chosen because Robinson knew that, given half a chance, the Aboriginals would return to their homes.

George Arthur was so pleased with Robinson's work that he raised his salary from £100 to £250 a year, with a £100 bonus and a grant of land. It was decided that a permanent Aboriginal establishment would be placed on Gun Carriage

AUSTRALIA'S NATIONAL PICTURE

Benjamin Duterrau (1767–1851) was an English painter who, after a successful career in London, moved to Tasmania at the age of sixty-five, in 1832, seeking new challenges. The fact that he would move to the other side of the world at such an age is in itself remarkable; however, Duterrau also went on to paint a picture, *The Conciliation*, that was to eptomize the era.

Settling in Hobart, Duterrau started painting portraits and landscapes; he also met George Augustus Robinson and was fascinated by the work he was doing. Robinson would take Aboriginals to Duterrau's Hobart studio, where the painter used them as models, and also made etchings and plaster sculptures of them. Painted in 1835, *The Conciliation*, which has often been referred to as Australia's "National Picture," depicts Robinson striking a noble pose amid a large group of Aboriginals.

One of the figures represents Truganini, although— and it seems typical of the controversy that surrounds this event in Tasmanian history—scholars disagree on which one she is. Some say she is the figure pointing to Robinson while pulling another Aboriginal by the hand; others that she is the woman standing closest to him.

The Conciliation hangs in the Tasmanian Museum and Art Gallery. As a further matter of controversy, a larger version of *The Conciliation*, which Duterreau painted in 1840, has been lost for over 150 years.

MUSQUITO: BANDIT OR REBEL?

In 1813, an Aboriginal man born in New South Wales, whom the English called Musquito, was sent to Van Diemen's Land on suspicion of murder, but released when it turned out he was far more valuable as a tracker of bushrangers. Not a lot is known about Musquito, except that he was, as the English said, "an admirable bloodhound." However, in 1818, he decided that his services were not properly appreciated and he ran off to join a group of Hobart Aboriginals known as the Tame Mob. These were men who had been exiled even by their own people, becoming, in effect, Aboriginal bushrangers. Musquito and his followers attacked settlers in the Oyster Bay area; it was said Musquito continually incited the Aboriginals to kill whites. His name became known and eventually a price was put on his head. In 1824, he was shot in the groin and captured, tried without benefit of defense council, and, finally, hung alongside a Tasmanian Aboriginal named Black Jack. The execution was followed by a number of revenge attacks on whites. George Robinson blamed the colonial authorities for bringing such a man to Tasmania to begin with: "Muskeeto murdered several in Sydney and was sent here to be out of the way. What a policy!"

(Vansittart) Island, in Bass Strait, and in March of 1831, Robinson landed there with a group now totaling fifty-one Aborginals. Huts were built and vegetable gardens planted. Then Robinson set off again.

Over the course of the next five years, Robinson made four more expeditions. Soon, the Aboriginals who inhabited the settled districts began to come out of the bush. In 1832, before setting out to conciliate the peoples of the far west—the fiercest, most independent groups—he asked for and received a thousand pounds from George Arthur, with three hundred payable up front. By the end of 1834, he had made contact with every group of Aboriginals in Tasmania. His strategy was always the same: first, provide food and presents to gain the Aboriginals' confidence; next, warn about the dangers of white settlers; and, finally, offer a place of refuge. Later—any time between a few months and a year later—he would return to collect his charges and lead them from the wilderness.

Over the course of his journeys, however, Robinson gradually changed. There was no question in his mind, as he acknowledged in letters to friends, that the Aboriginals had full rights to their lands. But he continued to feel that if he didn't bring them out of the bush, they would die. He wrote in his journal: "Patriotism is a distinguishing trait in the aboriginal character, yet for all the love they bear their country, the aboriginal settlement will soon become their adopted country … With these views I purposed acting accordingly and trusted to the goodness of providence for wisdom to direct me in what I had to do." Robinson wanted the Aboriginals to find a safe place, away from the depredations of white settlers; the fact that many Aboriginals did not share his view and wanted to stay in their homelands made him increasingly frustrated. He began, on occasion, to use guns to intimidate the Aboriginals into allowing themselves to be brought in. He never discharged the weapons, but the threat was there.

On February 3, 1835, Robinson reported to Arthur that "[t]he entire Aboriginal population are now removed." This was almost true: he had indeed rounded up the vast majority of surviving Tasmanian Aboriginals. What's more, he had made a series of epic, unparalleled journeys, going over and over again into daunting wilderness—something, in fact, that no other European was willing to do at this time without an armed escort.

Finally, in October of 1835, Robinson journeyed north once again to join the Aboriginals on Flinders Island, whence the settlement had been moved after Gun Carriage Island was found to be too small.

A PEOPLE MAROONED

Located in Bass Strait, about fifteen miles off the northeast coast of Tasmania, Flinders Island is named for the English explorer Matthew Flinders, and is approximately sixty miles long and twenty wide. Robinson got there in October 1835 to find about 120 Aboriginals waiting for him—almost two-thirds of the group had died in transit, much to his dismay. But even with this reduced number, Robinson felt he could still show the success of his experiment.

He set to work building his "Aboriginal Establishment," as he called it. There were quarters for the civilian staff, the military presence, and the convict laborers, and nine huge double huts for the Aboriginals. They were also given vegetable gardens and a common store of provisions, though it was to be administered by the Europeans. They were taught to farm. The fourteen children were separated from their parents (some were orphans already) and sent to school.

Robinson set about changing the Aboriginals' names. Woorrady became Count Alpha, because he was a chief and the first Aboriginal Robinson had met. Truganini became Lalla Rookh, meaning "the last survivor of her clan." Another Aboriginal chief became King William, after the reigning British king. Calling the Aboriginals by these names turned out to be popular—they all wanted a different name—and was also a clever way for Robinson to show the indigenous people that their society and power structure were actually quite similar to those of the British.

There was not a lot to do on the island. There was some attempt to educate the Aboriginal people, but only the promise of immediate rewards could persuade them to focus on such abstract matters. The women cooked and washed; the men were so little employed that they spent most of their time playing games the English had taught them: marbles and cricket. They spent two hours a day in church.

Gradually, people began to sicken. The Aboriginals were especially susceptible to bronchitis and pneumonia, and dysentery caused by an impure water supply. Their only meat, except what they could eke out from hunting muttonbirds, was salt pork, and the Aboriginal women boiled vegetables so thoroughly that most of the nutrients were leeched out. Consequently, they began to suffer from malnutrition, as Thomas Ryan, a doctor who examined them in 1836, recorded, adding presciently: "I tremble for the consequences; the race of Tasmania, like the last of the Mohicans, will pine away and be extinct in a quarter of a century." Ryan instructed Robinson to build a fresh water aqueduct to draw water from neighboring hills. But although this was begun, it was never finished; nor did Robinson ever provide fresh meat for the Aboriginals' rations.

Robinson seems to have grown as tired of living on the island as the Aboriginals did, and he made several trips to the mainland. In the meantime, his charges began to die. Robinson forbade cremation, the age-old custom of the Tasmanians, for fear that they would resort to using the bones of the dead as totems. He insisted on burying the dead as Christians, though even he could see that Christianity was not taking hold on as he wanted it to—the Aboriginals still practiced, albeit in secret, their old customs, maintained kinship structures, stole each other's women, and performed ceremonial dances. Robinson never used physical force to control them—unlike the convicts on the island, the Aboriginals were never flogged. But he coerced them by denying rations to some and encouraging others to spy on their fellows, thereby employing a kind of administrative behavior that is typical of prisons and concentration camps.

And then he left. In 1839, offered a job on the Australian mainland, Robinson took fifteen Aboriginals with him, and departed. When he had arrived on Flinders Island in 1835, there had been 123 Aboriginals living there. In the interim, 59 had died, although 11 had been born.

After twelve years on the mainland, Robinson decided, in 1851, to return to England, where he would die, a wealthy and respected man, in 1866. Before he left, he paid a final visit to the Tasmanian Aboriginals, who had in the meantime been moved to Oyster Cove, on the D'Entrecasteaux Channel, not far from Hobart. Only thirty were then alive, and Robinson was saddened to find that they did not greet him with enthusiasm. Nor were they hostile, however. They merely seemed indifferent.

LAST OF HER RACE?

By 1855, there were only sixteen Aboriginals left at Oyster Cove, living in a miserable collection of huts. One of them was Truganini. These Aboriginals were paraded out on ceremonial occasions and often sat for the new art of photography. In the photos, they seem stuffed into their Western clothes, stiff and impassive for the camera.

There then began a morbid watch to see who the "last Aboriginal" would be. The second last one, William Lanne (or Lanney), died in Hobart, on March 2, 1868. Because it was felt that his remains might be valuable, rival surgeons fought for them. To obtain his skull, one doctor crept into the mortuary, cut off Lanney's head, skinned it, put the skin on a head from a white cadaver, and put that head back on Lanney's body. In his haste, however, the surgeon put the skin on backward; the next morning, a colonial medical officer found "the face turned around and at the back of the head the bones were sticking out."

Truganini, now "the last Aboriginal," was horrified to learn of Lanney's fate and begged to have her ashes scattered in the ocean. But when she died in 1876, she was buried secretly in a vault behind Hobart Penitentiary. In 1878, she was dug up, her flesh boiled off her bones, and her skeleton put on display in the museum of the Royal Society of Tasmania. It remained there until 1947, when it was taken down. Finally, in 1976, she had her wish: her remains were cremated and scattered over D'Entrecasteaux Channel.

That year was the centenary of Truganini's death, and it was also the time when revisionist historians began to question official accounts of the island's history. The publication, in 1966, by historian N. J. B. Plomley, of the journals of George Robinson had initiated a new period of research into the era. Historians including Lyndall Ryan now asked whether the Tasmanian Aboriginals had really died out, pointing out quite accurately that communities like the ones consisting of sealers and Aboriginal women on the islands of eastern Bass Strait survived. These were not "full-blooded" Aboriginals. But were American Indians considered "not Indians" if they were one-half European? By the same token, would they be denied their "Europeanness" if they were part Indian?

The debate naturally led into a discussion of the fate of the Tasmanian Aboriginals. Had they been the victims of a deliberate policy of extermination—genocide—on the part of the colonial government? The ongoing dispute over this has in turn given rise to a wider discussion, relevant to historians the world over, about the validity of historical sources, the very methodology of historical investigation. It's a debate that will continue and could shape our future.

Truganini in old age. At the time of her death, George Augustus Robinson's loyal guide and sometime lover was wrongly identified as the last of her race.

The debate over George Robinson goes on, too. Was he a "con man," as one historian has called him, out to get as much money from the government as possible before abandoning the Aboriginals to a slow death? Or, was he sincerely seeking, as no doubt many others were at the forefront of similar clashes of cultures—elsewhere in Australia, in the Americas, Asia, and Africa—a positive, mutually beneficial way to resolve those differences, a way toward conciliation?

Almost certainly, Robinson did not consider the Aboriginals as fully human—or perhaps "fully adult" is a better way of putting it, for he treated them as if they were children, in a manner typical of even the most well-meaning Europeans of his era. He was a religious man who thought that bringing the Aboriginals to the European God was needed in order to save their souls; but in caring for their souls he neglected their bodies. And in the face of their steady demise, in the earthly civilization he had set up for them, he became strangely passive, for such an energetic man. And then he sailed away. If he can be indicted, it is here.

WILLIAM WALKER: AMERICAN PRESIDENT OF NICARAGUA

FILIBUSTER IS A DISTINCTIVELY AMERICAN TERM WHICH, LIKE ALL THINGS distinctively American, derives from somewhere else. The word is from the Spanish *filibustero*, first used in the eighteenth century as a name for the pirates who pillaged the Spanish West Indies. As a verb, "filibuster" subsequently came to mean "to sabotage" or "to interrupt"—in the U.S. Congress a filibuster is a last-ditch delaying tactic employed by minority parties to keep a bill from passing.

But in mid-nineteenth-century America, for a very short period of time—perhaps twenty years at most—filibuster had a far less civilized connotation. It applied to a breed of desperate adventurers whose goal it was to overthrow Latin American governments with small groups of heavily armed men, and turn those countries into American puppet states.

Filibusters were also known by a perhaps more descriptive term: freebooters, from the Dutch *vrijbuiter*, meaning "plunderer." And chief among these plunderers was a Southern gentleman named William Walker, who was five feet two inches tall, weighed 120 pounds, and had the coldest gray eyes that anyone who met him had ever seen. These gray eyes were described as all color, seemingly without pupil, and they never appeared to blink, not during pitched combat or forced marches through the steaming Central American jungle or even at the very end, when William Walker looked down the barrels of a firing squad.

A YOUNG GENIUS IN NASHVILLE
Thirty-six years before a volley of shots echoed over a Honduran beach, William Walker was born into genteel middle-class life in Nashville, Tennessee. The year was 1824. Walker's father was a Scottish merchant and insurance agent, his mother an

invalid. The family's life was centered around work and the Bible—no sports, dancing, or other frivolous activities were allowed. Despite or because of this, Walker turned out to be a brilliant, precocious student. He graduated from the University of Nashville at age fourteen, received his MA from the same school two years later, and then, overruling his parents' desire that he become a minister, left for Europe to study medicine.

After traveling through France and Germany, Walker decided that practicing medicine was not what he sought in life, after all. With the combined impetuosity and determination that marked most of his life's activities, he returned home, got a law degree, and was admitted to the bar in the state of Louisiana. He then decided that legal matters bored him and turned to journalism. By 1848, when he was twenty-four, Walker seems to have settled in as the editor of the New Orleans *Daily Crescent*, which was, by Southern standards, a liberal newspaper, advocating women's suffrage and abolition of slavery. In his editorials, Walker took a particularly tough position against expansionism, the understanding that it was the United States's Manifest Destiny to not only push westward across the continent, but also south to Mexico and Central America and east to Cuba.

These regions, expansionists claimed, were ripe for annexing, since they were run by lowly Latin Americans who were not smart enough to govern their own affairs. The southern expansionists by whom Walker was surrounded in New Orleans had it in their heads that slave labor could turn these countries into giant, lucrative plantations, thus adding to the power of the Southern states, which were already feeling the North outstrip them in terms of production and population. As one Southern apologist for expansionism cried in a popular journal, "We have New Mexico and California! We will have Old Mexico and Cuba!"

Around 1850, imperial powers such as Britain and Spain still had a toehold in Central America, but the United States was beginning to extend its influence.

LOVE AND DEATH IN NEW ORLEANS

Walker was a very private young man who was polite but did not smile much and kept to himself. He did have a few close friends, and one introduced Walker to a beautiful young woman named Ellen Galt Martin. Ellen was twenty-three years old, a vivacious and aristocratic New Orleans beauty who also happened to be a deaf-mute. She seems to have been a perfect match for such a private man as Walker and the couple fell in love. He learned sign language, and the two became inseparable. A date was set for the wedding, but then one of the cholera epidemics that plagued New Orleans descended upon the city and, on April 18, 1849, Ellen Galt Martin died at the age of twenty-four.

William Walker, ever the impenetrable man, left behind no private diaries or journals, so we cannot speak with exactitude about his state of mind, but friends of the time describe him as beside himself with grief. In February of 1850, he quit his job at the *Crescent* and decided, like thousands of Americans at the time, to leave his past behind him and head west to California. He took a steamship to Panama, traveled overland to the Pacific, then voyaged up the west coast of Central America and Mexico to San Francisco. Using his New Orleans connections, he got a job as an editor on the San Francisco *Daily Herald*.

But Walker had changed. Rather than the polite, judicious, and liberal newsman he had been before, he became aggressive and outspoken. In one instance, he suggested in an editorial that a probate judge had stolen funds from an estate; for his trouble, Walker was challenged to a duel by a friend of the judge, who shot and wounded him (Walker would fight three duels in his life and be wounded in two). Soon after this, he attacked another judge for being too soft on criminals and was sent to jail for contempt.

Those who knew William Walker in New Orleans would not have recognized this shrill and intemperate man. And worse was yet to come.

NARCISCO LÓPEZ AND THE INVASION OF CUBA

After Walker had arrived in California there occurred a bloody and quixotic invasion of Cuba in 1851 that was unmatched until 1962 and John F. Kennedy's Bay of Pigs incursion. It was led by Narcisco López, perhaps the most famous filibuster—until Walker came along. López was a charming and handsome former Spanish army officer who had moved to Cuba from Venezuela, gone broke there in the plantation business, and decided to lead a revolution to "free" the country from Spanish rulers, in 1848. In reality, like most filibusters, López was looking for loot and power.

López's attempt failed, and he fled to the United States. In 1850, he led a failed invasion of Cuba, but in 1851 returned with a force of over four hundred men. As with all freebooter armies, these troops were a decidedly mixed lot: former soldiers who had fought in the Mexican-American War of 1846–48, idealistic students who brought López's rallying cry of "López and Liberty!" and pure mercenaries out to earn the $4,000 López promised each of them if the invasion succeeded.

The invasion did not succeed. The local peasants refused to take up arms with López; in fact, most of them fought with the Spanish against him. After a pitched battle, fifty-one Americans under the command of a young Kentuckian, Colonel William Logan Crittendon, surrendered under promise of safe conduct. Instead, they were taken to a local fort and told they only had a half hour to write letters to their family before they were to be executed. All but one were then taken in groups of six, forced to kneel in the dust, and shot in the back. Crittendon refused to kneel or turn his back. His final words were: "A Kentuckian kneels to none except his God, and always dies facing his enemy."

López was captured in the interior of Cuba with the rest of his filibusters. The mercenaries were spared and sent to work in silver mines in a Spanish penal colony in Morocco. López, however, was taken to Havana and garroted in front of twenty-thousand screaming people.

Opposite: This drawing of William Walker highlights the pale eyes and intense stare that led to him being known as the "gray-eyed man of destiny."

When news of the execution of the American filibusters and of Crittendon's last words became public knowledge in the United States in September of 1851, there was a huge outcry. Riots broke out in New Orleans and armed bands of men called for the invasion of Cuba to avenge the deaths of these "patriots." Nothing ever came of this, and Cuba was spared—until the U.S. invasion during the Spanish-American War of 1898.

The fiasco in Cuba had an effect on William Walker in California, however. Changed forever by the death of his fiancée, Walker had become aggressively racist and profilibuster. In a book published a few years later, he wrote: "That which you ignorantly call "Filibusterism" is not the offspring of hasty passions or ill-regulated desire; it is the fruit of the sure, unerring instincts which act in accordance with laws as old as creation. They are but drivelers who speak of establishing fixed relations between the pure white American race … and the mixed Hispano-Indian race as it exists in Mexico and Central America, without the employment of force." This was the essence of filibustering—the white race taking over and controlling the red, brown, and black races—and Walker decided it was a cause worthy of his involvement. Since Cuba was too far away for him to invade, he set his eyes on a closer goal: Mexico.

WALKER'S FIRST INVASION

When war ended between the United States and Mexico in 1848, America had acquired both California and Texas in the Treaty of Guadalupe, but many American expansionists hungered for more. Just to the south of New Mexico and Arizona was the Mexican state of Sonora (part of which is now in present-day Arizona). The settlers who lived there—all of them Europeans and Mexicans, since the Mexican government refused to allow Americans to settle there—were preyed upon by Apache Indians, whom the Mexican authorities were unable to control. For a few years, potential filibusters had been raising a hue and cry about Sonora. Since the Mexican government had failed in its responsibility to protect the Sonorans, they said, it was America's "humane" duty to attack and conquer the state, to save its inhabitants from savages. In the event of a filibuster takeover, Sonora would be declared an independent republic, but, of course, under the protection of the United States. Its rich silver mining, then controlled by the French, under an agreement with the Mexican government, would be taken over by the United States as compensation for its intervention.

It's not surprising that William Walker chose Sonora for his first filibustering expedition. Having turned from the newspaper business back to working as a lawyer, Walker used contacts he had made in San Francisco's business community to raise money for an invasion. While this was going on, he went on reconnaissance to the town of Guaymas, Sonora, a small port on the Gulf of California. The Mexicans, however, had been forewarned about Walker and refused to let him into the interior of the country. Frustrated, he wandered about the town for a while before heading back to San Francisco. A traveler who happened to be there at the same time snapped this word-picture of the would-be filibuster:

> Below medium height, and very slim, I should hardly imagine him to weigh over a hundred pounds. His hair light and towy, while his almost white eyebrows and lashes concealed a seemingly pupilless gray, cold eye and his face was a mass of yellow freckles … His dress was scarcely less remarkable than his person. His head was surmounted by a huge white fur hat, whose long nap waved with the breeze, which, together with a very ill-made, short-waisted blue coat, with gilt buttons, and a pair of gray, strapless pantaloons, made up the ensemble … I will leave you to imagine the figure he cut in Guaymas with the temperature at one hundred [degrees].

THE NARROWEST ESCAPE OF ALL

If there were a prize for thinking quickly in the face of death, it would have gone to one David Q. Rousseau of Kentucky, a filibuster who was unfortunate enough to join Narciso López on his 1851 invasion of Cuba and then be among the fifty-one men captured along with William Logan Crittendon by the Spanish. When the fifty-one men were given half an hour to write last letters before being executed, Rousseau didn't have anyone close to whom he wished to write. With nothing to lose, he cast about and came up with an inspired idea.

Deciding that the Spanish were sure to read these missives, Rousseau pretended that American Secretary of State Daniel Webster was a close friend of his. His note began, "Dan, my dear old boy, how little you thought when we parted at the close of that last agreeable visit … that I should now be [confined] in the infernal hole of a dungeon from which I indite this. I wish you would send the Spanish minister a case of that very old Madeira of yours … and tell him of the silly scrape I have got myself into." Amazingly, the Spanish read this and decided it would be wiser not to kill Rousseau, since he had such powerful connections. While all the Americans with him were executed, he alone was spared and sent to the Spanish silver mines in Morocco. He was released after two years and returned to America, where he later served as a lieutenant for a Kentucky regiment in the Civil War.

And yet, his observer noted, it would be a mistake to underestimate Walker. "Extremely taciturn, he would sit in your company for an hour without opening his lips; but once interested, he arrested your attention with the first word he uttered and ... you felt convinced that he was no ordinary person."

It's hard for someone in the twenty-first century to understand William Walker's motivations. It is easy enough and true to say he was a racist and quite possibly a sociopath, and that he was often ridiculous—what potential conqueror, in his right mind, wanders the streets of a city he is planning to invade dressed absurdly and making conversation in cafés? Part of this was due to Walker's arrogance—these were only Mexicans he was dealing with, after all—and part to a courage born of naiveté, the kind of naiveté that would shortly lead him to double-cross one of the most powerful men in the world. But it also seems fairly certain that he was a man deranged by a grief that followed him then and for the rest of his life, and in turn caused him to disregard not only his fate, but that of others.

Back in California, Walker gathered his recruits—all forty-five of them. In this expedition and others he would make, he would find most of his "soldiers" among the dregs of society: miners washed up in San Francisco after the '48 Gold Rush went bust, skid-row alcoholics, former soldiers itching for action. In October 1853, he boarded his army onto an old steamer, the *Caroline*, and was forced to depart in a big hurry, having heard that the U.S. Army was about to seize his invasion force for violating U.S. neutrality laws. Once at sea, with almost no provisions, even Walker realized how silly it was to try to attempt to take over Sonora. So he decided instead to land on the nearly deserted Baja Peninsula, across the Bay of California from Sonora. He came ashore at La Paz, made a prisoner of the flabbergasted Mexican governor, and raised a filibustering flag of his own design. He then declared Baja a free and independent state and named himself "President of Lower California."

When news got back to San Francisco of Walker's triumph, more men decided to join him, encouraged by what one journal called "the go-aheadism of Young America." Over two hundred set sail to meet Walker who, however, was having a few problems. He had moved his forces to the port of Ensenada, in northern Baja, but there some Mexicans stole and burnt the *Caroline*. Fifty of Walker's men, sick and tired of his rigid discipline and the lack of rewards for their efforts, deserted and headed back to California. A Mexican warship was now at harbor in Ensenada, keeping Walker bottled in. And, to make matters worse, his forces were now being attacked by Mexican fighters under the command of a guerilla leader named Guadalupe Melendrez, who killed several filibusters in a sharp attack outside of Ensenada.

A HERO IN DEFEAT Despite all of this, Walker now grandly declared himself president of both Lower California *and* Sonora, without having yet invaded the latter. Blocked by the Mexican Navy and with Mexican guerillas harassing him, Walker decided the time was ripe to get out of Ensenada. In February 1854, he marched a force now numbering 135 men around the northern end of the Gulf of California to the mouth of the Colorado River—some two hundred miles over rugged, arid land. When he heard of a desertion plot among his followers, he unhesitatingly had two of the supposed conspirators shot and others whipped, displaying the harsh, Puritanical discipline for which he was to become known in Central America.

Walker and his men crossed the swirling water of the Colorado River, losing most of their provisions on the way, and reached Sonora, but were by now too weak and hungry to invade the country. Instead, harassed by Melendrez and his guerillas, they headed north. With the border in sight, Melendrez and his men spread out in a line, blocking Walker's ragged band from entering the United States. But the desperate Walker led an attack straight at the Mexican guerillas, his men shooting wildly and screaming, and Melendrez and his men galloped away. Near San Diego, Walker surrendered to two U.S. Army officers, saying: "I am Colonel William Walker. I wish to surrender my force to the United States." He had thirty-four men remaining.

The U.S. government, which had very mixed feelings about filibusters, tried Walker for having violated certain neutrality acts, the chief of which, passed in 1818, made it a crime for any U.S. citizen to attempt to overthrow a foreign government. Walker defended himself on hoary "humanitarian" grounds: he had been attempting, he said, to save the citizens of Sonora from the Apaches, since the Mexicans refused to do it. The jury went out and returned eight minutes later with its verdict: acquittal on all counts for Walker.

The case received enormous news coverage, and it was apparent to all that Walker had the support of the public. Californians considered him a hero. He subsequently dabbled in politics, being named a delegate to the 1854 state Democratic Convention. In fact, the United States did benefit from Walker's eccentric expedition. The Mexican government believed that the American government, despite its prosecution of Walker, had to some extent been behind him, and to forestall future expeditions it agreed to sell the northern part of Sonora to the U.S., a transaction called the Gadsden Purchase.

THE NICARAGUAN OPTION

The California Gold Rush of 1848 made the American West a very desirable place, but how to get there? Many Americans, of course, simply went straight across the plains, on horseback and in covered wagons, but this path was mainly for those who wished to ranch or farm and was in any event long, difficult, and fraught with peril. Another way was to board ship on the east coast of America and sail through the southern Atlantic and round Cape Horn, but this voyage, too, was lengthy and full of danger.

The eyes of American speculators began, in the 1850s, to turn to Central America, to Panama (then a region controlled by Colombia) and Nicaragua. One could, whether on the west or east coast of the United States, board a ship, sail to either country, quickly cross the narrow isthmus, and then board another ship to your destination. The overland trip through Nicaragua was shorter—twelve miles as opposed to twenty-eight through Panama. When the idea of a canal between the Caribbean Sea and the Pacific Ocean was suggested, Nicaragua still seemed the better option, partly because Nicaragua was lower in elevation—and the technology for lifting ships above sea level

Narcisco López, one of the most famous filibusters of his day. His failed invasion of Cuba ended with his public garroting.

Cornelius Vanderbilt, one of the boldest of the era's financial buccanneers. The withdrawal of his support was to have fatal consequences for Walker.

was still rudimentary—and partly because the route would lead across Lake Nicaragua, thereby reducing the amount of canal-building needed. So appealing was the Nicaraguan option that one of the most astute businessmen in America, Cornelius Vanderbilt, locked up the rights to construct the canal.

Known in America as "the Commodore" for the steamship lines he operated, the fabulously wealthy Vanderbilt was also known to be a ruthless and powerful man who thought nothing of crushing any businessman who opposed him. While the canal was still in the planning stage, he set up the Accessory Transit Company to transport passengers overland through Nicaragua, and between 1851 and 1857 moved one hundred thousand passengers. Around the same time, the United States and Great Britain, which also held and claimed land in Central America—including Nicaragua's so-called Mosquito Coast, where any canal would have to begin—hammered out an agreement under which they would share control of the proposed canal while allowing Vanderbilt to continue transporting his passengers. Both parties, along with Vanderbilt, were keen to prevent anyone intererfering in their lucrative and hard-won deal. But that was just what William Walker was about to do.

FULFILLING A MANIFEST DESTINY
William Walker quickly tired of politics and went back into the newspaper business, becoming an editor at the San Francisco *Commercial Advisor*. But filibustering now seemed to be in his blood, and it didn't take him long to sense the possibilities inherent in an invasion of Nicaragua. For one thing, the country was in terrific turmoil. It had gained its independence from Spain in 1831, but had spent almost all of the intervening years in civil war—between 1847 and 1855, the country had thirteen presidents. Even while Vanderbilt was shipping his travelers through the country in 1854, a bloody war raged between two political factions, the Legitimists, the party in power, and the Democratic Party, which opposed them.

After studying the situation, Walker concluded that Nicaragua was ripe for the plucking. Not only might the proposed canal be built there, but the country was rich in gold, copper, tropical hardwoods prized in American shipbuilding, and corn and other crops. Since much of the country's population of 250,000 was in either the Democratic or Legitimist armies, Nicaragua would be the perfect country into which to import slave labor, which would please Walker's supporters in the Southern states (he ignored the fact that Nicaragua had abolished slavery in 1824).

With help from a go-between, San Francisco newspaper publisher Byron Cole, Walker wangled an invitation to bring an army down to Nicaragua from Democrat leader Francisco Castellon, who promised each "settler" Walker brought with him 350 acres of land. And not only was Walker able to raise money for this expedition, but the U.S. government seemed to be supporting him: Major General John E. Wood, who headed the Pacific Army, met with Walker when he heard what the latter was up to and, far from issuing a reprimand, wished him luck. Wood's imprimatur was symbolic of Washington's ambivalent attitude toward the filibusters. On the one hand, America could hardly appear to sanction independent operators attacking foreign countries—and of course, there would be no question of even tacit approval if the foreign country in question were France or Great Britain. But, on the other hand, filibusters like Walker enjoyed much popular support among the Manifest Destiny crowd and in the South, and, after all, they did promise to bring more and more territories under American control. And since these territories were relatively weak and populated by brown people … Should Walker succeed, there might be a way to recognize him, if not enthusiastically, then at least in a quiet manner. If he failed, he was definitely on his own.

ON THE OFFENSIVE
On June 16, 1855, William Walker landed with fifty-eight freebooters at the small port of Realejo on Nicaragua's west coast. There he was reinforced by an army of about one hundred locals provided to him by the Democratic leaders. The next morning this force headed inland, through an extraordinarily beautiful and unspoiled tropical landscape. Walker's Americans, armed to the teeth with modern rifles and Colt revolvers and dressed in flannel shirts, blue cotton pants, and wide-brimmed black hats, towered over the Nicaraguan troops, who were barefoot and carried flintlock muskets and machetes.

Walker attacked Legitimist forces on June 29 in the town of Rivas. In typical fashion—military tactics were never Walker's forte—he simply led his men straight into the heart of Rivas, shooting and shouting. The Legitimists, who knew they were coming, had erected barricades, and fired from behind them. Walker's native troops broke and ran at the first gunshot, leaving the fifty-eight Americans to do the fighting. Surrounded and outnumbered, the freebooters waged a courageous house-to-house battle, but were forced to retreat, leaving six American wounded behind. As a foreshadowing of how vicious this war would become, the Legitimists chained these prisoners to a pile of wood and burned them to death.

Walker and his army retreated to the Democratic-controlled town of León to lick their wounds, but Walker was not going to be defeated this easily. Gathering more troops from the United States, and a more reliable local army, he seized the town of Virgin Bay, on Lake Nicaragua. There he waited behind barricades until he was attacked by Legitimist forces. With the lake behind his men, and no retreat possible, the filibusters won a surprising victory, killing fifty of the enemy. Then Walker, whose force had now swollen to 250 Americans, went on the offensive. In a brilliant tactical move, he seized a lake steamer belonging to Vanderbilt's Accessory Transit Company—overruling the American captain's protests by saying that he, Walker, was a representative of the Nicaraguan government—sailed it forty miles across Lake Nicaragua, and attacked the Legitimist stronghold of Granada, forcing it to surrender—partially by seizing and executing a Legitimist cabinet minister and threatening to kill more of the government.

The Legitimists capitulated and a peace treaty was signed on October 23, 1855. The new president of the country would be a moderate Legitimist named Patricio Rivas, Walker's Democratic ally Castellon having died of cholera. And General William Walker would become commander-in-chief of the Nicaraguan army.

WHY PANAMA?

Given that Nicaragua seemed a much more promising site, how did Central America's interoceanic canal end up in Panama? There are a number of reasons. One of them was the continued presence of the British in and around Nicaragua, which would have prevented the United States having exclusive control of the waterway. Another was the instability of Nicaragua: the country seemed to be in a constant state of civil war, thanks in part to troublemakers like Walker. There was also the little matter of a postage stamp.

In the 1870s, Nicaragua issued a five-centavos stamp that showed a picture of Mount Momotombo, a volcano on an island in Lake Nicaragua, in full eruption. This turned out to be a colossal error from a public relations point of view. Those who wanted the canal in Panama pointed to this as a grave danger, and ultimately won their case. After the French started a canal in Panama in 1898, the Americans bought it from them and finished it in 1914.

The present-day Nicaraguan government has not given up on the idea of a canal and proposes building one that would be roomy enough for some of the ultra-large ships that currently cannot make it through Panama's locks. But inevitable opposition from the United States and various environmental groups means this is unlikely to happen.

FORGING A MYTH

There was a legend among the Mosquito Indians of Nicaragua that a "gray-eyed stranger" would come to their land and become their leader. Hearing of this, Walker played it up in a propaganda newspaper he had published in Granada, *El Nicaraguense*, which was written partly in Spanish and partly in English. He referred to himself as "the gray-eyed man of destiny," and represented himself as being the country's sole hope for a revived and peaceful future.

Within a few months, Walker had clashed with, and had executed, his last opponent in Nicaragua, Legitimist General Ponciano Corral. With Rivas merely a puppet, Walker was in effective control of the entire country by the beginning of 1856. Even though American President Franklin Pierce had just issued a proclamation against filibustering, Pierce's minister recognized Walker's Nicaragua government, thus giving it some short-lived legitimacy. Walker was, as usual, a mass of contradictions. On the one hand, he refused to allow his freebooters to loot or rape; if anyone so much as touched a Nicaraguan woman, he was shot by a firing squad. On the other, he was ruthless in achieving his goals and lied consistently to the people of Nicaragua. Although he claimed he wanted peace with the other Central American states of Belize, Costa Rica, and Honduras, he was, at the same time, raising an army to attack them. In order to achieve this, he conspired with representatives of Vanderbilt's Accessory Transit Company to ship, free of charge, as many as one thousand American freebooters to train in Nicaragua for an expedition to take control of the rest of Central America and possibly Cuba.

In return, Vanderbilt expected Walker to stabilize Nicaragua for the Accessory Transit Company, and provide Vanderbilt's steamboats with exclusive rights in any other Central American ports Walker might subsequently capture. Unfortunately for Walker, no sooner had he made this agreement with Vanderbilt's representatives than he allowed himself to be persuaded to break it. It was a decision that would lead directly to his death.

DOUBLE-CROSSING VANDERBILT
In February of 1856, Walker made the mistake of allowing himself to be convinced by two of Vanderbilt's commercial rivals, Cornelius Garrison and Charles Morgan, that he could make more money and have more power if he seized Vanderbilt's Accessory Transit Company in the name of the Nicaraguan government. That he agreed to do this was a sign of William Walker's stunning naiveté. Garrison and Morgan made a killing on the stock market out of the deal, but once Vanderbilt found out, he simply warned passengers not to travel across Nicaragua, claiming it was too dangerous, and set up a new transit line through Panama.

Walker's troubles got a lot worse when the president of Costa Rica declared war on Nicaragua and invaded. Caught by surprise, Walker and his men fled to Granada and sustained two bloody losses in battles at Virgin Bay and Rivas. Had it not been for a dreadful cholera epidemic that killed ten thousand people in the region, Walker would have been ousted. Instead, he regained control of Nicaragua and actually had himself officially named president in June of 1856 after a sham election. One of his first acts was to repeal the 1824 Nicaraguan Emancipation Act. Slavery would once again be legal in Nicaragua, he proclaimed, much to the joy of his Southern supporters.

June of 1856, however, was the high point of Walker's time as a filibuster, and the good times couldn't last. For one thing, he had made too many enemies. Not only was most of Central America against him, but so were Cornelius Vanderbilt and the northern U.S. states of New England. Great Britain also coveted the territory Walker was eyeing up. A force of Nicaraguan rebels, aided by arms and money from Vanderbilt, attacked and defeated Walker at the Battle of San Jacinto in September 1856. With his men dying right and left, of bullets and disease, Walker retreated through Nicaragua to the Pacific port of San Juan del Sur, where he and sixteen officers abandoned the rest of his men and fled on a U.S. warship. Yet, amazingly, when he arrived home in New Orleans in May of 1857, Walker was granted a hero's welcome.

WILLIAM WALKER REDUX

Most Americans have no idea who William Walker was. Confirmation of this came in 1988, when President George H. W. Bush carefully chose an ambassador to El Salvador, hoping to calm the troubled waters in the region. Lacking a sense both of history and irony, he could not understand why people in Central America snickered at the mere mention of the man's name: William Walker.

For a time, indeed, the American public idolized William Walker. He was greeted in the South as a man who would bring the Southern way of life to Central America (Walker called it "Americanizing"). He was celebrated everywhere he went and even met with President James Buchanan in Washington. But then, as so often with Walker, things went wrong just when they seemed to be going right.

Walker made the mistake of publicly blaming the U.S. Navy for not helping him fight the Nicaraguan rebels, something which did not sit well with many. Then a ship carrying 140 of the men Walker had left behind in Nicaragua arrived in New York just as he was making a triumphal visit there. The wretched refugees accused Walker of abandoning them in a most cowardly fashion. Instead of answering these charges, Walker headed back to New Orleans to raise another army. In November of 1857, he took a small group of filibusters to Nicaragua. This time, however, President Buchanan, embarrassed by and fed up with Walker, sent the U.S. Navy after him. They caught up with him just as he was embarking to invade Nicaragua, this time on the Atlantic side near the port of Greytown, and took him prisoner. The commodore of the U.S. fleet, Hiram Paulding, summoned Walker to his cabin and told him: "You and your men are a disgrace to the United States. You have dishonored your country." Paulding claimed that Walker then broke down and wept "like a child."

But despite being disgraced in the United States, Walker had one last expedition in him. Having befriended the ex-president of Honduras, Trinidad Cabanas, he decided in 1860 to lead an attack on that country and gather support for Cabanas. Once he had assembled a power base, he intended to move on and conquer all of Central America.

Walker, as ever, was dreaming wild dreams. He and his men were ambushed near the town of Trujillo, Honduras, and Walker was wounded. Fighting furiously, they managed to hold off the forces attacking them until, in a seemingly miraculous fashion, a British warship, the *Icarus*, appeared in the harbor. On the condition that he and his men receive safe passage, Walker surrendered to the British captain.

But it was a trick. The British had decided to capture the troublesome Walker and his men and turn them over to Honduran authorities. The rest of the men were allowed to return to the United States, but Walker was condemned to death. Despite written protests and a plea he made to a reporter from the *New York Herald*, who was present, the sentence was carried out. William Walker died as he had lived, alone. He faced the firing squad with an impassive stare near Trujillo, on the morning of September 12, 1860. He was thirty-six years old when he died in a hail of gunfire. His corpse was left to lie where it fell as the firing squad marched back to town and onlookers cheered.

CASTING A SHADOW OVER CENTRAL AMERICA

William Walker was the last of the filibusters. The Civil War intervened in America, slavery was abolished, and American interests turned in other directions. Had he been able to establish an American republic in Nicaragua and other parts of Central America, however, it is possible Walker could have brought these countries into the United States as proslavery states, altered the balance of power in Congress, and postponed, at the very least, the Civil War.

Today, Walker is far better known in Central America than he is in the United States. Nicaragua and Costa Rica have numerous monuments to the battles won against this man who would be their king. In these countries, he's a symbol of American inference in the affairs of independent states, a poster boy for racism and predatory capitalism. His defeat and execution are celebrated as sources of regional pride, particularly in the light of U.S. interventions in more recent times, most notably in the 1980s under President Ronald Reagan. The Reagan administration not only interfered in a rebellion in El Salvador, but after the Sandinista revolution of 1979 overthrew Nicaragua's brutal, U.S.-supported Somoza regime, it secretly instructed the CIA to create a right-wing army in the country, the Contras. Despite the fact that the Contras had no support among the people of Nicaragua, Reagan spent $20 million trying to overthrow the Sandinista government. Not only that, but in an effort to keep government expenditures secret, Oliver North, military attaché to the White House, funneled guns through the government of Iran directly to the Contras. From Reagan's point of view, he was keeping "Communism" out of Central America, using whatever secret and shadowy means he could—and without regard for what the people of Nicaragua actually desired. Similar interventions took place in Grenada and Panama. Willam Walker would have recognized a kindred spirit in Ollie North.

William Walker was one of the most enigmatic figures in nineteenth-century American history: a racist, arrogant, but undeniably brave man who sought power for reasons we will never quite understand. The poet Joaquin Miller wrote of him that he was "part angel, part Lucifer," but he seems in some essential way to have been an empty man. Look at pictures of him and even from a distance of 150 years you'll see how curiously lifeless he seems. No one will now ever know whether he was born with this void or it was created by the death of the only woman he loved.

THE TAIPING REBELLION: THE SECOND-WORST CONFLICT IN HISTORY

HE TAIPING REBELLION, A PEASANT UPRISING THAT OCCURRED IN MID-nineteenth-century China, involved more combatants than any other war in the nineteenth century, killed more people than any other conflict apart from the World War II (estimates range from twenty to forty million), nearly overthrew a centuries-old dynasty, and changed the future of an entire country. Yet very few people outside of China have ever heard of it. Nor do many know of its messianic leader, Hong Xiuquan, who claimed to have had an apocalyptic vision that revealed he was Jesus Christ's younger brother.

There are fascinating parallels between this strange crypto-Christian peasant rebellion, which took place between 1845 and 1864, and Mao Zedong's Marxist peasant revolt of the mid-twentieth century. Like Mao's Red Army, Hong Xiuquan's Taiping army emerged from the hinterland, advocated equality between men and women, and instituted collectivist agrarian reforms. As with Mao, at the end of it all, the hands of Hong Xiuquan were drenched in Chinese blood. But although Hong Xiuquan failed in his attempt to gain control of China, his little-known rebellion was one of the reasons why Mao succeeded.

THE FIRST OPIUM WAR
By the 1830s, the Manchurian Qing dynasty had already been ruling China for almost two hundred years. Centered on the imperial city of Beijing, its massive bureaucracy spread across a mainly rural, generally impoverished China, whose population had reached four hundred million, more than doubling since the mid-eighteenth century. The imperial court was cultivated, but inward-looking, ruled by a figurehead emperor who was in turn controlled by powerful and hidden Mandarin advisers.

Foreigner traders, especially the British and French, were considered barbarians and confined to a special settlement outside the walls of the harbor city of Guangzhou (Canton). This did not, however, stop the British from supplying the Chinese people with opium. The East India Company imported tons and tons of the drug from its plantations in India, receiving tea and silk in return. And this despite the fact that the drug was banned in Britain. The effect on Chinese society was tragic: workers, addicted by the thousands, languished in opium dens.

In 1839, a brave Chinese imperial official destroyed British stores of opium in Guangzhou and persuaded the imperial court to threaten to cut off trade with the British if they did not cease bringing the drug into the country.

In response, in one of the most shameful episodes in its history, Britain attacked and, with its modern weapons, completely defeated China, in what has come to be known as the First Opium War. The Treaty of Nanjing of 1842, which brought the war to an end, awarded Britain most favored nation trading status with China, five open ports instead of one, and the resumption of the trade in opium, imports of which more than doubled in the next thirty years.

As a result of this humiliating defeat, the Qing dynasty was seen as weak and tottering by its own people. Around the same time, mass flooding of the Yellow and Yangtze rivers struck the country, causing famine conditions in the river valleys. The time was ripe for upheaval.

Interestingly, the same conditions—a corrupt Qing dynasty defeated in war, along with famine, and disease—were present at the beginning of the twentieth century as Mao Zedong was reaching manhood and his hero, Sun Yat-sen, was preparing the revolution that would overthrow the Manchu once and for all.

Qing China, 1864. The seeds of Hong Xiuquan's rebellion were sown in the southeast. The uprising then spread north through central China.

A MYSTERIOUS FOREIGNER

Hong Xiuquan, which means "son of heaven," was born Hong Huoxiu in 1814, in Guangdong Province, in China's southeast. His father was a farmer, as was his grandfather. Hong and his family were Hakkas, meaning, literally, "guest people"—the Hakkas originated in the central Chinese plains before gradually moving south in response to various civil wars and famines. The Hakkas spoke a different dialect than the other Chinese in Guangdong, and Hakka women did not bind their feet. As a result, no Chinese men of other tribes would marry them, and so the Hakkas remained culturally inbred.

Despite his family's humble circumstances, Hong could trace his lineage all the way back to the twelfth century. He was a precocious child who could read at a very early age, and whose family sacrificed a great deal so that he could become an imperial

WAYWARD OFFSPRING

The Christian missionaries would later be repelled by the blasphemy of Hong's Taiping theology, and angered when Hong would tell them that *his* religion was, in fact, the real Christian religion, not theirs. They were also horrified by the outcome of the Taiping Rebellion.

Yet it was their teachings, filtered through the prism of Hong Xiuquan's disturbed state and his Chinese cultural upbringing, that stoked the fires of rebellion.

In part, it was the result of a different interpretation of the Bible. The Chinese focused on the more apocalyptic elements of the Book of Revelation and drew parallels with their own society. God had a grand plan to save the Chinese people, according to Hong, and if a little bloodshed occurred, well, look at what went on in the Christians' holy book.

Most of the foreign missionaries could never come to grips with this, but the Welsh Congregational minister Griffith John did, writing in one letter to his fellow missionaries: "Protestant missionaries of China. This Insurrection is your offspring. For want of your parental care, it has grown wayward and deformed." John's warning would do no good, however. By then, the insurrection was beyond their control.

official. In the spring of 1836, having passed a qualifying exam in his village, Hong traveled to Guangzhou for the Confucian state exam. Passing this civil service exam was a huge honor for the Chinese at the time: any scholar who did so was not only assured of a job, but was acclaimed by those close to him—literally paraded through the streets of his village.

This may have been the first time the twenty-two-year-old Hong had been away from home and his close-knit family. It was certainly the first time he had been to a big city like Guangzhou. Like any country visitor, he walked through the teeming streets gawking. When he arrived outside of the examination hall, he came upon a curious sight. Two men were standing on a street corner, the first a local, the second a foreigner, who was, however, wearing Chinese clothes and whose hair was styled in a topknot. The foreigner looked directly at Hong and, through the Cantonese translator, said, mysteriously, "You will attain the highest grade, but do not be grieved, for grief will make you sick."

The strangely dressed foreigner than gave Hong a pamphlet which turned out to be a religious tract written by a Chinese author entitled "Good Words for Exhorting the Age." Hong, puzzled, thanked him politely, then walked away.

It is not known for certain, but the foreigner was very likely an American missionary by the name of Edwin Stevens, who liked to adopt Chinese dress, sneak or bribe his way into Guangzhou city proper, and proselytize the Chinese people. This was Hong's first encounter with a missionary, but it would not be his last.

Hong took his civil service exam. To his shame, he failed. On the way home, he glanced briefly at the pamphlet the missionary had handed him. The book was full of stories about a Christian God. As Hong later recounted it, he first noticed the word "Hong" in the table of contents. Hong means "flood" and the summary of the story said that it was about a flood that destroyed the entire world, save for a few animals and people herded onto a large boat by a man named Noah. Hong looked closer and saw that his flood had been ordered by a vengeful God named Ye-huo-hua. "Huo," which means "fire," was the first syllable of Hong's name, Huoxiu. Though it was at this stage only an idle observation, Hong thought to himself, "I have the same name as this God."

CHASING OFF THE DEMONS
Hong returned to Guangzhou to retake his civil service exam in 1837 and failed once again. Miserable, he went back to his home village, told his family and his young, pregnant wife, and took to his bed. He became ill and feverish, and his family thought he was dying. But in his fever, Hong had a dream, or rather, a vision, one so extraordinary it changed his life—and the entire course of Chinese history.

While he was lying in bed, Hong dreamed that demons had come to take him down to hell. He escaped them and a sedan chair miraculously appeared before him, and he got onto it. Borne by four attendants, Hong flew through the air and found himself in a place that was bathed in light. Men in glorious robes slit him open. But he was not afraid, for they were replacing his soiled inner organs with new ones. Then he was taken before a man whom he realized was his father, a man who wore

black dragon robes and a large hat and had a golden beard. As Hong prostrated himself before this man, he heard him say: "So you have come back up? Pay close attention to what I say!" The father, who appeared grief-stricken, went on to tell Hong that the Chinese people had been led astray by demons and that even the thirty-three levels of heaven wherein the father resided were beset by demons. At this, Hong leaped up and, wielding a mighty golden sword, chased off the demons.

Hong's father was grateful, but told him that he must now return to earth and battle the evil demons there. In order to help him do this, the father gave Hong a new name: Hong Xiuquan, which meant "heavenly king."

While all this was going on in Hong's fevered imagination, his family watched him writhe in bed, crying out, "Slash the demons!" When he finally came out of his delirium, he insisted that everyone address him by his new name. He told his father that he, Hong, was not his son, and denied that he was a brother to his siblings. And he wrote his experiences down, in both poetry and prose.

Everyone thought that he had gone mad and they watched him carefully. But as time passed, he seemed to calm down and although he insisted on being called Heavenly King, he was not anywhere near as volatile as he had seemed at first. Failing twice again to pass the civil service exam, he settled down to the life of a village school teacher. He became father to a daughter. The vision might have been only an isolated and puzzling incident in his life, had he not, seven years later, once again picked up the text of "Good Words for Exhorting the Age."

TURNING PREACHER

In 1843, after the horrible upheaval of the First Opium War, a friend of Hong's named Li Jingfang visited his house, saw the odd pamphlet, and asked if he could borrow it. Hong, who had still not read it, told him to go ahead. When Li returned, it was as if he were on fire. He insisted Hong read the book with him.

"Good Words for Exhorting the Age," although written by a Chinese author and itinerant preacher named Liang Afa, was a translation of selected stories of the Christian Bible, as spread by missionaries who were preaching throughout China. Mainly Protestants, and mainly American and British, the missionaries saw it as their goal in life to convert the Chinese from Buddha and Confucius and bring them to Christ. They were so intent on this that they decided, as a group, to put aside religious differences that might confuse the Chinese. Thus, they did not present themselves as Baptists, Methodists, or Presbyterians, but as one group of Protestants. Even before the First Opium War opened up the country to them, intrepid missionaries such as the Americans Edwin Stevens and Issachar Roberts had managed to make contact with many Chinese inland and spread the word of Christ.

Liang Afa was a printer who had been baptized in 1816 by the Scottish minister William Milne and who, after Milne's death, had spread the word of Christ through his written pamphlets. "Good Words for Exhorting the Age" was therefore Christianity second-hand, as seen through the eyes of a Chinese convert who imperfectly understood the doctrine and changed it to suit his needs, transcribing Biblical names into Chinese and giving the exhortations of Biblical prophets a fervent Chinese bent.

When he finally read the pamphlet, Hong, now twenty-nine, understood what his dream meant. He found out that this god, Ye-huo-hua, had a son named Jesus, and so he decided that he, Hong Xiuquan, must be Jesus's younger brother, the second son of God—God's Chinese son. He understood now about the demons: they were in these holy writings he was reading, for Liang had called the serpent in the Garden of Eden story "the serpent demon" and had said that it must be crushed. Hong finally understood, too, what God, the Father, was saying to him in his vision: that he had to begin preaching the cleansing word of his Father to those around him.

Hong's first convert was the man who read the book with him, Li Jingfang, whom he "baptized" as best he could, using hints of the ceremony that he found in "Good Words for Exhorting the Age." He then baptized a cousin, Hong Rengan, and began to add more and more followers to his little group. They used "Good Words for Exhorting the Age" as their holy book, pouring over it and discovering more and more descriptions that matched up with Hong's vision. They even had huge, three-foot-long swords made to echo the sword Hong wielded against the demons.

But the Confucian authorities in the village would not put up with this heresy. Hong lost his teaching job and no one would hire him. So he and his wife and a few followers set off on the road, hoping to make a living selling writing brushes and ink, and to preach the word of the heavenly kingdom as they went. In April 1844, they traveled west to the mountainous province of Guangxi, Hong preaching all the way. He told people he was the son of God and that he had been instructed by his

Opposite: A seventeenth-century painting on silk of a civil service exam. Hong Xiuquan's failure to pass these time-honored tests sparked the apocalyptic visions that created a revolution.

heavenly father to rid China of the "demon devils" ruling the country. This struck a chord with the poor Hakka people Hong was talking to, the farmers and coal miners, for not only was their lot in life a difficult one—burdened as they were by taxes and corrupt officials—but the locals also persecuted them as foreigners and they were plagued by bandits.

As a Hakka himself, and one with a message of hope, Hong found himself welcome in the province and his following grew and grew. It was not just rebellion he preached, but a new, different, and moral way of life. Men and women were to be equal, land was to be shared. The old clans would be abolished—"Human Fellowship … fellowship with people in the open," as Hong wrote, would help save the Chinese people. Harmony was the way to salvation.

But something else began to happen. As he wandered through the countryside, Hong stopped using the word "I" to refer to himself. Instead, he began to speak and write the word "Zhen," which means "I, the ruler."

Perhaps it was a scent of this incipient megalomania that put off American missionary Issachar Roberts, who met with Hong Xiuquan around this time. Hong was anxious to gain the approval of the missionary and even wrote out a statement asking Roberts to baptize him. But something happened that is unclear, and neither Hong nor Roberts ever explained it. A few days after their meeting, Hong left, and all Roberts recorded was that he was "not fully satisfied" with Hong as a baptismal candidate.

THE BATTLE OF THISTLE MOUNTAIN

By 1847, Hong and a small group of followers had gathered in a village near Thistle Mountain in Guangxi Province. The "God-worshipers," as they were now called, had become more openly hostile to the Confucians, even going so far as to stage protests in front of Confucian temples. Naturally, the authorities started to clamp down on them, accusing Hong of black magic and insurrection, and refusing his party entry to certain villages in the region. Passions became heightened when a local Hakka peasant claimed to be Jesus Christ and to have messages for his "younger brother" Hong. Hong, shrewdly, accepted this and listened to these messages, which proclaimed him as ruler and lord of the Taiping Tien-kuo, or "Heavenly Kingdom of Great Peace," that was to be built on earth.

Obviously, this heavenly kingdom left no room for the temporal one of the Qing dynasty, and the Manchu at court were becoming concerned. Accurate reports described how Hong's group, which now numbered forty thousand, was buying gunpowder and arming itself. It is unclear whether Hong always intended to attack the Chinese authorities, or if he was just protecting himself, as he claimed. Either way, it became inevitable that a battle would occur, and one did, in January of 1851, when seven battalions of the Qing Army attacked at Thistle Mountain and were badly beaten by the Taiping, or Heavenly Army, as they were now known.

This was just the beginning. Continuously defeating the Qing forces, the Taiping swept down from their Guangxi mountain base and drove northeast to the Yangtze River valley, Nanjing, and the port of Shanghai. Theirs was an army like no one had ever seen—in fact, an army whose like would not be seen again until Mao's Red Army swept down from its own mountain base to do battle with Chiang Kai-shek's Nationalist forces as World War II ended.

The Taiping soldiers were both men and women. The men grew their hair long, to their shoulders, thereby declaring their opposition to the Manchu, who shaved most of their heads and braided the remaining hair into topknots. They wore red tunics and blue trousers, and appeared to have absolute discipline.

The Taiping had given up their individual possessions and placed all their money in a common treasury. "When people of this Earth keep nothing for their private use, but give all things to God for all to use in common, then in the whole land every place shall have equal shares and everyone be clothed and fed," wrote Hong. Hearing this message, thousands and thousands of peasants began to join the Hakka core. The goal of their army became clear: to push the Manchu demons from China and establish an "earthly paradise."

CREATOR OF KINGS
It was only as the Taiping army began its march and started to swell in size that most Westerners in China took notice. At first, the missionaries were quite pleased, for here was what seemed to be a disciplined, Christian army marching against the corrupt dynasty of the Manchu, who had given the missionaries so much trouble. Even Issachar Roberts, who had refused Hong baptism, could write: "Behold, what God hath wrought ... one has risen up [amongst the Chinese] who presents the true God for their adoration and casts down idols with a mighty hand, to whom thousands and tens of thousands of people are collecting." Hong, who was nothing if not Old Testament in his approach, was ordering his army to destroy temples and idols. He banned prostitution, alcohol, opium, and gambling. Only a few missionaries sounded a warning. One puzzled American minister wrote, after hearing that Hong Xiuquan claimed to be the brother of Jesus, "he must mean something more by that expression than the scriptures authorize."

Hong Xiuquan was in his mysterious and megalomaniacal element as the leader of the Taiping Army. He appointed kings of the north, south, east, and west—the West King was the peasant who had been having visions with messages for Hong. Then there was the Shield King, Hong's cousin and second convert, Hong Rengan. Hong's two older brothers were named Peace King and the Blessings King.

The highly motivated Taiping soldiers continued to fight well. In October of 1851, Taiping forces took the walled city of Yongan and beat off ferocious Qing attacks. However, as the siege around the city grew tighter, Hong decided his army needed to break out, which they did, in the spring of 1852. Much like Mao Zedong's Red Army on its Long March, the Taiping Army wandered over the countryside, staying one step ahead of the pursuing Qing forces as Hong sought the earthly paradise that would become the center of his kingdom. The war now became extremely bloody. The Taiping reached the city of Quanzhou in May of 1852; there the South King was shot and killed by a Qing sniper. Enraged, the Taiping massed for attack and slaughtered everyone in the town, including noncombatants.

Shortly thereafter, heading up the Xiang River on makeshift vessels, the Taiping were ambushed and decimated by the Qing—ten thousand members of Hong's army, including many of the original Hakkas, were killed. Needing new men, Hong began to recruit less committed people, men who hated the Qing regime or the Confucian religion, but paid lip service to the God-worshipers' beliefs. The Taiping now sang:

Those with millions owe us their money …
Those with ambitions but no cash should go with us.

The original dedicated core of the Taiping Army was gradually being replaced with men and women who saw a chance to profit from the uprising. At first, however, this was not a problem, as many of the new recruits were former soldiers or bandits who knew how to fight and were willing to help take city after city as the Taiping army sent the Qing armies reeling back.

After fighting their way along the Yangtze valley, the Taiping troops finally stood in front of the massive city of Nanjing in March 1853. Approximately five hundred thousand strong, they attacked and slaughtered about thirty thousand Qing soldiers and fifty thousand civilians. Within a year, the Taiping forces would swell to more than a million strong, most centered around Nanjing. They had, at last, found a city to represent their earthly paradise. Hong Xiuquan decided to rename it Tien Ching, or "Heavenly Capital."

UNIMAGINABLE HORROR

On March 29, the Heavenly Capital having been subdued, Hong Xiuquan, wearing yellow robes and yellow shoes, the Chinese imperial colors, entered the city carried on a golden throne. Behind him on horses were thirty-two young women with yellow parasols—Hong Xiuquan, indeed, had already established his own heavenly paradise on the road to Nanjing. Despite forbidding "licentiousness" and adultery on pain of beheading, he had begun to take numerous concubines. He issued an edict that if these "sisters-in-law," as he called them, showed any jealousy of each other, they would be beheaded. And if anyone was heard speculating about Hong's relationship with any of these women, that person would also be beheaded.

Here, at the moment of the greatest Taiping triumph, lay the seeds of the rebellion's disaster—something similar was noted in a later era, when Red Army political elements cautioned that the behavior of the commanders had a direct influence on troops. In Nanjing in 1853, with a massive army behind him, Hong Xiuquan began a life of mysticism and indulgence that made him seem like a Chinese emperor of old.

The Taiping were to hold Nanjing for eleven years, from 1853 to 1864, and the war would now enter a period of unprecedented horror. In the summer of 1853, Hong sent an expeditionary force of thirty thousand soldiers to fight their way to Beijing, and they nearly captured the city before being surrounded and annihilated in 1855. The Qing and Taiping then fought a series of pitched battles across the breadth of central China. As the German writer W. G. Sebald has written, "The bloody horror in China at that time went beyond all imagining."

Millions of Chinese died. The once fertile Yangtze River valley was littered with dead bodies. Missionaries attempting to get into the area to find out what had happened described their boats bumping against corpses as they attempted to move upriver. One missionary watched a group of Chinese having a New Year's celebration while surrounded by the unburied dead of their village, as if the dead had become a grotesque backdrop no one noticed anymore.

Entire rural populations were killed, conscripted, or driven away by armies on both sides. Their crops lay rotting in the fields, leading to widespread famine. Massive makeshift refugee camps spread out all over the countryside, spawning disease. No longer disciplined, the Taiping soldiers raped, looted, killed, and burned wherever they went. Missionaries watched them drink and smoke opium and behead innocent citizens for the slightest infraction.

Back in Nanjing, Hong Xiuquan had become increasingly reclusive and paranoid, spending much of his time with his harem, while appointing his thirteen-year-old son, the Young Monarch, Tiangui Fu, as head administrator. Issachor Roberts managed to get into Nanjing to see Hong and was aghast at how strange things had become. While his former baptismal student was "a much finer looking man than I [remembered] … large, well-made, well-featured, with a fine black moustache," Roberts was disconcerted when Hong offered him three women as wives. He refused politely, but then heard someone shout "Kneel in the presence of the Lord." He knelt quickly, before he realized the person he was kneeling to was Hong.

HEAVENLY CONCUBINES

It was rumored after the rebellion was over and the Second Son of God dead that he had had eighty-eight concubines, and both Chinese and European sources record that this was in fact the case. Hong was obsessed with the number of wives a person could have, and set quotas. The East and West kings got eleven each; his own brothers, rather more junior kings, got six. Middling bureaucrats got two; commoners, of course, got one.

Unlike the court of the Qing, Hong's palace had no eunuchs; instead two thousand women ran the place, some working as administrators, some as cleaners, and some as concubines. Obviously, order had to be kept. Hong wrote a five-hundred-stanza poem in which he laid down the rules: no fighting, no jealousy, no loud gongs when people were trying to sleep. One group of women must prepare bath towels (scented) for Hong, another must trim his beard, wipe his nose, and clean "the area near his navel." Hong wasn't so specific about sex, but he did write, in his poem:

She who can truly ease the flame
repels the demon's snare,
She who can truly ease the
flame is my true wife.

Probably the most approachable member of Hong Xiuquan's administration was Hong Rengan, his bespectacled cousin who was Shield King. Well educated, he became a sort of apologist for Hong Xiuquan, a PR man to Westerners, while holding to the party line about Hong's original visions.

Hong began to proclaim that he was being visited by the ghost of the East King, Yang Xiuging, whom he had killed in a purge. He had also decided that he was inhabited by the spirit of Mechizedek, high priest and prophet from the Bible, although it is doubtful any Westerner knew this at the time.

The court was rife with corruption. In order to do the slightest bit of business inside Nanjing, ordinary citizens had to buy a "permit" from one Taiping official or another, just as they had previously done with the Manchu. Because of this corruption and because of the widespread death and famine, the Taiping regime began to lose its support among the people and among the Western missionaries.

DEMISE OF THE HEAVENLY KING
The Taiping army, under General Li Xiucheng, decided to make a bid for the port city of Shanghai in 1862. If the Taiping could capture this town, they would have ocean access, could transship to different parts of the country, and could trade with foreigners. But, surrounding Shanghai with seventy thousand men, Li Xiucheng was dismayed to discover that the Western settlements there intended to defend the city and fight him. Previously, the major Western powers—Britain, America, and France— had stayed out of the conflict, but they had now decided that their best commercial interests lay in fighting alongside the Qing dynasty.

Despite this, Li and his men continued the siege—which reduced some residents in the city to eating their pets—and prepared to launch an all-out attack. However, at this point a rare snowstorm hit Shanghai, making movement impossible—there were thirty inches of snow on the ground and the Taiping forces were not dressed for such weather. Finally, they were forced to leave.

In May of 1864, Nanjing was besieged by eighty thousand imperial Qing troops, as well as the soldiers of the "Ever-victorious Army," a highly discplined, well-armed brigade of Chinese troops drilled and trained by Western officers and led at Nanjing by British commander Charles "Chinese" Gordon. They dug huge tunnels under the walls of the city, where they planted explosives. In reply, the Taiping dug their own tunnels and desperate hand-to-hand combat took place deep beneath Nanjing. The residents of the town began to starve to death and there was panic in the court of Hong Xiuquan.

When told there was no food in the city, Hong replied: "Everyone in the city should eat manna. That will keep them alive." In other words, God would provide. When people complained that they could find no food, Hong Xiuquan, disgusted, showed them what to do by going into the palace grounds and pulling up weeds, which he cooked and ate. But subsequently he fell ill and, on June 1, 1864, he died. He was buried in a shroud of yellow silk, but with no coffin—given that he would rise up to heaven, what need did he have of a wooden box?

The city held out for over a month longer. When the Qing forces entered the city on July 19, it was a scene of unparalleled, almost apocalyptic horror. Not one of the one hundred thousand Taiping trapped in Nanjing surrendered. Thousands of them committed suicide in ways that are almost unimaginable—by setting themselves on fire and burying themselves alive, for example. The historian Orville Schell has written that there was something "numbing" about this final bloodbath, and it underlines the fact that the Taiping Rebellion was first and foremost a cult—one thinks, on a much smaller scale, of the followers of Jim Jones committing suicide in South America, or of the Branch Davidians immolated in Waco, Texas. But one can also make the comparison with the Jewish defenders at Masada, dying by their own hand, making their deaths their last, free act.

In the countryside around Nanjing, meanwhile, foreign mercenaries saw thousands of people executed on suspicion of being Taiping sympathizers as the Qing roamed brutally though the land, raping, looting, and burning. The Qing dynasty had triumphed, but the war had cost millions of lives and would have an extraordinary effect on Chinese history. The crop and property devastation and loss of life in the once-fertile Yangtze valley turned it into a desert for the next century. No longer able to heavily tax a land so harshly impoverished, the Qing rulers came to depend more and more on the customs fees they charged foreign powers. This, and a lack of a strong central government, allowed foreign powers to exert their influence, most notably Japan. Even the once rigorous Chinese civil-service examination system—ironically, the one that had repeatedly failed Hong Xiuquan—began to fall apart.

The country was ripe for the revolution that would succeed, beginning with Sun Yat-sen's uprising and the overthrow of the Qing in 1911.

HONORING A REVOLUTIONARY

Without the rebellion of the Second Son of Heaven would there have been a Chinese Communist victory? Almost certainly. But Mao and his early Communists learned a great deal from the Taiping, including the major fact that a peasant uprising based on an egalitarian impulse could work in China. It is interesting that both Mao and the Heavenly King used the same words in speaking of their enemies: "snakes," "beasts," "evil demons." Both movements were rigidly moralistic about sexual matters, while their rulers did whatever they pleased, and both rulers were paranoid in the extreme. Hong Xiuquan was more obviously insane, but, how is one to think of the Mao who instituted a cult of personality and purged millions during his rule?

Undoubtedly, Mao identified with Hong, for like the Second Son of Heaven, Mao Zedong was a Hakka. After he took control of China, he ordered that a museum called Hong Xiuquan's Former Residence Memorial Museum be built near Hong's birthplace in Guangdong Province. A tree was planted there in Hong's memory, and a replica of his former residence—the real thing was burned down by Qing troops—was built and called the "Study Pavilion." The museum plays up Hong Xiuquan's "revolutionary" activities, while allowing his Heavenly Kingdom to fade into obscurity. It remains a popular tourist attraction.

THE YOUNG MONARCH

One of the most pitiable aspects of the end of the Taiping Rebellion was the fate of Hong Xiuquan's son, Tiangui Fu, the Young Monarch. At the age of nine, his father had given him four wives and his own palace, and he was only thirteen when Hong Xiuquan, fading deeper into madness, made him administrator of the Heavenly Kingdom.

When the walls were breached by the Qing forces, the Young Monarch disguised himself in an enemy uniform and fled on horseback, along with Hong Rengan. Hong Rengan was captured and executed. The Young Monarch kept on fleeing deeper and deeper into the countryside. For a while, he was taken by a peasant and used as a slave. Finally, in the fall of 1864, he was captured by the Qings.

He told the authorities that he had had no wish to be administrator or even to be part of the Taiping Rebellion. All he had wanted to do, he said, was study ancient Confucian books, but his father had told him they were "demonic." If the Qings were to let him go, he said, he would become a scholar and study Confucian literature, just as his father had done before his visions. The court demurred and beheaded the Young Monarch, aged fourteen, on November 18, 1864.

JOHN WESLEY POWELL AND THE SHAPING OF THE AMERICAN WEST

N 1540, IN SOUTHWESTERN NORTH AMERICA, AN EXPEDITION OF PARCHED AND TIRED
Spanish conquistadores led by one García López de Cárdenas was guided by
Hopi Indians to the rim of a vast chasm, more than a mile deep. They stood there
open-mouthed and astonished, peering into the depths. At the very bottom of this
canyon was a river. The Spanish were so thirsty that they made several attempts to
make it down to the river, but each time retreated, since the descent was so precipitous.
Finally, they were forced to leave and make their way back to Mexico.

Two hundred years would pass before Europeans returned to the area, in the form
of isolated trappers and mountain men, who hovered around the fringes of the
canyon and sometimes lost their lives in the roaring rapids that led toward it. As far
as it was known, no Europeans had ever been deep inside the canyon, had ever
explored its towering sandstone and granite walls and hidden caves, had even been
close—although there is evidence, in wall paintings and stone artifacts, that ancient
Native Ameicans had ventured inside.

Even in the mid-nineteenth century, the canyon remained, literally, uncharted
territory, marked "unexplored" on maps. The aggressive western expansion of the
United States had bypassed not just the canyon itself—ten miles across, three hundred miles long—but the whole plateau around it, a thousand square miles in all,
bigger than some U.S. states and European countries. The chasm itself became
known variously and simply as "Big Canyon," "Great Canyon," and "Grand Canyon,"
as if its vastness was so awe-inspiring that a name could not quite be fixed to it.

Before his journey through the canyon via the Colorado River in 1869, John
Wesley Powell, the one-armed Civil War veteran, called it "the Great Unknown."
He went on to write: "What falls there are, we know not; what rocks beset the channel,

we know not; what walls rise over the river, we know not." *We know not*: words that have inspired many human adventures—trips to the moon or journeys deep into the depths of the ocean. Not just adventures, either, for, like space walks or deep-sea explorations, John Wesley Powell's journey was a scientific exploration as well as a physical one.

Because of Powell, maps were made of the Grand Canyon that form the basis for all current ones. His survey of the magnificent rock structures of the canyon was an influence on the formation of the U.S. Geological Survey, of which Powell became director; once there, he began working on the first complete topographic and geological maps of the western United States—maps not finished before his death, but still in use today. And out of his incredible journey came a landmark document of American environmentalism, his 1878 *Report on the Lands of the Arid Region*, which argued passionately for the preservation of the West's precious water resources and their use for the benefit of the people rather than big business.

A SELF-TAUGHT SCIENTIST

One of the wonderful polymaths ubiquitous in the nineteenth century, John Wesley Powell was an inspired amateur scientist. At that time, advances in geology, natural history, and ethnology went hand-in-hand with the exploration of the great unknown areas of the world and fired the imaginations of young men. In particular, with the seminal publication, in 1859, of Charles Darwin's *On the Origin of Species*, the world began to look to the scientifically-inclined research (if not to the biblically-minded treatise) like a far more fascinating and complex thought than previously imagined.

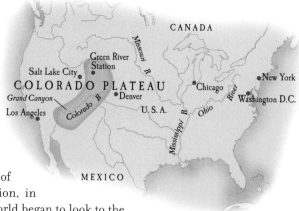

In 1869, despite the westward advance of thousands of pioneers, most of the vast, arid Colorado Plateau remained unexplored by Europeans.

Powell was born in 1834, in New York State, the son of a Methodist minister who moved his family around a great deal, first to Ohio, then to Wisconsin. The elder Powell was an avid slavery abolitionist, a stance so unpopular that John Wesley was subject to stoning by his classmates in Ohio, and finally had to be home-schooled. This turned out to be a blessing in disguise, as his tutor, a neighbor named George Crookham, gave him a thorough schooling in the natural sciences. Against the wishes of his father, Powell decided to become a scientist himself; when he was eighteen, he began teaching in schools to earn money for college, although he was ultimately only able to afford about a year at university.

In the meantime, Powell spent all his spare time exploring the Midwest, at one point even rowing alone along the entire length of the Ohio River. He was, essentially, self-taught: he became an expert on geology and conchology (the study of mollusk shells). So it was typical of him, when he saw the Civil War looming on the horizon, to make a study of military engineering. An impassioned abolitionist, Powell was one of the first to answer Abraham Lincoln's call for volunteers in 1860. He enlisted as a private with the Twentieth Illinois Regiment but soon rose to the rank of major, in charge of an artillery battery. During the Battle of Shiloh in April 1862, he held up his right hand as a signal for the guns to fire, and a Minnie ball struck his wrist. The wounds were so severe that the arm had to be amputated at the elbow and he was to endure surgery for years to come to ease the pain of the stump. Despite his suffering, Powell returned to his battery within six months and fought in other campaigns, most notably the siege of Vicksburg—where, as his men dug trenches, he searched for fossils in the deep, wet earth.

FIRST TRAVELS THROUGH AN ARID LAND

At the end of the war, Powell's father wrote to him, "Wes, you are a maimed man. Settle down to teaching … Get this nonsense of science and adventure out of your mind." But it was Powell's attitude that his missing arm was not going to stop him from doing whatever he wanted to: he would be defined not by what he lacked, but by who he was. Interestingly enough, in all his writings about his Grand Canyon adventures, it is only apparent to the most astute reader that Powell lacked most of his right arm.

Powell became a geology professor at Illinois Wesleyan University, in Bloomington, Illinois, but spent more time out of his office than in it. He, his wife, Emma—almost as adventurous as Powell—and groups of students began to take trips out West. In the early summer of 1867, they traveled by train, wagon, and horseback to Denver, climbed Pike's Peak (Emma Powell becoming only the second woman to do so) and stayed to explore the headwaters of the Grand River, one of the two massive rivers that eventually meet and form the Colorado. They then wintered in the Uinta Mountains, where Powell made friends with a tribe of Ute Indians and learned their language and customs.

During this extended trip, through much of what were then the Utah, Wyoming, and Colorado territories, Powell couldn't help but notice one thing: for mile after mile after mile, the American West was a bone-dry land. This was at odds with the way it was being sold to homesteaders by the government, railroad, media, and land speculators, whose slogans included not only "Go West, young man," but also "Rain follows the plow." In reality, settlers were finding out that there was barely enough water for crops and livestock—and their hopes and dreams were being dashed.

During his trip—hovering, literally, near the edges of the Canyon, peeking into the abyss—Powell became obsessed by the idea of conquering America's last unknown expanse by taking boats down the treacherous white waters of the Colorado. On the face of it, the proposition was absurd. Powell was a 120-pound, five-foot-six, one-armed geology professor in his mid-thirties, from the nineteenth-century equivalent of a community college, whose own sister referred to him as "the homeliest man God ever made." He had little experience with running rapids and no credentials as an explorer at all—and Western adventurers as experienced as John C. Fremont, the famous "Pathfinder," had refused to even attempt to ride down the Colorado into the canyon, a voyage, Fremont wrote, possessing "certain … prospect

POWELL THE ETHNOGRAPHER

It isn't widely appreciated, but John Wesley Powell was also a pioneering American ethnologist. He had a tremendous respect for the Indians of the West, and in journeys in 1868—before his Grand Canyon run—he spent a great deal of time with the Ute Indians. He learned to speak their language and traded buckskins for cultural artifacts. In 1870, when he was planning his second Grand Canyon journey, he headed southwest from Salt Lake City to a place about twenty miles north of the Grand Canyon and met the Shivwit people, an Indian group with little white contact. Powell suspected these Indians of killing three members of his first expedition but was never able to prove it. Remarkably, instead of trying to pin the crime on them, he stayed with them, leaned their language and customs, and later came back with a photographer to film them and other southwestern tribes. In 1878, Powell pushed Congress to establish the Bureau of Ethnology, of which he became the first director. Under his guidance, the agency compiled an important dictionary of American Indian tribes and a thorough classification of Indian languages. All of this helped lay the groundwork for the explosion of anthropological study of Indians in America in the twentieth century.

of fatal termination." What Powell did have going for him, however, was a steely determination forged in battle, as well as a love of mystery. And the Grand Canyon and surrounding areas were a deep mystery.

There was another, special attraction. Powell, the geologist, wanted to go deep back into time, into what he called "the unreckoned ages," to understand the powerful forces at work in nature. He had lost all of his childhood religion, but had found a new one: the religion of science. And he felt that nowhere would its workings be as apparent as in the natural cathedral of the canyon. Many people in the nineteenth century believed in the literal truth of the Bible, that the Earth was created in six days; even the educated, nonscientific point of view was that the world was about six thousand years old. However, geologists everywhere were beginning to prove that the Earth was far, far older than this—tens or even hundreds of million years old—an assertion that put them at odds with true believers, just as scientists today are at odds with creationists.

A JOURNEY FRAUGHT WITH PERIL

In actuality, the Grand Canyon itself was only the last and largest of many canyons Powell needed to traverse in order to make his unprecedented journey. He would first launch his boats into the Green River, in Wyoming Territory, itself a largely unexplored watercourse. He would follow the Green south and east to where it joined the Grand River, forming the Colorado River, which would, shortly thereafter, carry him into the canyon.

On May 11, 1869, Powell arrived at Green River Station, Wyoming Territory, on the newly laid Transcontinental Railroad. He brought with him four boats, seven thousand pounds of supplies (enough to last for ten months), and nine men. All except Powell and his brother, Walter (a surly Civil War veteran who had spent time in Confederate prison camps and was possibly unhinged), were experienced trappers and mountain men. None, however, knew anything about running rapids or handling boats in white water.

The first man Powell had selected was Jack Sumner, an ex-Union soldier (as were six others of the crew) who had guided for Powell when he arrived in the West the year before. Sumner was a smart, obstinate man who had survived numerous scrapes with death, including nearly being murdered by Ute Indians. He in turn enlisted several friends: Oramel Howland, a hunter and a printer, who would map the expedition; Howland's young brother, Seneca, a quiet young man who had been wounded at Gettysburg; another man known as Billy Hawkins, who would cook for the expedition (and may or may not have been a fugitive from justice); a mountain man named Bill Dunn, who dressed in buckskins and had hair all the way down his back; and another Civil War veteran, the acerbic and depressive George Bradley. The final two members of the expedition were men who just happened to wander by Green Station and offer their services: Andy Hall, the youngest expeditionary at age twenty, and Frank Goodman, an Englishman who had come west seeking adventure.

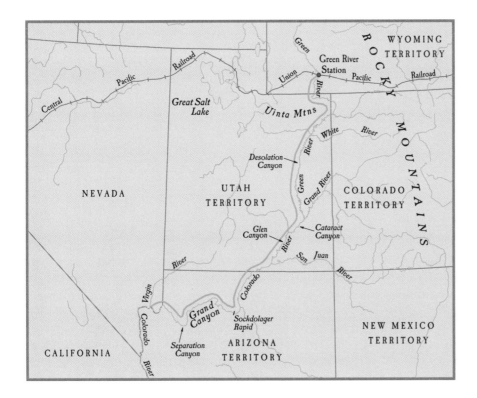

Powell's journey along the Colorado River took him from Green River Station in Wyoming Territory via a thousand miles of raging rapids and rugged canyons to the mouth of the Virgin River.

This somewhat makeshift expedition launched itself on the morning of May 24, to the cheers of onlookers in the little town, and to some good publicity back home. Samuel Bowles, the well-known editor of the Illinois paper *The Springfield Republican* was a friend and admirer of John Wesley Powell and, although he warned his readers that "whoever dares venture into the canyon will never come out alive," felt that the "resolute, gallant" Powell had as good a shot as anyone.

It's hard for a contemporary observer to imagine a group setting off on such a dangerous expedition with so little real preparation. The boats that the Colorado River Expedition—for so Powell grandly called it—rode in were not meant for white water, but had been built on the East Coast for ocean use. They were stable, heavy, round-bottomed wooden boats—fine for riding Atlantic coastal swells, but not for maneuvering on a dime around rocks in rough, rapid water. Not only that, but they were rowed by men sitting backward, in the traditional way, men unable to see what was coming at them, a terrible disadvantage in rough water, on a dangerous river.

Powell had planned a way around this problem. He would ride in a lighter boat, in front of the other boats, in order to find a safe path through the rapids. If he could not find one, he would signal to his men to pull over. They would then either portage the rapids, or "line" the boats through—a backbreaking process by which the men clambered to the shore on either side and pulled the boats across the water using ropes.

But the chief impediment to the expedition was this: Green River Station was 6,100 feet above sea level and Powell's destination—one of the two or three tiny trading settlements on the other side of the canyon—had an elevation of about 700 feet. He and his men were facing a river that dropped more than a mile in height. The question was, did it drop gradually, or like Niagara? This was a very real and pressing concern for these men, for, hemmed in by high cliffs that allowed no escape, they had no way of knowing if their doom lay in a roaring mist of white water, just around the next bend.

A MOUNTAIN DRINKING A RIVER
The Green River, at first relatively calm, took the men through arid badlands, which, nonetheless, were teeming with geological "life," including fossils and fascinating striations of rock. Powell established the precedent he would follow for the entire trip, of tying up whenever he could to hunt for fossils or to climb the towering cliffs that surrounded the river in order to see what lay ahead, taking a barometer with him to measure altitude. Meanwhile the other men hunted—they were notoriously unsuccessful hunters—repaired equipment, or simply napped.

On June 5, they reached the spot where the Green entered the towering Uinta Mountain range, and the trip began in earnest. Stopping for the night, they watched the river pour, seemingly, into the side of a towering cliff—"like a mountain drinking a river." They were at the entrance to a majestic canyon Powell called Lodore, where the cliffs rise two thousand feet on either side, so high that they block out the light. With the mist hovering around the canyon's mouth, the next morning, the place seemed to Powell like "a dark portal of gloom." They entered what Bradley called in his journal "the wildest rapids yet seen," filled with jagged rocks and foaming white water. One boat crashed, spilling its supplies, and three men were trapped on a sandbar and only just rescued from the rising water.

They had been under way only two weeks, but had already lost a boat and more than a ton of supplies. "The river in this canyon," Bradley wrote, "is not a succession of rapids … but a *continuous* rapid." Whenever they could, they would portage or line a rapid, but when they could not, they had to run it. They learned to look for signs, like any tracker following a wild and dangerous animal. A small bit of churning water, seemingly unconnected with anything, was a sign of rapids ahead. Hard rock, like granite, and narrow channels meant fast water; sandstone and wide channels, a slower, steadier stream.

Throughout the Uinta Mountains, they ran fast rapids—sometimes filled with whirlpools and cataracts—through canyons whose darkness was reflected in the names the explorers gave them—bleak names like "Desolation" and "Coal." Often, the small beaches at the sides of the river disappeared, so that the men found themselves in hurtling chutes of roaring water, hemmed in by towering cliffs that were the color, one expedition member wrote, of "muddy rainbows."

But one day, at the end of June, they suddenly shot out of the mountains; the Green widened and began to meander through a vast plain. Greatly relieved, the expedition members enjoyed a leisurely run through groves of cottonwood trees, sometimes covering as much as sixty miles in a single day. But there were disturbing portents of things to come: their food, mostly flour and dried bacon, was beginning to spoil from constant wetting and redrying, and game was scarce.

AN ANCIENT LANDSCAPE The expedition had now traveled about 250 miles in little over a month. They stopped in the Uinta Valley because from here they had their last chance to contact civilization—a federal Indian Agency outpost lay forty miles away, and Powell intended to replenish his food stocks there, as well as send letters home. Unbeknownst to Powell and the others at this time, a hoaxer had come forward saying that the expedition had been lost in the canyon, and that he was the only survivor. The news sped around America, and the whole country began to mourn—until Powell's wife, Emma, disproved the hoaxer's lies and then letters from Powell's crew started to reach their destinations.

Unfortunately, the agency had few supplies to spare for Powell, and it also resulted in him losing a man. Frank Goodman, the wandering Englishman who had signed up in search of adventure, told Powell that he had already experienced enough and was leaving the expedition. There was nothing for Powell to do but let him go. After living with Indians for a time, Goodman would eventually make his way to Utah, where he settled down and raised a large family.

On July 6, Powell and his men set off again, this time heading into territory where few Europeans had been before them. The expedition entered one canyon. And then another. And another. They were back in the rapids with a vengeance— and still had another 260 miles to go before they even reached the Colorado.

The days passed as the expedition sped through the white water, without mishap but with some close calls as men were dunked and supplies lost. At every opportunity, Powell searched for fossils and took notes on rock formations. The geologist in him noted the deep antiquity of the cliffs, the strata of different-colored rocks. "Cliffs of rock," Powell would later write, "terraces of rock, crags of rock—ten thousand strangely carved forms." It was a landscape that had been cut over millions of years by the river—living proof of the world's antiquity. Powell considered this an incontestable fact, and didn't even feel it was worth arguing about with those who adhered to the biblical view. But his companion Sumner, viewing the awesome landscape, wrote in his journal: "The testimony of the rocks cannot be impeached. I think Moses must be mistaken in his chronology of biblical history."

RIDING THE COLORADO

Finally, after twenty days more traveling, the explorers saw another river to their left: the Grand. It was the sign they were looking for, for soon the Green and Grand merged into one great river: the Colorado. Unfortunately for the expedition, this pivotal moment came at a time when their cohesiveness was beginning to shatter. Part of the problem was the scarcity of supplies. The only game they could find were scrawny geese, which barely provided a meal; they looked with longing at the wild bighorn sheep that stared with impunity from crags, out of reach of gunshot. Powell estimated that, from now on, each man would receive a pound of bacon and flour per day, no more. Tempers already frayed by the dangers of the expedition began to fray further. Powell and Oramel Howland began to bicker: Howland had fallen behind in his mapmaking duties, Powell complained. Howland griped back that Powell had neglected to bring enough food for the men.

Powell, it should be noted, was respected but not loved by the members of the expedition. He was not by temperament a warm individual and tended to treat his crew like hired hands—even though Bradley saved Powell's life on at least two occasions, Powell could never get his name straight, usually referring to him as "Bradey." In any event, most of the men sided with Howland in his dispute with Powell, Sumner writing acerbically in his journal that "military martinets and civilians very often disagree."

Internal disagreements aside, the men continued to be awed by the extraordinary scenery around them. They were in territory seen by few humans before them. From their vantage point on the Colorado, they could look up thousands of feet and see huge standing buttes on the rims of the cliffs, like sentinels pointing up to the sky: "a thousand spires point heavenward," wrote the religious Bradley.

This extraordinary landscape was like nothing they had ever seen. "Canyon walls that shrink the river into insignificance," wrote Powell, "with vast, hollow domes … all highly colored—buff, gray, red, brown, and chocolate; never lichened; never moss-covered; but bare and often polished."

The rapids of the Colorado began to get so fierce that the group portaged and lined the boats whenever they could—this despite the fact that the men had developed a taste for running rapids and wanted to do away with the brutally hard (and time-consuming) labor of manhandling the boats. They were now making only four or five miles a day and the temperature hovered around one hundred degrees Fahrenheit. They fought rapids filled with huge chunks of rock that had fallen off the cliffs. In some stretches of white water, waves rose twenty feet high; in others, they were "holes"—deep, sweeping whirlpools that could suck a boat down and hold it there. The specter of a huge waterfall haunted them: "We know that we have got about 2,500 feet to fall yet," Bradley wrote nervously in his journal. In the

No photographs of Powell's 1869 expedition were taken. But he led another trip along the river in 1871, and a photographer shot the expedition setting off, once again, from Green River Station.

HANGING BY THREADS

At least once a week, Powell would stop the expedition and go off with a partner, usually Bradley, to climb cliffs up to two thousand feet high to take altitude readings (judging the drop in altitude was the only way Powell could measure how far the men had come). These cliffs are a challenge for modern climbers with two hands. Powell had only his left hand and no ropes. Once, Powell found himself on a sheer rock face high above the water, his feet wedged in a tiny crevice, his hand grasping a rock above him. He could go no farther and called to Bradley for help. Bradley found his way to a ledge above Powell, but could not reach him. As Powell's grip grew shaky, Bradley finally hit upon a solution. He was wearing only long underwear and a shirt. He took off the underwear and lowered it to Powell. Powell then had to take his one hand off the cliff and grasp for the underwear which was dangling in thin air behind him. Then he hung on for dear life as Bradley pulled him to safety. Incidents like this occurred again and again, with neither man making undue fuss about them. After one climb, Bradley wrote in his journal: "On the way back, the Major's cut-off arm was on the rock side of a gulch we had followed up, and I found it necessary ... to place myself where he could step on my knee, as his stump had a tendency to throw him off balance. Had he fallen at these points, the drop would have been four hundred or five hundred feet."

midst of what the men called Cataract Canyon, they came upon three ferocious rapids that are known to modern-day rafters as Drop 1, Drop 2, and Drop 3. Tellingly, Drop 3 is also called Satan's Gut.

When Powell and his men set out to run Drop 1, one of the boats was immediately caught in a whirlpool and spun around and around, and it was all they could do to rescue it. Powell now had the men line the boats over the remaining rapids, but the work was so dangerous and difficult that it took them all day, and the boats, smashed against rocks, were leaking by the time they were through. That night, having made his usual climb to a rocky perch high above the river, Powell was caught in a desert thunderstorm; it produced a flash flood that roared down a side canyon and nearly killed him—he literally had to outrace it.

After the men left Cataract Canyon, they reached a beautiful spot they called Glen Canyon, where the cliffs were not as high and the river slowly meandered through multicolored sandstone walls. Deep in the canyon was an extraordinary natural chamber, two hundred feet high by five hundred feet long by two hundred feet wide. It was like a cathedral, and the men lingered in it, unable to tear themselves away from this magical place. Powell found that they were not the first people to have visited: they discovered the ruins of an Indian settlement (thought by modern-day scholars to be Anasazi) and spent an afternoon collecting arrowheads and pottery shards.

It was as if the river was giving them a respite before sending them, finally, into the howling wilderness of the Grand Canyon itself.

INTO THE CANYON

The Grand Canyon announced itself, on August 6: the river narrowed to fifty yards and the men faced tumultuous rapids that ran between towering vertical cliffs. For the next several days, the men portaged, lined, and shot the white water, overwhelmed by the canyon itself, by what Powell ecstatically called "the most sublime spectacle on earth." The Grand Canyon, he wrote, was a "library of the gods ... He who would read the language of the universe may read ... in a slow and imperfect way, but still so as to understand a little, the story of Creation."

But Powell's men had their thoughts on other, less sublime considerations. They were starving, wet—most of them had no changes of clothing left—and frightened by the magnitude of the challenge they were still facing after two and a half months on the water. Things were not getting better, but worse. The rapids came without ceasing, a never-ending series of them, as the river cut its way through terrifying canyons within canyons that were deep black in color—the color of the hard granite that caused the fiercest rapids.

Then they came to the wildest rapid yet, which they called (and is still called) the Sockdolager—a nineteenth-century colloquial term for a knockout punch. Sumner wrote: "We finally encountered a stretch of water and canyon that made my hair curl"—quite a statement from the laconic guide and former soldier who had been in cavalry charges and fought off Indian attacks. The canyon walls were close together, the rapids fell approximately thirty feet in about six hundred yards, the waves were fifteen feet high—and then the canyon turned hard left, concealing what lay beyond.

The only way to get through Sockdolager was to ride straight down the middle, and that is what the three boats did, shooting past rocks, getting caught in holes and whirlpools, the men bailing furiously. It has been estimated that the flow of the Colorado at this point is as high as one hundred-thousand cubic feet of water per second—the same rate as Niagara Falls. Pause a moment and consider what that might feel like, in barely controllable small boats, with jagged rocks reaching out for you.

The men survived Sockdolager, but then faced the forty-mile stretch of rapids now called Adrenaline Alley. Powell wrote: "Down in these grand, gloomy depths we glide, ever listening, for the mad waters keep up their roar ... the river is closed in so that we can see but a few hundred yards and what there be below we know not."

Bickering between Powell and the crew reached a new height of pettiness when Bill Dunn accidentally dropped a gold watch belonging to Powell into the river. Rather incredibly, Powell told him he would have to pay $30 for it. A few days later, Oramel Howland and Dunn got into a fistfight with Powell's brother, Walter, who had to be restrained from shooting them.

Something had to give, and it finally did. On August 27, the expedition ran another set of bad rapids, ones that "ran like a racehorse," Sumner wrote. Setting up camp that night, they realized they faced yet more white water just downstream. This was too much for Oramel Howland, his brother, Seneca, and Bill Dunn. They told Powell they were going to climb out of the canyon, through a side-canyon they had spotted, and try to make their way to the nearest Mormon settlement, perhaps sixty-five miles away. It is a sign of how desperate they were that they would rather have taken a chance on walking that far—at least forty-five miles of it through desert—than continue with the expedition.

Powell attempted to reason with them, but the minds of the three men were made up, and the next morning they left with water and what provisions they could carry. The last Powell saw of Dunn and the Howland brothers they were climbing the cliffs leading out of the canyon. The three men were never seen again and to this day no one knows for sure what happened to them. One story is that they were killed by Indians who mistook them for three men who had murdered an Indian woman. Another theory is that they were shot by Mormons, who feared outsiders. There is no hard and fast evidence for either speculation.

Now there were only six men left—men who were ragged, starving, and exhausted. The next morning, August 28, they set off with whatever water and provisions they could carry. The next day, after passing through two more sets of rapids, they found themselves, to their joy and astonishment, passing out of the Grand Canyon and into low, rolling desert country.

The first people they passed were a band of Indians who fled at the sight of them. But late on the afternoon of August 30 they came upon three white men fishing, who took them to their cabin and gave them food. "We laid our dignified manners aside," wrote Sumner of their first meal off the river, "and assumed the manners of so many hogs." After nearly one hundred days and one thousand miles on the river, the Colorado River Expedition had been delivered from peril.

An aerial view of Glen Canyon Dam and Lake Powell. Ironically, one of the most beautiful canyons that Powell traversed—Glen Canyon—was submerged by the lake that now bears his name.

A UTOPIAN VISION

John Wesley Powell came out of the Grand Canyon more convinced than ever about the Earth's immense antiquity. He published a book about his experiences that expanded on the journal he had kept, and went on a lecture tour—to the disgruntlement of men like Jack Sumner and Billy Hawkins, who, in a fit of jealousy, claimed that Powell had stolen money Congress had appropriated for the expedition (in fact, Congress had provided no funds for the journey whatsoever).

The expedition also placed Powell at the center of another debate important to the future of the American West. For his trip through the desert lands of Wyoming, Arizona, and Utah had shown Powell beyond any doubt that there was a limited supply of water in the West, and that it needed to be conserved. After a second journey through the Grand Canyon in 1871, one so hazardous that he felt compelled to end it halfway through, Powell stopped running rivers and started measuring them. As director of the U.S. Geological Survey, he decided to inventory how much water the West really had. He established the country's first river-gauge stations, trained water engineers, and invented some of the terms we use today to describe water resources, such as "runoff"—water that flows down mountains and slopes to reach waterways.

In 1878, Powell completed his *Report on the Lands of the Arid Region*, which was published as a congressional document and which laid out a strategy for settling the West without battles over scarce water. Essentially, Powell called for a slowing down of the homesteading. Powell wanted, instead, to set up carefully planned settlements based on the Mormon communities, where water was used cooperatively, and where settlers would be keenly aware of the dangers of pollution and overuse. He believed that this type of cooperative would also help small towns to organize and keep large communities from stealing their water.

Powell's was an admittedly utopian vision, based on self-reliance and communal good will, not government funding. Had it succeeded, big cities like Los Angeles, Salt Lake City, and Phoenix would be much smaller, or might not even exist—Phoenix, for instance, sits amidst a desert in the state of Arizona and has no natural water resources of its own. Modern-day environmentalists see Powell as the first man of his time to have had the foresight to recognize that western America's seemingly vast natural resources were finite, needed to be evenly distributed, and ought not to be hoarded by any one entity for profit. It is important to note here, however, that Powell was a *conservationist*, not a preservationist. In other words, he wanted to reclaim land, to irrigate it properly in order to grow crops and graze livestock on it; he wasn't interested in creating unspoiled wilderness areas.

Powell's ideas were not to succeed, of course. Western congressmen allied with the railroads and the big ranchers shouted it down, claiming it would interfere with free enterprise. In the end, passing its first laws three months before Powell's death, Congress began a century of massive western damming and irrigation, which fostered the development of huge farms, and led to communities like Los Angeles snapping up water rights from hundreds of miles away, since water was an entity that businesses could buy, like land, and sell to the highest bidder, leaving local farmers with dusty fields where they had once had rich cropland.

Powell died of a cerebral hemorrhage in 1902, at the age of sixty-nine. There is a final irony in his story. In the 1950s, the United States Bureau of Reclamation built a dam over Glen Canyon and the beautiful amphitheater that Powell and his men had found, as well as the Anasazi ruins and thirty-five miles of Cataract Canyon. Environmentalists were enraged. "To grasp the nature of the crime that was committed," Edward Abbey wrote, "imagine the Taj Mahal or Chartres Cathedral buried in mud until only the spires remain visible." Unperturbed in a way typical of massive government bureaucracies, the Bureau of Reclamation went on to name the 186-mile-long artificial lake that was created Lake Powell, in honor of John Wesley Powell's great journey into the unknown.

AN ENVIRONMENTAL BATTLEGROUND

In the early 1950s, the Bureau of Reclamation proposed a hydroelectric dam at the confluence of the Green and Yampa rivers, which would flood a part of Dinosaur National Monument and reduce the flow of the Colorado River. The Sierra Club, led by then-director David R. Brower, started a public awareness campaign to stop this dam, which caused thousands of letters to pour into Congress in protest. This was regarded as the first salvo of the environmental movement in the United States. But, ironically, it resulted in one of its worst defeats. In response to the campaign, the authorities proposed the damming of Glen Canyon as a compromise. Brower and other environmentalists accepted it, but Brower later said: "Glen Canyon died and I was partially responsible for its death."

Construction began in 1956 and the dam was officially opened in 1966, although it would take seventeen years for Lake Powell to fill completely. Before the dam opened, archeological crews were allowed in to photograph and film the soon-to-be-flooded canyon. Teams found hundreds of sites linked to ancient Americans, and brought out what artifacts they could. They even identified rock inscriptions left behind by John Wesley Powell's crew.

GUANO: HOW THE WHOLE WORLD WAS CHANGED BY BIRD DROPPINGS

IMAGINE YOU'RE WALKING DOWN THE STREET ON A BRIGHT SUNNY DAY, WHEN a shadow swoops over your head. You duck instinctively, but feel a wet plop on your shoulder, and find yourself, as wings flutter away, the proud bearer of a shining puddle of bird poo. Your immediate reaction might be to wonder aloud what you did to be singled out for such malign attention from the gods. But, wait: examine that odorous, milky-white (well, sometimes green) substance a little more closely. Because of what is in this little puddle, and billions of little puddles like it, nineteenth-century American overseas imperialism began, three South American countries went to war, and one ancient Pacific island culture was irretrievably devastated. This is not even to mention related goings-on in the twentieth century, including a murderous madman and his harem on a deserted island, secret U.S. airbases during World War II, the little matter of the 1961 Bay of Pigs invasion of Cuba, and chemical weapons dumps currently in the Pacific Ocean.

All this because of bird droppings, you ask, incredulously? Strangely, yes. For centuries, bird poo, or guano by its other name, was a highly prized and much sought-after fertilizer.

HUMBOLDT'S DISCOVERY
By as early as 10,000 BC, prehistoric peoples understood that heavily used land wears out and that fertilizing it with wood ash (potash), animal feces, and the like helps restore it. Much later, it was discovered that the natural fertilizer par excellence was guano—or, as it was originally named by the South American Indians who first used it, *huano*, meaning literally dried bird droppings ("guano" is a corruption of this word based on the English pronunciation).

The best guano is found in one particular part of the world: western South America. There the chilly Humboldt Current causes the sea to teem with cold-water fish like anchovies and herrings, perfect food for sea fowl such as gannets, gulls, pelicans, and cormorants, which, for thousands of years, have feasted and then alighted upon one or the other of the dozens of small, rocky islands off the coast of Chile and Peru and pooped their little hearts out. Because the Humboldt also cools the air and makes it more arid, the guano was not washed away by rainfall, as it was in other climates. By the early nineteenth century, guano on some of these islands had built up to be hundreds of feet deep—the uppermost layers a dry, yellow dust, the lower layers almost cement like in consistency.

From as early as 500 AD, the Moche Indians of Peru made the short trip offshore to the three small, rocky Chincas Islands, about fifteen miles from the present-day port of Pisco, to gather guano. Because of guano, the empire-building Incas who came later were able to grow crops in the barren soil of mountainsides and build a civilization that supported an estimated ten million people. The Incas understood how important bird droppings were: they set up a system that assigned different guano islands to different regions to facilitate distribution. It was a crime punishable by death to kill birds nesting on the islands.

When the Spanish came, they noted the importance of bird droppings to local agriculture, but, since they were far more interested in harvesting gold and silver than guano, they put their captive manpower to work in mines and the Incan farm system declined. The Indians continued to take their boats out to the guano islands and use the bird droppings on their small farm crops.

In 1804, the incredible bounty of land fertilized by guano was noted by Alexander Humboldt (for whom the aforementioned current would later be named) as he was touring Peru. He took samples of guano back to France with him, where they were analyzed by chemists and discovered to have a very high level of nitrate and phosphates. Scientists had already discovered that plants, while taking carbon and oxygen from the air, derive all-important nitrogen and phosphorus from the soil, and had been seeking for some time to develop a fertilizer rich in these substances.

A good fertilizer was desperately needed by farmers in a world by then driven by agriculture. Land in Great Britain and eastern North America was tired and farmed-out, even when rotated—a study of once-fertile land in upstate New York showed that an acre that produced thirty bushels of corn in 1775 produced, by the 1830s, only eight bushels. Fertilizer of all types was tried. Farm publications sprang up devoted solely to fertilizers, suggesting farmers try everything from human waste and putrefied animal remains to sawdust, hay, ground cow horns, and urine, both human and animal.

Despite Humboldt's glowing reports, guano remained virtually unknown. A few barrels turned up here and there in Britain and North America, almost as a specialty item, but there was no significant trade in the substance—until, in the late 1830s, two businessmen in newly independent Peru decided to try their luck at exporting it on a larger scale. The two men asked an English merchant living in Chile to send samples home to Britain, to be given to farmers for a free trial. Results were so encouraging that British traders ordered an entire boatload, which the Peruvians were only too happy to sell them.

PERUVIAN GOLD

The first shipload arrived in Southampton, England, in 1840. Unfortunately, as one historian has written, "the stench was so foul [that] the entire town took to the hills." Despite this, guano was a huge success. The cost to the British traders was only twelve pounds per ton; they sold it for twenty-four pounds, making a profit, on one shipload, of one hundred thousand pounds—an extraordinary markup at the time. In the next two years, the same Peruvian businessmen shipped more than eight thousand tons of it to Britain. Farmers began to talk about it in rapturous terms, swapping stories about how they had gotten their crop yield to increase three hundred percent and apple trees to bear fruit twice within a year.

The market grew so rapidly that the Peruvian government stepped in and nationalized the business, creating a monopoly and driving up the price. In response, the British began a mad dash to seek out other guano islands, a few of which were known to exist off the coasts of Africa and Arabia. In March of 1843, British merchants discovered that Ichaboe Island, off the coast of present-day Namibia, was covered with guano to a depth of approximately twenty-five feet; a year later, one hundred ships were carrying the guano away from the island. In January 1845, 450 ships and 6,000 men vied for Ichaboe's last few tons of guano, and pitched battles were fought with pickaxes and shovels. By May, the island had been mined out and was left, totally deserted.

Unfortunately, as the English were to discover, the African variety of guano was inferior, having had a good deal of its nitrogen leached away by rainfall. Peru still had a virtual monopoly on really good bird droppings.

By the 1850s, farmers in the United States were clamoring for supplies, but Peru and Great Britain had signed an exclusive trade deal, so Peruvian guano had to be imported to the United States from Great Britain, at significant expense. Despite this, the demand in America was so great that farmers had to beware of fraudulent peddlers, who sometimes visited farms carrying sacks filled with sand odorized by animal urine. As a result of this practice, the very first federal "guano inspectors" were appointed, to check out shiploads of guano coming into American ports and stamp grades on sacks.

Because of guano, or the lack of it, American farmers began to organize themselves, for the very first time understanding the power they could wield collectively (in 1850, eight out of every ten Americans lived on farms). Presaging the massive agrarian movement of the 1870s, groups of farmers went to their congressional representatives and demanded good guano at a reasonable cost. In 1850, Millard Fillmore became the first American president to mention bird droppings in an inaugural address, when he stressed the need for more guano at affordable prices. Beginning under Fillmore, the federal government attempted to pressure Peru into selling straight to American markets by establishing a series of price incentives and, later, tariffs. Nothing worked.

However, it was common knowledge, reported by sailors, that there were numerous small islands in the Pacific and Caribbean that were quite literally covered with guano. And there had to be even more guano islands out there that no one had found. What was to keep America—now expanding westward at a rapid pace, in keeping with its Manifest Destiny—from mining guano in these places, just as the British had in Ichaboe?

Well, there *was* the little matter of ownership, but that didn't seem to deter the American government. In 1856, the United States Congress passed the Guano Islands Act, subsequently signed into law by President James Buchanan, which stated: "Whenever any citizen of the United States discovers a deposit of guano on any island, rock, or key not within the lawful jurisdiction of any other government … and takes peaceable possession thereof … such island … may, at the discretion of the president, be considered as appertaining to the United States."

In bird poo begins imperialism. The American overseas empire was thus set in motion, almost accidentally, by a government seeking fertilizer for its farmers. Indeed, America's very first overseas possessions were not Cuba or the Philippines, but specks of guano-covered rock claimed by private citizens in the mad rush that ensued after the Guano Islands Act was made law. Businesses like the American Guano Company, United States Guano Company, the Pacific Guano and Fertilizer Company, and the Phoenix Guano Company—to name just a few—sprang up, financed by speculators. Guano expeditions were formed, cartographers hired, and clipper ships pressed into service, all to seek out islands where guano could be found.

Meanwhile in Peru, the mother lode of guano, there was no need to seek the stuff out. It was all around. The problem was getting it out of the ground.

A HELLISH OCCUPATION

By 1860, the most mined guano islands on Earth were Peru's Chincas Islands. These were the places from which Incan farmers had once ferried boatloads of guano, and they were now the focus of big business. Beginning in 1841 and lasting until the early 1880s, Peru would earn about eighty percent of its foreign exchange selling bird droppings. Yet, with few other sources of revenue, the government of Peru remained in debt, continually spending all the money it received from Britain for one year's crop of guano, while obtaining advances on the next year's.

THE MURDEROUS KING OF CLIPPERTON

Tiny Clipperton Island lies seven hundred miles southwest of Acapulco, Mexico. Desolate and subject to earthquakes and even tsunamis, it supports little life apart from sand crabs. It was discovered by Ferdinand Magellan in 1521 but not named until the eighteenth century, when the English pirate John Clipperton used it as a base. The American Guano Mining Company briefly mined it, but by the end of the nineteenth century it was in Mexican hands.

By 1914, there were about one hundred people working there. There was little to eat or drink, so every two months a ship brought provisions from Mexico. But during the Mexican Revolution of 1910, the island was, somehow, forgotten. By 1917, most of the inhabitants of Clipperton had died of starvation. The survivors were fifteen women and children and one man, the lighthouse keeper, Victor Alvarez. He declared himself King of Clipperton, and embarked on a grisly rampage of rape and murder, killing five women who refused his attentions before being killed by a sixth. On July 18, 1917, shortly after his death, a U.S. naval vessel happened by the island and picked up four women and six children, the last survivors.

Now administered by the French, Clipperton has been all but left to its voracious land crabs and is visited only occasionally by scientists and sports fishermen.

So the guano needed to keep coming. The problem was that mining guano was a hellish occupation and no native Peruvian wanted any part of it. The conditions were unspeakable. Most of the guano had been baked by the sun into thick rock that had to be chopped at with pickaxes and chisels. Workers dug trenches as much as one hundred feet deep, where they hacked out huge chunks of feces that were lifted out and carted away in wheelbarrows to the cliff edges, then dumped down slides or chutes into the cargo holds of waiting ships moored at the shoreline. Clouds of noxious yellow dust filled the air, choking even those workers who used primitive respirators made of hemp and tar. Anyone who spent any time on the Chincas suffered from diseases ranging from asthma and dysentery to far more serious ailments like histoplasmosis and shigellosis, gastrointestinal complaints caused by ingesting bird droppings.

To recruit workers, Peru resorted to draconian actions. The government sent ships to China, where Peruvian representatives (or the American or British ship captains paid to do the job) told illiterate peasants that they would be going to the gold fields of California. Instead, the Chinese were taken to the Chincas. As often as not, the Peruvian government hired slavers to simply kidnap Chinese and take them to Peru. By 1875, it has been estimated that about one hundred thousand Chinese had been brought to Peru, almost all under false pretenses if not in actual bondage. Some found relatively easy work on Peruvian plantations, but most were sent to the Chincas. There, on a diet of four unripe bananas a day, living in grass huts, they were beaten, whipped, and worked to death. If a man could no longer stand, he was given a job crawling through the guano, picking out and discarding pebbles. Many committed suicide: one favorite mode was to dive off the cliffs, headfirst, into the holds of the guano ships. Two American visitors to the Chincas in the 1860s noted, to their horror, shallow graves, from which the toes and fingers of dead men emerged.

Gradually, however, word began to get back to China to avoid Peruvian recruiters, and so a new source of labor was sought through a practice known as "blackbirding"—recruiting Melanesian or Polynesian islanders as workers. These men and women were promised three-year terms with good wages; on the Chincas, they got nothing but hard labor, illness, and death. In time, even the "contracts" given these workers were dispensed with, and they were simply kidnapped.

In early December of 1862, a fleet of eight raiding ships left Peru and sailed 2,400 miles due west to Easter Island. A force of about eighty sailors disembarked from the ships a few weeks later and displayed an array of trinkets and trade goods for the Easter Islanders, hundreds of whom gathered around to examine them. Then one of the ship captains fired a revolver in the air, and the raiders brought out guns and began corralling islanders to the ships. In the panic that followed, some islanders threw themselves in the sea, and others were shot and killed as they ran away. In all, the raiders captured almost all the males of working age on the island—about one thousand men, a third of the island's entire population, including the chief, the crown prince, and every priest who knew how to read Easter Island's ancient and still-mysterious hieroglyphics.

The men were taken to the Chincas Islands, where nine hundred of them died in very short order. These actions on the part of Peru were so outrageous that France, the United States, and even Great Britain—still the major beneficiary of Peruvian guano—complained, and, finally, the one hundred remaining Easter Islanders were repatriated. On the way, eighty-five of them died of smallpox, leaving fifteen to step ashore once again. Some of these fifteen brought smallpox with them, which further decimated the island's population. The catastrophe struck the last blow against the old culture of Easter Island and forever destroyed any chance modern scientists might have had of understanding the ancient civilization that once thrived there.

THE UNITED STATES OF GUANO
In the fifty years after the passage of the Guano Islands Act, American businessmen staked their claim to ninety-four small islands, some of them no more than rocky outcroppings, in the Pacific and Caribbean. About twenty-five of these places simply did not exist, being figments, deliberate or otherwise, of the imaginations of whaling captains, who were paid to remember specks of land they might have seen as they passed through the South Pacific. Entrepreneurs were not supposed to claim them without actually visiting them, but in the mad rush for guano, many did just that.

Over sixty of these island claims were recognized by the American State Department as "appurtenances," but of these, only twenty-two were actually mined. One of the first of the guano islands to be claimed in the central Pacific was remote Howland Island, 1,675 nautical miles southwest of Honolulu—about halfway from Hawaii to Australia. Howland was typical of the guano islands, in the sense that it was a place you wouldn't wish upon your worst enemy. Consisting of only about four hundred rocky acres, surrounded by sharp coral reefs, and with no safe natural anchorages, Howland was infested by rats brought to the island by

DWINDLING SUPPLIES

Guano is still a popular fertilizer today, particularly for people who eschew chemicals and farm or garden organically. Most organic guano is bat guano, which is harvested from bat caves in Asia, particularly the Philippines, and is very high in nitrates. It was already known to be potent in the nineteenth century, but the difficulty of getting it out of caves in large amounts made it uneconomical. The harvesting of bird guano on the Chincas and other islands off the Pacific coast of South America is still important to the local economy, although there is nowhere near as much guano as there used to be, in part because there aren't as many seabirds as there used to be—the mid-twentieth-century population of forty million birds is now down to two million. There are many suspected causes for this, among them the warming trend fostered by El Niño (which causes a decline in the cold-water fish the guano birds love to eat) and overfishing. Another possible cause is a lack of nesting sites. Some of the birds that produce guano also make their nests in it; as the guano continues to be depleted, potential breeding sites dwindle. In response, wildlife conservationists and scientists from Peru and around the world have begun a program that teaches the guano collectors, or guanaros, how vital it is to leave at least some of the guano for the birds.

some long-forgotten shipwreck. It was equatorial, blazingly hot, and had little rainfall. But Howland did boast a fair amount of good-grade guano and was thus claimed by both the American Guano Company and the United States Guano Company by 1857. Both attempted to occupy it with armed employees and shots were nearly fired, before the federal government stepped in and declared that the two companies should harvest jointly.

The island's guano was mined by Hawaiians, called by the Americans "Kanakas" (a word meaning "people" in Hawaiian), and while their working conditions were not as bad as those on the Chincas Islands, they were not good. Since there was no natural anchorage, the Hawaiians had to paddle boats full of guano to ships waiting offshore, thereby risking capsizing in the turbulent and shark-infested waters around the reefs. Men were choked by the guano dust and drinking water was extremely scarce. The thousands of rats got into food supplies, bit sleeping workers, and robbed birds' nests of eggs. Company records show that workers killed thousands of rats a week, to little avail.

However, there was money to be made. On Howland, Baker, and Jarvis islands, on Midway and Johnson atolls, tiny specks far out in the Pacific, tons of guano were harvested then shipped back to the United States at prices ranging up to $80 a ton, depending on demand. One historian has called the islands belonging to the American Guano Company alone the "Monstrous Guano Empire." By 1880, about ten million dollars worth of guano fertilizer was sold in America annually, although at that point the boom had started to gradually decline, mainly because of the discovery of huge deposits of rock phosphates in the United States, which, it was found, could be turned into perfectly serviceable fertilizer.

THE WAR OF THE PACIFIC

A certain amount of shooting and infighting was part and parcel of the rush for guano, but in 1879 a dispute over bird droppings led to an all-out war between three nations: Chile, Peru, and Bolivia. The dispute focused on huge deposits of guano in the Atacama Desert, on the Pacific coast. Bolivia claimed the land, but Chile disputed ownership. After a few provocations by both sides, Bolivia declared war against Chile. Peru, eager to have access to the valuable nitrates of the Atacama, backed Bolivia.

This was a mistake because Chile had the largest and most effective navy in the region and was easily able to blockade the coastline along the Atacama Desert. The naval campaign began with the Battle of Chipana in April of 1879 and ended with total Chilean control of the seas by October of that year. The land campaign took a little longer, but resulted in Chile conquering and occupying all of Bolivia and Peru—in the latter case, long-oppressed, conscripted Chinese guano workers rose to fight against the Peruvians.

Under the Treaty of Ancón, which ended the war in 1883, Chile received all the territory formerly claimed by Bolivia, which contained the valuable nitrate deposits. The loss of this coastal territory (although Chilean historians claimed Bolivia never owned it) is, to this day, a source of resentment in landlocked Bolivia. Peru also

The practice of kidnapping Pacific islanders to work in Peruvian guano quarries decimated the adult population of Easter Island.

suffered a national humiliation. With the whole country occupied for a time by Chile, its president fled to Europe, and, deeply in debt, with the Chincas Islands running out of guano, the country fell into a period of civil war and chaos.

LAST BASTIONS OF SLAVERY
The United States managed to avoid serious disputes with other nations over the Pacific guano islands, in part because of the vastness of the territory, but also because, in many cases, American maps were so poorly made that islands were mislocated and misidentified, with the ensuing result that no one else knew where or which they were. But this was not the case in the Caribbean, where many of the islands claimed by the United States were contested by other countries. Great and Little Swan Islands, for example, one hundred miles off the coast of Honduras, were claimed by that country but occupied by the United States. Navassa Island, about ninety miles south of Cuba, was considered by Haiti to be part of its territory; nonetheless, Americans hotly contested the claim and to this day hold the island.

Reputed to have been discovered by Columbus in 1493, Navassa was the third island claimed under the Guano Island Act of 1856. Rocky and cliff-edged, it contained large amounts of guano high in phosphates and had the advantage of being much closer to the American mainland than the Pacific appurtenances.

But Navassa also became significant in another way. The Thirteenth Amendment to the Constitution of the United States, ratified in 1865, banned slavery, but after the Civil War those who sympathized with the old Confederate cause sought to claim that those islands attached to the United States as appurtenances by the Guano Islands Act were exempt from this amendment—and that, therefore, on these islands, slavery was

DEADLY DEPOSITS

America's use of Johnson Atoll continues to arouse controversy. One of the nation's most closely guarded military compounds, it contains what the government calls the "Johnson Atoll Chemical Agent Disposal System." Although it probably does not hold nuclear weapons, the atoll stores, in underground tanks and bunkers, some thirteen thousand tons of chemical weapons at any one time, including two nerve agents, which are probably sarin and VX nerve gas.

These agents are apparently destroyed in one of nine huge incinerators on the island, or detoxified in other ways. Despite numerous protests, including one from member nations of the South Pacific Forum, which called Johnson Atoll "the toxic waste disposal center of the world," the U.S. military continues to use the atoll for this purpose.

legal. By the late 1880s, Navassa was being mined by black contract workers recruited in Baltimore, Maryland, many of them former slaves. They dug out the guano by pickaxe and sometimes dynamite, in fierce heat, all the time overseen by white supervisors who, emboldened by racism, treated the workers with great violence, sometimes punishing minor infractions by hanging men up by ropes attached to their wrists, with their toes barely touching the ground, for hours in the blazing sun.

In 1889, some of these workers suddenly rose up, seized arms from their white supervisors, and killed five of them. A U.S. warship put down the uprising, imprisoned forty of the men, and brought them back to Baltimore to stand trial for murder. A black fraternal society, the Order of the Galilean Fisherman, as well as what was probably the first black militant society in America, the Brotherhood of Liberty, raised money to defend the men. Prominent black lawyers, in a case that received wide attention, contended that because the men were treated like slaves, they were driven to riot, and, indeed, even had a duty to do so. Despite the defense's impassioned pleas, three of the men were convicted of murder and sentenced to die, while the rest were given prison sentences of varying lengths after being found guilty of manslaughter and rioting. However, a grassroots petition begun by black churches gained enough momentum to give President Benjamin Harrison pause, and he commuted the men's sentences to life in prison in 1891. Then, and partly as a result of the Navassa Island case, the Supreme Court issued a ruling in 1900 supporting the Thirteenth Amendment by explicitly prohibiting slavery in "territorial appurtenances," places that were "subject to the jurisdiction of the United States, but which are not incorporated into it."

ISLANDS OF INFLUENCE
By the beginning of the twentieth century, synthetic chemical fertilizers had been made cheaply and easily available, particularly in America, Great Britain, and other parts of Western Europe, and the demand for guano declined sharply. In 1898, the last year in which such records were kept, only 4,562 tons of guano fertilizer were imported into the United States, compared with four times as many in 1869. In the years preceding World War I, the American government decided that the guano islands had outlived their purpose and were, in fact, far more trouble than they were worth. It abandoned title to two-thirds of the claimed islands, and although the Guano Islands Act remained in effect (and does to this day), the State Department simply refused to process any further claims.

However ... after World War I, as America was beginning to adopt a more global outlook, the fate of the guano islands began to be reconsidered, and the State Department decided to hang on to eight of them as American territory. In the Pacific, they were Johnson and Midway atolls, and Baker, Howland, Jarvis, and Palmyra islands. In the Caribbean, they were the islands of Great and Little Swan and Navassa.

Some of these tiny specks subsequently played important roles in the shaping of our world. For instance, on Great Swan Island in the Caribbean, which America wrested from Honduras, the CIA, having leased the island in the guise of a dummy

corporation called the Gibraltar Steamship Company, set up an airstrip and radio station in 1960. The radio station, calling itself Radio Free Cuba, began broadcasting anti-Castro messages from "Havana Rose," a Cuban exile whose real name was Pepita Riera. On April 17, 1961, the station sent secret messages to the Cuban underground telling them that the Bay of Pigs invasion was about to begin.

In the South and Central Pacific, the guano islands became stopping points for American air routes across the Pacific and, more importantly, vital military bases. Howland Island became famous after its airstrip was prepared for the aviator Amelia Earhart to land on during her round-the-world trip in 1937, though she disappeared en route the U.S. Navy expanded the facilities, which were shelled by the Japanese during the opening months of World War II. The U.S. Navy also built facilities on Johnson Atoll, which was transformed into an important American military base.

None of these islands would be in American hands if it wasn't for guano. And but for the lead offered by those potent bird deposits, it might have taken farmers many more years to learn the secrets of fertilizers and, in the United States at least, understand the political power they themselves could muster. For want of guano, thousands were enticed to other continents, and countries came to blows. Because of guano, the Bolivian Navy remains confined to Lake Titicaca one hundred years after it fought for, and lost, its coastline.

It's hard to believe bird droppings ever had such value. It's a perspective you may want to think about the next time something unexpected lands on your shoulder.

In one of the fierce sea battles that characterized the War of the Pacific, the Peruvian warship *Huascar*, on the right, bombards the Chilean ship, the *Sarah*.

THE LAST AMAZONS: THE FIGHTING WOMEN OF DAHOMEY

WOMEN ARE NOT SUPPOSED TO HAVE MARTIAL INSTINCTS, RIGHT? It doesn't mean they don't get into a good catfight now and again, but when it comes to being part of a trained, aggressive force meant to kill or be killed in sustained warfare, well, that's best left up to the men. This is an attitude that still prevails in the highest level of the military in many countries. Just before the first Gulf War, for example, Marine Corp Commandant General Robert H. Barrow (retired) offered the following testimony in front of the U.S. Congress, during hearings about the advisability of putting American women into combat:

> Combat … is killing. And it's done in an environment that is often as difficult as you can imagine. Extremes of climate. Brutality. Death. Dying. It's … uncivilized! And women can't do it. Nor should they even be thought of as doing it … And I may be old-fashioned, but I think the very nature of woman disqualifies them from doing it. Women give life. Sustain life. Nurture life. They don't take it.

Anyone familiar with historical accounts of women in battle, which date back to antiquity, will find this statement highly problematic. But General Barrow is a product of his culture. And this culture isn't confined to the military. Many academics dispute the presence of warrior women in history: sure, there were the likes of St. Joan and Molly Pitcher, who dressed as men and fought in the front lines, but these were the exceptions that proved the rule. The legendary amazons of yore were merely myths or legends. Indeed, according to some feminist scholars, these warrior women were simply creations that justified men's castration fears, women made up to show men the dark side of womanhood. Abby Kleinbaum in *The War Against the Amazons* calls women warriors "a dream men created, an image of a superlative female," and goes on to write: "As surely as no spider's web was built for the glorification of spies, the amazon idea was not designed to enhance women."

In fact, there are numerous traditions of fighting women in history, and not all of these can be considered mythic. Any attempt to deny this long tradition of female warriors is to deny a significant part of women's cultural heritage. As David E. Jones points out in his study *Women Warriors*: "To be robbed of any element of what comprises the strength of mind, body, and spirit cripples the engines of personal freedom … Women as well as men hold a military history and a chivalrous tradition."

AMAZONS ANCIENT AND MODERN

Amazons were mentioned in Greek myths, including those relating to the lost city of Atlantis. But the Greek historian Herodotus claimed that these warriors actually existed. He used the name for a female army that invaded Greece in the fifth century BC from the Bosporus and attacked Athens, though it was eventually repulsed. According to Herodotus, these warriors wore long pants and leather boots and carried small round shields and double-headed battle axes. Supposedly, they cut off one breast to facilitate shooting a bow and arrow and killed all their male offspring. In referring to the amazons, Herodotus clearly assumed everyone would know what he was talking about, and recent archeological finds in the area around the Don River show that at least twenty percent of the women skeletons dating to the fifth century BC were buried with weapons like those he described. So, even though not all the legends associated with these female warriors are likely to be true—just as not all the legends that have sprung up around the 1956 Brooklyn Dodgers are true—it seems that Amazon warriors did exist.

This is unsurprising when you consider how often similar forces have appeared throughout history. In the second millennium BC, women warriors such as Queen Iati'e and Queen Tabua were celebrated in Arabia for their martial prowess, and Queen Boudicca was the scourge of the Romans in England in the first century AD. In the sixteenth century, Spanish explorers lost deep in the Brazilian wilderness while descending a massive river fought a battle with a group of women warriors; since even conquistadores knew their classics back then, they called the women "amazons" and named the river after them. A few years earlier, when Francisco Pizarro's men fought the Inca in Peru, they were met by women soldiers hurling

Under kings Gezu and Glele, the West African kingdom of Dahomey (in modern-day Benin) rebelled against the region's dominant Yoruba states. But by 1880, it faced a new foe: France.

Previous pages: *The Battle between the Amazons and the Greeks*, by Pauwel Casteels, from the late seventeenth century. Herodotus claimed this battle occurred in the fifth century BC.

stones from slings. North American Indians were also recorded as having women warrior societies. And numerous examples from the sixteenth, seventeenth, and eighteenth centuries can be found of women who lusted to fight and went to extraordinary lengths to disguise themselves so that they could join the army.

In modern times, women guerilla fighters saw action for Mao Zedong's Red Army and in Vietnam; other women fought and died for the American armed forces in both Gulf Wars. Despite this, few modern societies are yet ready to see their women fighting and dying in war. Most polls taken in the United States, for example, show that war is still considered a man's business.

THE CRADLE OF WOMEN WARRIORS

The place where the greatest number of women warriors has been recorded is Africa. Herodotus described fighting women he saw on his journeys in North Africa, who wore red leather armor and drove chariots. Archeologists in Ethiopia have found bas reliefs showing bow- and spear-wielding women dating to about 170 BC. Members of the Portuguese explorer Vasco da Gama's mid-sixteenth-century expedition along the west coast of Africa described a king who had six thousand armed women soldiers. The Herero of southwest Africa fielded large forces of women fighters: one queen named Kaipkre led a women's army against British slave traders in 1721.

But probably the best-documented women fighters in history are the women warriors of Dahomey, the southern part of what is now Benin, in West Africa. These amazons, as they were called by all Europeans who observed them or had the unsettling experience of opposing them, fought for the kings of Dahomey, in particular Gezu, or Gezo (1818–58), and his son Glele (1858–89), under whom their numbers swelled to around twelve thousand in the mid-nineteenth century.

The women were known as *ahosi*, "the king's wives," but, in most cases, that was in name only, since most Dahomey amazons remained celibate. They were not people you would particularly want to meet in a dark alley: one of the weapons they carried was a two-foot-long razor blade capable of slicing a man in two. Even without weapons they were formidable, as one French soldier found out when a wounded amazon tried to tear out his larynx with her teeth.

It is typical of the place that Dahomey's origins are shrouded in myth—and blood. No one is quite sure how this West African nation got started. The most common explanation is that, in the mid-seventeenth century, Wegbaja, king of a small nation called Abomey, began conquering neighboring states including Allada and Whydah, countries bordering what would later be called the Slave Coast (prime real estate for doing business with European slavers). After killing a rival chief named Dan, Wegbaja was so thrilled he built his palace right over Dan's grave and called it "Danhome," which means, "in the belly of Dan."

The Fon people—the main ethnic group of Dahomey—have an extraordinary oral history that dates back hundreds of years. Once, in the late nineteenth century, when a Dahomean king complained to the French about an incident, he referred casually to something that had occurred two hundred years earlier, as if it had happened yesterday. In this oral record, the amazons first appear as a regiment of elephant hunters working for the king of Dahomey. They would creep up on the animals and then attack in a group, felling the mammoth beasts while inevitably losing some of their number to swinging tusks. Perhaps because of the ferocity and courage they demonstrated, the amazons subsequently became the king's bodyguards.

In the eighteenth century, this palace guard became a regiment or squadron in the king's army. Various European accounts tell how they fought in small wars and trained on the parade grounds of the Dahomean royal palace in the town of Cana. One French traveler in 1777 described "a great number of armed women, forming a sort of square battalion … As they paraded they fired a musket volley … Soon they formed into two lines, and kept up a general fire which was very well executed."

The kings of Dahomey, no doubt sensing the European fascination with the amazons, liked to have these warriors practice drills for visiting French or British dignitaries, as well as stage ferocious mock attacks, in which the amazons would hurl themselves at barricades made of thorns and bushes—the kind of barrier used by most palisaded villages in Africa at the time—and defeat and capture the enemy, who were played by other amazons. Sometimes actual captives were used, in which case they were shot and stabbed.

But for all of the eighteenth century, the amazons numbered 1,500 at most. It was only in the early nineteenth century, following a coup by King Gezu, that they became a force to be reckoned with in West Africa.

KING GEZU'S AMAZONS

In 1818, Gezu overthrew his brother Adandozan and took over the throne of Dahomey. At the time, Dahomey was a totalitarian state run by the godlike figure of the king, who had absolute power of life and death over his subjects. The state depended heavily on the slave trade, but that may not have been the only reason why it sought so many captives in war; another was for human sacrifices. The Fon people believed in direct contact with ancestors who had words of wisdom to provide to the living. Executed captives—usually women and children or injured warriors, who could not be sold as slaves—were first given messages for the dead, and then either beheaded or killed in various draconian ways. A favorite method was to tie a captive in a huge wicker basket and then dump him from a raised platform into a bloodthirsty crowd of Fon, who would then tear the prisoner from limb to limb.

The ready availability of carcasses led to novel uses for human remains. If you've ever seen an old movie where an African kingdom was represented by a king sitting on a crown of skulls, holding a staff made out of a leg bone, it was probably based on Dahomey. Special groups of women boiled the skin off the bones and placed these raw materials in the hands of Dahomean builders, who used them for thrones, platforms, wall-coverings, and the like.

Prior to Gezu's coup, Dahomey had been a tributary kingdom of the far larger

A TRUE AFRICAN QUEEN

One extraordinary African woman warrior was Queen Zinga Mbandi, who was born in the kingdom of Ndongo in Central Africa in the seventeenth century. After the deaths of several male members of her family by her hand, Zinga became Queen of Ndongo. Almost immediately, she was attacked by the Portuguese. She defended herself with both male and female armies, but was defeated, whereupon she marched to the neighboring kingdom of Matamba, took it over, and began an eighteen-year war against the Portuguese. The Dutch, rivals of the Portuguese, became her allies and were able to observe her rule.

One chronicler describes watching her perform a ritual sacrifice of a captive. She dressed in men's clothes and danced in front of her victim, ringing an iron bell. Then she leaped at him, lifted up his arm, and rammed the blade of her sword into his heart. After she cut off his head, she drank his blood.

Zinga had style. She kept a harem of fifty men to satisfy her needs, making some of them wear women's clothing. The Portuguese were unable to defeat her in three small wars in the mid-1600s, until they captured her sister, after which she agreed to make peace in order to secure her sister's freedom. Queen Zinga died at the age of eighty-one. Her last request, which puzzled but was still fulfilled by her court, was to be buried wearing the habit of a Catholic nun, with a crucifix and rosary clutched in her hand.

Yoruba kingdom of Oyo, which spread through most of what is modern-day Nigeria. The Yoruba outnumbered the Fon ten to one; both nations were rivals in the lucrative slave trade, capturing men, women, and children from villages further inland and bringing them to European slavers on the coast.

Gezu, however, decided to refuse to pay tribute to the Yoruba. This meant war, and this war was the probable reason for the expansion of the amazon force, from a small fighting unit to a major component of the Dahomean army. In part, this development occurred of necessity: Dahomey simply did not have the male fighters to be able to stave off an army from the far larger population of the Yoruba.

This stylized 1851 depiction of the warriors of Dahomey got one thing right: the amazons liked to behead their fallen enemies whenever possible.

SELECTION AND TRAINING
In order to be able to fight wars, capture slaves, and execute captives, amazons had to possess a certain toughness and esprit. While these qualities could be instilled through training, it is clear, according to Western accounts, that Gezu's recruiters sought out women who had already displayed assertive or aggressive behavioral traits—mischievous or disobedient servants or daughters, women caught in adultery, even women who nagged their husbands too much. Other amazons were foreign captives whose lives were spared on condition that they fought in the regiment.

The first thing an amazon had to do was to leave her past behind and go to live in the royal palace compound with other women fighters. For many, this was not a difficult thing to do: they were, after all, exchanging a life of hard labor and early death for a chance of glory, although it, too, carried with it the possibility of premature demise, and a bloody one at that.

Another attraction was that amazons were revered in Fon society. When a female warrior walked about the streets, she was preceded by a slave girl ringing a bell, which told men to retreat a certain distance and avert their eyes. If a man so much as glanced at an amazon, it could mean his death, since every amazon was, at least nominally, the wife of the king. One European traveler in the middle of the nineteenth century wrote with some irritation that his journey through a Fon city was slowed down because he "continually met gangs of the amazons with their bells, causing our progress to be a succession of tacks from side to side, instead of making a straight course." On the down side, amazons had to give up all chance of sexual pleasure and motherhood. The king insisted that amazons be celibate and it seems they probably were: given that they were the king's "wives," it meant death for them and their lovers if they were caught.

There is a good deal of European testimony regarding the training of the amazons. The women drilled separately from the male warriors, but just as diligently, practicing marching, maneuvering, shooting, and stabbing. Their dress varied, but generally the amazons wore a short tunic, underneath which was a pair of pants that reached to just above the knee. A belt held the outfit together and carried ball and powder boxes. Most amazons wore caps bearing images of crocodiles—an intimidating symbol of their ferocity.

Fascinatingly, the Dahomeans made scale models of the fortified towns they had defeated in battle. These were used to help recount successful campaigns, often to Europeans, and in training. On a larger scale, the Dahomeans would also reenact successful battles, right down to the order of attack, setbacks, and final victory, when the amazons would drag their "captives" before the king. This of course had a ritual element, but also helped train the women in tactics and instill esprit.

For most of the eighteenth and nineteenth centuries, the favorite weapon of the Dahomean amazons was the flintlock musket (although the fighters received breech-loading and repeating rifles just before their final defeat by the French in 1894), with which they could shoot off a round in thirty seconds, a very decent rate of fire. On one occasion, King Gezu invited an Englishman named Duncan to observe a demonstration of amazon musketry. Armed with long Danish or English rifles loaded with two or three iron balls at a time, the amazons blazed away at a succession of live animal targets, blasting goats and ducks out of existence with startling accuracy.

Despite this, the amazons were probably more feared for their blades. Their basic weapon was a short sword that looked like a cutlass or machete, about twenty inches long and four inches wide. More terrifying were the huge razors that the explorer Richard Burton called "portable guillotines." They were about thirty inches long and came folded into a black wooden handle. At the touch of a hidden spring, the blade sprang out, a little like a modern-day switchblade; the razor was then swung with both hands, to deadly effect.

The amazon corps was organized around specialization in the different categories of weapons: razor wielders, riflewomen, archers, and so on. It came to occupy a central position in the Dahomean army, but retained its own women officers, and answered only to them. The only allegiance amazons owed to any man was to the king.

WAR WITH THE YORUBA
For most of the forty years of his reign, King Gezu was at war either against the Yoruba or against many of the smaller nations that surrounded Dahomey that were allied with the Yoruba. The Yoruba sent delegates to Gezu in the early 1820s, to find out why he hadn't paid his tribute. His response was to behead one of the ambassadors, a clear enough reply. The Yorubans then attacked and Gezu defeated them.

Gezu used the amazons sparingly in these early battles, but, probably because of manpower shortage, he threw large numbers of them into the next campaign, against the Mahi people, allies of the Yoruba. The amazons overran numerous towns. One victory was against the Mahi town of Kenglo, situated on a formidable hill, with cliffs on three sides and a stone rampart on the fourth. Amazon women scaled this rampart and captured the palace. The victory was commemorated by a bas relief in Gezu's palace, showing the women raising a flag in victory. Other bas reliefs showed them beheading their Mahi prisoners.

In 1840, the Dahomean army attacked a larger Mahi trading center called Atakpamé. They were defeated, but had it not been for the amazons, who rallied the army, the defeat would have turned into a rout. Nine years later they attacked the same town again and this time were victorious. There then occurred an intriguing

Women warriors of Dahomey pose with weapons in front of a visiting African king. The amazons also put on such displays for European visitors.

dispute. According to two Englishmen who were present, the amazons and the male troops got into a bitter argument in the presence of King Gezu about who had played the greater role in the victory. An amazon warrior named Akpadume claimed that some male soldiers had wandered off, leaving the amazon flanks exposed to a Mahi attack and that the amazons had had to save the day. Gezu let the two sides bicker for a while before ending the argument—an indication that he knew the value of competition between the soldiers of both sexes.

But it was two epic, though unsuccessful, battles that King Gezu's amazons fought against the Yoruba of the town of Abeokuta that really brought them to the attention of Europeans and, thus, of the wider world. Abeokuta was an unusually large trading town in what is now Nigeria. In the early 1850s, it had a population estimated at fifty thousand, including Anglican Christian missionaries. The Yoruba of Abeokuta, known as the Egba, surprised and defeated the Dahomean army in a battle that resulted in the deaths of numerous amazons and the capture of King Gezu's personal stool and his umbrella, which was hung with magical talismans. This meant war.

Two British officials, consular officer John Beecroft and Royal Navy officer Frederick Forbes, heard that there might be a Dahomean attack on Abeokuta and visited Gezu in his capital city to inquire about this in June of 1850. Gezu advised them to move the missionaries out of Abeokuta. During their visit, the officials heard the amazon women, fired up, singing a song in which they urged Gezu to let them attack the Yoruban town.

The British did not remove their missionaries, and indeed, resolved to fight to defend the city against the Dahomeans. In March of 1851, Gezu set out to attack Abeokuta with a huge force consisting of sixteen thousand soldiers, of whom four thousand were amazons. They faced a formidable challenge: a town ten miles in circumference surrounded by a high earthen wall and a ditch filled with thorn bushes. Abeokuta's forces had fifteen thousand soldiers armed by the British, who watched the attack from a hill within the city—probably the first time Europeans watched a massed attack by the amazons.

The usual Dahomean mode of attack was to travel at night to a village, move up silently on it, and then strike at first light, but in the attack on Abeokuta an over-confident Gezu dispensed with these precautions—an error that would cost him dearly—and attacked in daylight. The women fighters advanced ahead of the men and, according to the British account, simply passed right over the thorn bushes and fearlessly attacked the wall, some women making it over and into the city before being cut down. A fierce battle then raged, but, with the help of their massed fire-power, the Egba were able to force the women to retreat. The Dahomean army lost three thousand soldiers, of which two thousand were amazons—an indication of the ferocity with which the amazons carried forward the attack.

In 1858, Gezu was killed in a skirmish and his son Glele took over. By the time he attacked Abeokuta again, it was 1864. The intervening thirteen years had only increased the anger of the amazons and their desire to avenge their defeat. In February, attempting to catch Abeokuta by surprise, Glele marched his army of twelve thousand, of whom three thousand were amazons, in a wide circle around the city. But the Egba had again been forewarned, and were well prepared, having shored up their defenses and added British light artillery to their firepower.

The Fon army showed up at the walls of the city early one morning, with the amazons singing and dancing, and throwing their rifles from one hand to another in a show of insouciance. Then they attacked, the amazons leading with typical ferocity. Reaching the wall, they fired their muskets right down into the faces of the defenders and even managed to plant a flag on the wall. But this was to be the high water mark of their advance. With superior forces and firepower, the defenders of Abeokuta cut down the Dahomean army. Only four Dahomean soldiers made it into the city; all of them were amazons.

FIGHTING THE FRENCH
Much to their chagrin, the Dahomeans were never able to capture Abeokuta, and in the next thirty years their kingdom would change forever. Almost immediately after this defeat, Glele attacked numerous smaller towns that supported the Egba. In each case he was victorious, taking up to three thousand prisoners at a time, who were either sacrificed or—since the slave trade with Europe had ceased—sold to Arab countries to the north.

However, the Dahomeans began to clash with the French, who were expanding

SONGS OF THE AMAZONS

Although they made up the smaller portion of the Dahomean army, the women warriors were its heart and soul when it came to morale. Through their impressive fighting ability, they not only showed the men that they were their equal, but they also gave them backbone. Another way they stirred up courage was by singing songs they had made up themselves. In 1930, an aging amazon sang this bloodthirsty ditty for some French observers:

> The blood flows,
> You are dead.
> The blood flows,
> We have won.
> The blood flows, it flows, it flows,
> It flows.
> The enemy is no more.

IT'S ALL SHOWBIZ

Once the French began fighting the amazons, it was only a matter of time before impresarios like P. T. Barnun sat up and took notice. A Barnum-sponsored "Dahomean dance troupe," featuring twenty-four "amazons," took Paris by storm in 1891. It turned out that only half of them were from Dahomey, and almost certainly none of these were real amazons, but the military drill "dances" and sham fighting displays they performed to the beat of heavy drums drew thousands. The troupe toured Europe for two years. More recently, television's *Xena: Warrior Princess* has brought fighting women to a (mostly male and mostly adolescent) modern audience—former U.S. Secretary of Defense Madeleine Albright jokingly called Xena "one of my role models." And in the multimillion-dollar business of video games, let's not forget gunslinging British digital character Lara Croft.

their trading operations in the area and building more and more forts. In 1887, Dahomeans attacked a French trading post run by a Senegalese merchant. When they found the French flag there, an amazon beheaded the Senegalese and forced his wife to wrap the head in the flag and take it to King Glele. In December 1889, Glele died and was succeeded by his son, Behanzin. In January 1890, the French Navy moved in on the Dahomean port town of Cotonou. They had previously paid the Dahomeans for the right to operate here, but now began arresting Fon officials and set up a fort.

In response, a Dahomean force including several thousand amazons attacked the town very early on the morning of March 4. The French legionnaires were astounded by the bravery of the women, who tore logs out of the defenders' stockade with their bare hands, in order to shoot through the gaps. A teenage amazon beheaded a French gunner, and it was here that a *tirailleur*—a native soldier fighting for the French—had his throat bitten by an amazon. The battle lasted for hours, until French gunboats lying offshore began pouring fire into the ranks of the attackers and the Dahomeans were forced to retreat, leaving hundreds of dead and wounded behind.

In another battle a few months later, the Dahomeans attacked a French column near the village of Atchoupa. This time the Dahomeans had the French out in the open and actually outnumbered them, but the advanced firepower of the French gave them the edge. The legionnaires and their native auxiliaries were armed with breech-loading rifles which could fire more rapidly than the weapons of the amazons, and were accurate at a greater distance: three hundred yards as opposed to the one hundred yards of the Dahomean muskets. The result was a slaughter of the Dahomeans.

Shortly thereafter, a peace treaty was signed on terms advantageous to the French, but peace did not last for long. In 1892, the second and last Franco-Dahomean war began after Fon warriors raided French-controlled villages. Seizing upon this provocation, the French set out to destroy the Fon. They had already built up their forces and blockaded the coast of the country to keep the Dahomeans from receiving any arms from smugglers. On September 14, French forces at the fort of Dogba were attacked, the first of twenty-three separate engagements over a seven-week period that would spell the utter destruction of the Dahomean army and kingdom. The amazons were at the front of all these attacks, and died literally on the points of French bayonets.

Increasingly, the French found that their amazon attackers were drunk. Sometimes, touring a battlefield after a skirmish, French soldiers would find amazons passed out in holes or behind bushes, reeking of gin and brandy. Alcohol had long been handed out to Dahomean soldiers before battle, but this excessive indulgence seemed to indicate a falling apart of amazon esprit in the face of almost certain destruction by the French. The French soldiers, for their part, were fascinated by the amazons. They called them "black virgins" whose fingernails were painted "red with the blood of victims." There is a strange sexual element in the French descriptions of amazon corpses that survive from the time: "a little amazon, quite young, almost pretty, her big eyes open, glazed by a short agony," and "two seemed very young, fourteen or fifteen years old; they were very beautiful, strongly muscled, but finely, too." The French were now using Lebel small-bore rifles, which fired bullets with great velocity, making tiny entrance wounds but ripping apart the women's bodies. These wounds, too, were described with loving attention to detail.

The last battle took place at a village near Cana, the old royal capital. The Dahomeans were routed by a French bayonet charge—a tactic that consistently beat the amazons, who did not use bayonets—and the war ended. According to French estimates, possibly fifty or sixty unwounded amazons remained out of about twelve hundred.

THE LAST AMAZON?

After the war, the surviving amazons, who may have numbered about three hundred, including those recovering from wounds, attempted to assimilate back into village life. One scholar has traced the histories of several of them and found that, like almost any combat veteran, man or woman, they had trouble adjusting to peacetime. Some married and had children, but most remained single. One elderly amazon was seen by a British traveler hovering near the tomb of Glele in 1934. She was described to him as "the last amazon." But yet another traveler, eight years later, met a different woman also said to be the last amazon. And one African scholar, Amelie Degbelo, met an ancient woman in 1978 who said she had been an amazon. She claimed to be 102 years old. Degbelo believed her.

Some writers have suggested that the way to truly instill an amazon fighting spirit in the armed forces of the present day would be to create all-women units. So far, no modern army has tried this. American and NATO forces have integrated women into their ranks and many women, especially American women in the Gulf Wars, have seen combat as part of mixed units. In Israel's 1948 war, women were in mixed combat units that blew up bridges and saw fierce fighting against the Lebanese in Jerusalem. Almost immediately thereafter, a women's army corp was created—but specifically exempted from combat. Only in 2003 were women soldiers integrated into Israeli combat units, a move that met with protests from some male Orthodox Jewish soldiers.

Yet one of the reasons why the Dahomey amazons were so successful was because of their cohesion as all-female regiments, who lived, worked, ate, and fought together. Perhaps the best examples of all-female units in modern times were the three regiments of the Russian Air Force who saw combat against the Germans on the Eastern Front during World War II. Some of the women flew Yakolev fighters, or Yaks, some short range bombers, and some flew night-bombing missions over German positions using ancient biplanes. Up against modern German aircraft like Stukas and Messerschmitts, the Russian women were extraordinarily successful.

The amazons are gone now. But their legacy will live on, as long as people are able to accept that, far from being a myth, the woman warrior is a fact of history—and likely to be a fact of the future.

BRINGING THE IRISH WAR TO AMERICA: THE STORY OF JOHN DEVOY

I N 1800, THE POPULATION OF IRELAND WAS ABOUT FOUR AND A HALF MILLION people. By the summer of 1845, it was eight million, five million of whom were small farmers dependent on one single crop for their very existence: the potato. The summer of 1845 was unusually fine and hot, with hardly any rain until August, when the skies opened up with torrential downpours. A Dublin newspaper, the *Freeman's Journal*, wrote on August 20 that, despite the rain, the potato crop was proving to be bountiful. But then on September 11, 1845, the *Journal* wrote a report that now echoes through history. The potatoes being harvested in the north of Ireland were afflicted with a "cholera," their roots "all blasted and unfit for the use of man or beast."

No one knew what caused the potato plague that spread all over Ireland. Excess rain was blamed, electricity from the thunderstorms, even the new "guano manure" (see p. 236) in use in certain parts of the country. The culprit, undiagnosed at the time, was a killer fungus called *Phytophthora infestans*, which would proceed to play havoc with the Irish potato crop for the next four years. Other crops were raised, of course, as well as livestock, and the fungus did not affect these. But the British landlords who ran the country assumed that all Irish peasants needed for subsistence was the potato, and took their payment in grains and sheep. If the Irish used these to feed themselves, they were ousted from their plots of land. If they paid the rent, they starved to death.

Between 1845 and 1849, up to one million Irish died. Aside from a few ineffectual gestures, like importing Indian corn from America to feed the starving, the British government did little. The same *Freeman's Journal* wrote in 1847: "Do we live under a regular or responsible government? Is there justice or humanity in the world that such things could be, in the middle of the nineteenth century, and within twelve hours' reach of the opulence, grandeur, and power of a court and capital [London] the first upon the Earth?"

Those Irish who did not die left the country at a rate of more than a quarter million a year. By 1851, more than a million and a half had emigrated, about a million of those to the United States. These included people who had watched their families die and been ousted from their homes and wandered roads covered with the corpses of old women and children. When they arrived in America they brought with them a profound bitterness against the British government, which awaited a spark to set it off.

That spark would be John Devoy, an Irish rebel who worked tirelessly to make sure the flame of resentment did not go out in subsequent generations of Irish Americans and that, as they grew wealthy and powerful in the United States, these people would never forget a struggle taking place three thousand miles across the ocean on the small island that had been the home of their ancestors.

John Devoy was to live in America from 1871 to his death in 1928—nearly sixty years of tempestuous history both in Ireland and in the United States. He transformed himself from a man cracking rocks in a grim British prison to a politician who advised presidents such as William Henry Harrison and influenced historical figures like Charles Stewart Parnell. He lived modestly, however, either alone or with a sister in New York and Chicago tenements, and after his death was overshadowed by other, more flamboyant Irishmen of the same period—by Parnell and Eamon de Valera, by Jeremiah O'Donovan Rossa and Michael O'Connell. Consequently, most people today have never heard of him. Yet through his work, hundreds of thousands of dollars flowed from Irish-American pockets to the battle for independence in Ireland, resulting, finally, in a free, if partitioned, Irish Republic after 1921. As a result of his efforts, the struggle for freedom in Ireland was brought to the forefront of American consciousness and stayed there, right through the twentieth century, through the bloody fighting in Northern Ireland in the 1960s and '70s, and up to the present day.

John Devoy's travels took him from Ireland, through Europe and North Africa, and, like millions of other Irish people, to a new home in North America.

THE YOUNG REBEL The Irish had been battling for their freedom from the English for at least two hundred years before John Devoy was born in a little cottage in County Kildare, in 1842. Irish rebels had fought the English in the great rebellion of 1641 and in the Jacobite War of 1689–92. In the rebellion of 1798, an army of Irish peasants was led by an Anglo-Irish lawyer named Wolfe Tone, who made league with the French, and appeared to have a very good chance of overthrowing the British until a storm destroyed the French Army as it sailed to invade Ireland.

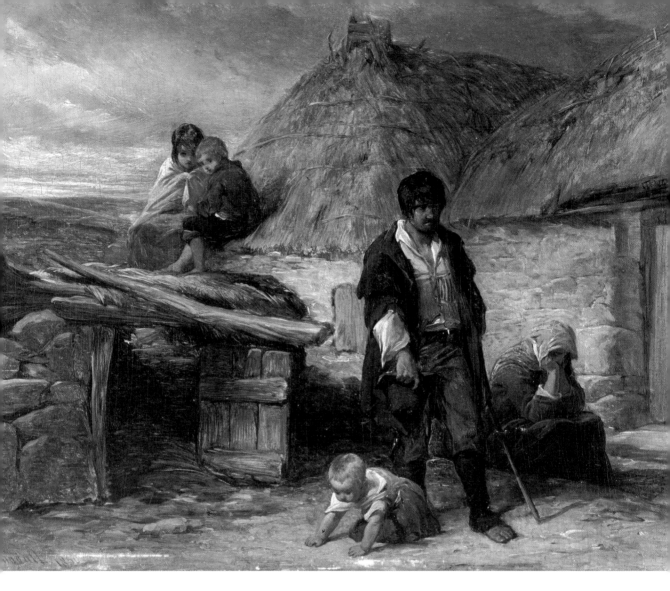

The rebellion of 1798 was a bloody and gruesome fight in which an estimated forty thousand Irish died, many of them tortured to death by the British, although the rebels committed their share of atrocities as well. This was an important rebellion in the history of the country and in John Devoy's personal history, since his great-uncle Johnny Dunne fought in it and he grew up hearing stories of Dunne's narrow escapes from the British.

John Devoy was one of eight children of William and Elizabeth Devoy, who worked a small plot of land belonging to the English Lord Mayo. William was a devoted Irish nationalist, a follower of "the Liberator," Daniel O'Connell, a famed orator who held peaceful "Monster Meetings" of hundreds of thousands of people in the Irish countryside. These meetings helped force Britain to repeal the Penal Laws, which barred Roman Catholics from election to the House of Commons and forbade the Irish from passing land on to a single heir, forcing them to split up farms between many children and thus shrinking the size of the plots, in many cases, down to less than the roughly three acres needed to sustain a family. This meant that when the famine hit, the Irish were even more vulnerable.

Like so many thousands of others during the famine, William and Elizabeth Devoy were forced off their land. They took their family to Dublin, where, through his political connections, William found work as a brewery clerk. John was sent to an elementary school; in his first recorded act of rebellion, he refused to sing "God Save the Queen," and was beaten by the headmaster. When the beatings continued on subsequent days, John turned on his tormentor, attacked him, and was expelled.

By the time he was sixteen, in 1858, Devoy had enrolled in Gaelic classes held in the editorial offices of a radical newspaper—a political act since the language was outlawed by the British. The next year he dropped out of school and began working at the brewery where his father was employed, but work became secondary to politics in his life. He joined the National Petition Movement, which collected half a million signatures to demand self-determination for the Irish. More importantly for his future as a radical, he became a member of the clandestine Irish Republican Brotherhood (IRB), the group that would evolve into the modern Irish Republican Army, or IRA.

THE FENIAN BROTHERHOOD

The IRB, began on St. Patrick's Day, 1858, when a group of friends, brought together by a man named James Stephens, gathered in a small room in Dublin and swore a solemn oath to "renounce all allegiance to the Queen of England and to take arms and fight … to make Ireland an Independent Democratic Republic." Stephens was a veteran of the so-called Rising of 1848, a short-lived rebellion against the British during the height of the famine. Now, he and his fellows would plot armed revolt against the British oppressors.

Shortly after forming the IRB, Stephens went to America to visit a comrade in arms from the 1848 rebellion, a Gaelic scholar named John O'Mahony. Together they formed an American twin to the IRB, named by O'Mahony the Fenian Brotherhood, after the ancient and legendary ancient Irish warriors known as the Fianna. Both secret organizations were divided into groups called "circles" of up to eight hundred men. Supposedly, only one man from each circle was to know one other man. Since the Fenians in America could operate openly, this was the public name given to both organizations.

An IRB recruiter came to John Devoy's Gaelic class and secretly swore in Devoy and his friend James J. O'Kelly. Devoy was now nineteen years old. His father, a moderate, nonviolent nationalist, was so upset about his son becoming a Fenian that he threatened to disown John if he didn't quit. In typical fashion, John not only did not quit, but he decided to join the French Foreign Legion, where he thought he could get some military training. This act was typical of John Devoy, for his entire life was marked by his stubbornness and his firmness of will, which were both admired and abhorred by friends and enemies alike.

A picture of him taken a few years later, when he was twenty-three, shows a man with an unusually wide brow, short-cropped dark hair, and a very firm jaw. He was only five feet six, but square-shouldered: his picture gives the impression of pugilistic strength and a low center of gravity. His eyes seem to stare off in the distance, like those of a dreamer, but Devoy looks this way in his photographs because he was severely myopic—by the time he reached his seventies, he could only see shadows.

A SUCCESSFUL INFILTRATOR

Although he could not speak a word of French, Devoy made his way across the English Channel to Paris, where he went to the Ministry of War and somehow talked his way into the Foreign Legion, being sworn in on May 2, 1861. He was sent to Algeria, where, to his disappointment, he saw no military action, but did learn discipline and a fair amount of French. He was discharged—or possibly deserted, the record is not clear—a year later, and returned home, where he met James Stephens. Very quickly, this determined young man, who could now claim some knowledge of military affairs, became Stephens's assistant, helping him prepare for an extraordinary moment: when Fenians on both sides of the Atlantic would rise to attack the British in Ireland.

An invasion of Ireland by American Irish may now seem like a far-fetched notion, but it was not at the time. The American Fenians under Mahony had raised as much as two hundred thousand dollars for the Irish cause and Fenians openly toured military camps on both sides during the Civil War, seeking war-hardened veterans who would fight in the coming battle. Stephens claimed to have an army totaling thirty thousand soldiers in Ireland and America. A date was set for the uprising in late 1865, and Stephens gave Devoy a job that would make him legendary among the Fenians: he became the chief Fenian organizer within the British Army.

Donning a British uniform, Devoy would pretend to be a soldier and make his way into barracks to persuade Irishmen who were in the British Army to secretly swear an oath to the Fenians. This derring-do was typical of Devoy who, all his life, was willing to take risks when he thought the outcome would be worth it. Highly persuasive, he moved through the barracks like a union organizer in a factory, making numerous converts to the Fenian cause, who would work as a fifth column when the rebellion started. "Out of a British garrison [in Ireland] of twenty-five thousand," Devoy wrote in his memoirs much later, "some seven thousand were sworn Fenians."

The British finally identified Devoy and put a price on his head. In the meantime, Stephens, who had already been arrested by the British once and escaped, kept putting off the date of the uprising, fearful that he did not have the support he needed. By the time he finally decided to move, an informing American Civil War veteran in the employ of the British, had moved into the organization. Wholesale arrests were made, including a massive crackdown within the British Army in Ireland. It is a sign of how deeply Devoy had infiltrated the British regiments in the country that most suspected collaborators were simply shipped to garrison duty in distant parts of the Empire—the British government realized that it was impossible, and would in any event be a public relations disaster, to arrest everybody.

The five Fenian revolutionaries who were released from British prisons and exiled to New York aboard the steamship *Cuba*. John Devoy, notable for his broad forehead, is at far left.

On February 22, 1866, Devoy, in the company of several deserted soldiers and IRB men, was cornered by police and soldiers in the back room of a Dublin pub. He was indicted for treason and, a year later, pled guilty and was sentenced to twenty years in Millbank Prison, in London. With Devoy in Millbank, briefly, were seven other Fenians—Irish soldiers, most recruited by Devoy—who soon found themselves shipped to a notorious penal colony in Fremantle, in Western Australia. Devoy saw them leave Millbank in 1867; he was certain he would never see them alive again.

RELEASED INTO EXILE
John Devoy remained in Millbank Prison, on the banks of the River Thames, within earshot of Big Ben, until January of 1869. He lived in a nine-by-eight-foot whitewashed cell, with a plank bed. He and the other Fenians were forbidden to speak to each other, but

THE IRISH INVADE CANADA

It sounds like a headline in a newspaper mocked up as a practical joke, but in fact, this is what happened in the spring of 1866. The idea for an Irish invasion of Canada had been dreamed up in February of that year, when a dissident branch of the American Fenian Brotherhood met for a public convention in Pittsburgh, Pennsylvania. Having broken off from John O'Mahony's more conservative wing, this fiery group resoundingly passed a resolution to collect funds to build up an army to attack British-ruled Canada. No effort was made to keep the plan secret—the results of the convention were reported in newspapers all across the United States—yet the U.S. government, under President Andrew Johnson, looked the other way. The British, after all, had supported the Confederates during the Civil War, and Confederate raiders had even attacked the U.S. from Canada. The British took the threat seriously, as did Canada, but Johnson did nothing. Wild rumors began to circulate in Canada—that the Fenians had one hundred thousand troops, that they would attack along a thousand-mile front. In the end, all the Fenians could muster was about seven thousand troops under the command of John O'Neill, a former Civil War officer, like many of his troops (in fact, many of the soldiers under Fenian command still wore their Union uniforms). On May 31, 1866, O'Neill and eight hundred of his men crossed the Niagara River not far from Buffalo, New York, and landed in Canada. They took over the small village of Fort Eire, putting up American and green Fenian flags, and then moved on to the town of Ridgeway. There, on June 2, they defeated a force of about eight hundred Canadian volunteers, killing twelve and wounding forty, and incurring losses of eight Fenians killed and twenty wounded. At this point, the U.S. government finally roused itself and sent Civil War heroes Ulysses S. Grant and General George Meade to upstate New York. They stopped a reinforcing army of three thousand Fenians, cut off O'Neill's supply lines, and forced him to retreat to the United States, where he was placed under arrest. His men were allowed to return home, however, and even given free passage by the sympathetic leader of the Irish political machine at Tammany Hall, Boss Tweed. In the end, the invasion was a public relations disaster for the Fenians, who appeared ridiculous and divided. However, it did have the unintended consequence of speeding up the creation of the Dominion of Canada in 1867.

communicated by knocking on their cell walls, much as downed American flyers did in North Vietnamese prisons a century later. Devoy tried numerous times to escape, and lost weight on the bread-and-water punishment rations he was given each time he was caught. After three years, he was transferred to Chatham, a prison reserved for truly unrepentant Fenians like Devoy. Chatham was notorious for repetitious labor: not only breaking rock, but darning socks, one pair after another, for sale in England. And the diet, if anything, was worse than at Millbank.

Then, to his surprise, he and four other Fenians—Jeremiah O'Donovan Rossa, Charles O'Connell, John McClure, and Henry Mulleda—received a letter from the office of British Prime Minister William Gladstone. In it, they were offered a choice: stay in prison or pick permanent exile in America. Gladstone was responding to vehement protests by the people of Ireland, who had read reports of the horrendous prison conditions in Millbank and Chatham and other prisons like them. He was willing to exile Devoy and his ilk—if they promised never to come back again. From the British point of view, this turned out to be a very bad decision indeed.

All five men chose America, naturally, and, still in a state of shock, found themselves in January 1871 crossing the Atlantic aboard a Cunard Line steamship, the *Cuba*, heading for New York City. Devoy and his fellow prisoners arrived in New York City to a rousing, Fenian-promoted welcome. Once on shore, the prisoners were given a parade and welcomed warmly by the powerful Irish-dominated Tammany Hall political machine that ran the city. Celebrations went on for two weeks, culminating in an official reception in Washington, D.C., where the men met President Ulysses S. Grant. The former Commander in Chief of the Army of the Potomac, Grant had still not forgiven the British for supporting the Confederacy during the Civil War; this little show of welcome for the Fenians was meant to humiliate the Queen Victoria and her ministers.

Everyone, in other words, had an agenda, and Devoy did too. His body might have been exiled from Ireland, but his mind and spirit weren't. He was still a revolutionary, and he had come to America to start a revolution.

CLAN NA GAEL Despite the show of welcome put on by the Fenians, the brotherhood in America had fallen on hard times. In one of the splits that would bedevil the Irish movement, a more radical Fenian group had broken away from founder John O'Mahony and begun to prepare itself for war—with Canada. In one of the strangest episodes in American history, an army of Fenians, many of them Civil War veterans, invaded Canada, near Niagara Falls, in June of 1866, and captured the Canadian town of Ridgeway. The purpose was to strike a blow at Britain by striking Canada. But the invasion was quashed and the Fenians humiliated. Episodes like this tore the brotherhood apart and significantly reduced its power.

When Devoy first arrived in New York, he took a job as a Wall Street clerk, and found a room in a tenement hotel in the notoriously violent Five Points district of lower Manhattan, so vividly depicted in Martin Scorsese's movie *The Gangs of New York*. He also joined a little-known Irish organization called the Clan na Gael, the "Family of the Irish," which had been founded by an Irish American newspaperman some five years earlier. The Clan was a small, supersecretive organization, but Devoy saw it as an opportunity to build a power base of his own, away from the squabbles of the Fenians. He then cast about for an opportunity to publicize the Irish cause in America.

In early 1874, one fell right into his lap. Devoy was contacted by one of the Fenians with whom he had been in Millbank Prison, a man named James Wilson. Wilson was one of the soldiers who had been transported to Australia for life. He had somehow seen a newspaper clipping of Devoy's triumphant arrival in America and had smuggled out a painful letter that began: "Dear friend ... this is a voice from the tomb." Wilson begged Devoy for rescue, although he suggested using "your tongue and pen ... your brain and intellect" to lead a protest to influence a release. Instead, Devoy formulated an audacious plan: he would hire a ship, have it sailed to Australia, and help the men escape their bondage. The Catalpa Affair, as the rescue is now known, would be the making of John Devoy in America.

THE CATALPA AFFAIR

After months of persuasion, Devoy managed to get the Clan na Gael to give him the money to buy an old whaling ship, have it refurbished, and hire a crew. Working incessantly and in the deepest secrecy, he went to New Bedford, found the ship he was looking for—the *Catalpa*—and hired a mainly Portuguese crew with an American captain, the cocky twenty-nine-year-old George Anthony.

The *Catalpa* sailed for Western Australia in April 1875; in the meantime, Devoy sent a Fenian named John Breslin, then living in California, to Australia to pose as an Irish American looking for mining opportunities. Breslin arrived in Fremantle well ahead of the *Catalpa*, and seemingly, aroused no interest as he poked around the town (staying, somewhat amusingly, at the Emerald Isle Hotel) and watched the prisoners coming and going in work parties around the harbor. The convicts, it turned out, were not closely watched—with only unpopulated scrub or ocean every way they turned, there was really nowhere for them to run.

Devoy remained in New York, where he received intermittent telegrams from Breslin and waited anxiously. In the meantime, he worked on various Clan na Gael schemes, such as the one proposed by a fellow Irishman to get "a half dozen real good [Irish American] fellows" appointed to West Point Military Academy, where these "moles," as we might term them today, could be trained as future officers of an Irish Republican army. The plan came to nothing.

The *Catalpa* finally arrived in March 1876, almost a year after it had set out. Breslin and Captain Anthony made contact, and Breslin in turn passed a secret message to the Fenians while they were out on a work party. At the appointed hour, the jubilant Fenians threw their pickaxs aside and raced for the wagon Breslin had rented. He drove the horses pell-mell to the beach, where Anthony himself was waiting with a lifeboat.

After about five hours rowing, they reached the *Catalpa*, set full sails, and raced away; unfortunately, smoke puffs on the horizon showed that they were being followed by a British military gunboat whose steam could easily outrun the *Catalpa's* sails. Anthony hove to, and waited for the British. The gunboat's captain demanded the return of the prisoners. Anthony told him there were none aboard, whereupon the British officer threatened to open fire on the *Catalpa*. And here Anthony endeared himself to thousands of Irish Americans who later saw the story played out in newspapers around the country: "We sail under the protection of the flag of the United States," he shouted over his megaphone. "Fire on us and you fire on the American flag."

The British captain backed down and the *Catalpa* went on its way. When the Irish in America and Ireland found out about the rescue that summer, they exploded into a frenzy of celebration. "Soon the world will know what you have brought about," an old friend of Devoy wrote him. But Devoy was less interested in being known to the world than persuading the Irish in America to help bring an end to British rule in Ireland. And now, because of the plan he had hatched, he was the leader of the most powerful group of exiles in the country.

The extraordinary Fenian submarine, dreamed up and built by John Holland and funded by John Devoy, became a model for future U.S. Navy submarines.

THE FENIAN SUBMARINE

Shortly after the *Catalpa* rescue, John Devoy was approached by John Holland, an Irish-born former Christian Brother who taught elementary school in New Jersey. Holland was obsessed with the possibility of using submarine warfare against Britain. His brother, a Clan na Gael member, had told him to speak to Devoy. Holland showed Devoy a few sketches and convinced Devoy that a well-built submarine would be able to destroy Royal Navy warships almost at will. Impressed, Devoy dispensed Clan funds totaling almost $60,000 to Holland to build a prototype, which he did quite openly, watched by the New York press as well as British agents, in an ironworks on the west side of Manhattan.

In the spring of 1881, Holland and an assistant spent three hours underwater in the sub, which the press called the *Fenian Ram*. By July, Holland was taking the vessel for regular trips under New York Harbor, surfacing to frighten and entertain local shipping. The British government made increasingly urgent requests to the American State Department to put a stop to this "Fenian Torpedo Boat." Finally, the State Department confiscated the boat, and the *Fenian Ram* never fired a shot in anger.

But the American government was so impressed with Holland's work that they bought his designs and had him build them two more subs. And, in tribute, the first U.S. Navy submarine was named the USS *Holland*.

A NEW DEPARTURE By 1878, Devoy was a reporter for the *New York Herald*, a job secured for him by his old IRB colleague James J. O'Kelly, also a New York newspaperman. He still lived in a cheap hotel and worked tirelessly for the cause. But he had changed. He had not given up on the idea of armed confrontation with Great Britain and in fact had recently helped establish, within the Clan, a General Military Board to organize and train an Irish militia in America for a possible invasion of Ireland. But he strongly disagreed with the tactics advocated by his old fellow prisoner Jeremiah O'Donovan Rossa, who wanted to use money from what he called the Clan's "Skirmishing Fund"—Devoy later changed the name to the more sedate "Nationalist Fund"—to plan a series of terrorist dynamite attacks on Great Britain itself.

Rossa's dynamite campaign was not Devoy's idea of the future. He reasoned that civilian bloodshed would only alienate an American Irish community who, at this point, saw Devoy and his fellow revolutionaries in the same light as America's own Revolutionary War heroes. Now two million strong, the Irish Americans needed an issue to grab hold of, with which to empathize. The issue, Devoy decided, would be Irish land reform.

In 1877 and again in 1879, the Irish potato crop failed, due to extremely wet summers, and the Irish were once again evicted from their farms in droves by their English landlords. Famine was prevented only by an enormous relief operation mounted both in America and Britain. An Irish Fenian named Michael Davitt, who had lost his right arm as a twelve-year-old working in an English industrial mill, seized upon the issue of organizing the Irish to demand rent reductions, an end to evictions and, eventually, Davitt hoped, transfer of land from the British to the Irish. Davitt also managed to enlist to the cause Charles Stewart Parnell, a wealthy young Irish member of the British Parliament (whose mother was American). Parnell began to make fiery speeches in Parliament, defending the rights of Irish farmers.

Davitt then went to America in 1878, where he looked up John Devoy and asked him to take a stand on land reform—something Devoy had already decided to do. Calling the fight for land a "New Departure" for his movement, Devoy took Davitt on the road in America, giving speeches to Irish groups in New York, Boston, Philadelphia, and Chicago. He met with Irish politicians, teachers, and priests. He hammered home the need for money to carry on the "Land War," as they termed it, that Parnell and others were already fomenting in Britain.

Devoy had previously told intimates that he thought the Clan na Gael (which had approximately ten thousand members at its peak) was too small and too secretive a group. He wanted to take the Irish independence movement out of what he called "the ratholes of conspiracy" and into the sunlight of the American mainstream. This he now did with a vengeance.

"The land question is the question of questions in Ireland," Devoy said, "and the one upon which the national party must speak out in the strongest terms." Instead of talking about the establishment of an Irish republic, he was speaking about the "curse" of the landlord system, which brought misery to so many Irish. American Irish audiences, especially the wealthy, middle-class ones, responded to this and began to contribute thousands of dollars.

In March of 1879, Devoy took the extraordinary step of sneaking back into Ireland in order to see for himself the conditions there and to check the strength of the IRB membership; for despite his championing of land reform, he wanted to be able to count on an Irish Army. Once in Ireland, Devoy secretly visited his father and then, ducking constables and British detectives, attended numerous land reform rallies, met with clandestine IRB circles, and watched as the rain continued to fall and the crops began to fail. Davitt and Parnell now formed the Irish Land League, with Parnell as its president. And Parnell, at Devoy's invitation and supported by his not inconsiderable organizational skills, went on a speaking trip through the United States in the fall of 1879.

When he landed in New York, Parnell announced that he would be raising money not only for the Land League, but for famine relief as well, since Irish farmers were in even worse straits now that the cold weather was closing in. Traveling with Parnell were his three sisters and mother, who gave interviews and met with women's groups throughout his visit. Parnell made his first speech at Madison Square Garden, where he spoke to ten thousand wildly enthusiastic Irish Americans. He proclaimed that the Irish Americans were "virtually the arbiters of the Irish question"—the ones who, through their money and influence, could bring about Irish independence.

Land League supporters demonstrating at a forced sale of cattle in Ireland. The strategy of the Land League was to refuse to pay rent to British landlords.

Charles Steward Parnell, painted by Sydney Prior Hall in 1892. Despite his forced resignation and tragically early death, Parnell is remembered as an effective politician and great patriot.

Parnell was subsequently invited to speak to the U.S. House of Representatives and then undertook a sixty-two-city tour of America, taking in Midwestern cities such as Des Moines, Chicago, Cincinnati, and Columbus, as well as cities in the Northeast. By the time he left in March 1880, Parnell had raised hundreds of thousands of dollars for the cause and he and Devoy had established the American Land League.

Devoy took control of the American Land League, as he knew that it would be a powerful tool for victory against the British. Despite the fact that the organization was officially set up to funnel money to the Irish Land League in Dublin, Devoy saw to it that all contributions went to a priest, Father Lawrence Walsh, who in turn gave the money to IRB members in Ireland. Walsh's involvement would presage the unofficial involvement of the Catholic Church in the twentieth-century independence movement, when contributions to the IRA were funneled through certain parishes.

A year after Parnell left, the American Land League had 1,500 chapters throughout America. Within two years, it had sent an astonishing $500,000 to Ireland. Just as important, it had raised the level of the debate about "the Irish question." Congressmen rose on the floor of the House of Representatives demanding to know what the U.S. government was going to do about Ireland (the government, playing its typical game with the British, seemed to sympathize, but did nothing). James Redpath, a famous American abolitionist, returned from a trip to Ireland to proclaim that the Irish were every bit as enslaved as blacks had been pre-Civil War.

SHORT-TERM FAILURE, LONG-TERM SUCCESS

In 1881, the Land Act was passed in the British Parliament, mitigating some of the worst landlord excesses. The following year, however, Parnell was arrested for speaking out against the British government and the Land League was suppressed. As part of a deal subsequently made by Parnell and the government of William Gladstone, Parnell was released and brought the so-called Land War to a halt. Instead, he began lobbying for home rule, but not in the form of an independent Irish Republic, just a degree of self-determination for Ireland within the United Kingdom.

For Devoy in America, this was disastrous. Some Clan members reviled Parnell as a collaborator and Devoy with him. Once again, the movement splintered, with a Chicago faction of the Clan battling for more violent attacks on Britain, and Devoy himself was caught up in these factional battles. In 1887, a plot to blow up Queen Victoria during her Diamond Jubilee celebration was foiled by the British police, and forged letters linking Parnell with violent militants were used to discredit the politician. Parnell recovered from this, but his reputation was destroyed—and the Irish home rule movement along with it—by the revelation of his long-term adulterous affair (which bore three children) with Kitty O'Shea, the wife of a colleague. Worn-out by stress, Parnell died suddenly at the age of forty-five, in 1891.

The legacy of the Land League lived on, however—even longer than John Devoy. His career was by no means over after Parnell's death. He built the Clan back up to ten thousand members by 1900, so that it remained a potent force in American politics over the next twenty years. In 1904, at the age of sixty-one, he started the *Gaelic-American*, a newspaper which, although it had a circulation of only thirty thousand, was influential in the Irish American community. He continued to lobby ceaselessly for the formation of an Irish Republic; during the World War I, he conspired with Sir Roger Casement to bring arms from Germany via submarine to supply the volunteers during the 1916 Easter Uprising. With the rest of the Irish, he mourned the deaths by firing squad of the poets and intellectuals who had led the revolt—his former assistant, Tom Clarke, was among the first to be executed. When the Irish Free State was finally established in 1921, and a violent civil war broke out that saw Irishmen killing Irishmen, Devoy was seventy-eight years old and almost deaf and blind, yet still fiery enough to speak out against President Eamon de Valera, whom he considered a traitor to the Irish cause and blamed for the death of the young Irish leader Michael Collins.

It was the Land League that was Devoy's most lasting and significant contribution to the cause. It inspired ordinary Irish Americans, soon to be generations removed from their "homeland," to think of the rebellion on this small island as *their* rebellion, *their* war of independence. It reached right through the community, from workers to presidents. Although the American Land League had been dissolved by the beginning of the twentieth century, the nationalist dream it fostered entered what the writer Andrew Greeley has called "the preconsciousness" of modern Irish Americans. Many historians believe that Irish American opposition to the U.S. League of Nations proposed by President Woodrow Wilson after World War I was decisive in quashing it. Wilson, whom an aging but still powerful John Devoy called "the meanest man who ever filled the office of the President of the United States," had spent too much political capital supporting Great Britain.

As historian Eric Foner has said, the Land League "was the first nationalist organization to unite the Irish American community. The land issue had an impact no other could rival." For decades after, whenever the IRA war against the British peaked, hats would be passed in Irish-American bars in Irish neighborhoods of New York and Boston, collecting funds for the IRA. And even more people gave to the American Ireland Fund, which funneled money to relief activities, particularly in war-torn Belfast. It's likely that many of the Americans contributing money to the Irish cause in the 1970s did not understand that the battle in Northern Ireland was in some ways quite different from the battle that created the Irish Free State in 1921; to them it was simply a matter of continuing the fight against the British—life and liberty in the "ould country" was still at stake.

After making one last symbolic visit to Ireland—his first as a free man in over half a century—John Devoy died on a visit to Atlantic City in 1928, at the age of eighty. He had outlived all his contemporaries, including every man who had been with him in Millbank Prison. Many other Irish patriots left a lasting legacy in Ireland, but Devoy's truest legacy was in America, where he showed generations of Irish Americans that the cause of freedom in that small nation three thousand miles away across the Atlantic Ocean mattered and was worth their steadfast support and their sacrifices.

THE JUBILEE PLOT

One of John Devoy's most unfortunate actions was his recruitment to the Fenian cause of a strange adventurer named F. F. Millen, who turned out to be a British informant. Millen was a decidedly unsavory character who had left Ireland to fight in Mexico's War of Independence. He was initially recruited to join James Stephens's attempted revolution in Ireland. When this failed, Millen escaped back to New York, then offered his services to the British as a spy.

Millen was still working for the British in 1887, when he and Jeremiah O'Donovan Rossa planned a dynamite attack on a fireworks display being held to celebrate Queen Victoria's Diamond Jubilee, an attack that they hoped would eliminate the queen and her cabinet. The bombers were thwarted, and several given life in jail.

As far as history knew, for the next hundred years, that was the story. But, as recounted in his fascinating 2004 book *Fenian Fire*, Christy Campbell went deep into British classified archives to discover that in fact Britain's police and intelligence services had asked Millen to come up with the bomb plot, which the spy did, quickly convincing the volatile Rossa to attack. This was all part of a quite byzantine British intelligence scheme to discredit Charles Stewart Parnell by linking him with Irish terrorists. After the plot and the attempted smear failed, the British helped Millen escape back to New York. But when it looked as if he might talk, they murdered him.

QUEEN MIN
AND THE BATTLE TO SAVE KOREA

O NE OF THE FEW WESTERNERS TO MEET THE KOREAN QUEEN MYEONGSEONG Hwanghu, or Queen Min, as history knows her, was the famous British travel writer Isabella Bird Bishop, who was granted an audience with the queen in January of 1895, only ten months before Min's famously savage murder. Bishop, known for the accuracy of her impressions, wrote that the queen was "a very nice-looking, slender woman with glossy, raven-black hair and very pale skin." She went on to say that "her eyes were cold and keen, and the general impression [she gave was] one of brilliant intelligence."

This is one of the few descriptions we have of Min. There are no verified photos of the queen, and few images which we can say with any certainty bear any kind of likeness to her. In fact, a great deal about Queen Min remains uncertain. We don't even know what name she went by. Myeongseong Hwanghu was a posthumous name given to her so that the living might speak the name of the dead. Her birth name may have been Cha Young, which means "Purple Beauty," but no one knows for sure. After she became queen, she was simply called "Her Palace Majesty."

Despite this, her fame, or notoriety, endures. Some say that Queen Min was prepared to sell her country out to foreigners, notably the Chinese and the Russians, so that her clan, the Mins, could stay in power and grow wealthier. Others see her as a neglected symbol of early Korean nationalism, a woman bent on helping Korea progress into the twentieth century, who was assassinated by the Japanese because she was a threat to their imperialistic designs on her country.

Either way, her untimely death in 1895 cast a long shadow over the history of the twentieth century in East Asia. Had her plans been successful, Japan's ambitions might have been stymied, Korea might have been opened up to Western culture sooner, and World War II may have turned out quite differently. But Queen Min died in the dark of an early October morning, the true facts of her death obscured by the mists that floated through the pine forest outside Seoul's Gyungbok Palace—and the mists that, for centuries, kept Korea hidden from the world's view.

THE HERMIT KINGDOM

Korea is a mountainous country roughly the size of Great Britain. Geographically, it is a peninsula, but it has acted throughout history as if it wished it were an island nation, like its arch-nemesis, Japan. The first Dutch sailors to be shipwrecked in Korea, during the fifteenth century, found that it was all they could do to escape with their lives, so hostile were the locals.

A British naval vessel dropped anchor on some Korean islands in 1816, but the captain found that "their chief anxiety was to get rid of us as soon as possible." Another traveler of about the same time wrote that the Koreans deflected every inquiry with one question: "What time do you think to depart?"

Koreans learned from long experience that xenophobia had its advantages. For centuries, their peninsula was the object of the attentions of the Chinese and the Japanese. During the so-called Three Kingdom period of Korea's history, roughly the first millennium AD, the country was divided into three separate entities, the northernmost state being heavily influenced by the Chinese, the southern two interacting with the western Japanese islands.

In AD 918, the great warrior Wang Ko unified these three nations into one—Koryo, as he called it, meaning "high mountains and sparkling water"—from which comes the modern name of Korea. Wang Ko's dynasty lasted until 1392, when it was replaced by the Chosen dynasty, which would endure until 1910, but was really brought to an end the morning the knives flashed over Queen Min's bed.

Korea in 1895, surrounded by the imperial powers of China, Russia, and Japan, all of which had designs on the peninsula.

Despite its isolation, Korean culture advanced rapidly. By the mid-thirteenth century, far in advance of Europe, Korea had invented movable-type printing. Borrowing from the Arabs and Chinese, Korean scientists created astrological clocks, improved forms of gunpowder and artillery, and even an encyclopedia of medical science.

Yet, at the same time, Korea was, and still is, a country where superstition is a powerful force. Sorcerers and witches abound in its history: spells are cast, nature is alive with spirits, and ghosts routinely walk the land. Even in the nineteenth century, some thought Queen Min a witch.

THE MURDEROUS PRINCE SADO

After Queen Min, probably the most famous royal member of the Chosen dynasty was Prince Sado, an heir to the throne born in 1735. If the word "sadist" hadn't been derived from the Marquis de Sade, it could have come from the prince. By the time he was twenty-three years old, he had begun to murder court eunuchs just for the sheer pleasure of it: he loved decapitating them and once came into his wife's bedroom carrying a dripping head. He told his father, King Yongjo, that he killed because his father did not love him, something Yongjo, not having the benefit of Freudian theory, did not understand. The king did nothing to stop the killings—after all, the Chosen royalty were above the law.

Sado, who had hallucinations and would today probably be diagnosed as schizophrenic, went on to murder shamans, physicians, and anyone who brought him bad news. He also raped Buddhist nuns. By 1760, he was going into nearby towns in disguise and killing people at random.

Finally, the king had had enough. One day, he ordered Sado to commit suicide. Sado repeatedly tried to strangle himself, but kept on failing. His father yelled, "Aren't you ever going to kill yourself?" Growing impatient, Yongjo had his son placed in a large rice chest, which was left in a courtyard, in the broiling sun. Thirteen days later, the mad Sado finally expired.

CHILD KINGS AND DOWAGER QUEENS

In the nineteenth century, the Hermit Kingdom's isolation was the result of a deliberate policy of exclusionism. Korea continued to rely on China as an ally, but refused to have anything to do with its old enemy Japan, and generally avoided contact with any European power or the burgeoning sea forces of the United States. This was a policy that might have worked had the Chosen rulers remained as powerful as they were in the sixteenth century, when they had beaten off a Japanese invasion, but the beginning of the nineteenth century coincided with the decline of the Chosens.

In 1800, the ten-year-old King Sunjo ascended to the throne, beginning an era that came to be known as the period of "in-law" government, during which Korea was ruled by child kings and powerful dowager queens and their close-knit clans—in the first half of the century, the Andong Kims held sway. It seemed to matter little who the king was—often it was a distant relative of the ruling family—as long as the clan could easily control him.

As well as controlling the regent, the Andong Kims embezzled funds from the treasury, placed family members in the most powerful government positions, and executed or drove into exile their rivals. This and an apparent disdain for the Korean people resulted in numerous peasant revolts, all of them violently put down. Catholicism had taken root in Korea during the reign of a relatively benign late-eighteenth-century Chosen ruler, but from 1801 onward severe anti-Catholic persecutions also took place.

The Chosen dynasty was determined that foreign influences would not be allowed into Korea. In a sense this is understandable, given the way foreigners behaved. In 1866, for example, a heavily armed American merchant ship, the *General Sherman*, sailed up the Taedong River determined to trade, ignoring requests from the

Opposite: No verified likenesses of Queen Min exist, but this portrait may show the young queen. It seems to capture her fierce and elusive spirit.

King Kojong, husband of Queen Min. Some argue that Kojong's failure to oppose the Japanese, or at least form alliances against them, helped bring about the death of his wife.

Koreans that they leave. An angry crowd gathered on the riverbank and the crew of the *General Sherman* fired on them. The Koreans then killed the entire American crew and burned the ship—which is probably what the Americans would have done had a Korean ship sailed up the Potomac, blithely firing away at U.S. citizens.

In response, America began what was known at the time as the "Little War with the Heathens," in which two warships and a landing force of about seven hundred marines sailed to Korea and engaged Korean troops in a fierce battle on Kanghwa Island, north of present-day Inchon. About six hundred Koreans died, but the Americans, not knowing quite what to do with themselves, and having exacted a punishment that would play well in the popular press at home, simply turned around and sailed back across the Pacific.

PRINCE OF THE GREAT HOUSE

In 1864, King Cholchong died suddenly, without heirs. Queen Kim, his wife, wanted to appoint the new king, but another dowager, Queen Cho, wife of a former king, schemed to put the eleven-year-old son of Prince Hungson on the throne. This boy became King Kojong; his father, the prince, became the all-powerful regent with the title Taewongun, or "Prince of the Great House." Almost certainly, Queen Cho had engineered this move to place her clan in ascendancy over the Andong Kims, and for a time this strategy worked.

The Taewongun essentially ruled the country from 1866 to 1873, before Kojong came of age. Despite the fact that he had a reputation as a drunk and wastrel, he became a firm ruler with a sense of history, who sought to bring back the glory days of the early centuries of the dynasty. He began to rebuild Gyungbok Palace in Seoul, the city that had been Korea's capital since the beginning of the Chosen dynasty. The former home of the Chosen kings, the palace had been almost completely destroyed in fighting with the Japanese in the sixteenth century. But to finance the rebuilding, the Taewongun levied heavy taxes, which made him highly unpopular with the poor, and extorted so-called "voluntary offerings" from the well-to-do, which made him an enemy of the rich, as well. He also increased Korea's isolationism just as other countries in Asia were opening up their harbors for trade with the West.

The Taewongun turned out to be a brilliant regent—and not a bad artist, for he developed quite a reputation as a calligrapher and a delicate painter of orchids—but he made a crucial error in 1866, when he chose as a wife for his thirteen-year-old son the future Queen Min of the Min clan. She was fifteen at the time of her marriage. Both her parents had died when she was eight, which suited the Taewongun, as it lessened her ability to form a power base. The wedding was a sumptuous royal festival. The slender Min could barely support the wig that usually adorned the head of royal brides—an attendant had to stand behind her to hold it up.

The young queen was stepping into a highly charged and complex situation. On the one hand, she was the wife of the future ruler of the country. On the other, she was not from a ruling clan and was also subjected to some of the restrictions traditionally imposed on women in Korea. Women were kept rigidly secluded, and could not even go outside until about eight in the evening, when a bell tolled to signal that men should clear the streets, after which women were allowed to walk abroad for three or four hours. Queen Min had to endure other restrictions, too. Her comings and goings within Gyungbok Palace were continually monitored. Her face was hidden from almost all men. Even the queen's male Korean doctors were forced to take her pulse by tying a string around her wrist and then retreating to another room to feel her lifeblood pulsing through the thread. She even had to place her tongue through a slit in a screen for a physician to examine it.

Despite this, Min was a formidable presence, and the Taewongun sensed it quickly, writing that she was "a woman of great determination and much poise of manner." Noting that the young Queen read a good deal—usually history, and in particular histories of the royal families of China—the Taewongun said, sarcastically: "She evidently aspires to be a doctor of letters; look out for her." This was prescient, for the Taewongun and the queen soon became rivals, then deadly enemies.

For five years after her wedding, the queen was unable to give birth. During this period of infertility, the Taewongun provided another woman for the king, a court lady, by whom he did have a son. Then, on November 9, 1871, Queen Min gave birth to a son. But he died within three days. Maddened with grief, Min invited hundreds of shamans to the palace to help the spirit of her child reach the other world. Thousands of Buddhist monks prayed for the child's soul for weeks without stopping. Next, Queen Min—and is it any wonder there were some who thought her a sorceress?—ordered the shamans and diviners to work their magic to discover who had killed her son and heir. The shamans claimed that their divining had told them that it was the fault of the Taewongun, that he had poisoned her child. And so Queen Min decided to have her revenge.

THE QUEEN'S REVENGE Queen Min was just twenty years old at the time and yet, from what can be gleaned from the record, began to act like a veteran of political intrigue. She had probably realized early that her husband, King Kojong, was afraid of his father, the Taewongun, yet longed to step out from his shadow and rule the country himself. Seeking to undermine her father-in-law, she now brought together members of the Min clan, and, with the permission of her husband, put them in strategic positions of power in the government. She even managed to secretly gain the support of her husband's neglected older half brother—whom the Taewongun was apparently fond of referring to by a Korean phrase that means "the blockhead." Later, he would act as a spy for her in his father's court.

Then, in October of 1873, a Confucian scholar and philosopher named Cho'oe Ik-hyon wrote a letter to King Kojong in which he proclaimed that the Taewongun was "without virtue." Whether this was prearranged by the king and Queen Min is not known, but the king had previously received the philosopher and appointed him to a high position in his court. Predictably, the Taewongun protested, and even sent assassins to try to kill the man. King Kojong quickly sent Cho'oe into flight, but not before the philosopher wrote one more letter, in which he said: "the Taewongun is the father of the king, and it is the law to respect him, but he can't rule the country forever. The king has grown up and must take the throne himself." In a society in which scholars like Cho'oe were held in high repute—they were akin to those biblical prophets to whose advice and chidings ancient kings cocked an attentive ear—these letters had an extraordinary impact.

On November 5, the king announced that he was taking over the throne. Later that afternoon, the entrance to the Taewongun's palace was bricked over. It's not known who gave the command to do this, but it seemed very much like the work of an angry Queen. The ousted regent moved to his house in Seoul to lick his wounds. A week later, there was an explosion in the queen's sleeping quarters that caused a fire, although no one was hurt. Soon after, a beautiful box was delivered to Min Sung Ho, the queen's closest relative. The box exploded when opened, killing Min and his mother. Queen Min had no way to prove it—and in any event, by Korean law, the father of a king could not be arrested—but she was sure that the Taewongun was taking his own revenge.

THE HERMIT KINGDOM NO MORE

Korea could not resist the future forever. In the 1860s, Japan, which had grown in military might under the Meiji government, had sent representatives to Korea claiming that, due to wars that occurred even before written records existed, Korea was, in essence, a tributary state of Japan, and therefore needed to pay Japan large sums of money every year. Not surprisingly, the Koreans—then still under the control of the Taewongun—had rejected this demand, arguing that, since the only true emperor was in China, the Japanese king held the same rank as the Korean king, and there could be no question whatsoever of paying tribute. Not only that, but—what time did the Japanese envoy think to depart?

The Japanese renewed their demands in 1873. On this occasion, the Koreans noted with amusement that the Japanese representatives were dressed completely in Western clothing. People dressed in this fashion should not even be considered Japanese, a Korean prefect told them (and being Japanese was to be already pretty low in Korean eyes). Once again, the Japanese were forcibly removed from of the country.

The following year, after Kojong's accession, Cho'oe Ik-hyon and fifty scholars, each carrying an ax, marched to Gyungbok Palace to convey their feelings on the matter. Telling Kojong that the Japanese were "wild animals that only crave material goods and are totally ignorant of human morality," they begged the king to keep them out of the country and offered the use of their axes to cut off Japanese heads.

Unfortunately, Kojong decided—against the wishes of Queen Min, who was no fan of the Japanese—that the best way to contain Japan was to cooperate with it, and so he signed a treaty in 1874, giving the Japanese trading rights. This was all the Japanese needed. In 1875, they deliberately sailed a gunship, the *Unyo*, into an area that the Koreans had declared off-limits to foreign ships. When Korean shore batteries opened up near the island of Kanghwa, the *Unyo* destroyed them, and then went on to attack a fort in Inchon. Shortly thereafter, the Japanese landed a force of marines and took over Kangwha, and then threatened a far larger invasion.

Despite being urged by Queen Min and some advisers to fight the Japanese, King Kojong again signed a treaty with them in early 1876, known as the Treaty of Kanghwa, which marked the beginning of the end of Korea's status as Hermit Kingdom—and which would ultimately lead to Japan's annexation of Korea in 1910. The Japanese demanded and received rights to establish five new Korean ports, to survey Korean waters, to trade without interference, and to have Japanese nationals in Korea be subject only to Japanese law. The Koreans received nothing.

Once change came to Korea, it proceeded rapidly. In 1882, what the United States called "The Corean-American Treaty of Amity and Commerce" was signed at Inchon. Between 1882 and 1888, similar treaties followed with Germany, Italy, Russia, Great Britain, and Austria-Hungary. All of these were trade agreements that gave these countries consular representation, fixed tariffs, and port concessions in Korea. In return, Korea *thought* it would gain protection against Japan. But this did not occur.

Historians are uncertain about how much influence Queen Min had over her husband at this point; but by signing agreements with so many foreign powers so quickly after the treaty with Japan, it seems apparent that Min, who strongly disliked the Japanese, was trying to protect her country. Meanwhile, she and King Kojong were busily modernizing their country. After the signing of the Corean-American Treaty, American companies were invited in, and Seoul became the first East Asian city to have water, electricity, telephones, and trolley cars simultaneously. By 1900, there would be one hundred American firms doing business in Seoul.

THE TONGHAK REBELLION

By 1884, Queen Min had given birth to a son, Prince Chok, who would become the last king of the Chosen dynasty, and her Min clan had taken over much of the government, which increased her power in the court immeasurably. People knew that in many matters, while King Kojong gave the orders, Queen Min formulated them. Unfortunately, like the Andong Kims, the Mins were corrupt, venal, and vindictive in power. At one point in 1884, a short-lived revolt of the Korean military ousted the king and queen from power and they were forced to take refuge, ironically enough, in the Japanese embassy.

A much more serious revolt ensued in 1894: the Tonghak, or "Eastern Learning" movement. This was a revolt of peasants, led by village schoolteachers, who could no longer bear the burden of being taxed on almost everything—there were land taxes, fallow-field taxes, cloth taxes, taxes for the military, taxes on having a baby, even a tax on dying—and began attacking tax collectors and government officials. The movement was tinged with isolationism. A favorite slogan was "Drive out the Japanese dwarfs and the Western barbarians and praise righteousness." Thousands of peasants rose up against the government of Seoul, won victories in the field, and took over a provincial capital.

ROYAL FASHION

Isabella Bird Bishop did not spend all her time commenting on Queen Min's intellect. Much of her description was devoted to the forty-four-year-old queen's clothing. One of the queen's outfits was described in elaborate detail:

> She wore a very handsome, very full and very long skirt of mazarine blue brocade, heavily pleated, with the waist under the arms, and a full-sleeved bodice of crimson and blue brocade, clasped at the throat by a coral rosette, and girdled by six crimson and blue cords, each clasped with a coral rosette. Her head dress was a crownless black silk cap edged with fur, pointed over the brow, and with a coral rose and a full red tassel in front, and jeweled aigrettes on either side. Her shoes were of the same brocade as her dress. As soon as she began to speak, and especially when she became interested in conversation, her face lighted up into something very like beauty.

Overleaf: An 1895 woodblock print showing a naval encounter during the Sino-Japanese War.

Urged on by Queen Min, King Kojong asked the Chinese for help—a miscalculation, unfortunately. For when the Chinese entered the war, the Japanese did too, claiming that the Chinese presence was a pretext for a land grab. Ignoring Kojong's protests, both countries began to feed troops into Korea, which became a battleground between the Chinese and Japanese. Japan won victory after victory. The peasants launched a major attack against Japan near the end of 1894—some sources put peasant forces at as many as one hundred thousand—but they were no match for Japan's modern army, which crushed them and left their bodies all over the countryside.

The Sino-Japanese War lasted a year, ending in total defeat for the Chinese. Their relationship with Korea, and whatever help they might have been able to provide, was over. Japan was now the power to be reckoned with in East Asia.

MIN'S RUSSIAN GAMBLE
The Japanese now imposed a constitution and parliament on Korea, peopling the latter with Japanese sympathizers. It wasn't quite a puppet government, however, and many Koreans who had been oppressed by the Min clan welcomed its arrival. Queen Min, naturally, did not. To make matters worse, the Japanese now began to conspire with her old enemy, the Taewongun. He did not like the Japanese, but the Japanese knew, and counted on the fact, that he hated his daughter-in-law even more. Isabella Bird Bishop met the Taewongun around the same time she met Queen Min, later recording her impression of the seventy-five-year-old former regent: "Able, rapacious, and unscrupulous [...] his footsteps have always been bloodstained ... I was much impressed by the vitality and energy of his expression, his keen glance, and the vigor of his movements, even though he is an old man."

By the time Isabella Bird Bishop paid her visit, Queen Min had less than a year to live. An American missionary with medical training, named Lilias Underwood, had been allowed to act as the queen's doctor on occasion, and she described her as "slightly pale and quite thin, with somewhat sharp features and brilliant piercing eyes. She did not strike me at first sight as being beautiful, but no one could help reading force, intellect, and strength of character in that face."

In the twenty years during which Queen Min had helped rule Korea, the country had changed dramatically. In some respects, as with the modernization of the nation's infrastructure, it was for the better, but in others, such as the pernicious influence of Min corruption, it was not. Although Min had urged her husband to resist Japanese expansionism, her clan's misdeeds had helped facilitate the takeover by foreigners. The queen realized that the danger of the Japanese had to be countered. She also understood that, in the wake of the Sino-Japanese War, the Russians were alarmed by the spread of Japanese influence. So she began to cultivate close contacts with the Russians, asking members of the Russian legation to meet with her, attracting Russian students to Korea to study, encouraging the military to visit, and importing Russian architects and engineers. It was also around this time, shortly before her death, that the queen began meeting with foreign missionaries, such as Underwood and Bishop. It was as if the captive queen was starting to show her face to the world. But it was too late.

OPERATION FOX HUNT

By the fall of 1895, Min had become a seemingly immovable obstacle to Japanese expansion, and the Japanese decided that extreme measures were required. Their ambassador to Korea, Miura Goro, secretly began planning her assassination. The arrogance of this decision to murder the sovereign queen of a foreign nation is striking, although not unheard of—one need only look to the U.S.-backed assassination of Salvador Allende of Chile. But the way in which the Japanese carried out the assassination was unparalleled in its brutality and misogyny.

Calling the plot "Operation Fox Hunt," Miura put together a mixed force of Japanese and Korean assassins to attack the queen's quarters at Gyungbok Palace early in the morning. Another squad was sent to collect the Taewongun, to have him ready to take over the government. At 5:30 a.m., on the morning of October 8, the operation began. Perhaps about fifty killers—Miura may even have been among them—attacked the palace, with much shouting and shooting. Most of the Korean guards ran away; the majority of the remainder were Japanese and they simply let the assassins go by.

The killers first came to the king's sleeping quarters and took him captive, then went to the queen's sleeping area. According to an eyewitness report from Sergei Shabatin, a Russian architect who worked within the queen's palace: "Having been seized by soldiers myself, when I was standing in the courtyard I saw ten to twelve court ladies being dragged by the hair before they were thrown out the window. Not a single lady let out a cry to break the complete silence. In the last moments … I stood in the courtyard, five Japanese men … dragged out one court lady by her hair." This last woman was apparently Queen Min.

For the next hundred years, it was believed that the Queen was then stabbed to death outside the palace and taken to a nearby pine forest, where her body was burned. However, documents recently uncovered by researchers in the records office of Japan's Ministry of Foreign Affairs paint a fuller, more brutal picture. Most damning was a report which was written by one of the killers, Isujuka Eijoh.

Isujuka's report states that the killing was planned by Miura, the Japanese ambassador, right down to the last detail, and that the Japanese troops guarding the palace were more directly involved in the murders of the queen and her ladies than previously understood. It goes on to describe how "We rushed deep into the royal chamber and dragged out the queen. We stabbed her several times and stripped her naked. We examined her genitals [to dishonor her]." The queen was then taken to a nearby chamber and her body placed on display so that several of the foreigners present, especially the Russians, would know that she was dead. Then, according to Isujuka, "we poured oil on her body and set her on fire." Then the assassins took the body to the forest, where they burned it again and scattered the ashes.

At 9:30 a.m., a telegram was sent to the Japanese Army Chief of Staff which read "Queen dead and king safe." Operation Fox Hunt had been a success.

PUBLIC APOLOGIES

In 2005, two Japanese descendants of the assassins who killed Queen Min returned to Korea to pay homage to the tomb of the murdered queen. One of them was an eighty-four-year-old doctor, Tasumi Kawano, the grandson of Shigeaki Kunitomo, a key figure in the assassination. Another was a woman named Keiko Ieiri, the wife of the grandson of another assassin. The two were part of a group of descendants tracked down by a society in Japan seeking to redress the wrong of Queen Min's death. Their visit was paid for by a Korean television station.

Dr. Kawano claimed that when he was young he used to play with Queen Min's key bag, which his grandfather had brought back from Korea. His grandfather had died before he was born, but the murder was talked about in the family as a patriotic act. Dr. Kawano's grandfather had been right in the center of the assassination, apparently pointing his sword at Queen Min and saying, "Are you the empress?"

Although he expected to be a focus of hostility in Korea, Dr. Kawano thought it was important to come to the country and make amends for the actions of his grandfather. When he visited the grave of Queen Min, he told a reporter: "I want to get on my knees and apologize that my grandfather did not understand the truth about Empress Myeongseong. She was simply using Russia for Korea's national interest."

Dressed in traditional uniforms, soldiers at Seoul's Gyungbok Palace, home of the Chosen dynasty and site of Queen Min's assassination, perform the Changing of the Guard.

JAPAN UNLEASHED After the death of Queen Min, King Kojong and his son were unofficially held prisoner by the Japanese and the Taewongun until February. To add insult to injury, the Taewongun tried in the immediate aftermath of the assassination to force the king to sign a decree robbing the queen posthumously of any royal rank. The king refused. On February 11, 1896, he and his son fled to the Russian embassy, dressed as palace women, and stayed there almost a year.

Initially, the Japanese denied any involvement in the crime; but finally, following international protests, the government punished a few of the minor participants. However, a show trial held at Hiroshima acquitted Miura and others for "lack of evidence." In the meantime, with Kojong practically a prisoner in the Russian embassy, Moscow and Tokyo agreed to carve up Korea, in an odd foreshadowing of the country's contemporary divisions. Although they did not quite finalize their agreement, it was decided that a buffer zone should be created between Russian forces that had entered the country and the Japanese—in other words, a demilitarized zone like the one in place today.

In 1897, King Kojong, emboldened by Russian support, returned to his throne and declared himself not just king but emperor. Seemingly unhinged, he forced subjects to bow to him as many as nine times. He also spent "a fortune" having the remains of Queen Min properly buried, even though they consisted of just one finger bone. None of the foreign observers could understand why such a mourning procession—which included 5,000 soldiers, 650 police, 4,000 lanterns, hundreds of scrolls testifying to the queen's virtue, and giant wooden horses intended for her use in the afterlife—was necessary. But it appeared that the king, however ineffectual he had been, had loved his queen, and also wanted to reassert her royal rank, in part to spite his father. Her funeral procession was a way of telling the world that Min was truly a queen.

The death of Queen Min ended any possibility of an alliance with Russia that might have protected Korea from Japan. After Japan defeated Russia in the 1904–05 Russo-Japanese War, Korea was annexed by Japan, and the Chosen dynasty, by then headed by Min's son, Chok, was brought to an end.

Japan's ambitions in East Asia then went unchecked. The only major power not involved in World War I, Japan concentrated on colonizing Korea and stationing a large army there. It became the first invasion force for the Japanese thrust into northern China in the 1930s, which in turn prompted a confrontation with Western powers and the spread of World War II to the Pacific region. During the war, Koreans died by the thousands—it is a little-known fact that over ten thousand captive Korean laborers perished at Hiroshima and Nagasaki.

Had Min succeeded in her efforts and the Russians gained control of Korea, they might have been able to block Japanese expansion. A Korea controlled by the Russians during World War II would have had a powerful effect on Pacific Rim history in numerous ways—placing a check on Japan in her ambitions against China, for instance, but also extending the Iron Curtain around the whole of Korea immediately after the war.

In Korea, starting in the 1990s, there has been a resurgence of interest in Queen Min. A musical called *The Last Empress* portrays her as a heroine fighting the Japanese and her father-in-law, the Taewongun, as a villain. Television documentaries have been made about the queen and the new evidence about her death. Today, in some circles, Min is seen not only as a nationalist patriot, but as a beautiful and moral woman. That isn't quite right; in reality, Queen Min stood for the power of the royal throne and a dying way of life. But she fought ferociously to achieve her aims in a society in which women were extremely limited by conventions.

THE EXTERMINATION OF THE HERERO: THE FIRST MODERN GENOCIDE

I N 1944, AS THE NAZI ATROCITIES AGAINST THE JEWS WERE REACHING A horrifying peak, a new word entered the English language: genocide. The word was coined by Ralph Lemkin, the Polish-born scholar and adviser to the U.S. War Ministry, who saw what was happening to the Jews and Gypsies in Nazi Germany at the time and felt that the phrase "mass murder" was inadequate to describe the situation, and that, as he put it, "new conceptions require new terminology." In his book *Axis Rule in Occupied Europe*, Lemkin put together words from two different languages: the Greek *genos*, meaning "race" or "tribe," and the Latin suffix *-cide*, "to kill," to create a word that defined a coordinated plan for "the destruction of an ethnic group."

But the Nazi "Final Solution" wasn't the first example of genocide in history—nor the first in that century of slaughter—and sadly it wouldn't be the last. It was not even the first time that the Germans had perpetrated such a crime against another race.

Between the years 1904 and 1907, in the colony of German Southwest Africa, now known as Namibia, the Germans, in the words of the historian Thomas Pakenham, "turned a small war into a great catastrophe." Under the lunatic iron hand of General Lothar von Trotha—whose very name reeks of monocle and riding crop—German forces herded the people of the indigenous Herero tribe into the arid wastes of the Omaheke Desert and refused to let them return. They built forts along a three-hundred mile front to keep them out, poisoned waterholes, and pushed them back into the desert like cattle. Whenever a few women and children managed to straggle out of the sandy bush, there were scenes like this one, reported by a translator traveling with the German army:

On our return journey, we again halted at Hamakari. There, near a hut, we saw an old Herero woman of about fifty or sixty years digging in the ground for wild onions. Von Trotha and his staff were present. A soldier named Konig jumped off his horse and shot the woman through the forehead at point-blank range. Before he shot her, he said, "I am going to kill you." She simply looked up and said, "I thank you."

In this fashion, sixty thousand Africans, mainly the Herero people and their southerly neighbors and old enemies, the Hottentots (or Nama, as they were also known), were exterminated.

Scholarly debates still go on as to whether this qualifies officially as genocide—some scholars say that a massacre is not a genocide unless the death toll surpasses sixty thousand and that in this case the figures were anyhow inflated. However, most definitions of genocide focus on *intent*. In their seminal 1990 work *The History and Sociology of Genocide*, Frank Chalk and Kurt Jonassohn write: "Genocide is ... one-sided mass killing in which a state or other authority intends to destroy a group as that group and membership in it are defined by the perpetrator." And this was certainly the case in German Southwest Africa. The Herero were killed because they refused to become slaves and because they had something the Germans wanted—grazing land—but also because they were considered to be subhuman— "baboons," as German soldiers and settlers routinely called them. This same pattern of dehumanization is quite familiar in the slaughters of the Armenians, the Jews, the Bosnians, the Cambodians, the Tutsi of Rwanda.

In the end, quibbling over the definition of the word "genocide" is merely a distraction. What matters today is that we keep these stories alive—horrifying though they may be—and learn from them.

The colony of German Southwest Africa took shape toward the end of the nineteenth century, after the arrival of a small group of German traders in the 1880s.

BEFORE THE GERMANS
Life wasn't simple before the Germans came to southwestern Africa in the early 1880s, but at least the people who lived there were free. The Herero lived in what is the present-day country of Namibia, in a land so dry that, initially, no major European power was interested in colonizing it. One early German traveler said of the coastline: "Everything looked so dead, so bleak, so deserted ...".

There were no perennial rivers, only ones that flowed, perhaps, twenty times a year. If you landed on the coast—and it was hard to land, because there was only one natural harbor in eight hundred miles of coastline—and you wanted to bring cargo inland, you first had to traverse the hostile Namib Desert, seventy-five miles across and inhabited only by a few "Bushmen," who had long since adapted to a land that receives less than one inch of water yearly. Once you got across the desert, you reached the central plateau, essentially a vast, semiarid grazing area. And if you traversed the plateau, you found yourself in the Omaheke Desert, an offshoot of the vast Kalahari Desert to the east.

For several hundred years before the arrival of Europeans, the Herero had inhabited the central plateau. Their life, and love, was cattle—the Herero language contains over a thousand words to describe just the physical appearance of cattle. According to Herero creation myths, cattle were given to humans by God. The whole point of the Herero existence was to take care of cattle and breed more of them. Though they occasionally sold or traded their cattle, Herero did not eat the animals, except to draw blood to mix with milk and wild berries. When a cow died, it was as if a member of the family had passed away.

The Herero repeatedly moved their homes to find better grazing land, which they shared as a communal asset. The population was divided into nine tribes, which were in turn subdivided into lesser units. By the time the Germans arrived, there were perhaps eighty thousand Herero in all. Travelers were impressed by the Herero, in ways both good and bad. They were described as tall—often over six feet—

A CENTURY OF SLAUGHTER

In 1948, the United Nations attempted to refine Ralph Lemkin's definition of genocide. The UN Genocide Convention decided that genocide was any act committed with intent to destroy, in whole or part, a national, ethnic, racial, or religious group. It also asserted that genocide normally included "imposing measures to prevent births within the [victim] group" (such as the Nazis' attempts to sterilize members of groups they considered undesirable). Though scholars still argue over the precise definition of the term, the following are widely accepted as the major genocides of the twentieth century:

ARMENIA, 1915–23: Roughly one million Armenians were murdered by the Ottoman Turkish government during and following a mass deportation (see p. 296).

UKRAINE, 1932–33: Three to four million peasants starved to death in the Ukraine after the Soviet Union seized the entire 1932 crop in response to Ukrainian rebellions against Stalin's rule.

NAZI GERMANY, 1939–45: The Nazis were responsible for the deliberate extermination of an estimated five to six million Jews and approximately 250,000 to 500,000 Gypsies.

INDONESIA, 1965–66: About half a million members of the Indonesian Communist Party were massacred by the army and paramilitary government forces.

CAMBODIA, 1976–79: After the fall of Cambodia to the Khmer Rouge, about eight million people were placed in "reeducation camps." About 1.8 million of these people were shot, starved, beaten, or worked to death.

RWANDA, 1994: The Hutu people of Rwanda killed half a million members of the rival Tutsi ethnic group. Another half a million people subsequently died of starvation and disease.

---

and handsome. They were also, as one observer wrote, "exceedingly filthy in their habits … the exhalation hovering about them is disgusting." They were brave, but could be cruel: if a man was caught stealing cattle, the Herero routinely tortured him before cutting his throat.

By the middle of the nineteenth century, the Herero had, to some extent, been Christianized, due to the influence of missionaries who had moved in after the first European hunters had arrived in the early 1800s. The Herero's rivals for the central plateau, the Hottentot people, who lived just to the south, where the plateau rolled down into arid steppes, were Christianized as well, mainly through the auspices of the Dutch Reform Church. Beginning in about 1830, the Herero and Hottentots fought a war over cattle grazing land that raged up and down the plateau for decades. They used guns sold to them, in some cases, by missionaries, and raided each other's cattle herds.

One thing these conflicts had done was to give each people more of a sense of national identity. The Herero were led by one chief, Maharero, whose son would lead the resistance against the Germans twenty years later. The leader of the Hottentots was an extraordinary figure named Hendrik Witbooi, a brilliant warrior who was also so fanatical a Christian that, when his daughter had killed an illegitimate child because she had feared her father's wrath, he ordered her put to death (her life was saved at the last minute by missionaries).

The Herero and the Hottentots were still fighting when the Germans arrived to change the entire equation.

THE ACCIDENTAL COLONY
Because of the near-constant warfare and relatively inhospitable conditions, southwestern Africa was not generally seen by Europeans as a favorable location for settlement; but there were some who wanted to try their luck. By the early 1880s, a small number of German traders and settlers had arrived in the region. There were probably no more than fifty of them, but that still made them the predominant European force there. One of them was a trader named Adolf Lüderitz, who had his eye on the grazing land of the central plateau. He was a man with good political connections, and managed to gain the ear of Otto von Bismarck, the German Chancellor. Bismarck was not a believer in colonization, but for some reason—and various theories have been suggested as to why—he agreed to give Lüderitz imperial protection if the trader managed to acquire land and create a safe harbor on the coast.

Lüderitz managed to do both, before drowning accidentally in 1884. His work was carried on by other traders, who bought land from the Herero with marks and rifles. After that came agents of the German government, who signed "treaties" with various Herero chieftains. To the Africans, it did not seem like a bad deal at all. In return for simply agreeing that Germany could "protect" them, the Herero chiefs received money and status and continued their pastoral life, as always. Everyone signed up, except for Hendrik Witbooi, who continued to fight the Herero and resist the Germans.

Under the new South African Imperial Commissioner, Dr. Ernst Göring (the father of Nazi leader Hermann Göring), who arrived in April 1885, the Germans spent the next several years strengthening the colony. The somewhat inept Göring was replaced in 1889 by Captain Curt von François, a military man, who arrived with twenty-one soldiers. By 1892, more German settlers had arrived and were becoming firmly entrenched. For better or for worse, Southwest Africa was now, officially, a German colony.

In 1892, the last war between the Herero and Hottentots ended, mainly because Hendrik Witbooi realized that the real threat to his land was not his traditional enemy, but the Germans. Still unwilling to sign a peace treaty, he begged the Herero to turn on the foreign intruders. He even sent a letter, written in his archaic Dutch, to an English magistrate in a neighboring colony, complaining that "the German ... makes no requests according to truth and justice and asks no permission of a chief. He introduces laws into the land ... [which] are entirely impossible, untenable, unbelievable, unbearable, unmerciful, and unfeeling."

But at this point, the Herero had been taken over by the young Samuel Maharero, son of the old chief, and Maharero was cooperating with the Germans. They were paying him two thousand marks a year to keep peace in his tribe, and had even, helpfully, executed two Herero who were his rivals for the chiefdom. With Witbooi now isolated, von François saw that he had an opportunity to get rid of him, once and for all. He attacked and shelled Witbooi's camp, killing fifty women and children.

But Witbooi escaped with his men into the night, then swung around behind the German forces and made off with their horses. This left the Germans unable to advance; meanwhile, Witbooi and his men ranged far and wide over the southern

German soldiers guarding graves near Okatumba. Victory over the Herero was not achieved without significant costs.

half of the colony, raiding and stealing equipment and livestock. Having been made a fool of, von François slunk back to Germany, to be replaced by a very decent colonial administrator named Major Theodor Leutwein.

Leutwein was a stocky, bespectacled, square-jawed man whose rigid appearance hid his classical education and humanist sympathies. He was a soldier, to be sure, but one who felt that martial power was best used to keep peace. By August 1894, he had convinced Hendrik Witbooi to surrender by offering him generous terms. With peace in hand, he was able to buy land from the cooperative Samuel Maharero, on which he could begin construction of a railroad into the interior—a huge selling point for prospective colonists.

But what would colonists do there? The country was too arid for farming, and studies Leutwein commissioned showed there was little in the way of mineral resources. That left only one thing: cattle grazing. Leutwein was well aware that German colonists would soon displace the Herero as southwestern Africa's cattlemen—it was simply inevitable, a manifest destiny—but he was determined to try to do this as peacefully as possible, to ease the Herero into a future where they would work as laborers on their own land. Above all, he wanted to avoid bloodshed.

THE EVE OF THE STORM

By December of 1903, Leutwein could congratulate himself on having succeeded, under difficult circumstances, in keeping the peace and expanding the colony. In this he had had a helping hand from rinderpest—cattle plague—which had swept into southwestern Africa from the east in 1897 and destroyed thousands of the Herero's precious cattle.

To keep themselves alive, the Africans began to sell land to German settlers to pay for food for their families and vaccinations for their remaining cattle. After the rinderpest came typhoid and malaria, and after these, a plague of locusts. All of this had the result, by 1900, of putting forty thousand head of cattle in the hands of a few hundred German settlers. By the end of 1903, almost a quarter of Herero land was in German hands.

Leutwein was certain that the Herero were far too weak to rebel, and that this gradual weakening, like a dying man slipping slowly into a peaceful coma, would continue until the Germans owned the entire colony, lock, stock, and barrel. But it turned out that he did not really know the people he had so prided himself on understanding. He thought, for instance, that Samuel Maharero, chief of the Herero, loved German things—the good suits, the rancher's hats, the brandy—too much to rebel. But Maharero surprised him. This former apologist for the Germans had begun to understand that his land was slowly being destroyed. It was not just that Herero territory and cattle were disappearing, bad though that was; it was the German attitude. As one Herero put it to a German settler: "The missionary says that we are the children of God like our white brothers, but just look at us … Dogs, slaves, worse than baboons on rocks … that is how you treat us."

Most of the German settlers regarded the Herero as barely human. On one occasion, when a member of the Social Democratic Party of Germany rose in the Reichstag to declare that blacks in German Southwest Africa had souls, he was howled down by the conservative side of the house. Many settlers assumed that the blacks would be their virtual slaves, an attitude that led, in a colony of four thousand white men and very few white women, to frequent rapes of Herero women.

Ironically, the spark that ignited the Herero revolt was created when Leutwein tried to resolve what he considered to be one of the Herero's chief problems: the fact that traders loaned money to them at usurious interest rates, and then foreclosed on their land or cattle when they could not pay. On November 1, 1903, Leutwein decreed that German traders had to collect all outstanding debts within a year or forfeit them. He had hoped this would discourage the practice of lending, but in the short run, the traders went on a frenzy of debt-collecting, simply stealing cattle from the Africans as a way to get their money back quickly.

"LET US DIE FIGHTING!"

It is impossible to say for certain, but it seems probable that Samuel Maharero discussed the idea of a revolt with his chiefs as early as the spring of 1903. By the late fall, a plan emerged to attack German outposts, tear up the railroad to disrupt communications, and attack outlying settler ranches, burning them down, killing the men, and making off with their cattle. Maharero gave his men orders not to touch missionaries, women, or children and these orders were carried out to the letter—it would not be the Herero who would massacre noncombatants. Maharero also sent a letter to his old enemy, Hendrik Witbooi, now eighty years old but still a fierce warrior, begging him to join him in throwing off the German yoke and driving their common enemy out of their lands: "All our obedience and patience with the Germans is of little avail for each day they shoot someone dead without reason. Hence I appeal to you, my brother, not to hold aloof from the uprising, but to make your voice heard … Let us die fighting!" But Hendrik Witbooi did not receive this letter: it was intercepted by Africans loyal to the Germans and brought to them.

The Herero waited until Leutwein was in the south with half his forces, attending to a minor revolt of another tribe, and then struck. On the night of January 12, 1904, outlying farms were attacked by the Herero, who killed the male settlers (but, as ordered, didn't touch the women and children) and made off with the cattle. They placed the main German towns—Okahandja, Omaruru, and Windhoek—under a sort of siege, not actually attacking them but using small squads to keep watch on them while the main body of Herero marauded through the countryside.

At this time, there were about 750 German soldiers in the colony, armed with Model 88 rifles, capable of killing a man up to half a mile away, as well as rapid-firing Maxim guns and mountain artillery. They were opposed by about eight thousand Herero warriors. For the first two weeks of the revolt, the Herero had the colony pretty much to themselves. They roamed up and down the plateau, shooting any male settlers they found outside the forts, stealing cattle, and burning ranches.

By the end of January, Leutwein had returned, and was ready to negotiate with his former old friend Maharero; he was certain that a compromise could be worked out. But Leutwein failed to understand that it was too late for compromise, not only from the point of view of the Herero, but from the point of view of the Kaiser, as well.

THE KAISER'S REVENGE

In Berlin, Kaiser Wilhelm II couldn't believe what he was hearing. How dare a ragged band of subhumans revolt against German forces, kill German settlers, and parade around a German colony as if, well, as if they owned it! The Kaiser, as well as the screaming German popular press, thought that the reason for the uprising was that the colonial government of German Southwest Africa—meaning Leutwein and his aides—had been too lenient on the Africans. This would go on no longer. As Leutwein's replacement and head of a German expeditionary force, the Kaiser named General Lothar von Trotha, a career officer who had earned a reputation in China and German East Africa for being ruthless. Von Trotha set sail in May; when he arrived in German Southwest Africa in June, he told Leutwein: "His Majesty the emperor and king only said to me that he expected that I would crush the uprising with any means necessary." Von Trotha was fully prepared to do that. He had brought with him two thousand men (and, in the coming months, the German presence would swell to twenty thousand troops). Some of his eager officers brought with them hunting rifles, cigars, and champagne: they were out to bag themselves some "baboons." Leutwein and his seasoned colonial troops looked at these newcomers with dismay. They had fought against the Herero and respected their abilities as warriors.

By August, most of the Herero had made a strategic withdrawal, with their vast flocks of captured cattle, to the Waterberg Plateau, on the western edge of the

ANNIHILATION OF THE ISAAKS

Between 1988 and 1990, the government of Somalia carried out genocide against members of the Isaak clan, who, it was claimed, were fomenting rebellion. Approximately sixty thousand Isaaks died, both civilians and insurgents, at the hands of the Somalian National Security Service and certain government-supported paramilitary groups.

The Somalian artillery forces would often shell entire villages if they were thought to contain groups of Isaaks. At other times, paramilitary forces would sweep through villages, separate the non-Isaaks from the Isaaks, force the non-Isaaks to flee, then burn the village down, and kill the remaining inhabitants. The soldiers were also given lists of "enemies" and directed to hunt down and kill prominent Isaaks.

A few exiled Isaaks are pressuring the Mogadishu government to admit complicity in this act, but as recently as 2003, the government has claimed that such a genocide simply did not occur.

A dramatic but inaccurate reconstruction of the Herero offensive against Windhoek in January 1904. In fact, the Herero made no direct attack, merely besieging the settlement.

Omaheke Desert. Maharero had with him six thousand fighting men, as well as forty thousand women and children. He seems to have thought that he could hole up and beat the Germans, but had placed himself in a strategic dead-end. By August 11, von Trotha had him surrounded by 4,000 troops, 36 artillery pieces, and 25 machine guns. Significantly, von Trotha deliberately surrounded him on three sides only, leaving one lightly defended escape route—into the desert.

Von Trotha then gave the signal to attack. The Herero beat off numerous advances, but they hadn't bargained on the terrible toll that German artillery would take on the fifty to sixty thousand of them enclosed in an area just five miles wide and ten miles long. Demoralized, the Herero broke and ran—and von Trotha did not try to stop them, as long as they ran east, into the desert. They left behind the sick and the wounded, the old and the very young, all of whom were butchered by the Germans.

EXTERMINATION ORDER

The trail into the desert was littered with hundreds of bodies, but von Trotha was not going to stop there. During the rest of the month of August he set up fortified positions along a front several hundred miles long, facing the desert. Whenever small bands of Herero tried to move back onto the central plateau they were killed or driven back into the Omaheke. The desert wells were poisoned by German patrols, giving the Herero the choice of drinking and dying, or simply dying.

On October 2, von Trotha issued an official order, the *Schrecklichkeit*, meaning "Extermination," which was signed "The Great General of the Mighty Kaiser:"

> I, the great general of the German troops, send this letter to the Herero People. Herero are no longer German subjects. They have murdered, stolen, they have cut off the noses, ears, and other body parts of wounded soldiers, and now, because of cowardice, they will fight no more … All the Herero must leave the land. If the people will not do this, then I will force them to do it with the great guns. Any Herero found within the German borders, with or without a gun, with or without cattle, will be shot. I will no longer receive any women or children. I will drive them back to their people or I will shoot them. This is my decision for the Herero people.

Outside of the Holocaust, there is almost nothing in twentieth-century history to rival this very open and very public order. It was not that the other European states, and the United States, had not engaged in brutal tactics during their empire building—a 1904 report on the Belgian atrocities in the Congo, for example, deplored the dreadful treatment of the indigenous population, though it claimed that drastic methods were necessary to reclaim the country "from its natural state of barbarism." It's just that this is the first time anyone in a position of authority from a European state was so very, very clear about their intentions.

And thus the genocide of the Herero began. They died far out in the desert, where their bodies were found for some time after, piled around the waterholes or lying alone in the desert. Anyone found still alive, the Germans killed. About three thousand survivors, including Samuel Maharero, desperately battled their way across the Omaheke, and found refuge in the British colony of Bechuanaland.

As it turned out, the *Schrecklichkeit* created quite a stir. Leutwin first cabled the Foreign Office asking to be given the authority to countermand von Trotha. When he was refused, he asked to be relieved of his duties.

In Berlin, the Social Democrats protested vociferously and, finally, the newspapers in Britain and the United States published the order, which so alarmed the German Chancellor, Bernard von Bulow, that he asked the Kaiser to revoke it. The Kaiser, concerned that Germany's enemies had been given a weapon against her, ordered Von Trotha to cancel his order. But the damage had already been done: the Herero were in the process of being destroyed.

ONE MORE REBELLION

The day after von Trotha issued his infamous order, eighty-year-old Hendrik Witbooi finally and belatedly decided to enter the fray against the Germans. His reasons for doing so were typically strange and complex. He had met a strange visionary prophet from the Cape, an African named Sturmann, who claimed that God had sent him to drive the whites from Africa. His rallying cry was: "Africa for the Africans." This mystic appealed to the fanatical Christian in Witbooi, who proclaimed that he would "put on the white feather" (get ready to fight) because Christ, through Sturmann, had proclaimed it was time to save Africa.

On October 3, 1904, as the Herero starved and died in the desert, Witbooi and his Hottentots launched attacks all over the southern part of the colony, burning and killing. There were only about five hundred German troops there and they had a hard time surviving, until von Trotha hurriedly sent reinforcements. Witbooi then waged a true guerilla war, using hit-and-run attacks against what were now about fifteen thousand German riflemen. Witbooi had perhaps three hundred men, but they used the barren Kalahari as a staging area, slipping into and out of the desert with ease, attacking German positions and fading away. Indeed, they managed to run circles around the Germans for an entire year, until Hendrik Witbooi was mortally wounded on a raid in October 1905. His dying words were: "It is enough. With me it is all over. The children should now have rest." When he heard this, von Trotha responded, "What a beautiful message!"

With Hendrik's death, the Hottentot rebellion came to an end. Although fighting continued in a scattered way until the end of 1905, the war was essentially over. Von Trotha was recalled and given the Order of Merit by the Kaiser. Leutwein had already resigned and returned home to write his memoirs. In the meantime, about six thousand starving Herero and two thousand Hottentots had been taken prisoner and sent either to labor for the colonists or to an infamous camp on Shark Island in the Atlantic Ocean. So many tried to escape from the island, possibly just to commit suicide, that it was routine to find Herero or Hottentot bodies washed up on the shores of the colony in the mornings. Over half of the Herero or Hottentot prisoners died in the camps, according even to a German count.

During the conflict, the German army suffered 2,348 men dead, missing, or wounded. The Herero were about eighty thousand strong at the beginning of 1904. According to the best estimates of modern historians, between twenty and thirty thousand were killed from the start of the rebellion in January 1904 to the end of the Battle of Waterberg. Between fifty and sixty thousand fled into the Omaheke, with about three thousand making it to Bechuanaland. After the repeal of the *Schrecklichkeit* order, more Herero surrendered and were taken to Shark Island; here, the surviving women and children outnumbered the men two to one. According to even an official German count taken in 1911, there were only 15,130 Herero left in German Southwest Africa. In other words, the population had been reduced by approximately sixty thousand, or eighty percent.

In 1911, the camp on Shark Island was closed, and the surviving Herero returned to the population as common laborers. Blacks were forbidden to own land or cattle, and could be whipped for transgressions, either by their owners or at the order of German magistrates. There were over sixteen hundred official (judicial) whippings in 1911 alone.

REMOVED FROM THE RECORDS
Following the controversy surrounding the *Schrecklichkeit* order, the Social Democrats in Germany continued to make such a fuss about the treatment of the Herero that, in 1906, Chancellor von Bulow dissolved the German parliament and went directly to the German people, asking for a mandate for the authorities to continue to administer the German colonies as they saw fit. In the resulting election, the Social Democrats were heavily defeated. When Germany became mired in the prolonged struggle of World War I, the Herero war quickly faded from the national consciousness.

In 1915, the British invaded and occupied German Southwest Africa. While British forces were in control, two officers were assigned to investigate the killing of the Herero. Their report, delivered in 1918, was explicit, accurate, and damning. But in 1920, the League of Nations awarded control of German Southwest Africa to South Africa, and it was in the interests of all involved—including the British and the numerous German ranchers and farmers in the region—that the genocide be swept under the rug. Therefore, on July 19, 1926, the South West Africa Legislature adopted a resolution that the British officers' report be labeled an "instrument of war"—in other words, a politically biased document—and that it be removed from official files and from public libraries and destroyed. This was done.

The Herero who had escaped into Bechuanaland grew into a larger and larger group and gradually began filtering back into what was now called South West Africa. After a struggle against South Africa in the later part of the twentieth century, the territory gained its independence, as Namibia, in 1990, and more Herero returned. Today, there are about one hundred thousand Herero in the country, most of whom work on farms. Recently, they have returned to haunt their former oppressors by demanding that Germany pay reparations for its crime.

In the long run, if any lessons from the forgotten lives and deaths of the Herero are to be gleaned, it is that genocide must always be remembered—be it the genocide of the Herero, the Armenians, the Jews and Gypsies, the Cambodians, or the Tutsi—lest it continue to happen.

SEEKING REPARATION
The nation of Namibia has long sought an apology from Germany for the massacre of the Herero. In 1998, the German President Roman Herzog visited the country and expressed regret, but stopped short of an apology and would not discuss reparations. On the hundredth anniversary of the revolt, in 2004, the German developmental aid minister visited the country again, and this time did apologize, but once again ruled out action on reparations.

The Herero in Namibia are now suing Germany in a lawsuit brought in U.S. courts. In the meantime, the life of Samuel Maharero, who died in exile in Bechuanaland (modern-day Botswana) in 1923 but was brought back to Namibia to be buried, is celebrated every year in late August, on Herero Day.

CONTAINING AN EPIDEMIC: THE SAN FRANCISCO PLAGUE

LIKE A BAD ACTOR CONSTANTLY REINVENTING HIMSELF, THE GERM KNOWN as *Yersina pestis* has gone by many names: the Plague of Athens, Justinian's Plague, the wandering sickness. A relatively young germ, perhaps twenty thousand years old, *Yersina pestis* originated as a bacterium that caused a nasty stomach flu, but nothing more. Yet it evolved into something that has repeatedly and irrevocably changed the course of human history.

Its most famous performance was as the Black Death, in fourteenth-century Europe, when it killed one out of every three people. This remains the second-worst catastrophe in history—World War II has the dubious honor of being first. In fact, according to a study commissioned by the United States Atomic Energy Commission, the Black Death got the closest any event has come to nuclear holocaust in its "geographical content, abruptness of onset, and scale of casualties."

By Victorian times, many people considered *Yersina pestis* a disease of the past. But in the mid-1890s disturbing news began to spread around the world, news of a sweeping epidemic of plague in Hong Kong, China, and parts of India. Even so, those who lived in predominantly white, affluent, Western countries believed this was something that happened to other people—people of a different color—and not to them. The plague was worthy of a shudder while reading the morning newspaper, a fresh cup of coffee, then a sigh for those poor souls perishing ... somewhere—but not here. But, in fact, although it is little discussed today, plague did strike here, in the West, right in the polite parlors of Victorian America, in the heart of downtown San Francisco, at the beginning of the last century.

For any reader acquainted with public health crises of the twentieth century—the devastating Spanish flu pandemic, AIDS, and the SARS and bird flu scares—the sequence of events in San Francisco will have a familiar ring: death, disbelief, more death, governmental (or corporate) intransigence and cover-up, and then, finally, so much death there can no longer be a cover-up. In San Francisco, the only saving interruption to this vicious cycle was a handful of men—two in particular—who fought to save numerous lives. Together, they may have kept the city from being the launching point for an American bubonic plague outbreak of horrifying proportions, and set a precedent for the successful containment of major epidemics.

THE YEAR OF THE RAT

San Francisco was an emergent and boisterous city, the year that the twentieth century began. The town had been a miner's camp only fifty years before, during California's famous Gold Rush, and had then grown by leaps and bounds, becoming both a port of embarkation for the United States military and a port of entry for immigrants from all over the Pacific Rim. By 1900, San Francisco had 340,000 inhabitants, was ranked the eighth largest city in America, and was known for its shining Beaux Arts buildings.

One of the most fascinating areas of San Francisco was Chinatown. It was as if a village from the Manchu dynasty had been picked up and placed down whole in the center of the city—complete with temples and open-air fruit markets. The population was predominately made up of male, working-class immigrants, who wore bowler hats as a nod to the West, but braided their hair into long Manchu pigtails known as queues.

San Francisco in 1900. Chinatown, the focus of the plague outbreak that began in that year, lay close to the center of the city.

San Francisco's Chinatown had its beginnings in the Gold Rush, when laborers came from China to work in the mines. The Chinese called California "Gold Mountain." When America's great westward-reaching railroads were being built, more Chinese came. Many workers were attracted by brochures sent out by American recruiters, which read: "Americans are very rich people. They want the Chinese to come, and make him very welcome."

After the gold ran out and the railroads were built, the Chinese stayed on in Chinatown to roll cigars, provide laundry services, and work as cooks, butlers, and doormen. By the late nineteenth century, Chinatown was home to a population of close to thirty thousand—almost one-tenth of the city's population—massed in a twelve-block area. Although there were wealthy Chinese businessmen in San Francisco—Chinese owned half the city's cigar factories and nearly all the town's slipper factories—the living conditions of most Chinese immigrants were terrible. Observers wrote of a dozen men working in spaces fifteen feet square, and sleeping under their work benches as another shift took over.

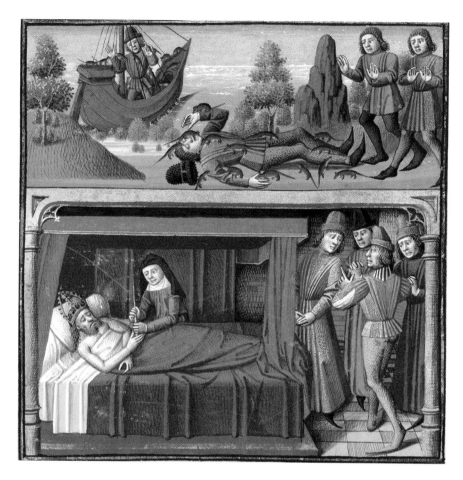

A fifteenth-century illustration showing the horrors inflicted by bubonic plague. The Black Death of the mid-fourteenth century is thought to have killed twenty-five million people in Europe.

Toward the end of the nineteenth century, as the country fell into economic depression, whites began to claim that the Chinese were usurping jobs. In a familiar pattern, the Chinese were first accused of moral corruption (running opium dens and whorehouses), then attacked and beaten on the street by white gangs—their pigtails were a favorite target of knives and scissors. San Francisco newspapers fanned the flames by publishing "Chink" cartoons featuring racial stereotypes.

Adding to this atmosphere of smoldering racial resentment and fear were the reports coming out of Asia of a plague epidemic, of thousands dying in Hong Kong and Bombay. Although no one at this point knew exactly how plague spread, people in San Francisco began to look at the Chinese population with ever more distrust. The Chinese themselves became terrified by an incident that occurred in Honolulu's Chinese district in 1899. When a few suspected cases of plague were discovered there, the city ordered that the plague-affected houses be burned. The flames, taken by the wind, touched off stored fireworks, destroying the homes of six thousand Chinese.

SAVED BY THE STOMACH OF A FLEA?

The efforts of Joseph Kinyoun and Rupert Blue helped ensure that plague was contained in San Francisco during the outbreak of 1900. Still, scientists have wondered why that plague was not more virulent—after all, the same plague epidemic killed thousands in Asia around the same time.

Some experts feel that the plague that broke out in San Francisco and other areas in the late nineteenth century was not the same as the Black Death of the fourteenth century. Outbreaks of plague in the late nineteenth century tended not to kill as many infants and children as the Black Death, which mercilessly scythed down the very young, and the initial infection rate in modern outbreaks was much slower than in medieval times. (A little known fact is that medieval populations tended to develop at least some limited immunity to the disease as each infestation continued.) It is also possible, however, that the answer may lie with the flea. *Xenopsylla cheopis*, the Indian or Oriental plague flea—probably the flea that transmitted the Black Death—is particularly suited to imparting a nasty plague bite. That's because *X. cheopis* has a bundle of sharp little spikes inside its belly. Every time it drinks blood, a clot forms, full of plague germs, and the little creature vomits it right back up onto its human victim. Then, because nothing has stayed in its stomach, the starving *X. cheopis* keeps on drinking—and regurgitating lethal plague germs.

X. cheopis was present in San Francisco, but the most common flea in the city was *Nosopsyllus fasciatus*, the northern European rat flea, which has a normal digestive system. Its bite, while nasty, is less potent.

Around Christmas Day of 1899, a four-masted steamship, the *Australia*, sailed through the Golden Gate, carrying cargo and passengers. The *Australia*'s last stop had been Honolulu. It was held briefly in quarantine while federal health officers searched the ship and its passengers for any trace of infection. None was found, and the ship was allowed to dock. By chance, she moored close to where the sewers from Chinatown emptied into the Bay. In a month or two, the Chinese began seeing large numbers of brown rats dying in their alleys. No one knew why, and no one then made the connection to the *Australia*. The dead rodents were, however, seen as an evil harbinger by the Chinese. Back in their homeland, entire families would abandon their houses at the sight of a dead rat. But here, in Chinatown, there was nowhere to go.

Soon it was February, time of the festive Chinese New Year celebrations. Quite by coincidence, the coming year would be the Year of the Rat.

ASHES, ASHES, WE ALL FALL DOWN
The first casualty of the plague in San Francisco was a forty-one-year-old lumber salesman named Wong Chut King, who lived in a flophouse called the Globe Hotel. His illness started in early March, with a pain in his groin, which the Chinese healers he consulted treated as a bladder or prostate ailment. But Wong soon grew delirious. The plague germs released fatal toxins into the tissues of his liver, spleen, and heart. He began to hemorrhage internally, causing purplish black splotches on his skin—the black marks of the age-old children's plague song "Ashes, ashes, we all fall down." Finally, septic shock set in and Wong Chut King fell into a coma and died.

San Francisco's Chinatown in
1895. The community consisted
mainly of male, working-class
immigrants who had come to
seek their fortune in California.

It doesn't take more than a few plague bacteria to cause infection, but the fact that Wong died so quickly—within a matter of five days—suggests that this was a powerful variety of the disease (though still relatively mild compared to the Black Death, which usually killed people in two or three days).

Because Wong's death was considered a puzzle, his body was turned over to the police, who called a city health official, who in turn called a young doctor named Wilfred Kellogg, a practitioner of the new science of bacteriology. After an autopsy, Kellogg extracted lymph fluid, put it under a microscope, and saw bunches of short, rod-like germs with rounded tips that resembled closed safety pins. He immediately recognized them as plague bacilli.

What Kellogg found was so explosive that he knew he needed an expert to confirm his results and do further tests. The ideal person was right there in San Francisco: Joseph Kinyoun, chief quarantine officer of the U.S. Marine Hospital Service, the government agency that inspected ships for disease and set up maritime quarantines. Kinyoun was stationed on Angel Island, in San Francisco Bay, and had a sophisticated laboratory set-up.

A pudgy, prickly, brilliant thirty-nine-year-old, Joseph Kinyoun was misplaced as a public health official, and might have better spent his life in a laboratory, behind a microscope. He was one of the first of a very modern breed: a germ hunter. Raised in the South after the Civil War, he became a doctor just as the new science of bacteriology was being developed by Joseph Pasteur, and later studied at the Pasteur Institute in Paris. Here he learned the basic procedure for proving that a germ causes a disease: first, isolate the germ; second, grow it in a pure culture; third, inject it into a lab animal; and then, finally, if the animal dies, isolate the germ from the animal.

Kinyoun joined the Marine Hospital Service in 1886 and, while stationed in New York, became the first scientist in the world to isolate the organism that causes cholera. He was well on his way to a comfortable career on the East Coast when he was sent with his wife and children to be chief quarantine officer on windswept Angel Island. It was not the posting he would have chosen, but he went.

THE MONKEY DIES

When Kellogg brought Kinyoun the slides from Wong Chut King's autopsy, Kinyoun set to work finding out what had killed the man. He isolated the germ and then injected it into lab animals, including a monkey. In the meantime, as a precautionary measure, the San Francisco government set up a *cordon sanitaire* around Chinatown. This panicked the Chinese, who were certain their homes might suffer the same fate as the homes of the Chinese in Honolulu. Their fears were heightened when they realized that white-owned stores within the borders of Chinatown were exempt from the quarantine.

Passions began to run high. The local papers and the city government ridiculed the Chinese, the plague fears, and health officials like Kinyoun. Yes, precautions might be taken and microbes might affect "the Chinaman," squashed into his tenement hovel, but it was certainly nothing for most ordinary citizens to worry about. But then it was found out that all the animals Kinyoun had injected had died of bubonic plague. And then more human beings began to die. A week after Wong Chut King's death, a twenty-two-year-old workman passed away, then a thirty-five-year-old cook, then another laborer, all infected with the plague. Kinyoun wired his superiors in Washington for instructions, using a secret code, and was told to employ preventative methods: quarantine, burning "pest houses," spreading lime, destroying rats, inoculating potential victims.

The bacterium for plague had been identified in 1900, but the way in which it entered the human body was still a mystery. There was a growing feeling that rats were spreading the plague from seaport to seaport, but how it leaped from rodents to humans was by and large unknown. Scientists in Sydney, Australia, found plague bacteria in the stomach of a flea in 1900, right around the time that a Pasteur Institute bacteriologist named Paul Simond demonstrated that the bite of the flea was the culprit.

But possibly because of racist thinking—the plague kept happening in what would now be called "the developing world"—no one really paid any attention to these reports, until about 1906, when Simond's findings were finally accepted by the British Plague Commission in India.

Joseph Kinyoun did what he could with the limited resources of the Marine Hospital Service. He called for quarantine of Chinatown, burned refuse, flushed toilets with chemicals, and sent his men to inoculate the suspicious Chinese against the plague. But he was losing the battle, both on the medical front and the public relations front. The only plague inoculation available, Haffkine's vaccine, employed a small amount of plague bacillus to spark an immune reaction. Unfortunately, it had severely painful side effects, and sometimes even caused death. It was especially dangerous to a person who had already been exposed to the plague but was not yet symptomatic. The Chinese knew this, so when Kinyoun's health officers swarmed through Chinatown with inoculating needles, they hid from them.

Kinyoun was soon nicknamed "the wolf doctor," someone who preyed on helpless people. To make matters worse, from the Chinese point of view, the government decreed that any Chinese person who died of pneumonia or any suspicious respiratory illness be autopsied—something the Chinese abhorred for religious reasons. Kinyoun was in some ways his own worst enemy. He had a choleric temperament that erupted at criticism; and was known to refer to Chinese as "chinks," a slur that did not endear him to the people of Chinatown.

By spring, nine people had died of plague. Only cases of bubonic plague had been observed so far, but Kinyoun was afraid the disease would mutate into the virulently contagious pneumonic plague, the only form of plague that can be spread from person to person, and the main cause of fatalities during the Black Death. His worst fears were realized by the case of Anne Roede, a white nurse working in Chinatown. Roede was tending to a teenage boy suffering from what she thought was diphtheria. Without warning, the boy suddenly vomited straight into her face. Forty-eight hours later, her throat became sore; then her breathing became labored and she started running a high fever. In three more days, she was dead.

THE THREE FACES OF PLAGUE

Most people think of plague as a single disease, but there are in fact three forms of it. *Bubonic* plague is the most common form. It's transmitted by a flea bite, has a two- to six-day incubation period, and causes classic symptoms: an egg-shaped bubo at the site of the flea bite and black-purple bruises from internal hemorrhaging. In medieval plague cases, it also gave rise to an almost indescribably foul stench which seemed to come from inside the victim; for reasons no one quite knows, this has not been observed in modern victims. Left untreated, bubonic plague has a mortality rate of 60 percent. The second form of plague is *pneumonic* plague, the only form that can be spread from human to human. It starts off as bubonic plague, but then bacilli escape the lymph system and invade the lungs, causing the victim to cough up blood. Relatively uncommon today, this was the main form of plague during the Black Death. Left untreated, it will kill up to 95 percent of its victims. The third and most deadly form of plague is *septicemic* plague, wherein massive amounts of plague bacilli move directly into the bloodstream. No one survives septicemic plague if left untreated, and death has been known to occur within fourteen hours of the onset of symptoms. Fortunately, all forms of plague can now be treated effectively with intravenous antibiotics, such as streptomycin, tetracycline, and doxycycline.

Rupert Blue, the far-seeing and energetic chief quarantine officer, whose vigilance and ingenuity helped stem the tide of the plague in San Francisco.

Doctors said the cause of Roede's death was diphtheria—until Kinyoun's autopsy discovered pneumonic plague. The boy who had infected her had also died, but had been buried without an autopsy or proper diagnosis. Convinced that he had a serious epidemic on his hands, and that more deaths were being hidden than actually reported, Kinyoun stepped up preventative measures. In response, the city of San Francisco, fearful that continued bad publicity would harm the city's reputation and businesses, mounted an extraordinary campaign of character assassination against Kinyoun. As 1900 drew to a close, the head of the chamber of commerce called him "a menace to our trade and commerce." The *San Francisco Chronicle* urged his ouster in a headline which read: "The Doom of Kinyoun." Mayor James Phelan dispatched telegrams to forty American cities, telling them that there had been just one isolated case of plague, and that visitors had nothing to fear.

In an unprecedented attack, Henry T. Gage, Governor of California, made a speech suggesting that Kinyoun had actually planted the plague in San Francisco: "Could it have been possible that some dead body of a Chinaman had innocently *or otherwise* received a post-mortem injection … by someone possessing the imported plague bacilli?" Governor Gage then led a delegation to Washington, where he called on President William McKinley, and Kinyoun's boss, Surgeon General Walter Wyman, to remove Kinyoun from duty. Wyman bowed to pressure and transferred Kinyoun to Detroit. On the eve of Kinyoun's departure, the authorities made one more attempt to destroy him: the police tried to arrest him on a trumped-up charge of murder. The charge was so patently untrue that Kinyoun simply refused to allow himself to be taken into custody, and the courts eventually dropped the matter.

TURNING TO BLUE Kinyoun was ousted, but the plague would not go away so easily. Despite the fact that plague infections usually decline in winter—the rats, and their fleas, go underground for warmth—six Chinese people died of bubonic plague in San Francisco in early 1901. One University of Michigan researcher, trying to make vaccine from samples of the San Francisco bacillus, contracted pneumonic plague and very nearly died.

A year after the *Australia*'s visit, thirty people were dead. Because only two of them were white, and because of the massive misinformation campaign promulgated by the city's business and political elite (not to mention the state government), San Francisco feigned indifference as it readied itself for a state visit from President McKinley and his wife. Ironically, the First Lady turned out to be suffering from typhoid and most of the visit had to be canceled.

Into this false peace came the new chief quarantine officer of the U.S. Marine Hospital Service, Dr. Rupert Blue. Thirty-three years old, Blue was the antithesis of Kinyoun: handsome, well-built (an amateur boxer), and extremely courteous and cordial. Although not a bacteriologist of Kinyoun's stripe, Blue had experience dealing with plague outbreaks in Europe, and knew how essential it was to contain them.

In a sense, Rupert Blue was handed a gift the minute he set foot in the city. For the story had finally come out that Governor Gage and Surgeon General Wyman had conspired to keep the news of the plague secret. Gage had initially succeeded in convincing Wyman to let California take care of its own dirty little secret, thereby avoiding any kind of trade quarantine around San Francisco. But when it emerged that it was against an 1893 federal law to conceal the presence of a communicable disease in any U.S. port, Wyman had no choice but to release a heretofore secret report confirming the presence of bubonic plague.

Blue rolled up his sleeves and dove right in. The first thing he did was personally inspect Chinatown's cellars, back alleys, and markets. He was horrified by the lack of sanitation—the raw sewage in basements, the heaps of rotting garbage in back of meat markets, the swarming vermin—and began convincing Chinese merchants to start cleaning up. He was puzzled by the sudden low death toll in Chinatown—death for whatever reason—for even with very few infants and children, whose presence normally drives mortality rates up, the Chinatown "bachelor population" normally had a death rate possibly fifty percent higher than white San Francisco. He became convinced that the Chinese were shipping their dead across the bay to Oakland, or secretly burying them in the country, to avoid autopsies and the stigma that comes with having the plague.

In contrast to Kinyoun, Blue showed great respect and empathy for the people of Chinatown. It helped a great deal that he hired a man named Wong Chung as his translator. Wong knew his way around Chinatown and, quite literally, could take Blue to where the bodies were buried.

Blue needed every ounce of his energy and charm during that summer of 1901. First of all, plague broke out in a Japanese whorehouse, killing three women. Then, during a Chinese festival in August, a man who worked in a cigar factory was found to have pneumonic plague. One cough at work could have infected a dozen coworkers, but when Blue and his men went to test them, all the Chinese simply vanished from their jobs. To make matters worse, the state, while publicly supporting Blue's program, obstructed him at every turn. He complained ruefully about the state Health Board doctors who persisted in trying to diagnose every new case of plague as cholera, even in the face of classic symptoms like buboes and hemorrhaging.

MAKING HEADWAY Would Blue have been able to maintain his level of energy if he had known that it would take years for him to stamp out plague in San Francisco? It's hard to say. What is known is that, for the next four years, Rupert Blue worked as tirelessly as possible to help eradicate the disease, even while undergoing personal upheaval in the form of a painful divorce from his actress wife. The stresses of the job were enormous. Ever at risk of sickness themselves, Blue and his men injected each other with Yersin's antiserum, an antiserum drawn from the blood of horses infected by the plague. Not only could this antiserum cause severe immune reactions, but it was also costly and scarce.

Despite their best efforts, by 1902 the plague had started to spread out from Chinatown. It infected a seamstress in a hotel one block north, and a sailor who had come into the city but had not visited Chinatown. By August of that year, another white victim had died. Now people were starting to pay more attention. A national board of state health organizations demanded to know what was going on in San Francisco. Governor Gage did not have good answers for them, or for the citizens of California, and was defeated in a subsequent election and replaced by George C. Pardee. After that, Blue was able to work, if not with active government support, at least with far fewer impediments.

Although Blue would not know until at least 1907 that fleas carried plague from rats to humans, he and others understood that there was a strong connection between *Rattus norvegicus* (the Norway, or brown, rat) and plague—the fewer rats, the fewer cases. So he began ratting in earnest. Hiring scores of the unemployed, Blue sent them fanning throughout Chinatown, setting traps bearing succulent morsels (cheese, bacon, bread) laced with arsenic. He also initiated a massive cleanup. He sent inspectors door-to-door, checking for vermin infestation and unsanitary conditions. In one week, they inspected 1,916 rooms. They condemned places they considered hopelessly infected, burned trash, had houses scrubbed, and, most importantly, cemented cellars so that vermin could not break in.

They were making headway, although people continued to die: a fifty-four-year-old Chinese actor who became ill on stage; two seven-year-old girls, close friends who died within three days of each other; an Italian railroad man who scavenged wood filled with fleas (the disease also killed his mother). As a result of these last deaths, Blue extended his campaign from Chinatown into the new Latin Quarter (now North Beach).

By February 1905, there had been 121 recorded cases of plague in San Francisco, causing 113 deaths, a very high mortality rate, even for the plague. But one hundred days then went by without a plague death. Then six months. By New Year's Day, 1906, it seemed that the plague had finally been eradicated. Blue, by this time quite a popular figure in San Francisco, decided to wind down his campaign. Surgeon General Wyman posted him to Norfolk, Virginia, to care for sick sailors there.

That would have been the end of the San Francisco plague story, except for one inconvenience: a very large earthquake.

THE RAT RETURNS
On April 18, 1906, at 5:12 a.m., the ground beneath San Francisco began to shake convulsively. Building after building collapsed. Those on the waterfront literally sank, drowning their inhabitants. Huge fires broke out all over the city, and since the water mains had ruptured it was nearly impossible to put them out—the air rang with explosions as dynamite was used to set backfires. Probably close to 3,000 people died and 250,000 were left homeless. And then, from the rubble, came the rats, hordes of them, pouring over the city, feasting on the detritus of the city and its inhabitants.

Within a few days of the disaster, Rupert Blue was sent back to San Francisco. He visited refugee camps in the shell of the city and found deplorable sanitary conditions that encouraged typhoid, scarlet fever, smallpox—and plague. Almost immediately, an Italian teenager named Louis Scazzafava fell ill with fever and buboes. Although he survived, it was a warning shot. Blue cautioned a colleague from Washington: "The campaign is likely to be a long one, and infestation will be fifty times more difficult [to eradicate] than before …" This was mainly because rats had now spread to so many parts of the ruined city.

Undaunted, Blue set up a headquarters and established his "rattery," a laboratory filled with narrow, metal-topped tables. He sent out rat crews to trap rats all over the city; when they brought the dead creatures back to the rattery, Blue and his

DOES PLAGUE STILL EXIST?

The answer is an emphatic yes. Pockets of plague persist all over the world. Cases are reported every year in Brazil, Congo, Madagascar, Myanmar, Peru, and Vietnam—twenty-five thousand cases occurred during the Vietnam War, spread mainly along the animal–fleas–humans chain. A dozen or so cases arise in the southwestern United States each year. If treated promptly with intravenous antibiotics, people who contract bubonic plague today usually survive. Plague germs have also been cultivated by developers of biological weapons. During World War II, the Japanese dropped infected plague fleas on Manchuria. However, it was the Cold War that was the boom era for plague weapons. The United States attempted to make plague, but abandoned the project when germ cultures in test tubes lost their potency over time. Despite this, one young American chemist working for the army nearly lost his life to plague in 1959. (A British scientist working on a *Yersina pestis* project at the time died of pneumonic plague.) The Soviets were more successful. After the Cold War ended, defectors reported a Russian arsenal of twenty tons of pure plague serum.

men dissected them, looking for signs of plague. It was a nasty, dirty, dangerous business. By 1907, Blue knew of the connection between rat fleas and human plague, and so each rat caught alive was dipped in kerosene or boiling water. Still, there was always a chance of a stray flea finding a laboratory worker and biting deep into his skin.

By October, Blue and his men were killing and dissecting thirteen thousand rats a week, a truly astonishing number. Yet plague cases kept on coming: a sixteen-month-old baby, a five-year-old girl, the mother and father of two young boys who had been playing with a dead rat carcass on the street (the boys survived, orphans). There had now been sixty-five cases of plague, with thirty-eight people confirmed dead. And the dead were from all races.

On April 18, 1906, compounding the destruction wreaked by the famous earthquake, fires raged through central San Francisco.

Blue encouraged the city to replace the surviving wooden docks and wharves with cement ones, and to establish more effective rat guards on the hawsers that moored ships to the docks. He cleaned up Butchertown, the stinking meat market area that had long been a home to rodents. And he stepped forward into the public arena, making speeches wherever possible, encouraging people, whatever their station in life, to eliminate rats. Eventually, at his instigation and at the urging of the umbrella civic organization, the Citizens' Health Committee, fifty-four neighborhood improvement clubs sprang up around the city, as well as more than sixty women's clubs, all of them focused on "municipal housekeeping," a nice euphemism for killing rats.

In the next two years, Rupert Blue effected a total turnaround, not just in the plague in San Francisco, but in public awareness, for he instilled in the people of the newly rebuilt city a sense of civic pride in public health. By 1909, eleven thousand houses had been disinfected, over 250,000 square feet of wooden side-walk had been replaced with concrete, and an estimated two million rats (five times the human population of the city) had been killed.

In San Francisco, the human cost was 190 dead of the plague, out of 281 infected. The first outbreak, prior to the earthquake, had had a mortality rate of 93 percent of those who contracted the disease; this fell to fifty percent after the quake, due to superior diagnosis and treatment—and good sanitation. As Blue and Kinyoun knew only too well, the plague thrives when hygiene breaks down. During the outbreak of the disease in Bombay—where one British plague commissioner described even the hospitals as being filthy and overcrowded—over nineteen thousand people died from August 1896 to February 1897.

San Francisco paid a high price for denying the disease that afflicted its citizens, and it is possible that it learned its lesson. When the AIDS epidemic broke out eighty years later, the city responded swiftly and compassionately. Many other cities and nations constrained by the same sort of commercial and political pressures that affected San Francisco, such as countries in AIDS-stricken Africa or China in the day of SARS, must, it seems, learn this harsh lesson all over again.

Rupert Blue's predecessor, the prickly Joseph Kinyoun, served as an epidemiologist for the U.S. Army and died in 1919 at the age of fifty-eight; he is today recognized for his pioneering bacteriological work. Blue himself had a stellar career after his sojourn in San Francisco, becoming Surgeon General of the United States from 1912 to 1920, in which role he fought for universal milk pasteurization and advocated, vainly, a national health insurance system. He lived to the ripe old age of eighty. His one regret, when it came to fighting the plague, was his failure to persuade the U.S. government that squirrels could spread the disease into the countryside outside San Francisco.

His fears were well founded. Bubonic plague now exists in squirrels, chipmunks, and prairie dogs in the western United States—warnings are issued to hikers in these areas. It is the very same strain of plague that nearly brought a great city to ruin at the beginning of the twentieth century.

SOGHOMON TEHLIRIAN: BLESSED ASSASSIN OF THE ARMENIAN NATION

Who today, after all, speaks of the annihilation of the Armenians?
Adolf Hitler, 1939

N July of 1922, in Tiflis, in the Georgian Soviet Socialist Republic, a man walking down the steps of a public building was approached by three men who emptied revolvers into him without a word, then turned and fled. Standing nearby at the time was the soon-to-be notorious Lavrenty Beria, brutal head of the *Cheka*, or Georgian Communist secret police. As the echoes of the gunshots died away, Beria turned to a friend and muttered, *"Eda Dashnakski terror*," meaning, "It is the Armenians."

The man shot in Tiflis was Ahmed Cemal Pasha, one of a trio of Turkish leaders known as the Ittihad Triumvirate, the "committee of three," who had been the chief engineers of the massacre of more than one million Armenians, beginning in 1915. His assassination was the latest in a series of carefully planned attacks. A year earlier, in July 1921, another high-ranking Turk had been shot dead in Constantinople as he exited a theater. In December of that year, in Rome, Sayid Halim Pasha, former prime minister of the Ottoman Empire, was assassinated as he drove his car along the Via Eustacchio. In February 1922, two former Turkish high officials were killed, together, on a main thoroughfare in Berlin, shot by two men who disappeared into the night.

The killing that started this series of assassinations also took place in Berlin, on March 15, 1921, on a quiet street in the city's Charlottenburg district. A stocky, middle-aged man wearing a long gray overcoat walked down an avenue, swinging his cane, the picture of wealth and confidence. He was approached by a young man with dark hair and large dark eyes, a man who, in his photos, bears some resemblance to the writer Franz Kafka. This young man was prone to epileptic seizures and fainting spells, and struck his German landlady as nervous and fearful. She sometimes heard him weeping quietly to himself in the middle of the night. His name was Soghomon Tehlirian, and he was the only survivor of a slaughter by the Turks of a column of thousands of Armenians that included his mother, two brothers, three sisters, and a niece.

Although the man with the well-to-do appearance had papers identifying him as Ali Sahih Beh, his real name was Mehmed Talat Pasha. A former minister of the interior for the Ottoman Empire, he was another of Turkey's Ittihad Triumvirate, and the man most reports blamed for the decision that set in motion the Armenian massacre.

Soghomon Tehlirian locked eyes with Talat Pasha as he passed him, then turned, whipped out a revolver, and shot the Turk once in the back of the head. He started to run, but was quickly cornered by a mob of local people, some of whom began to beat him. The Armenian cried out, in broken German, "I foreigner, he foreigner, this not hurt Germany," but it did no good. Finally, the police came to take him into custody. It is one of the many ironies of this story that Soghomon Tehlirian was beaten by the citizens of a country that would soon perpetrate another slaughter, one that, incredibly, would surpass even the beating, shooting, stabbing, bludgeoning, drowning, and starving to death of one million Armenians.

Turkey in 1915, showing the Armenian heartland. Using World War I as a smokescreen, the Turks moved to eliminate all Armenians within its borders.

COUNTRY AT A CROSSROADS

Soghomon Tehlirian was born in 1897 in western Armenia, in the village of Pakarij. Armenia lies on the plateau that separates Turkey and the rest of the Middle East from Central Asia. It has long been a crossroads of cultures and an obstacle to the expansionist aspirations of empires. The ancestors of present-day Armenians have inhabited the region for at least eight thousand years, but the first Armenian state was not born until about two hundred years before the birth of Christ. It reached its height of power as a well-known trading kingdom about 100 BC, when its borders touched on the Mediterranean, Black, and Caspian seas, but by the time of the birth of Christ the Romans had conquered the country. Thereafter, it remained a focus of contention between Rome and Persia, a land where great armies battled. Between the fourth and the nineteenth centuries, the territory was ruled by Persians, Arabs, Mongols, and, finally, the Turks. After the Russo-Turkish war of 1828–29, the Ottoman Empire ceded eastern Armenia to the Russians, but retained the western part of the country, where Tehlirian was born.

"Young Turk" Mehmed Talat Pasha. As minister of the interior of the Ottoman Empire, he was largely responsible for the genocide of the Armenians in 1915.

In the late nineteenth century, Armenians, with their distinct culture and Nestorian Christian religion, lived within the mainly Muslim Ottoman Empire as what the Turks referred to as a *millet-i-sadkika*, a "loyal nation." However, the Armenians were accorded fewer rights than other Turkish citizens: they could not testify in court, could not bear arms, could not rise in the army beyond the position of enlisted men, and were harshly taxed. By 1885, the first Armenian political parties had been born and Armenian nationalists had begun to raise their voices against these injustices. When they did, Turkish troops, along with Kurds (whom the Ottomans often used to attack Armenians), began to assault Armenian villages. When the Armenians armed themselves and fought back, the Turks killed so many of them—some estimates of Armenian deaths in the period 1894–98 are in the hundreds of thousands—that even Western powers became alarmed and condemned the Ottoman leader, Sultan Abdul Hamid II.

In 1908, it seemed that things would get better for the Armenians. A political group that called itself the Committee for Union and Progress—later known as the "Young Turks"—forced its way into power in Turkey and insisted that Abdul Hamid give religious and political freedom to all subjects of the empire. In 1909, a bitter civil war ensued between forces loyal to the Young Turks and the followers of Abdul

Hamid. The Armenians lost thirty thousand people in this war, mainly during a massacre by the forces of the sultan near the city of Adana. The Young Turks finally gained full control of the Ottoman Empire in 1913, when they formed the Ittihad Triumvirate of Enver Pasha, Ahmed Cemal Pasha, and Mehmed Talat Pasha, all men in their thirties.

At first, the Armenians were overjoyed. Now, it seemed, there was a Turkish government that would bestow upon them true citizenship, possibly even independence. But their hopes were quickly dashed. The Young Turks were nationalists desperate to revive Turkey's faltering economy and antiquated transportation systems; while suspicious of the intentions of most European states, they began to look toward Germany as a model nation-state whose militarism was to be emulated. The Young Turks decided that the only way for Turkey to reclaim its former greatness in the face of modern economic competition was to revive the dream of a pan-Turkic empire that extended all the way to Central Asia. To achieve that they would not only have to deal with the Jews, Greeks, and Bulgarians in the country, but also with the largest minority group, the two million Armenians.

THE "ARMENIAN QUESTION" What the Young Turks called "the Armenian Question"—there are obvious parallels here with Hitler's "Jewish Question"—stemmed in part from the growing nationalist aspirations of the Armenians, who were by this time clamoring for improved living conditions and greater participation in government. The Turks were also unhappy that the Armenians were beginning to make their plight of subjugation and poverty known in other states with Christian populations, such as France, Italy, and Russia—states that might use the issue as an excuse to invade Turkey. In addition, the strong ethnic differences between the Armenians and Turks meant that the former were a major obstacle to the dream of a homogenous pan-Turkic empire.

The outbreak of World War I gave the Turks the excuse they needed to begin eradicating the Armenians. The Ottoman Empire allied itself with Germany and, in response, was invaded by Russia, fighting in support of France and Great Britain. The Russian advance into eastern Turkey was backed by many Armenians. To "protect" other Armenians from the Russians, the Turkish government decided to remove them from the region. A plan was secretly conceived, to be managed by the Turkish Ministry of the Interior under Talat Pasha. It involved deportation, execution, and starvation.

The plan was put in motion on the night of April 23, 1915, when six hundred Armenian intellectuals, including writers, artists, priests, journalists, and doctors, were roused from their beds in Constantinople, taken to remote areas, and murdered. The aim was to prevent these cultural leaders urging their people to resist what was about to happen. A list of names had been drawn up for Minister of the Interior Pasha by an Armenian traitor named Harootiun Mugerditchian.

Throughout the summer and fall of 1915, villages all over Armenia were emptied, usually with only three days' notice. Some of the Armenians were moved by train, some were able to bring their wagons, but most were forced to walk. Long,

snaking lines of deportees headed south toward the Syrian Desert. But only about a quarter of those ousted from the central plateau would make it there. So-called "Special Organization" troops eliminated able-bodied men along the way, either by shooting them outright or forming them into "labor battalions" and starving and working them to death.

Gradually it became clear that the deportees were being driven out into the open simply to be killed. At remote sites along the route, they were set upon by units of Kurdish cavalry who shot and stabbed them in a frenzy.

Those who made it to the desert faced the final part of the Turkish plan: extermination by starvation. No shelters had been prepared for them. Men and women dying of thirst were shot for trying to drink from the Euphrates River. Tens of thousands died in the heat. Finally, at a remote place in the desert called Deir el-Zor, units of Turkish forces and Kurds moved in and, in a final carnage, butchered tens of thousands. By 1916, nearly all the Armenians had disappeared from the central plateau.

MARCH FROM ERZINCAN

The genocidal Turkish forces caught up with the eighteen-year-old Soghomon Tehlirian and his family in June of 1915, in their home near Erzincan. The Turks ordered that the entire population of the town—about twenty-thousand in all—turn over their valuables to the Turkish authorities and form a column. They were then marched away by Turkish soldiers. With Tehlirian were his mother, his three sisters, his sister's husband, his two brothers, and a two-year-old niece. After marching for several hours, they heard gunfire coming from the head of the column. Suddenly, all was chaos. Turkish troops descended on Tehlirian's group, shooting, clubbing, and stabbing. Tehlirian's mother was shot dead. His sisters were dragged away into the bushes and raped. An ax cleaved Tehlirian's brother's skull right in front of him. And then something smashed into Tehlirian's head and he fell unconscious.

When he awoke, it was dark. He felt a heavy weight on him and pushed against it: it was the corpse of his brother. As well as having been clubbed in the head, Tehlirian had been shot in the arm and bayoneted in the knee, and then left for dead. He staggered around and found his sisters' corpses in some bushes and his mother's lying nearby.

Overwhelmed with horror, he realized that he was the only survivor from the column. According to Tehlirian, he found his way to a remote mountain village, where a kindly woman gave him clothes to replace his bloodstained ones. After resting a short time, he began a long journey eastward toward the Russian border, traveling only at night, in the company of two other Armenian refugees. Sometimes the trio only had grass to eat. One of them died. The exhausting trip took two months.

Tehlirian then found his way to Tiflis in Georgia, where he joined the Armenian Revolutionary Federation (ARF), an Armenian nationalist group that was forming partisan units to fight the Turks. At first, Tehlirian worked as a medic, but the hatred growing inside of him was too strong and he eventually became a guerilla fighter.

For the next three years he helped battle the Turkish forces. At the end of the war, weak and suffering from the aftereffects of typhus, and haunted by dreams of his mother (in which she begged him to cover her corpse), he went to Constantinople. He got a job as a shoemaker, and fell in with a group of Armenian refugees. Like many other Armenian survivors, he put advertisements in newspapers, seeking any relatives who might have survived the deportation. But it seemed an entire nation had disappeared.

In the meantime, with the war over, the Western powers put pressure on the new puppet Turkish government to punish those responsible for the genocide, which had been reported throughout the war by some news organizations, the *New York Times* prominent among them. The new sultan installed by the British, Muhammad VI, declared an extraordinary military tribunal, before which sixty-one members of the Young Turk government were tried for atrocities against the Armenian people. The trials began in January 1919 and a good deal of evidence was brought out to show Turkish involvement in the killings. In the end, though, the only Turk who paid a high price was Governor Kemal Bay, who was charged with organizing the killings of

MODERN ARMENIAN TERRORISM

The revival of Armenian terrorism was triggered in 1973 when an elderly survivor of the genocide, who had lost his entire family in the massacre, killed two Turkish diplomats in America. In 1979 and 1980, a group called the Justice Commandos of the Armenian Genocide assassinated the Turkish ambassadors in Vienna and Paris and were responsible for many smaller incidents, including bombings of Turkish tourist spots. A group calling itself the Armenian Secret Army for the Liberation of Armenia (ASALA) seized the Turkish Consulate in Paris in 1983 and held twenty hostages, killing one and wounding thee others. Four years later, ASALA occupied the Turkish Embassy in Ottawa, although the Turkish ambassador managed to escape. No further attacks occurred, possibly because of internal schisms. The ASALA leader, Hagop Hagopian, was assassinated on an Athens sidewalk in 1988. His assailants were never caught; intelligence experts suspect either dissident members of ASALA, or possibly members of a secret ultranationalist organization of Turks known as the Gray Wolves.

the Armenians of an entire district. His defense was typical of those involved in genocides, such as the Nazi officers who organized the Holocaust: he "only carried out orders," he said. Bay was hung; numerous underlings were given prison sentences.

The three Young Turk leaders, Talat, Enver, and Cemal, had escaped to Odessa in a German submarine at the end of the war. The military tribunal sentenced them to death in absentia, but no attempt was made to track them down and carry out the sentences. As far as the Turks and most of the Western powers were concerned, the matter was now closed.

However, it was not closed for the ARF. Meeting in Boston in 1919—many Armenians had fled to America—the organization's central committee decided that it was not satisfied with the outcome of the military tribunal and would take the matter into its own hands. It decreed that the three Young Turk leaders and others would be killed. The committee cast about for a potential assassin for Talat Pasha, the first of the targets, who had been spotted both in Russia and Germany. They found him in Soghomon Tehlirian.

LEARNING TO KILL While living and working in Constantinople, Tehlirian had noticed that many of the Armenian refugees with whom he spent his time in cafés were trying to forget the genocide, to banish the awful memories, to move on with their lives. Tehlirian was unable to do this. The images of his murdered family were with him everywhere. He began to have epileptic seizures that were almost certainly a result of the blow he had taken on the head. He bought a pistol and carried it around with him.

In 1919, Tehlirian met an older woman, a teacher named Yeranoohi Danielian, who became a good friend to him and listened to his troubles. One day, they walked by a house and Yeranoohi told Tehlirian that the man who lived in it, an Armenian named Harootiun Mugerditchian, was the man who had supplied the Turks with the list of intellectuals to be arrested and killed on the first night of the genocide.

Tehlirian became obsessed with Mugerditchian, and could not believe he was living the good life while his victims moldered in the ground. He found himself returning again and again to Mugerditchian's house, watching through the window as the man entertained his friends. Finally, one day in April of 1919, without conscious premeditation, while Mugerditchian sat at a table surrounded by ten guests, Tehlirian pulled his gun out of his pocket, aimed it at the informer, and shot through the window. Mugerditchian died the next day. Tehlirian escaped, and was pleased and gratified when his fellow Armenians reacted with great rejoicing.

The ARF heard about Tehlirian through Yeranoohi Danielian, who had meanwhile migrated to America, and paid Tehlirian's way to Boston, where he finally appeared in front of the central committee. They asked him a lot of questions—about his past life, about his shooting of Mugerditchian, about his feelings with regard to the genocide. It became apparent that they were sizing him up. At last, he was put in the hands of a secret committee with the code name of Nemesis (the goddess of retribution in Greek mythology). There, he was asked if he would be

willing to commit another assassination, this time of Talat Pasha, who was now in Europe, although the ARF did not know yet exactly where. Tehlirian agreed and was then sent back overseas, to a safe house in Geneva, Switzerland. There, he received a letter stating that his target was in Berlin.

With the help of ARF operatives, Tehlirian was able to get an apartment almost across the street from where Talat was staying. He began to stalk his quarry. But he was an amateur assassin, and clearly mentally disturbed. On one occasion when he saw Talat from his window and decided to kill him, the lock on his door stuck and he was unable to leave his room in time to reach his target. He drew attention to himself by pacing back and forth and talking to himself at all hours, drinking cognac at breakfast, and having Armenian friends over, with whom he played the mandolin and sang sad songs. Twice, while on the trail of Talat in Berlin, he had epileptic

Many of the massacres of the Armenians were carried out once the refugees arrived in what is now Syria. These Armenians were murdered in the town of Aleppo.

seizures. He also followed Talat's wife, a well-known beauty, to the Berlin Botanical Gardens, and found himself transfixed by her loveliness. When he left his room to shoot Talat on March 15, Tehlirian had not planned any escape route, and in fact, lingered to stare at the corpse of his victim, which is why he was caught.

Soghomon Tehlirian, in a photograph taken in 1921, around the time of his trial for the murder of Talat Pasha.

KILLER WITH A CLEAR CONSCIENCE

After he was arrested, however, Tehlirian realized fairly quickly that his only hope of avoiding the guillotine was to portray the crime as a personal act of revenge against the man he thought responsible for the deaths of his family, rather than as a cold-blooded act of political assassination. Therefore, he hid his connection with ARF and glossed over certain personal details—for instance, in telling the story of his escape after the massacre of his family, he hid the fact that he had been an Armenian guerilla fighter for three years. The murder had exploded in the German press, making all the front pages. Some newspapers were sympathetic to the Armenian, but others decried the killing of a former head of government of a former ally in broad daylight on a Berlin street.

As Tehlirian waited for trial, he was often heard singing songs to himself in his cell. Sometimes an Armenian priest visited, but they were not allowed to converse in a foreign language, so they merely sat together in silent comfort. Three attorneys were appointed for Tehlirian, the lead one being an experienced and intelligent German lawyer named Adolf von Gordon. Tehlirian was examined by psychologists and neurologists for the defense and prosecution. When his case began, on July 2, 1921, the courtroom was overflowing with spectators and journalists. Tehlirian wore a black suit as he sat at the defense table. Looking around, he saw Talat's widow, staring at him from the seats. He turned away.

By this time, Tehlirian was certain that he would be found guilty and executed. But the judge was not unsympathetic and Tehlirian's testimony was moving and horrifying, as the official transcript makes clear:

DEFENDANT [SOGHOMON TEHLIRIAN]: While we were being plundered, they started firing on us from the front of the caravan. At that time, one of the gendarmes pulled my sister out and took her with him. My mother cried out, "May I go blind." I cannot remember that day any longer. I do not want to be reminded of that day. It is better for me to die than describe the events of that black day.
PRESIDING JUSTICE: However, I want to point out to you that, for this court, it is very important that we hear of these events from you. You are the only one that can give us information about those events. Try to pull yourself together and not lose control.
DEFENDANT: I cannot say everything. Every time I relive those events … They took everyone away … and they struck me. Then I saw how they struck and cracked my brother's skull with an ax.
PRESIDING JUSTICE: Your sister, the one whom they pulled and took with them, did she return?

DEFENDANT: Yes, they took my sister and raped her.

PRESIDING JUSTICE: Did she return?

DEFENDANT: No.

PRESIDING JUSTICE: Who cracked your brother's skull with an ax?

DEFENDANT: As soon as the soldiers and the gendarmes began the massacres, the mob was upon us too and my brother's head was cracked open. Then my mother fell.

PRESIDING JUSTICE: From what?

DEFENDANT: I do not know, from a bullet or something else.

PRESIDING JUSTICE: Where was your father?

DEFENDANT: I did not see my father; he was in another group ahead of us, but there was fighting going on there too.

PRESIDING JUSTICE: What did you do?

DEFENDANT: I was struck on the head and fell to the ground. I have no recollection of what happened after that.

The judge gradually led Tehlirian through these recollections and then arrived at the morning of March 15:

PRESIDING JUSTICE: When did the idea first occur to you to kill Talat?

DEFENDANT: Approximately two weeks before the incident. I was feeling very bad. I kept seeing over and over again the scenes of the massacres. I saw my mother's corpse. The corpse just stood up before me and told me, "You know Talat is here and yet you do not seem to be concerned. You are no longer my son."

PRESIDING JUSTICE: What feeling did you have, seeing Talat Pasha dead before you? What were your thoughts?

DEFENDANT: I do not know what I felt immediately after the incident.

PRESIDING JUSTICE: But after a while you must have realized what you had done.

DEFENDANT: I realized what I had done after they brought me to the police station.

PRESIDING JUSTICE: Then, what did you think of what you had done?

DEFENDANT: I felt a great satisfaction.

PRESIDING JUSTICE: How do you feel about it now?

DEFENDANT: Even today, I feel a great sense of satisfaction.

PRESIDING JUSTICE: You are aware, of course, that under normal circumstances, no one has the right to be his own judge, no matter how much one has suffered.

DEFENDANT: I do not consider myself guilty because my conscience is clear.

PRESIDING JUSTICE: Why is your conscience clear?

DEFENDANT: I have killed a man. But I am not a murderer.

The trial would last only two days. The German prosecutors tried to highlight Tehlirian's connections with Armenian dissidents, but failed, while von Gordon returned repeatedly to Tehlirian's epileptic attacks, the massacre of his family, and his visions of his mother. The defense also brought in some by-then infamous

IN DENIAL

Just as there are many people who deny that the killing of six million Jews by Germany did not take place—a prominent denier of the Holocaust, Englishman David Irving, was sentenced in 2006 to prison in Austria for two years—so the world abounds with deniers of the Armenian genocide.

It is claimed on several internet sites that the Armenian genocide was "falsified." Some claim that Tehlirian was a guerilla fighter with the Russians before the 1915 killing of his family. It is also claimed that he had no sisters, just three brothers; that he lied about his father's presence in the convoy—supposedly his father was away on business in Belgrade at the time; that Tehlirian wasn't even present at the convoy scene; and that only his mother and one brother were killed, accidentally, during the "process of relocation."

There are actually some inconsistencies in Tehlirian's testimony—it is not apparent if his father was really there, and Tehlirian may have been trying to hide his father's real whereabouts—but the details of the massacre as described by Tehlirian are identical to the verified details of many other massacres of the Armenians, and there is no doubt that these massacres occurred. Proving your story is difficult when you are the only one left to tell the tale.

THE WRATH OF ISRAEL

One can't help but draw parallels between the assassins of Nemesis, the ARF assassination wing, and the gunmen sent out by the Israeli secret service, Mossad, to take revenge on the Black September terrorists after the murder of Israeli athletes at the 1972 Munich Olympics. Even the name of the Mossad operation, Operation Wrath of God, echoes that of Nemesis.

Only a few short months after the Olympic massacres, in December of 1972, the PLO's representative in Paris was killed by a radio-controlled bomb. In the next eight years or so numerous PLO operatives associated with the massacre were killed. Some claim that the revenge effort went on for more than twenty years. Recently, however, some intriguing questions have been raised about Operation Wrath of God.

In his book *Striking Back: The 1972 Munich Olympics Massacre and Israel's Deadly Response*, Aaron J. Klein claims that Mossad succeeded in assassinating only one terrorist directly associated with the massacre, and killed him as late as 1992. Mainly, says Klein, only minor Palestinian activists were killed, while the real planners of the operation escaped to Eastern bloc countries, out of the reach of Mossad. Israeli officials do not comment on this, claiming only that any activity which disrupted terrorism was to the good.

telegrams from Talat Pasha, in which he specifically ordered the deportations and massacres, and called as witnesses Armenian massacre survivors, who testified to the horrors of the genocide. It was one of the first times these accounts had been heard in a court of law. The jury and spectators listened silently.

On the afternoon of the second day of the trial, the judge charged the jury and sent them to deliberate. To everyone's astonishment, they returned in an hour. The court reporter's transcript catches the chaos of the moment:

FOREMAN: I avow with honor and clear conscience to the verdict of the jury. (*Proceeds to read jury's findings.*): Is the defendant, Soghomon Tehlirian, guilty of having intentionally killed a man, Talat Pasha, on March 15, 1921, in Charlottenburg? No. Signed Otto Reinecke, Foreman of the Jury.
(*There is a great deal of commotion and applause in the courtroom.*)
PRESIDING JUSTICE: I now sign the verdict and I ask the clerk to do the same and read the verdict out loud.
(*The secretary reads the verdict and it is translated for the defendant.*)
SECRETARY: The defendant is acquitted at the expense of the state treasury. (*Renewed commotion and applause.*) In accordance with the decision of the jury, the defendant is not guilty of the punishable act with which he has been charged.

Then the following decision was announced.

PRESIDING JUSTICE: The order of imprisonment as regards the defendant is hereby annulled.
(*The defendant is congratulated by his defense attorneys, his compatriots, and the public in attendance.*)

FORGETTING AND REMEMBERING
Soghomon Tehlirian was acquitted, in German legal terms, because of Article 51—essentially, because the jury thought that he had acted "in a state of insensibility or morbid disturbance." In other words, he had been temporarily insane at the moment he pulled the trigger. At the same time, everyone, including the jury, knew that Talat had been killed for his role in the Armenian genocide.

Tehlirian's verdict was a great victory for the Armenian people. Nemesis unleashed further assassins, killing five Young Turks; every one of the assassins either escaped capture or was acquitted in a court of law for the same reasons as Tehlirian. Enver Pasha, the last living member of the Ittihad Triumvirate, was killed in a battle with Red Army solders in August of 1922, in Soviet Turkestan, where he had gone to try to foment a rebellion against the Bolsheviks.

Tehlirian's acquittal, along with the acquittals of the other Nemesis killers, raised a thorny ethical dilemma still pertinent today: is it morally defensible to kill in cold blood to revenge a wrong? The United States has resorted to assassination of terrorist figures (and attempted or planned assassinations of national leaders such as Fidel Castro and Saddam Hussein), claiming it is defending itself from future attacks. The same holds true for Israel, both in the past and in its more recent killings of Hamas leaders. But is it ever moral to kill purely for revenge? Moral or not, it is understandable. Whole communities of Armenians simply disappeared after the genocide. No family was left intact, and most of the survivors were orphans and widows. Had it not been for a massive 1920s relief effort organized by the Americans for "the starving Armenians" (refugees who had made their way to Russia and parts of the Middle East), it is possible that, as a people, the Armenians would not have survived. Severed from their historical homeland, with their wealth gone, the Armenians dispersed across the world.

As time passed after Tehlirian's trial, the world began to forget the Armenian massacre, and the Turks mounted a campaign to discredit Armenian accusers. The Turkish government refused to admit that it participated in the genocide, claiming that the numbers of dead were not large, that they were killed accidentally during a genuine effort to relocate them for their own safety, or that they were eliminated because they were partisans fighting for the Russians.

Because people forgot, or denied the massacre, others with similar agendas became emboldened. In 1939, eight days before he invaded Poland and initiated a genocide of his own, Hitler told a gathering of his generals, "Who today, after all, speaks of the annihilation of the Armenians?" At the same time, the trial of Soghomon Tehlirian was a watershed for opponents of tyranny. Attending the trial was a twenty-three-year-old law student named Robert Kempner, a German Jew who later fled to America. Kempner said that the trial had an extraordinary effect on him and on the way he viewed crimes against the world community. After World War II, he became one of the chief American prosecutors at Nuremberg, where he helped punish the perpetrators of the Holocaust.

The eastern part of Armenia became a republic of the Soviet Union in 1923. In the 1970s, Armenians around the world again resorted to terrorism against their former oppressor (see Modern Armenian Terrorism, p. 302) in an attempt to get Turkey to acknowledge its guilt in the genocide. Since becoming an independent republic in 1990, Armenia has continued to call, in the United Nations, for the Turks to accept responsibility for the massacres, which Turkey still refuses to do.

After his trial, Tehlirian left Germany and ultimately emigrated to the United States, where he married, had children, and lived until the age of sixty-five, dying in 1962, in Fresno, California. Although he kept a low profile for fear of Turkish retaliation, he was revered by the Armenian community, and his memory still is. On a visit to the large Armenian population of Fresno in 2005, His Holiness, the Catholicus Karekin II, patriarch of the Armenian Christian Church, made a point of stopping at Tehlirian's grave. In this day and age of terrorism, the Catholicus's office was reluctant to draw too much attention to this gesture, merely stating in a press release that "Soghomon Tehlirian's memory is connected with the mastermind of the Armenian Genocide, Talat Pasha (Berlin, March 15, 1921)." For Armenians that was all that needed to be said.

WILLIAM BEEBE AND OTIS BARTON: EXPLORERS OF THE DEEP

Ever since the beginnings of history ... thousands upon thousands of
human beings had reached the depth at which we were now suspended,
and had passed on to lower levels. But all of them were dead ...
William Beebe, *Half Mile Down*

ETWEEN 1930 AND 1934, WILLIAM BEEBE, A NATURALIST, SCIENTIST,
and early environmentalist, and Otis Barton, a rich and eccentric deep-
sea dilettante, made a series of dives in the Atlantic Ocean off Bermuda in
a strange vessel, called a "bathysphere," that Barton had designed himself—essentially, a hollow metal ball suspended from a ship on a cable. Before this, no human
being had ever dived deeper than a few hundred feet.

Beebe and Barton made it all the way down to 3,028 feet, becoming the first men
to arrive "beyond the level of humanly visible light," as Beebe was to write, and
return alive. There they saw a world far stranger than Jules Verne or any other novelist could imagine—so strange, in fact, that Beebe was accused of writing fiction
when he described the creatures who swarmed past the bathysphere's windows.

Although they themselves are all but forgotten, the influence of Barton and
Beebe endures to this day. Not only did they pave the way for subsequent deep-sea
exploration in a variety of similarly bizarre craft, they—particularly Beebe—were also
pioneers in a field of scientific study that is hugely popular today: marine ecology.
For they were the first scientists to truly explore what many researchers now believe
to be the largest ecosystem on the planet: the depths of the sea. However, despite
their successes and the attractive alliterative coupling of their names—sounding so
much like a Park Avenue law firm or an upscale haberdashery—Barton and Beebe
were an odd couple, who very quickly got on each other's nerves, both inside the
cramped bathysphere and out. After their last dive together, on September 11, 1934,
they shook hands on a Bermuda dock and never spoke to each other again.

DOWN IN THE DEEP BLUE SEA
Water covers two-thirds of the surface of the Earth, and the average depth of the ocean floor is 12,450 feet, or four and a half times the average height of the Earth's surface above the water. The first human beings to go underwater did so simply by dint of holding their breath and were probably able to dive down as much as one hundred feet—only after learning the art of returning to the surface slowly, however, because a rapid return results in decompression sickness, or the bends.

But to spend any time underwater—to explore, to salvage, to seek treasure—one needs an artificial way to breathe. Aristotle reported on Greek divers as early as the fourth century BC, men who inverted buckets or cauldrons over their heads, thus trapping air temporarily, before entering the water. Aristotle and others also told the story of how Alexander the Great had himself lowered deep in the sea in "a very fine barrel made entirely out of white glass," so desirous was he of observing underwater life. Supposedly, he saw a sea monster so large it took three days and nights to pass in front of him. A lovely legend, but modern scientists point out that there were no chains heavy enough for this in an era of primitive metallurgy.

Nevertheless, legends like this reflect a long-standing fascination with undersea exploration. In the sixteenth century, the Italian inventor Guglielmo de Lorena created the first diving bell, a watertight chamber open at the bottom, in which a man was lowered into the shallow depths of Lake Nemi, near Rome, in an unsuccessful attempt to recover the sunken pleasure galleys of the Emperor Caligula. Lorena's diving bell covered the top of the diver's body and incorporated glass ports to allow the diver to see out; the person inside could also extend his hands from under the rim.

The modern diving bell was invented by none other than Edmond Halley, the astronomer and mathematician for whom Halley's Comet is named. In 1690, he designed a diving bell that would allow divers to spend extended periods under the sea. The bell consisted of a trapezoid-shaped, weighted structure built of wood, with a glass top; it was fed by barrels full of air, which were also weighted and sunk alongside the diving bell and linked to it by pipes. Halley claimed that he and four assistants remained underwater for about two hours in this device, descending to a depth of approximately sixty feet.

By the late nineteenth century, divers were using helmets into which air was pumped. By the 1920s, full diving suits allowed divers to descend three hundred feet; however, the bends were a problem, despite the fact that new prevention techniques, such as decompression chambers, were starting to be employed.

UNITED STATES OF AMERICA

APPALACHIAN MOUNTAINS

Boston

Martha's Vineyard

New York

Washington D.C.

ATLANTIC OCEAN

Raleigh

Cape Hatteras

BERMUDA

Just off the coast of Bermuda, the Atlantic Ocean drops to a depth of two miles, offering deep-sea conditions close to the east coast of North America.

luy auoit faicte qui l'estoit / sain: sauf descendu a terre

This fifteenth-century illuminated manuscript shows Alexander the Great being lowered into the sea in a primitive diving bell, said to have been made of "white glass."

THE NEW FRONTIER OF SCIENCE

Even before William Beebe set foot in his bathysphere—at the age of fifty-one—he had a career that most men would envy. Born in Brooklyn in 1877 to a well-to-do middle-class family, Beebe was raised in New Jersey and spent most of his summers traipsing the wilds of Pennsylvania and Canada. He had a flair for writing and was intensely interested in anything natural: he built snow houses, aquariums, and boats, identified flora and fauna, and taught himself how to stuff bird specimens. When he graduated from high school, his mother, seeing a scientist in the making, took him to New York and convinced two curators at the American Museum of Natural History to supervise his education. With their help, he enrolled in the Department of Zoology at Columbia University, where, frustrated by formal education, he seems to have taken few courses, but sat in on many lectures. Whatever happened, he must have impressed people: three years later, in 1899, despite not having obtained a degree, he was offered a job as assistant curator of ornithology at the Bronx Zoo.

Almost immediately, he began publishing articles on ornithology in such periodicals as *Harper's,* the *Ladies' Home Journal,* and the *Atlantic Monthly.* At the same time, his writing began appearing in various scientific journals, such as *Science*, *American Naturalist*, and *Zoologica*. He became a natural writer who straddled both the popular and academic worlds, much like the late Stephen Jay Gould. While he kept his curator job at the Bronx Zoo for the rest of his life, he branched out from ornithology to become an early ecologist, traveling to Asia, the Caribbean, and South America. Beebe was ahead of his time in that he wasn't just interested in plucking specimens from the jungle and examining them: he wanted to know how an organism functioned *within its environment*, a tenet of the modern science of ecology.

By the mid-1920s, Beebe had made a hugely successful career for himself. He had published ten books, hundreds of articles, and had thousands of fans in America and Great Britain. He lived in a penthouse in New York City and was a well-known figure in the city's "Roaring Twenties" social scene. He numbered among his friends Rube Goldberg, the cartoonist, and the celebrated and much-married Fannie Hurst, and had been a close friend of former U.S. President Theodore Roosevelt before his death in 1919. Beebe was tall, thin, and balding, but radiated intellectual charisma, and was known for his stormy relationships with women. By the mid-1920s he had been through a bitter divorce and then been married again, to a writer of popular novels named Elswyth Thane, who was twenty-seven years his junior.

Around this time, Beebe became more interested in ocean exploration. He had begun to explore shallow waters off the Atlantic coast in a copper diving helmet, and write about these adventures for his myriad fans. From this, he segued into going helmet-diving in the Sargasso Sea and around the Galapagos, and from then on he was hooked. He wanted to go deeper—far deeper than the technology would then allow—for he now saw the ocean as the newest frontier of scientific study.

Little scientific exploration had been carried out in the ocean since the first real scientific study of it, the 1872 HMS *Challenger* expedition. The *Challenger*, which carried a team of British naturalists, towed cables and nets that could dredge the seafloor to a depth of five miles. Using this equipment, the scientists established that the sea bottom was marked with ravines and peaks, just like the Earth's surface. Furthermore, numerous specimens of previously unknown fish brought up by the *Challenger*'s nets revealed that, far from being too cold to sustain life, as prevailing theory had it, the deep sea contained a broad and diverse range of sea creatures.

But no one had ever gone far enough below the surface to view this marine life. Beebe was determined to be the first. He recalled an idle conversation that he had had with Teddy Roosevelt before the latter's death, in which they discussed the ideal shape a diving tank should be. Roosevelt thought it should be a sphere, but Beebe had thought that it should be shaped like a cylinder. By 1926, he had begun to design one along these lines. Ever the publicist, he told New York newspapers that he would have it made and use it to become the first man to see the creatures of the deep.

MEANS TO DESCEND
Otis Barton, who was to become Beebe's scientific companion and ultimately his bête noire, was born with a very large silver spoon in his mouth in New England, in 1899, which made him

twenty-two years younger than Beebe and a lot richer. Barton's father had made a fortune in New Hampshire's textile mills before dying young and bequeathing it to Otis's mother, who moved the family—Otis and his two sisters—to Boston. The Bartons were soon in the company of the Lowells, Cabots, and Coolidges, the city's aristocratic families, and Barton was raised accordingly. He went to Groton and later Harvard, and spent his summers on Martha's Vineyard.

Handsome, with a shock of dark hair, Barton had the rare gift of an eidetic memory: one look at a page of writing or a picture and he could later recall it in precise detail. This helped him enormously with his academic studies, but may have created a barrier between him and other students; in any event, he was a day-dreamer and a loner.

The place where Barton felt most at home was the ocean. During his childhood summers on the Vineyard, he practiced walking underwater weighted with steel shot in bags around his waist and sucking air from a garden hose held by an accomplice in a boat, but discovered that his lungs were not strong enough to suck enough air once he reached a depth of six feet or so. Having seen pictures of Alexander the Great's supposed descent, he even practiced going underwater with a washtub over his head, its handles tied to his shoulders. He could breathe, but the washtub was so buoyant that he kept floating back to the surface. When he was still just sixteen, he designed his own diving helmet—a wooden box with a glass panel at the front—which received air via a hose and pump. A local craftsman made it for him, and he found out that it actually worked. With his brother Francis manning the pump, he would walk for half an hour at a time around the bottom of the local harbor, a feeling he described as like being in church.

After graduating from college in the spring of 1922, Barton wandered the world for a year, shooting big game in Africa and reef-diving in the Philippines, and then went to New York to attend graduate school in engineering at Columbia. But he continued to research the idea of deep-sea diving, and had begun, in his spare time, to sketch out a design for a diving chamber that could go deep beneath the surface and withstand the ocean's overwhelming water pressure.

Its spherical shape would distribute the stresses more evenly, and it would contain trays of soda lime and calcium chloride that would absorb the byproducts of human respiration (carbon dioxide and moisture), as well as two oxygen tanks that would provide enough air for about eight hours. It would be made of two-inch-thick steel and have three eight-inch viewing windows, each consisting of two panes of quartz fused together, which would create a strong yet brilliantly transparent port-hole that could withstand pressure of up to seven thousand pounds per square inch. The doorway of the tank would be so heavy that it would have to be lifted off with a block and tackle. And the whole thing would be lowered into the sea via steel cable four thousand feet long and an inch thick. When Barton was done, he was so certain he had a diving tank that would work that he commissioned a marine architect to turn his drawings into a finished design. Then, in the fall of 1928, he wrote to William Beebe at the Bronx Zoo and asked to see him about a certain matter of interest.

Opposite: Otis Barton stares out of the bathysphere prior to the first dive in 1930. For Barton, the descent was the culmination of more than a decade of research and experimentation.

THE FUTURE UNDERWATER

William Beebe was convinced that scores of bathyspheres would spread out across the sea in the future, providing humans with a true picture of the ocean deep's habitats. But this did not happen, at least not as he envisioned it. In the 1950s, Japan and the Soviet Union used bathyspheres, not to study ecosystems as Beebe would have done, but to observe fish behavior and thereby maximize the possibilities of commercial fishing. After the deep dives of Jacques Piccard, undersea technology turned in another direction, to the work of Jacques Cousteau, who developed the aqualung and experimented with undersea habitats, where divers spent several weeks at a time. (In 1965, former U.S. astronaut Scott Carpenter spent thirty days in one of these habitats, at a depth of 205 feet.) By the end of the twentieth century, undersea research had turned to remote-controlled submersibles— Remote Operated Vehicles, or ROVs— which bear grappling arms and highly sophisticated video cameras. These have already provided a much fuller picture of the world only glimpsed by Barton and Beebe.

Barton had followed the famous Beebe's diving adventures with keen interest, and knew from reading the *New York Times* that the scientist intended to build a cylindrical diving tank. He also knew that this would not work as the conical shape would not properly distribute the pressure of the ocean. Getting to Beebe was a problem, however. Beebe did not respond to his letters and finally Barton had to use his social connections to enlist the help of a *New York Times* reporter in arranging a meeting with Beebe. On the appointed day, in December of 1928, Barton showed up at Beebe's office at the Bronx Zoo, with blueprints under his arm, and made his pitch. Beebe was immediately impressed by the younger man's engineering knowledge and by the professionalism of his design. So he made a deal with Barton. Barton would pay for and supervise the construction of the diving chamber, and, once it was made, own it and all its equipment. In return, Beebe would make their deep-sea diving venture an official Zoological Society Expedition, which would help them raise money for the trip and for chartering a boat with a winch big enough to lower the … the what? What would they call their diving tank? After a few days, Beebe called Barton with the answer: they would call it the *bathysphere*, from the Greek words for "deep" and "ball."

Having found a hydraulic company in New Jersey that could produce the bathysphere, Barton threw himself enthusiastically into supervising its construction, paying for it with his sizable trust fund. The first steel ball he came up with weighed five tons, much too heavy for the winch that would have to raise and lower it. The next one weighed half that, but its inner diameter was only four feet nine inches, a very cramped space for two men. However, if Barton made it any larger he knew the bathysphere would have to become heavier, so he settled on that size. Adding now to the sophistication of the design was a coil made of strong and flexible rubber, inside of which were two lines, one for the headsets by which Barton and Beebe would communicate with their ship, the other for the electricity that powered the 250-watt searchlight mounted on the side of the bathysphere.

Throughout 1929, Barton perfected his design, while Beebe mounted a publicity campaign and managed to raise funds from rich friends such as Marshall Field, Coleman du Pont, and Bill Boeing. In the meantime, he had decided that the best place to lower the bathysphere into the sea was off tiny, uninhabited Nonsuch Island, off the coast of Bermuda. Beebe loved Bermuda, and, typically, was good friends with its governor. The governor felt the presence of a famous naturalist could only help his colony's tourism industry, and so he gave Beebe the use of the island indefinitely. There was a good dock on Nonsuch and a few buildings (including a former yellow fever quarantine hospital). Even better, ten miles south of the island, the mountain whose summit was Bermuda dropped rapidly to a depth of almost two miles.

ANOTHER BLUE WORLD

On June 6, 1930, a huge barge, the *Ready*, was towed out of Nonsuch Harbor by a tugboat. The *Ready* bore the bathysphere, William Beebe, Otis Barton, a crew of about twenty, and numerous of Beebe's young research assistants. By now, it was apparent that Beebe and Barton were oil and water. During the tests and preparations on Nonsuch, Beebe worked

nonstop from dusk to dawn, while Barton held to a much more leisurely schedule and, refusing to live in the island's primitive accommodations, returned to Bermuda each night to stay in the St. George Hotel.

Still, at this point in their relationship, they each had something the other needed: Beebe's marine expertise and connections, and Barton's knack for fixing almost anything mechanical. Within the bathysphere, Beebe would do most of the observing through the portholes, while Barton would be mainly concerned with checking the oxygen levels and refilling the trays of lime and sodium chloride.

When the moment was ready, each of them squirmed through the fifteen-inch circumference of the hatch—an extremely painful procedure that involved scraping their bodies over rough metal and projecting steel bolts—and put on their telephone headsets. In response to a thumbs-up signal from Beebe, the crew of the *Ready* lifted the steel door into place and hammered home the bolts that secured it, an ear-

About 130 feet long and very stable, the former Royal Navy water carrier the *Ready* was the perfect platform from which to launch the bathysphere.

shattering process for the passengers. It was so claustrophobic inside the bathysphere that each man attempted to be as still as possible, Beebe practicing deep-breathing techniques to calm himself. Through the tiny porthole, they could see the crew walking about, then they heard the winch creaking and felt the bathysphere being lifted. For a moment, Beebe nearly panicked as the sphere dangled over the side of the ship; the quartz windows were so clear it made it seem that they were about to hit the side of the *Ready*. Voices over their headsets assured them they were a good fifteen feet away.

The bathysphere started sinking through the water. At first they could see the hull of the barge, then that passed away and they soon went below fifty feet, the deepest Beebe had ever dived. At one hundred feet, the sea, which had been lit up bright green by the sun's rays, began to darken. At four hundred feet, to their horror, Beebe and Barton noticed a trickle of water on the wall right beneath the hatch. Thinking quickly, Beebe decided that higher pressure would actually seal the leak, and so he asked that the bathysphere be lowered more quickly. It was, and the leak stopped.

They now reached 525 feet, the greatest depth any person had ever reached alive. At six hundred feet, as the water grew darker, it took on a shade of blue, Beebe later wrote in *Half Mile Down*, that no person had ever seen. It was an otherworldly glow, a sort of twilight before the final dark: "The indefinable translucent blue [passed] … through the eye into our very beings. It seemed to me that it must be like the last terrific upflare of a flame before it is quenched."

Beebe called for a halt to the dive at eight hundred feet—"some mental warning," he wrote later, told him that this was enough for this trip. They were raised back up to the surface. Beebe had been so absorbed in what he was seeing that he didn't notice that he had been sitting on a monkey wrench during the entire dive. Its imprint endured on his buttocks for several days.

After having the door sealed more tightly, Barton and Beebe made another dive four days later. But only 250 feet down, their telephone line failed and the crew, unable to communicate with the adventurers, hauled them back up. On June 11, they tried again. This time they tied a dead squid to the side of the bathysphere, hoping to lure some undersea life. At a depth of just over six hundred feet, Beebe saw a jellyfish inches away from his face, "its stomach filled with glowing masses of luminous food." Soon the men realized that turning on their floodlight was unnecessary and distracting, for the creatures in the water around them had evolved to emit light. Beebe and Barton became the first human beings to see a living hatchetfish, a small fish that glowed like tin foil, and a golden-tailed serpent dragon, an eel with transparent, glowing fins. Previous to this dive, some of these creatures had been dragged up by deep-sea trawlers, but many scientific researchers had questioned whether what looked like light organs actually emitted light. Now Beebe and Barton knew that they did.

They reached 1,426 feet, a quarter of a mile down, where the pressure against the bathysphere was about 6.5 million pounds, or 650 pounds per square inch. Beebe, tranquilly watching the surreal marine life, had the near-hallucinatory thought (perhaps produced by an excess of oxygen) that he might open the window and simply swim out among the creatures. Reality set in as he realized that "the first few drops [of water] would have shot through flesh and bone like steel bullets."

Having returned from a world they likened for its alienness to the planet Mars, Beebe and Barton would spend the next two years apart before reuniting for their next dive, in September of 1932.

FRONT-PAGE NEWS

On the day after their last dive, June 12, Beebe wrote a story which he filed under his own byline for the *New York Times*. It appeared on the front page, above the fold, and began: "I descended with Otis Barton yesterday in a steel ball five miles south of Nonsuch Island to a depth of 1,426 feet, checked and double-checked."

After this, the avalanche of publicity began. The two men appeared in scores of newspaper stories and on newsreels. It was a time when adventurers were big business: men and women were flying higher and longer, driving faster, and now, diving deeper, than ever before. However, to Barton's chagrin, his role was widely perceived to be that of a sidekick, as the first line of Beebe's *Times* article had implied (perhaps unintentionally, perhaps not). Beebe seemed to be getting all the credit, partly, of course, because Beebe was the one doing all the writing, and Barton was seen as the rich guy along for the ride.

So Barton looked around for his own niche, and decided that the bathysphere was his entrée to Hollywood. He convinced himself that he could make movies like Frank Buck, the legendary animal trainer who liked to film exciting real-life animal battles between lions or crocodiles, so he trained himself to use a camera and practiced underwater filming in the Caribbean.

In the meantime, Beebe stayed at the research station he had by now developed on Nonsuch Island and continued to study marine life. He did this by taking a trawler out to pull in specimens in nets from predetermined depths, in order to find out where sea creatures were most active. He also pioneered a process called contouring, in which he would enter the bathysphere alone and have the *Ready* drag it through the shallow waters just off Bermuda's coral reefs. There, he studied the ocean bottom, watching the way the life forms changed as the level of the seafloor changed. In all this work, Beebe was again pioneering the observation of organisms within their environments, which would become standard practice among future ecologists.

Both men were busy in ways that underscored their differences and, soon, both of them needed another dive: Barton to advance his film career, and Beebe to further his scientific ambitions.

In September of 1932, the two men clambered into the bathysphere and dived deep into the sea once again. This time, however, they were accompanied by a national American radio audience, for they had agreed to make the first live radio broadcast from the deep—with Beebe announcing, of course. A live lobster was attached to the bathysphere as bait; as the men descended past their old mark of 1,426 feet, they could hear tugboat whistles of celebration over the headsets. The next thirty minutes would be broadcast to millions, and Beebe took full advantage of it, describing a school of

WILLIAM BEEBE'S SEA CREATURES

During the dives in the bathysphere, William Beebe made numerous notes on the strange and exotic species he saw, most of which had never been identified by scientists. With his penchant for the colorful, Beebe gave them extravagant names such as pallid sailfish, abyssal rainbow gar, scimitar mouth, great gulper eel, long-finned ghostfish, exploding flammenwerfer shrimp, and untouchable bathysphere fish. And he claimed to have observed a six-foot-long sea dragon.

Some scientists who reviewed *Half Mile Down* scoffed at Beebe's claims—one wrote that Beebe must have been viewing his luminescent fish "through a misty film breathed into the quartz window by Mr. Beebe's eagerly appressed face"— and the existence of many of these fish is disputed even to this day. Some scientists believe that Beebe willfully made them up, but this does not fit in with his rigorously honest scientific method. It is true, however, that most of the fish described by Beebe have never been spotted again. Yet, as recently as 2001, one scientist claimed that "most of [Beebe's] descriptions fit creatures we know [that] today inhabit the middle layers [of the ocean] just as he saw them. For example, his 'untouchable bathysphere fish,' in fact, [has been verified to be] a new species of dragonfish."

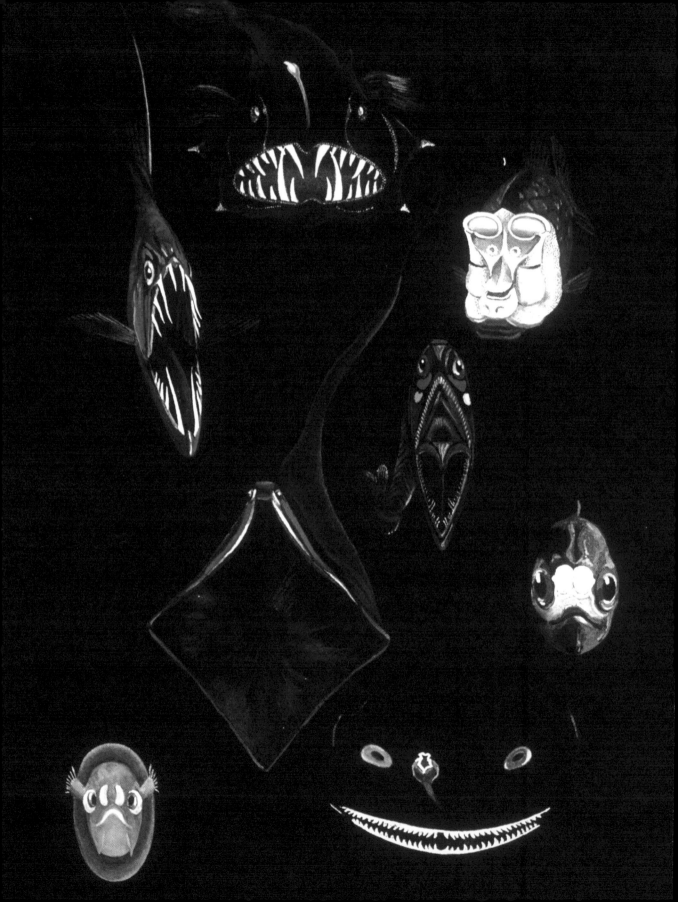

"brilliantly illuminated lantern fish with pale green lights." At 1,700 feet, he reported, they had passed "below the level of humanly visible light, beyond sunlight." He described a ten-inch-long saber-toothed razorfish and reported that he saw a six-foot-long "sea dragon," the existence of which scientists would later question. He also described for the radio audience the feelings he and (presumably) Barton were experiencing, referring to the "utter loneliness and desolation," and the fact that their journey was "akin to a first venture upon the Moon or Venus."

At 1,950 feet the *Ready* began to sway in a heavy swell. The cable jerked and Barton and Beebe were tossed about the bathysphere, Beebe cutting his lip and forehead, and Beebe's radio comments became slightly incoherent: "Cut lip on window ledge, Barton struck head hard on hatch. The sea is boiling with lights and I can make out jet-black comets." At 2,000 feet he reported: "The greenest light seen yet. Loads of little ... I don't know what they are."

At 2,200 feet, both Beebe and Barton were suffering from severe pressure headaches and were also bleeding from their injuries, so Beebe made a final effort and signed off: "Otis Barton and I bid you farewell from a depth of 2,200 feet beneath the surface of the Atlantic Ocean off Bermuda."

LAST DIVES Beebe and, to some extent, Barton, were now more famous than ever. In May of 1933, Beebe and the bathysphere became star attractions at the Chicago World's Fair, where Beebe shared billing with Auguste Piccard, who held the altitude record (51,783 feet) for ascending in a pressurized aluminum sphere lifted by hydrogen balloon. Barton, in the meantime, banked his celebrity—and a large portion of his trust fund, which had dwindled as the Depression set in—on making an underwater movie.

Unfortunately, the bathysphere had been notably neglected during its stint at the World's Fair: it had rusted and its once-fine quartz windows were clouded. Both Beebe and Barton knew that if they were to make the half-mile mark on another dive—they had been four hundred feet short before and Beebe was already working on a book he called *Half Mile Down*—they would need to find funds to overhaul it.

Beebe looked to Gilbert Grosvenor, publisher of the *National Geographic Magazine*, to whom Beebe had already sold two articles about his journeys into the deep in the bathysphere. The National Geographic Society had funded such adventurous trips as Robert Perry's journey to the North Pole and Piccard's balloon ascents. Grosvenor agreed to provide $10,000 for the overhaul, if the expedition would now be "carried out under the name 'National Geographic Society–William Beebe Expedition.'" To this Beebe readily agreed and so did Otis Barton, although the emphasis on Beebe disturbed him (he had already begun to write to newspapers decrying their focus on Beebe and demanding his own interviews).

The two, who had spoken only once since their last dive, entered the overhauled bathysphere on August 15, 1934, to take their last and longest dive together. Reaching 1,600 feet, Beebe saw red shrimp that darted toward his window and seemed to explode, so bright was their internal light. At 2,500 feet, he noted a large,

Opposite: As imagined by artist Else Bostelmann for the *National Geographic Magazine*'s coverage of the dive, the creatures Beebe identified seem to swarm out of a child's nightmare.

dim shape swimming off in the distance, and surmised that it was a whale, which must have "some chemical adjustment of the blood" to allow it to dive so deep (this is in fact true, although recently scientists have discovered that older whales can suffer from decompression sickness if they dive too deep). And, finally, Barton was able to make an identification of his own: a sighting of the first living *Stylophthalmus*, which has eyes at the end of long, periscope-like stalks.

At 11:12 in the morning, Barton and Beebe stopped at 3,028 feet, more than half a mile down. Their journey together was ending, but, as a result of their dives in the bathysphere, many new journeys into the deep and explorations of undersea ecosystems would now begin.

BEEBE AND BARTON PRODUCTIONS
After Barton and Beebe shook hands at the dock in Nonsuch and departed, they never spoke to each other again, but they were consistently aware of each other's presence in the world. Barton irritated Beebe no end by finally making his magnum opus, *Titans of the Deep*, an undersea B movie cobbled together from surface shots of the bathysphere, murky footage of shark attacks, and a few really strange scenes of a girl wearing a diving helmet trying to shoot barracuda with a .22 rifle. To make matters worse, the movie proclaimed that it was a "William Beebe & Otis Barton Production," when Beebe had had nothing to do with it. Furious, he wrote letters to every newspaper in New York when *Titans* opened, to correct what he called "the rather vital misconception" that he was connected to the movie.

Beebe's book, *Half Mile Down*, became a bestseller, even though certain scientists (who to some extent had always resented his celebrity status) questioned his description of the exotic fish he saw through his quartz window. Beebe did not dive deep again, but spent the rest of his life in scientific research, living mainly in Trinidad and making studies of ecosystems there. One of the things he liked to do was segment off an eight-mile-long section of the Atlantic Ocean and study it thoroughly, all the way down, observing life on different levels. He died, much-loved and revered, on June 4, 1962.

Barton lived on until 1992, dividing his time between New York City, California, and his childhood home on Martha's Vineyard. He served as a wartime photographer in the navy and tried to make more movies, but none came to fruition. In the late 1940s, he returned to the idea of deep-sea diving, and invented a successor to the bathysphere, the "Benthoscope," which had extra-wide windows to facilitate photography. It was still connected to the surface by a cable, but had the advantage of being able to roll across the bottom of the sea on wheels. He paid $16,000 of his own money to have it built.

Finally, off the coast of California, on August 19, 1949, fifteen years and a day since the bathysphere had last gone down, Barton took his Benthoscope into the deep blue sea, on his own, and descended to 4,500 feet, breaking his and Beebe's depth record. At last, Barton had bested Beebe.

POINTING THE WAY DOWN

The legacy and influence of Barton and Beebe are underappreciated, for a number of reasons. First of all, the attendant publicity surrounding the descents of the bathysphere, as well as the celebrity status of the "bathynauts," tended to put off serious scientists who might have followed in their footsteps. Secondly, World War II intervened and deep-ocean resources were devoted to building stronger, sleeker, and faster submarines.

In 1960, however, the scientist-adventurer Jacques Piccard, son of the pioneering balloonist who had appeared with Beebe at the 1933 World's Fair, was inspired by Beebe and Barton's adventures to plan another incredible journey. Along with an American submarine officer named Donald Walsh, Piccard took his bathyscaphe *Trieste II* (as opposed to the bathysphere, a bathyscaphe is a submersible vessel that can travel under its own power, like a tiny submarine) 35,810 feet down into the Pacific Ocean, to what is known as the Challenger Deep in the Mariana Trench, the deepest known point on Earth. Walsh and Piccard rested on the ocean floor for twenty minutes, the only human beings to have ever gone so deep.

Beebe and Barton's bathysphere was also a model for *Alvin*, a submersible operated by the Woods Hole Oceanographic Institute, which in the 1970s carried undersea explorers down to the smoking volcanoes, or "black smokers," that lie at the bottom of ocean trenches. Among these explorers was Robert Ballard, who pioneered the use of ROVs, or Remote Operative Vehicles, with which he later discovered the wreck of the *Titanic*. In his book, *The Eternal Darkness: A Personal History of Deep-Sea Exploration*, Ballard devotes his first chapter to Barton and Beebe, calling them "the first human beings [to have] entered the world of eternal darkness and returned alive." The intellectual Beebe, especially, might have approved of Ballard's goal: to explore the deep sea using "telepresence [in which] a mind detaches itself from the body's restrictions and enters the abyss at will."

Furthermore, Beebe's thoroughly modern approach to the study of marine life set new standards in ecology; like most scientists today, he was aware that the best way to learn about particular organisms was to immerse himself—literally in this case—in their environment. Among the first to realize this was the famous American scientist and environmentalist Rachel Carson, who dedicated her study of the oceans, *The Sea around Us*, to Beebe, in 1951. Today, many more, but by no means all, modern ecologists are aware of how much they owe to Beebe and Barton, and their bathysphere.

THE FATE OF THE BATHYSPHERE

Barton and Beebe's bathysphere had a long and interesting journey after they were done diving in it. At one point, Barton turned the machine over to the New York Zoological Society, and from there it was somehow loaned to the U.S. Navy, which used it to measure the effects of pressure waves created by underwater explosives during World War II.

After the war, the bathysphere was taken back to the Zoological Society, where it stayed until it was finally put on display in the New York Aquarium at Coney Island Amusement Park in 1957. It remained there until a renovation of the exhibit in 1994, when it was dumped in an outside storage yard underneath the Cyclone rollercoaster. There it sat, among piles of scrap, until the Wildlife Conservation Society resurrected it and placed it once again on display at the aquarium, in 2005.

NAZIS IN TIBET: THE SEARCH FOR THE ORIGINS OF THE ARYAN RACE

I N Nazi Germany, a group of brutal politicians combined a belief in racial purity and superiority with a highly efficient bureaucracy to mastermind the cold-blooded killing of millions of Jewish men, women, and children, as well as other "undesirables" such as Gypsies, homosexuals, and the mentally challenged. Today, we are careful to watch for the advent of these racist attitudes in modern-day societies, lest another Third Reich occur, in whatever country. Moreover, the term "racial cleansing" has become a widely used phrase to denote the destruction of a people to "purify" bloodlines. But many people do not know about the occult origins of Nazi racial philosophy—about the mystical theory that a race of light-skinned warriors once existed deep in the icy vastness of the Himalaya. These "Aryans" (a word derived from the Sanskrit word *arya*, meaning "noble") were, depending on which legend you consult, the survivors of a series of floods or ice ages, or even superhuman warriors cataclysmically released from frozen entombment by heavenly thunderbolts; in any event, they spread outward across the globe to found the great civilizations of the world, like those of ancient Sumer and Persia.

Sheer nonsense, of course. Except that men like Adolf Hitler and SS founder Heinrich Himmler took it very seriously indeed. So much so that in 1938, Himmler, the architect of the "Final Solution," sent a scientific expedition to Tibet to seek out traces of this master race.

NAZIS AND THE OCCULT
The occult beliefs of the Nazis came from a mishmash of sources. Many Nazis were members of the protofascist Thule Society, founded in 1910 and named after the mythic northern land of Hyperborea-Thule, which was first mentioned by Herodotus and supposedly

existed in the far north. The Thule Society believed that Germans were descendants of the Thuleans, who had spread south from Hyperborea-Thule and were destined to become the master race that would rule the world. (The German philosopher Friedrich Nietzsche began his 1895 book *The Antichrist* with the lines: "Let us see ourselves for what we are. We are Hyperboreans.")

In 1919, the German Workers' Party arose as a direct offshoot of the Thule Society. In fact, it was Dietrich Eckart, one of the founding members of the Thule Society, who brought Adolf Hitler into the party. The German Workers' Party later became the National Socialist German Workers' Party, or the Nazis, with Hitler at its head, and Hitler would return the favor to Eckart by dedicating *Mein Kampf* to him.

Another influence on Hitler was a lecturer and writer named Karl Haushofer, a former German senior officer in World War I. Haushofer began visiting Hitler and his deputy, Rudolf Hess, while both were in prison after Hitler's failed *putsch* of 1923. Haushofer expounded on his notion of "racial geopolitics," which stated that the Aryan race, for its continued existence, needed to expand and conquer the inferior races of Eastern Europe, Russia, and Central Asia. In 1933, when Hitler became chancellor, he named Haushofer as special adviser to the Nazi Party.

But probably the truest believer in the existence of a historical Aryan race was Heinrich Himmler, the mousy-looking man who was second only to Hitler in power in the Third Reich. Himmler, who founded the SS as a special Aryan brotherhood, believed in a lot of strange things. He thought, for instance, that he was the reincarnation of a tenth-century German king named Heinrich I (Henry the Fowler). He believed in telepathy, hypnotism, and the strange power of Venus figures unearthed in places such as India and Mesopotamia. Himmler was also a follower of the nineteenth-century religious charlatan Madame Blavatsky, founder of the Theosophical movement, who taught that humans had evolved through different stages of world existence, each stage ended by a flood. Blavatsky claimed that an elite priesthood had escaped from the lost continent of Atlantis and found its way to Tibet, and that it was this race that became the Aryans.

Tibet was an independent state in 1938, but was seen as a key territory by imperial powers, many of whom sought to gain favor with its rulers.

All of these strange threads of occult history came together in 1935, when Himmler, with the blessing of Adolf Hitler, founded the *Ahnenerbe*. The name stood for "Ancestral Heritage Organization" and the department was set up to study the roots of the Aryan race. Most people in the world, not to mention a large number of Germans, and even some Nazis, did not believe in the notion of an Aryan master race. But Himmler did, and he wanted to prove the truth of his ideology by

Hans Günther, the anthropologist whose theories about the origins of the "Nordic man" influenced leading Nazis, including Heinrich Himmler and Adolf Hitler.

establishing a comprehensive history for the Aryans, as well as a geography. And he wanted to do this scientifically, so that no one could question the veracity of his claims. So he cultivated anthropologists such as Hans Günther, who believed, after fieldwork in which he took thousands of anthropological measurements of the physical characteristics of people in Europe and Asia—heads, noses, lips, ears—that a pure Indo-Aryan racial type existed. This "Nordic man," however, was constantly in danger of mixing his genes with those of the impure, lesser races of the Semitic, Asiatic, or Negroid peoples. Therefore, as Günther wrote in his bestselling *Racial Lore of the German People*, "the question put to [the Nordic man] is whether we have courage enough to make ready for future generations a world cleansing itself racially and eugenically." The seeds of the Final Solution lie in this sentence.

Günther went on to say that he had traced the origins of the Nordic race back to Tibet, where certain Tibetan nobles whose pictures he had studied (he, himself, had not been to the country) had what he considered a "Nordic appearance," and might in fact be the last remaining Aryans of the lost race. Should this be proven scientifically, it would be a great boon to the Nazis, adding legitimacy to their claims.

Himmler began sending out small teams of Nazi scientists around the world, seeking evidence of Aryan origins. Such expeditions were sent to both the North and South poles, and also to Greece, heartland of European civilization, where Himmler hoped traces of an Aryan past might be found. But the biggest expedition of all was the one he sent to Tibet in 1938. And its leader was to be one of the Third Reich's most promising young scientists: Ernst Schafer.

A BORN HUNTER

Ernst Schafer, who lived until 1992, is a dark and complex figure. He was an explorer who, by the time he was twenty-five, had made two expeditions to Tibet during a period when the country was a decidedly dangerous place to visit—rife with banditry, feuding warlords, and skirmishes between the opposing armies of Chiang Kai-shek and Mao Zedong—and he was a brilliant naturalist, zoologist, and ornithologist.

But he also liked to drink the fresh blood of the animals he killed, and carried a gun with him almost everywhere—an interest that would lead to tragedy. And although he later claimed not to have shared Nazi sentiments about a master race, that he was merely an ardent German nationalist, he joined the SS of his own volition, and enthusiastically allowed himself to be used by Himmler to further the ideology of the Third Reich.

Schafer was born into a wealthy family in Cologne in 1910. He was a natural hunter, killing rats in his family cellar with a slingshot at the age of three. Like many a budding scientist, he established a menagerie cum laboratory in his bedroom; however, his family didn't agree with his habit of cutting the tails off mice to see if they would breed tailless offspring, and sent him away to a rather draconian boarding school when he was twelve. Its headmaster had the habit of taking his young charges out and leaving them in a local forest on their own, without food and water, for twenty-four hours at a time. Unlike some, Schafer thrived in this regime.

It was around this time that he first learned of German explorer Wilhelm Filchner's expedition to Tibet, where he met the Dalai Lama and took pictures of the so-called "Forbidden City," or "Holy City" of Lhasa. This fired Schafer's imagination; from then on, he knew that, one day, he, too, would go to Tibet. In the meantime, he studied zoology at Gottingen University, while Germany was undergoing massive changes. By then, 1929, the global economic depression had set in and Hitler's National Democratic Socialist Party, previously banned, was winning elections. Anti-Semitism was prevalent and a new nationalism was in vogue, but Schafer did his best to avoid politics as he concentrated on his studies. Then, in 1930, he met a rich young American, and his life changed completely.

ON THE TRAIL OF THE GIANT PANDA
Brooke Dolan, the twenty-one-year-old son of a wealthy Philadelphia family, was in some ways Ernst Schafer's psychic twin. Equally as brave, but far more reckless than Schafer, the severely alcoholic Dolan—known to the American press as "the Boy Explorer"—wandered Asia on self-financed expeditions to hunt rare animals, and later fought against the Japanese as a member of the American OSS. He died under mysterious circumstances in China in 1948, possibly a suicide.

Dolan traveled to Germany to recruit hunters for an expedition to the wild borderlands between China and Tibet to shoot giant pandas. He happened to meet Schafer, and the two of them hit it off. Traveling with other naturalists and hunters, Dolan and Schafer journeyed to China in the fall of 1931, and began an incredible expedition up the Yangtze River, then west toward Tibet. The border between western China and Tibet was rough country in the extreme; the men traveled continually on foot, while their belongings were carried on the backs of mules. Searching for the elusive pandas, both Dolan and Schafer, highly competitive with each other, left the expedition and set off separately through the bamboo forests that covered the mountain slopes above them. In May of 1932, Schafer won the race, becoming only the second white man to shoot a giant panda.

Moving ahead of their bulky supply train, Dolan and Schafer entered eastern Tibet in June, although they did not venture far into the country. They found burning villages and dead bodies, signs of attacks by the Chinese Nationalists on villages controlled by rebel Chinese warlords. The Tibetans Schafer saw on this journey seemed dirty and sick, and they often begged the Europeans for medicine. Observing the Buddhist prayer flags that were ubiquitous in Tibet, Schafer noticed that they often bore the swastika. A traditional symbol of good fortune in ancient cultures from India to the American Southwest, it was first used in Germany as the emblem of the Neo-Pagan movement of the late nineteenth century, but had also been adopted as the official symbol of the Thule Society and, in the early 1920s, of the Nazis.

As they continued through Tibet that June, Schafer shot an eagle out of the sky and had his servants spread the bird's wings for a dramatic picture. This, and his killing of the panda, may offend our modern sensibilities, but as far as Schafer was concerned he was collecting scientific specimens for later study. Less excusable, even given the

Ernst Schafer, leader of the Nazi expedition to Tibet. Schafer's earlier visits to the country had whetted his appetite for exploring its most remote regions.

prevailing anthropological climate, was the fact that he sneaked into a graveyard at night and dug up a Tibetan skull to take back to Germany, where he arrived in early 1932, after traveling south through eastern Tibet, Burma, and India.

A year later, Schafer joined the SS, which, at the time, was seen as an elite organization of professionals. Because thousands of Germany's bright Jewish professionals had already fled the country, the SS was trying to attract young doctors, lawyers, and scientists to replace them. Schafer later said that he had been forced to join, but there is no evidence of this. Sponsored by a friend of his father, and no doubt with an eye on his own career, Schafer became an *Untersturmführer*, the lowest level of commissioned officer, the equivalent of a second lieutenant in the U.S. Army.

PREPARATIONS MARRED BY TRAGEDY
Schafer was to make one more expedition to Tibet with Dolan, in 1935, when they penetrated even farther into the country, reaching its northern edge, near A'mne Machin, the sacred "Mountain of the Gods." There, they were prey to constant fears of attack by the violent and nomadic Ngolok people who controlled the area. The pressure seems to have put Dolan under what Schafer called in his journal "a nervous strain," and the Boy Explorer simply left Schafer and his other companions behind and walked out of the mountains disguised as a Tibetan trader. After an arduous journey, Schafer made it out, too, and floated back down the Yangtze to Shanghai. He never trusted Dolan again.

After returning to Germany, Schafer was lionized as a veteran explorer of Tibet and published a book about his experiences, *Unknown Tibet*, in which he called for a German scientific expedition to the country. In his foreword he wrote: "Our task is to make science a new vehicle for robust German manhood. Thus we do not only want to proclaim objective science, but be self-confident soldiers of the German spirit."

As a result of the publication of *Unknown Tibet* and newspaper articles on his adventures, Schafer came to the attention of Heinrich Himmler. In the summer of 1936, as Germany prepared for the Olympics, he met with Himmler in his offices in Berlin. At the meeting, it was agreed that a German expedition to Tibet should occur, sponsored by the *Ahnenerbe* and comprising SS scientists, and that it would be Schafer's job to organize the expedition and choose a team of scientists, with Himmler's approval.

Neither Himmler nor Schafer kept a record of exactly what was said in the meeting. But after his capture by the Allies in Munich in 1945, Schafer told American interrogators that Himmler had expressed his belief in an Aryan race descended fully formed from heaven—or possibly thawed from a deep freeze in icy Himalayan mountains by celestial thunderbolts. Schafer told his interrogators that he found this laughable, although it was fairly certain he did not laugh in Himmler's face. Furthermore, while Schafer probably did not believe in the most far-fetched racial notions of Himmler or others, he did believe in self-advancement. A Himmler-approved journey to Tibet, with a reliable, all-German scientific group, of which he, Schafer, would be the head, could be his making in the Nazi hierarchy. And there would be other benefits: a chance to explore some of the largely unvisited sections of Tibet, opportunities to bring back new animal specimens, and, finally, the prospect of visiting the Holy City of Lhasa, a chance rarely afforded Europeans.

In a state of great excitement, Schafer set about his task. Interestingly enough, when Schafer asked for about sixty thousand reischsmarks to finance the expedition, he found that the *Ahnenerbe* did not have the money, nor was it forthcoming from the SS, possibly because the canny Himmler wanted to be able to disavow responsibility for the expedition to Hitler if things went awry.

Once Schafer got over this disappointment, he found it to be a blessing in disguise. Himmler had asked him to take along certain men Schafer considered undesirable, such as a strange SS officer and writer named Edmund Kiss, who wrote novels about the lost city of Atlantis. But since Himmler was not even paying for the expedition, Schafer felt he could refuse—and thus began a relationship in which he often stood up to the Nazi leader.

Schafer managed to raise the money for the expedition by himself, and quickly, partly from his father's business contacts, partly from his own by-now fairly extensive contacts, and even partly from Brooke Dolan, who put in $4,000, perhaps because he felt guilty about abandoning Schafer during their last expedition.

Schafer then went about finding the scientists he wanted to take along with him. All SS officers, they were Ernst Krause, a botanist and entomologist who doubled as the expedition cameraman; Karl Wienert, a geophysicist who was an expert at measuring the earth's magnetic fields; Edmund Geer, the expedition's manager; and Bruno Beger, an anthropologist. The most controversial choice for the team, Beger was a disciple of Hans Günther; in a proposal he wrote to Schafer, he stated his contribution to the expedition would be "to study the current racial-anthropological situation through measurements, trait research, photography, and molds … and to collect material about the proportion, origins, significance, and development of the Nordic race in this region." In later years, when Schafer preferred to portray the expedition as a purely scientific undertaking untainted by National Socialism, the work of Beger got in his way, partly because the "racial science" practiced by Beger in Tibet would end up having disturbingly direct links to the Auschwitz concentration camp.

On the eve of his departure, Schafer was enjoying life. But it was at this time that an incident occurred that was to scar him for the rest of his days. His patron, Himmler had invited him into inner SS circles, and Schafer often hunted in some of the fabulous private game reserves of Hitler's elite. On November 8, 1937, he was out on a lake in a remote forest estate, hunting ducks with a large party of SS officers and their wives. Accompanying Schafer was his wife, the tall, blonde, and beautiful Hertha Voltz Schafer, whom he had married in 1936. In the boat that afternoon, Schafer stood up to fire as some ducks sped through the sky. He stumbled; his rifle fell against the oarsman's seat and discharged. Hertha, shot in the head, died an hour later. Everyone present testified that it was an accident, but Schafer, wracked by guilt, was never to be the same again.

SEVEN YEARS IN TIBET

Heinrich Harrer, who died in early 2006, was another German who had a strong connection with Tibet during World War II. A champion German climber (the first to conquer the north face of the Eiger), Harrer, like Ernst Schafer, joined the SS probably so that he could advance his chosen career.

In 1939, he was part of a German climbing expedition to the Himalayan mountain Nanga Parbat. After World War II started, he was interned by the British authorities in India as an enemy alien. However, he escaped in 1944, crossed the high passes into Tibet, and spent seven years as a friend and occasional tutor to the young fourteenth Dalai Lama.

After the Chinese occupied Tibet in 1950, Harrer returned to Europe, and wrote a bestselling memoir, *Seven Years in Tibet* (which was made into a movie starring Brad Pitt in 1994). He continued to make magnificent mountain ascents in places ranging from Alaska to New Guinea. The fact that he took up golf in 1958, at the age of forty-six, and became Austrian amateur champion, attests to his amazing athletic abilities. Like Schafer, Harrer denied any knowledge of Nazi war crimes. Given that he was far from Germany during the war, this was probably true.

THE EXPEDITION BEGINS In November of 1936, Adolf Hitler had signed an anti-Soviet pact with Japan; by the time Schafer's expedition was ready to embark, Japan was invading China and German explorers were not exactly welcome in the region. Unable to approach Tibet along the routes he had used on his two previous expeditions, Schafer's only approach was through India. And to travel that way, he needed the permission of the British. In March of 1938, as World War II crept closer, Schafer went to London, aiming to convince the British Foreign Office to allow him to travel into Tibet.

He provided a letter to the Foreign Office in which he claimed, with great disingenuousness, that he only wanted to make a scientific survey of a few border areas of Tibet, and requested that "perhaps the Survey of India would be good enough to attach a land-surveyor to our expedition as interpreter, because I could imagine that the Indian government might attach great importance in having this scarcely known land thoroughly cartographed."

Tibet, however, was a vital buffer zone for the British, situated as it was between British India and the Chinese, Japanese, and Soviets. And while the British did not control Tibet, they *did* control her western approach and did not want any Germans there (especially one that they had more or less decided was a spy). So Schafer's request, while not officially denied, was simply shelved. But Schafer was not a young man who took "no" for an answer. One of his numerous friends among the pro-German factions that existed in Great Britain just before the war advised him to do something very simple: go to India and sneak across the border into Tibet. And this he did.

He and his party arrived in Calcutta, India, in June of 1938 to find that they had had a lucky break: powerful British Nazi sympathizers had prevailed upon the British Foreign Office to allow the German Tibet Expedition into Sikkim, the tiny state nestled in the Himalayan foothills. From here, as the British and Schafer well knew, the forbidden land of Tibet could be accessed through a mountain pass called Natu La.

Schafer and his four fellow SS officers and their porters—about twenty men in all—fought their way through the arduous terrain of Sikkim during the monsoon season, the torrential rain and mudslides exacerbating the already inhospitable conditions, in which thrived diseases such as anthrax and rinderpest, and a strange illness called the black plague, which caused symptoms like malaria. On the plus side, the land glittered with a fabulous array of giant butterflies, which pleased Ernst Krause, and there was much game—Schafer shot a vulture and an eagle.

Bruno Beger immediately began measuring the facial characteristics of the people of Sikkim, looking for characteristics that might be the traces of the once-mighty Aryan race: blue eyes, a straight nose, a firm chin. He even set about making plaster casts of their faces. Unfortunately, one of his first subjects was a Sherpa who had recently suffered a bad head injury. The man had an epileptic seizure as the wet plaster covered his face—Beger had neglected to place straws in his nostrils so he could breathe—and nearly died, convulsing, until Beger tore the mask off.

The Holy City of Lhasa as seen in *Secret Tibet*, the documentary film made by Schafer and his team. At the time, very few Europeans had set foot in Lhasa.

During the next several months, Schafer and his expedition slowly climbed through Sikkim until they were high in the Himalaya, just fifteen miles from the Tibetan border. Fall was setting in and the weather turned bitterly cold as they made camp at twelve thousand feet near an alpine lake. Schafer hunted for specimens to take back to Germany. He spent weeks in the snowy wilds tracking the legendary shapi—a black, goatish creature worshiped by some of the Himalayan tribes as a god—finally becoming the first white man to bag one (it and many of Schafer's other specimens were later displayed in Berlin's Museum of Natural History). But Schafer could not be delayed for too long by his hunting, and, as the cold weather deepened, he put in motion his plan to sneak into Tibet.

ACROSS THE PLATEAU TO THE HOLY CITY

In December 1938, Schafer and his party wended their way through the freezing air of the Natu La Pass. It was a very steep climb, up the side of a mountain nearly to its top, and the footing was treacherous. Schafer had hidden his rifles and most of the expedition's equipment in boxes on the backs of their mules; the expedition was now masquerading as a group of "tourists"—somewhat ridiculously given that it displayed a swastika flag and Schafer wore a pith helmet with the jagged SS lightning marks emblazoned on its side.

In the ensuing weeks, the expedition descended to the main plateau of Tibet, where they entered forested valleys dotted with small villages and monasteries. The area had a picturesque quality that reminded the Germans of the Alps, reinforcing

Schafer and his team at a camp on the Tibetan Plateau. The explorers were awed by Tibet's landscapes but appalled by the living conditions of its people.

Beger's preconceptions about a shared Aryan culture. The expedition could not bring out its equipment openly, especially since the British had trade consulates in some of the larger towns, so at night Wienert took out his magnetometer to take astronomical sightings in order to fix altitude, latitude, and longitude. Schafer chafed because he could not hunt, but he had larger goals in mind: he wanted to reach Lhasa, which relatively few Europeans had seen.

Proceeding across the plateau, the explorers traversed undulating grasslands where yaks grazed by the thousands. They passed through the towns as quickly as they could, finding them to be impossibly filthy and grimy, their streets filled with beggars and the mentally ill, who were not cared for and were generally starving. Signs of Buddhism were everywhere. Schafer referred to the religion, disparagingly, as Lamaism; as far as he was concerned, it was a "degenerate" form of religion that had corrupted a once-strong (and presumably Aryan) warrior class of Tibet.

Soon, mountains began to loom in front and to the side as they traveled the last hundred miles to Lhasa. The scenery was extraordinary: far above rocky slopes colored red, yellow, and ochre, the sun gleamed on impossibly high, snow-clad peaks.

On January 19, 1939, they approached the city of Lhasa, the sacred home of the Dalai Lama. They passed the flocks of thousands of black holy cranes that surrounded the city, and pilgrims making their way along, prostrating themselves every few steps. They entered through the western gate and were met by Tibetans clapping, which heartened Schafer, until he was told by the porters that they were clapping to rid the city of the evil spirits the foreigners had undoubtedly brought with them.

At this point, Lhasa was at a critical juncture in its history. The thirteenth Dalai Lama had died in 1933, and the fourteenth, a three-year-old child, had only recently been found in a village near the Chinese border and was about to be brought to the city for enthronement. Political maneuvering on the part of the various imperial powers was reaching a peak. In the face of continued Chinese attempts to seize their territory, the Tibetans were seeking help from Britain; but while the British much preferred an independent Tibet, they did not want to occupy the country and find themselves in the precarious position of having to defend it. The Japanese, too, were making inroads: unbeknownst to Schafer or the British, a Japanese spy disguised as a Buddhist monk was even then touring the country.

The British continued to keep a close eye on Schafer. Although they could not oust him from the country, they attempted to make his life difficult by forcing him to conduct himself like the tourist he claimed to be and by reporting any possible scientific activities to the Tibetan authorities, hoping to convince them that the Germans were there under false pretenses. This had little effect. The Germans, with Schafer as their chief, began making inroads into Tibetan politics. They asked for and received a meeting with the regent who ruled the country in the absence of the Dalai Lama, and were surprised to find him quite receptive. In fact, after several meetings, he asked them if the German government might be able to provide guns to the Tibetan Army, to help them fight off Chinese or Japanese invaders (the British were not willing to arm the Tibetans). Clearly and intriguingly, the Tibetans saw Schafer and his party not as tourists or even scientists, but as emissaries of the German government. Schafer, however, refused the regent's request, which would have brought the Chinese and British down on his head, but he realized that Tibet was an area the Germans could exploit.

RETURNING HEROES
By mid-March, however, it was time to leave Lhasa, partly because of the political situation in Europe. Hitler had invaded Czechoslovakia and a wider war seemed imminent. If Schafer stayed too much longer, he ran the risk of the British interning him. So he and his party left the Holy City, heading first northeast across mountain passes, then south, through the ancient Yarlung Valley. They now had a permit from Tibetan authorities to make scientific observations and they did so with a vengeance. Beger took out his eye-color charts and the swatches of hair he carried to help place people in racial categories. With his calipers, he measured noses, ears, and chins; he made plaster casts of faces. All told, he gathered information on nearly 400 Tibetans, fingerprinted 350, and made 25 facial casts; he also took 2,000

DOCUMENTARY EVIDENCE

Schafer and his colleague Ernst Krause shot a movie in Tibet, entitled *Geheimnis Tibet (Secret Tibet)*, which is a strange and troubling document. Finally released as a documentary in Germany in 1942, and narrated by Schafer, it shows the usual travelogue scenes of Tibetan landscapes and festivals. It also attacks the British government for its "vicious calumnies" against Schafer and his team and for its "exploitation" of the ancient civilizations of India and Tibet. But then it goes further.

Showing scenes of Beger measuring men and women for his study, it talks of Tibet as an ancient warrior land that was ruined by a bastard religion (namely Tibetan Buddhism). The clear implications are that the Germans and their way of life are being weakened by the influence of the Jewish religion, and that if they don't take measures, they, too, will go the way of the abject Tibetans seen in the movie. The complete film footage, which is now in the United States Library of Congress, shows that some unsettling edits were made. One scene in the movie shows Beger measuring a young woman who is smiling at him. The full version shows the woman struggling and trying to push him away, and finally hitting him in the face as he tries to measure her body with his calipers.

photographs. Wienert made voluminous sets of geomagnetic studies; Krause studied the Tibetan wasp. Schafer hunted, burdening the expedition with skins to be carried back to Germany—three thousand in all. And Krause and Schafer took moving pictures, thousands and thousands of feet of film that covered sky burials (in which corpses were exposed and cut up, then left to be eaten by vultures), New Year celebrations, and Beger's measuring of Tibetans. Krause also took forty thousand photographs.

Finally, they headed south, back through Sikkim, and then into India. It was now late July, 1939, and war was inevitable. Indeed, the British had already begun to build internment camps in which they planned to house foreign nationals caught in India. Just in the nick of time, Himmler sent flying boats to Calcutta to ferry the expedition to Baghdad; from there it flew to Berlin.

Once in Berlin, the expedition members were feted and toasted by Hitler himself. Schafer received the SS's death's-head ring, the *Totenkopfring*, from Himmler. This was not an official military award, but instead a sign of Himmler's personal favor, given out only to SS men who performed truly heroic services. As the standard citation read: "The Death's Head reminds us that we should be ready at any time to lay down our lives for the good of the Germanic people." Newspapers around the Reich trumpeted the success of their expedition and Schafer was lionized. The Nazi propaganda machine stopped short of claiming that the origins of the Aryan race had been found, but played up the fact that German scientists had been searching diligently for them. The headlines also emphasized that the adventurous Schafer and his men had reached the city of Lhasa right under the nose of a none-too-happy British government.

But after completing the film of the expedition with Krause, Schafer found that he was sidelined by the more pressing issues of the war. Other members of the expedition—Beger, Krause, and Wienert—became a part of the SS military machine. Schafer himself was made head of the Inner Asian Research Department in the *Ahnenerbe*. (He also got married again.) By 1942, however, he had become extremely troubled by the SS's involvement in mass murder—if he hadn't known earlier, he certainly became aware of it during a trip to Poland, where he learned about Himmler's plan to liquidate Polish Jews. Although he was more of a Nazi than he let on, Schafer was not a murderer, and he tried as best he could to keep his involvement with the camps to a minimum. But, still, he *knew*.

Schafer spent the last part of the war fomenting an absurd idea for the invasion of British India by Tibetan guerillas, and, fittingly enough, seeking the origins of a mythical red horse with a white mane, which Himmler had read about in an ancient Nordic fairy tale and was sure was an ancient Indo-Aryan symbol.

THE DANGERS OF SCIENCE Schafer was arrested by the Allies, but he was able to convince them that he had nothing to do with genocide, that he was "merely" a scientist, and he was let go with a fine. In 1949, he moved to Venezuela to start a wildlife preserve with his second wife and three children, and he lived there until he died in 1992, aged eighty-two. Those who knew him said he never came to terms with his Nazi past. He had been a young man who had seized an opportunity to go on an adventurous expedition, but had ended up working for an evil and racist regime.

Himmler committed suicide after his capture by the British in 1945. Wienert, Krause, and Geer went back to civilian life and no more was heard from them. But Bruno Beger was a different case. His studies in Tibet made him the *Ahnenerbe*'s racial expert. In the spring of 1943, he arrived at Auschwitz to select 115 prisoners to measure, looking in particular for ones with "Asian" characteristics. He stayed there for eight days, carrying out his studies. After he left, the men and women he had studied were gassed and their corpses preserved and sent to the anatomy department of Strasbourg University, over which a friend of Berger, a Dr. Hirt, presided. But some of the heads of the bodies were missing, and there is circumstantial evidence that these may have found their way to the *Ahnenerbe*.

It took a while for war crimes authorities to catch up with Beger, but they finally did when his visit to Auschwitz was discussed during the trial of Adolf Eichmann in 1961. Beger was tried for the murder of the camp inmates in 1971, but he claimed that, while he did measure the doomed prisoners, he had no idea they were going to be killed. He was given a three-year suspended prison sentence.

Although Beger was the only one of the German expedition to Tibet who was directly connected with Nazi war crimes, all of its members were, in a sense, guilty of supporting, with their "science," an ideology that led to the mass murder of so many millions. And therein lies the cautionary tale. For by bringing a veneer of respectability and an air of scientific authority to otherwise unsubstantiated theories, scientists can help turn outlandish notions into destructive reality. Nineteenth-century "scientific" beliefs that blacks were not fully human helped make slavery an institution. The "scientific" notion that lobotomies and forced sterilization were the proper treatment for mental illness destroyed many lives in the United States and other Western countries up until quite recently.

Even today, there are people who believe that the Nazis were a sort of supernatural cult and that the cult still survives—in secret bases in Antarctica, some say. Books are published and web sites created, which deny the Holocaust and claim that the "master race" is simply waiting for a return when the time is right—from whatever frozen outpost, or even from a spaceship circling in the heavens. Ridiculous, right? Except that equally ridiculous ideas, and a few ambitious scientists willing to support them, helped the most evil regime in history destroy millions of lives.

HITLER LIVES

Almost before World War II had ended, people were claiming that Adolf Hitler had escaped, that he lived on in a secret base somewhere. One of the first to write about and publish this notion was an eccentric Chilean diplomat named Miguel Serrano, whose books *The Golden Ribbon* and *Adolf Hitler, The Last Avatar* postulated that Hitler was alive in Shambhala, which Serrano located in an underground base in Antarctica. From there, Hitler, now in contact with the gods of ancient Hyperborea-Thule, would eventually emerge to lead a fleet of UFOs against the world, and start a Fourth Reich. Today, Serrano's philosophies are perpetuated by the American Academy of Dissident Sciences, which claims that Nazis, while they still have a colony hidden in Antarctica, have also branched out to explore the surfaces of the Moon and Mars.

THE MALAYAN EMERGENCY: A LESSON NOT LEARNED

FOR A FEW WEEKS IN MAY OF 1948, A GROUP OF YOUNG CHINESE MEN AND WOMEN gathered deep in a thick jungle in Pahang, the largest of the eleven states that then made up the Federation of Malaya, a protectorate of Great Britain. The jungle was not a comfortable place to be. It was filled with biting insects and thorn bushes that left suppurating tears in legs and arms. If you spent any time at all beneath the triple canopy, the dampness and perpetual shade induced an almost deathly pallor, immediately noticed by others when you stepped back into civilization.

But the men and women of the Malayan Communist Party (MCP) were used to that. Communism had been introduced to Malaya in the 1920s when members of a radical faction of the Chinese Kuomintang immigrated to the country. The party became a legitimate force in Malayan politics, gaining control of a large portion of the labor movement, but when the Japanese invaded in 1942, the MCP began calling itself the Malayan Peoples' Anti-Japanese Army (MPAJA) and went deep underground in the jungles. With close support from the British, including arms, ammunition, training, and officers, the MPAJA turned into a formidable guerilla force and emerged, by the war's end, with a powerful and almost mythic reputation among the people of Malaya, due in part to the ruthlessness with which it had dealt with anyone suspected of collaboration with the Japanese.

The man in charge of the fateful May 1948 meeting in the jungle was a former MPAJA leader named Chin Peng. He was twenty-three years old. For his valor in fighting the Japanese, his former allies had awarded him the Order of the British Empire. Which is what makes it doubly ironic that he was meeting in the jungle with other former members of the MPAJA—which had by now reverted to its prewar name of the MCP—to plan a war that would drive the British out of Malaya once and for all.

THE FEDERATION OF MALAYA
After the Second World War had ended, the British returned to Malaya—just like the Dutch in Indonesia and the French in Indochina—to reclaim their long-held colony. Their control of the peninsula dated back to 1814, when the Netherlands had ceded the territory under the terms of the Anglo-Dutch Treaty. In those early days, the British ruled Malaya with a far looser hand than they did, say, India, controlling the colony mainly through trading arrangements set up by the East India Company. However, after the opening of the Suez Canal in 1869, which had the potential to bring more competition to the area, the British stepped in with a firmer hand, setting up a protectorate. In return for British military aid, the powerful sultans who made up the loosely arranged confederation of Malay states agreed to trade only with Great Britain. This turned out to be a highly profitable arrangement for both parties, especially after rubber became a valuable world commodity in the late nineteenth century.

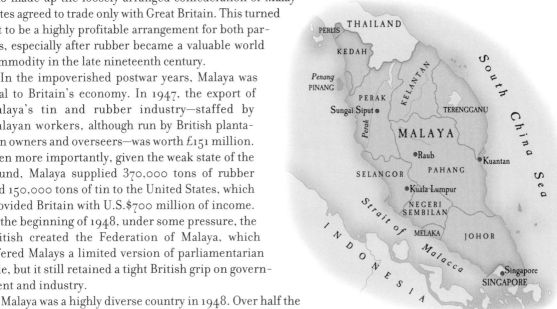

In the impoverished postwar years, Malaya was vital to Britain's economy. In 1947, the export of Malaya's tin and rubber industry—staffed by Malayan workers, although run by British plantation owners and overseers—was worth £151 million. Even more importantly, given the weak state of the pound, Malaya supplied 370,000 tons of rubber and 150,000 tons of tin to the United States, which provided Britain with U.S.$700 million of income. At the beginning of 1948, under some pressure, the British created the Federation of Malaya, which offered Malays a limited version of parliamentarian rule, but it still retained a tight British grip on government and industry.

Malaya was a highly diverse country in 1948. Over half the population of about five and a half million were ethnic Malays. Another large group were Indians, who had lived in the country for centuries, mainly as merchants and traders. There was also a sizable community, numbering about six hundred thousand, of ethnic Chinese, who had lived in Malaya since the late nineteenth century, when they had emigrated from their native land to work in the rubber plantations. The Chinese were among the poorest and most downtrodden members of Malay society, and it is not surprising that it was they who swelled the ranks of the MCP.

Unlike the Communist parties of Indonesia and Indochina, the MCP, returning from the war, did not at first resort to armed conflict. Their leader at the time was not Chin Peng but a charismatic Vietnamese immigrant, Loi Tek, a fierce anti-Japanese guerilla leader who also went by the nom de plume of "Mr. Wright." Under Loi Tek, the MCP organized a series of highly effective labor strikes which crippled British

British Malaya in 1948. For the United Kingdom, the colony was a valuable economic resource, but also a powderkeg of unrest.

rubber plantations, mainly worked by the Chinese "tappers." The British responded with the repressive Trades Union Ordinance, which required all unions to register with the British military government in Malaya. Increasingly, British planters found a newly hardened attitude on the part of their Chinese and Malay workers, who previously would have dismounted their bicycles and bowed if they saw a British person coming. Many of the planters responded by working their men harder, and cutting the wages of those who were in unions, and even beating and whipping strikers.

Still, and surprisingly to some onlookers, there was no armed rebellion. The reason for this became clear on March 3, 1947, when Loi Tek disappeared and took a large amount of the MCP's treasury with him. It was then discovered that Loi Tek had been not only a double agent, but a *triple* one. He had worked for the British Special Branch intelligence forces before, during, and after the war, gathering information on the MCP and passing it to London—it was through his auspices that the MCP had opted not to take up arms. But, to the horror of both the British and the MCP, it turned out that Loi Tek had also worked for the Japanese intelligence service, the *Kepeitai*, during the war. Moreover, while he was dealing ruthlessly with collaborators, he himself had facilitated a massacre by the Japanese of senior MCP leaders, who had been surrounded, captured, and beheaded. This had been Loi Tek's way of making his rivals disappear.

Loi Tek was never heard of again. He had left the MCP in ruins. The only way for his successor, Chin Peng, to reclaim control of a weakened and demoralized party was to turn to its militant wing, which had previously been kept in check by Loi Tek, and plan a guerilla war. In this, he was aided, ironically, by the fact that Loi Tek had eliminated most of the senior members of the party; those who remained were the younger rank and file who had done the most jungle fighting and were the most radical.

It was this group that met with Chin Peng in May of 1948, deep in the jungle, to plan a guerilla war. It was a war that would not end for another twelve years and would feature the birth of the first successful Western counterinsurgency techniques—strategies that might have changed the course of the war in Vietnam, had the United States paid attention. And it was a war that, although soon forgotten in Great Britain, had a powerful effect on Malay society, resulting in a vast movement of hundreds of thousands of people, universal suffrage for the Chinese, and the creation of the modern state of Malaysia.

FIRST SHOTS
At about 8 a.m. on July 16, 1948, about twenty miles from the tin-mining town of Sungai Siput in northern Malaya, a British rubber planter named Arthur Walker, fifty years old, was sitting in his office attending to some paperwork, when three young Chinese men rode up on bicycles. A Malayan worker standing outside saw them enter Walker's office and heard them say, politely, "*Tabek, Tuan!*" or "Salutations, sir!" Walker replied with equal courtesy. But within moments, two shots rang out, then the men walked unhurriedly to their bicycles and left. The worker found Walker slumped in a chair, shot twice through the heart. About an hour later and ten miles away, twelve armed Chinese guerillas walked into

Opposite: Three captured Communist insurgents photographed by their British captors. At the start of the war, such British triumphs were rare.

the office of a rubber plantation and shot and killed a fifty-five-year-old estate manager and his twenty-one-year-old assistant. Another British planter was targeted but escaped because his jeep broke down while he was making his rounds and the guerillas assigned to kill him grew tired of waiting.

These murders took place in remote areas of the country and were followed within the next few days by a spate of brutal attacks aimed at the Chinese workers and foremen who helped keep the rubber plantations going. A head laborer in the state of Johor, in southern Malaya, was shot fifteen times. A Chinese contractor was murdered near Sungai Siput. And, on the outskirts of a large rubber plantation, also in Johor, five guerillas dressed in green uniforms with red stars on their caps appeared at the door of the foreman of the rubber tappers and demanded fifty cents a week from him and his men as a "subscription" to help the MCP wage their war. When he refused, they tied him to a tree and cut off his arms.

The rebellion continued like this, with brutal, isolated attacks. British intelligence later learned that Chin Peng's plan was to produce a wave of terror in the outlying areas, which would in turn cause British planters to abandon their land and also attract new recruits to the Communist cause. The killings of planters and workers represented the first phase of the planned MCP offensive. In the second phase, the areas evacuated by the British would be declared "Liberated Areas," and guerilla bases would be set up there. Phase three would see a growing MCP army attack the British in battles for the larger cities, and emerge victorious.

But, because of the swift response of the British colonial administrators, the MCP offensive stalled in phase one. On July 18, Britain declared a state of emergency covering the whole of Malaya. Carrying unauthorized firearms became a capital offence, the entire adult population was registered and given identification papers, "seditious" publications were banned, and people could be detained and even deported, or "banished," without trial. This was excessive and paranoid, but typical of the times. In both Malaya and London, the British attributed the insurgency to an international Communist conspiracy, which was perhaps understandable, given that the Cold War was just beginning. Czechoslovakia had been taken over by a Soviet coup d'état and, in June, the Soviets had surrounded the city of Berlin, trying to gain control of it by starving the population, which resulted in the Berlin Air Lift. The British Labour Party under Prime Minister Clement Attlee feared that war with the Soviets was inevitable, and was already developing, with the United States and other nations, the Western military alliance that would become known as NATO.

The British saw the Malay uprising as part of a plot hatched by Joseph Stalin to take over Asia, now that he was meeting with resistance in the West. A British intelligence official in Malaya wrote in a secret report widely circulated in the Attlee administration, that "the [MCP] campaign is part of a broader Soviet-inspired drive to obtain control of what is strategically and economically one of the most important areas of Southeast Asia ... On instructions of the Cominform, the MCP started a campaign of murder, sabotage, and terrorism designed to paralyze the government and develop into armed revolution." Later historians have seen this as an example of Cold War paranoia. Chin Peng's revolt was fired by a homegrown version of Communism mixed with nationalism. True, almost every guerilla was ethnic Chinese, with the exception of a few Malays, but these young Chinese were almost entirely born and bred in Malaya. They took orders not from the Comintern, but from their internal leadership, and their armed revolt was a response to the situation in Malaya and, in particular, the situation the party found itself in after the disappearance of Loi Tek.

In the first year of the "Emergency," as it became known, Britain labored mightily to convince the United States to help it against the Malayan rebels—at one point almost begging to buy arms at a reduced rate—but America, perhaps burned by its failed commitments in China, refused to become involved. If it had, it might have learned some vital lessons that could have influenced the outcome of the Vietnam War, twenty years later.

AN UNDECLARED WAR

During the course of the next twelve years, Great Britain would commit twenty-three regiments and one commando brigade to quelling the uprising in Malaya. In all, some fifty thousand men would see duty there. The conflict would cost the British alone 1,800 killed and 2,500 wounded. The loss to civilian life was about 2,500 killed. Insurgent losses are harder to estimate, but of Chin Peng's forces of about 12,000 guerillas, probably around 7,000 were killed and 2,800 wounded.

Despite this, the British continued to insist on referring to the conflict as an "emergency" and not a war. They had sound economic reasons for doing this. The planters and tin miners in Malaya were not covered by insurance for property damage due to war, only to losses during "riot and civil commotion," and if the insurance companies would not pick up the costs, the cash-starved British government would have to. For the same reason, for the first few years of the war, the British publicly referred to the insurgents as "bandits." Unfortunately, this is exactly what the Japanese had termed the armed opposition during the Second World War, which led some Malays to equate the British occupation with that of the Japanese. Realizing this, the British introduced the all-purpose term of "Communist terrorist," or CT for short, which continued to be used throughout the war.

Of course, another reason for calling the war an "emergency," was to keep the population in Britain—which had just been through an enormous and costly conflict—from becoming alarmed. It was the same strategy used by the United States in referring to its participation in the Korean War as a "police action."

Unfortunately for the CT guerillas, most of the Malay population, with the exception of a few of the ethnic Chinese, never supported them, in part because CTs so often either targeted the Malays with violence or forced them to pay "subscription" fees in support of the conflict. But despite this, and despite being driven back into jungle bases, the CTs fought ferociously, sending out dozens of columns to attack British forces guarding small villages or British convoys on narrow jungle roads. Since the British did not know when they were going to be hit next, they spread their forces thin.

THE MAN IN BLACK

Counterinsurgencies tend to spawn colorful and violent characters. One such man who became famous during the Malayan Emergency was Police Superintendent "Two Gun" Bill Stafford. Built like a bull—in pictures, he oozes aggressiveness—Stafford had, before World War II, served as a stoker in the British Navy. One of his claims to fame was pulling both Charles Lindberg and his wife out of the Yangtze River when their plane started to sink there in 1931. During the war, he parachuted fifteen times behind Japanese lines in Burma. As a police superintendent in the early part of the Emergency, he led numerous guerilla attacks on CT outposts. He insisted on dressing completely in black. He wore two revolvers, one under each shoulder, and carried a rifle. His Chinese "killer squad" called him *Tin Sau-pah*—"The Iron Broom."

On one occasion, Stafford led a charge on a secret CT camp, in which he personally shot and killed Lau Yew, the irreplaceable chief military strategist of Chin Peng; he then fought off a counterattack by insurgents almost single-handedly. Amazingly enough, Stafford survived the Emergency and found his way back to England.

Robert Thompson, pictured in 1943, during his distinguished service against the Japanese in Burma. In Malaya, he led the first successful armed response to the Communist insurgency.

The British civilians, even those isolated deep in rural areas, proved remarkably resilient. Their spirit was exemplified by Peter Lucy and his wife, Tommy, who ran a rubber plantation called Amherst Estates, only eight miles from Kuala Lumpur, but deep in the jungle. They had lived there in the more idyllic, pre–World War II days and Peter, who had spent four years in a Japanese prison camp, merely wanted to return to overseeing the plantation. But he and his wife became the target of repeated attacks by CTs, who sprayed their living quarters with gunfire almost nightly. To protect himself and his wife, then pregnant with twins, as they traveled locally, Peter stripped steel plating off rotting Japanese tanks and armored the family Land Rover. When Tommy began to go into labor during a CT attack one night, the two of them climbed into their homemade armored car and drove pell-mell to the hospital, with Tommy firing a Sten gun out of the window. They made it, and Tommy gave birth to twin boys.

Initially, however, the British struggled to contain the rebellion. They had neither the resources—only four thousand widely dispersed troops—nor the knowledge to fight this kind of war. Increasing numbers of planters were murdered, and the CTs began an attempt to cripple production on rubber plantations by targeting tappers as they worked. By 1950, hundreds of civilians, both British and Malay, had been killed, and while perhaps six hundred CTs had died, there were still many more raiding villages and plantations and ambushing military columns almost daily. In mid-1950, guerilla attacks, which had numbered fewer than one hundred a month in mid-1949, reached a peak of four hundred a month.

In this period of crisis, before the British were able to organize themselves more fully, one man made a huge difference: Robert "Bob" Thompson. At the time of the first attacks, Thompson—who would later be knighted by the British government and, significantly, write an influential book called *No Exit from Vietnam*—was the British Chinese affairs officer in Malaya and just thirty-two. He was, however, an experienced guerilla fighter, having won the DSO and Military Cross battling the Japanese with irregular forces in China and Burma. Thompson planned the first British response to the CTs by forming what he called a "Ferret Force" of small platoons, led by British former World War II commandos. Their job was not to defeat the CTs, who then outnumbered the British forces, but to surprise and harass them in the jungle, which they considered their own territory. This they did quite effectively, with small, nighttime ambushes, which might kill only one CT, or none at all, but, according to the testimony of defectors, kept the enemy on edge.

POLITICAL SOLUTIONS
The situation began to turn in Britain's favor following the arrival of a new high commissioner, Sir Henry Gurney. Gurney had been chief secretary in Palestine and had seen politically motivated civil war there. Once he arrived in Malaya and joined up with Thompson, they came up with several strategies that would change the course of the war. To begin with, Gurney decreed that, since this was a war of ideologies, the army needed to support political solutions. Despite opposition from the British armed forces, he gained support for this approach from Whitehall.

Gurney's first momentous action was the creation of the so-called "New Villages." There were about six hundred thousand ethnic Chinese living in jungle areas of Malaya, and Gurney and Thompson decided to resettle them in guarded and fortified villages. This was a huge undertaking and initially resented by the Chinese—it involved relocating about ten percent of the colony's entire population. However, from the British point of view, it not only isolated the population most likely to be influenced or terrorized by Chin Peng and his men, but it also removed a prime source of the MCP's financial support. The initiative might not have worked—and indeed, it did not work later, when it was tried by the Americans in Vietnam—had it not been for an understanding that there had to be a carrot attached to the stick. Chinese who went to the New Villages were not only given land, but were eventually granted the right to vote, which the previous British administration had refused them. Round-the-clock protection also meant that they could finally go about their business undisturbed.

The process took eighteen months, and was not achieved without problems. Chief among them was the fact that Malaya's sultans were reluctant to give up land for the New Villages. In order to win them over, Gurney and Thompson had to painstakingly flatter, cajole, and sometimes even bribe these regional rulers. In the short run, this plan was highly effective against the MCP. In the long run, it created segregated Chinese communities that still exist in modern Malaysia. (In 2002, the New Village population was 1.25 million, of which 82 percent are ethnic Chinese. These communities have contributed to a heightened sense of Chinese identity in Malaysia, but some suggest that they ghettoize the Chinese population.)

Another of Gurney's initiatives was to offer a series of sizable rewards for information leading to the capture of top insurgents. With the British also offering amnesties for MCP members who surrendered, this had the interesting effect of causing some insurgents with prices on their heads to surrender in order to obtain the reward for their own capture (although the monetary sums were halved in these cases). As Bob Thompson wrote, "there is nothing like establishing prospects where an individual can go from terrorist to capitalist in two easy moves."

SHOCKED INTO ACTION
The measures taken by Gurney, Thompson, and other members of the British government—eventually referred to as the Briggs Plan, after the new director of operations in Malaya, Sir Harold Briggs, who helped implement them—brought a violent response from Chin Peng. He was especially angered by the British attempts to register all Malay civilians, and, in response, ambushed and murdered government registration teams, and tortured workers discovered carrying ID cards. The CTs began to employ jungle-fighting techniques new to the British raw recruits, such as concealed pits full of sharpened bamboo sticks. They also stepped up their war against the swelling British forces, blowing up troop trains or attacking supply convoys. And, continually scarce of arms, they set up ambushes whose sole purpose was to kill British troops for their weapons.

Members of a British "Ferret Force" study their plan of action before commencing an operation to drive suspected terrorists out of neighboring jungle.

One of these ambushes was laid on the morning of October 6, 1951, by about forty guerillas, on the road to Frasers Hill near Raub. The guerillas were hidden in the hills around an S-curve, waiting for a military convoy to arrive. None did, and they were about to leave when a three-car convoy drove into view. The CTs sprayed the cars with machine-gun fire. The British guards began to shoot back, but, for some reason, one of the passengers in the central car of the convoy opened his door and got out just as the firing was at its most intense. He walked calmly from the car to the shoulder of the road, almost as if he were on a stroll, but was then cut down by CT fire. This was Sir Henry Gurney.

After a few moments, the CTs withdrew and the skirmish was over. It turned out that Gurney had left his car in order to draw fire away from his wife and secretary, who remained crouched in the back seat, unhurt. Although, almost certainly, the CTs were not waiting for Gurney in particular, and did not even know for a while who they had killed, the assassination of the British high commissioner had seismic effects in London. If the Emergency hadn't been taken seriously before, it was now. Winston Churchill became the new prime minister a few weeks after Gurney's death, and he went on record as saying he wanted someone to clean up the problem in Malaya—immediately. "If Malaya goes," he said, "all the Far East goes."

The man he chose as the new high commissioner was General Sir Gerald Templer. Fifty-four years old and with a distinguished combat record in World War II and Palestine, Templer was quite different from the gentlemanly Gurney—abrupt, profane, and temperamental—but he was to get results.

HEARTS AND MINDS

Another objective of the Briggs Plan was to win the "hearts and minds" of the Malayan population, and Templer pursued this energetically. He opened schools and hospitals, arranged for Malayan orphans to be educated in Britain, and worked to create a home guard force made up of Malayan soldiers. In areas that were thought to have been cleared of Communists, he lifted curfew restrictions and restored many of the other freedoms that had been curtailed at the beginning of the war. Observing these "White Areas," as they became known, more and more people began turning in insurgents.

Templer's next move, beginning in 1952, was to conduct an extremely successful leafleting program. Over the course of the next eight years, millions of leaflets were dropped from the air over the Malayan jungle. Their content was carefully thought out; as Templer put it, they had to be "both attractive and fair, but not too lenient and vague." Some promised rewards if CT leaders were turned in; others showed pictures of guerillas who had gone over to the government side and were obviously well fed and well treated. One leaflet promised "good treatment, food, cigarettes, and medical attention" and further read: "Many of you who are now fighting for the Communist leaders in the jungles of Malaya are not hardened criminals but youths who were tricked and intimidated into following the wrong path. I would rather you lived to serve the common interests of the people of Malaya than died like wild beasts in the jungle." Gradually, more and more guerillas, some clutching leaflets, began surrendering their weapons to government troops.

Another of Templer's successes was the Special Operational Volunteer Force (SOVF), which consisted of platoons of ex-insurgents who had switched sides and were now fighting with the British against Chin Peng. The SOVF was not large, but had a profound psychological effect on CTs who saw their former comrades fighting against them.

By May of 1954, Templer, building on the work of Sir Henry Gurney and Bob Thompson, had helped pass laws that gave citizenship to more than a million Chinese and allowed the Chinese to work in the Malayan civil service, and also instituted free primary education for all Malayans—a first in the colony. Finally, he announced that the Malayans would hold their first national election in 1955, paving the way for independence, which would come on August 31, 1957.

Not everything was done through hearts-and-minds programs, of course. The CTs were worn down by relentless, intense fighting in the jungles, at enormous cost in blood, sweat, and tears. Realizing that the CT could not be defeated by standard military means, the British re-created the Special Air Service (SAS), which had first seen action in World War II. This jungle commando unit would send out three- or four-men patrols—the more sophisticated "Ferret Force"—who could live on their

A VOICE FROM ON HIGH

These days called "psyops," psychological warfare is such a part of modern conflict that it is written into battle plans. Affecting the hearts and minds of the enemy certainly did not start in Malaya, but the British did begin to write the book on how to win over a jungle-based enemy.

One method was to broadcast propaganda from a circling airplane. After some experimentation, the British used one of the large, stable World War II vintage Dakota bombers which they flew very slowly (about seventy miles per hour) in squares over areas of the jungle. The messages aimed at the CTs were recorded in studios in Singapore and repeated not only in Malay, but in various Chinese dialects, including Hakka, Mandarin, and Cantonese.

The content of the messages varied—rewards for surrender, descriptions of the killings or captures of well-known terrorists—but the main principles adhered to were twofold: that threats should never be used, and that all statements needed to be true. For those living in the densely canopied jungle, it must have sounded as if the voice of God had spoken. As one British commander later said, "I also heard the 'voice aircraft' asking the Communist terrorists to throw in the towel. I couldn't see the plane and it was weird to hear this booming voice coming from somewhere up above the trees."

own for days at a time and pinpoint enemy positions. The SAS used indigenous Sakai people to help them track down the CTs; like other peoples the Sakai had been angered by the CTs' attempts to extort food from them. The British also used helicopters on a large scale for the first time, to move small groups of soldiers quickly from one point in the country to the next, foreshadowing the massive helicopter deployments used by the Americans in Vietnam. In another foreshadowing of that later conflict, the British used napalm on suspected guerilla positions, although it was never as widespread or indiscriminate as in Vietnam.

In 1955, Chin Peng offered to negotiate a peace settlement, but it was rejected by the British, and by 1958 almost all hostilities had ceased. In 1960, Chin Peng, who had been moving back and forth across the Malay–Thai border for years, moved with a small group of guerillas to Thailand, where he continued a small-scale campaign for the next twenty-five years.

MODEL STRATEGIES In defeating the MCP, Britain became one of the few Western countries to successfully suppress a Communist uprising. As other nations found themselves facing similar situations, they studied the Malaya Emergency for lessons on how to fight a political war. Most notably, with America bogged down in Vietnam in the 1960s, some U.S. military planners sought to learn from Britain's handling of the Emergency.

There were significant differences between the situations in Malaya and Vietnam, of course. First of all, as the British were more than ready to admit, the insurgency of Chin Peng was nowhere near as effective as that of the Viet Minh. Secondly, Chin Peng had alienated the largest group of potential supporters—Chinese workers—by terrorizing them. Thirdly, his rebellion began in reaction to a crisis within a political party rather than as a result of a call to national unity and did not therefore attract as many adherents. Finally, Chin Peng was not, nor did he have, a genuine military leader who knew how to bring the battle out of the jungle and into urban areas.

Yet, drawing on their experience with civil insurgencies dating back to Palestine, Ireland, and even to the Boer War of 1899, the British did put together a successful formula for winning a political war. And their strategies for defeating the enemy politically as well as militarily were highly effective. So why didn't the Americans profit from this experience? After all, the history of the Malaya Emergency could easily be studied—during the Vietnam War, American military staff had even visited the British jungle-warfare training school in Johor. Most likely it was because, as Robert Thompson, who became a counterinsurgency adviser to Presidents John F. Kennedy and Richard Nixon, put it in *No Exit from Vietnam*: "[M]any Americans made studies of the British success during the Emergency … but they were largely superficial. It was never comprehended as a whole."

Americans, in other words, knew the letter of the law but not the spirit behind it. Indeed, their imitation of British methods took on a dark twist. They, too, used the phrase "hearts and minds," but only in the way that Lyndon Johnson used it in his famous statement, "Grab them by the balls and their hearts and minds will follow."

THE FATE OF CHIN PENG

Chin Peng continued to lead attacks against Malaya from his base in Thailand, until he signed a peace treaty with Malaysia in 1989. Peng's soldiers were allowed to return to Malaysia without penalty, but Peng was barred. In 2004, Peng published a memoir, at the age of seventy-nine, which became a controversial best-seller in Malaysia .

In *Chin Peng: My Side of History*, he describes himself as a sort of anti-colonial warrior, out to free Malaya from imperialist masters. He comes close to apologizing for some of his actions by saying "I was young, in a very different age that demanded very different approaches," but also denies claims that he fostered or took part in terrorism. All he wants, he says in the book, is to return to Malaya to pay his respects to the graves of his parents and his ancestors.

His demands have created quite a controversy in Malaysia. The government refuses to let him back in, claiming that he is a "terrorist who has murdered in cold blood," and others, too, have written letters to newspapers remembering the babies impaled on stakes, civilians beheaded, and entire villages burned. Peng sees it differently, writing, "It is ironic that I should be without the country for which I was more than willing to die." But it is unlikely that he will ever be allowed to return home.

General Sir Gerald Templer, the British high commissioner, whose steadfast attempts to win the hearts and minds of the Malay people helped turn the tide against Communist insurgents.

The New Villages of the British became the "Strategic Hamlets" of the Americans, where people were cordoned off as if they were POWs. The counterparts of the British SOVF units were America's "Kit Carson" scouts—North Vietnamese and Viet Cong turncoats molded into fighting units—except that most of these poorly controlled squads were known more for terrorizing than soldiering. Above all, with their indiscriminate bombing and killing, the Americans alienated the very population they were supposed to be supporting. As one commander said, tellingly, of the destruction of Hue City: "We had to destroy it in order to save it."

Had America studied the Malaya conflict more fully it might have learned the lessons needed to defeat North Vietnam. But perhaps not. The massive wealth and power of the United States was not geared toward the more subtle political, social, and economic methods that the British—at least partially as a result of a lack of economic strength directly following the war—were forced to invent. With less firepower, and more brainpower, they were able to win their war.

WHEN THE WORLD WASN'T LOOKING: THE DEATH OF THE MEXICAN COUNTERCULTURE

EXTRAORDINARY THINGS HAD A WAY OF HAPPENING IN THE 1960S, when each year was packed with enough cultural change and political upheaval to be worth, say, the entire decade of the 1950s. Yet, even in this context, 1968 was a tumultuous twelve months. In January, a U.S. B-52 Stratofortress bomber crashed in Greenland, discharging four nuclear bombs that, through a miracle, did not go off. That same month the Tet Offensive began in Vietnam, with the Communist North Vietnamese and Viet Cong attacking numerous South Vietnamese cities, resulting in vicious street-fighting in Saigon and Hue. In March, police responded violently to a huge demonstration in London's Grosvenor Square against the Vietnam War, arresting two hundred and leaving ninety-one people injured. On April 4, Martin Luther King, Jr. was assassinated in Memphis, Tennessee. In May, it seemed that an international revolution was starting, the so-called "Paris Spring" of political libertarianism, with exuberant student strikes in Paris and Prague. In June, American Democrat senator Robert F. Kennedy was assassinated in Los Angeles. August saw Soviet tanks roll into Prague, ending the Paris Spring there. Also in August, students clashed with police on the streets of Chicago during the Democratic National Convention, in a stormy battle over the war in Vietnam and what they saw as a corrupt and irrelevant electoral process.

It wasn't all violence, of course. All across the world, millions of young people made love, not war. The musical *Hair* premiered on Broadway, and an Englishman named Alec Rose sailed single-handed around the world. An impresario bought London Bridge for a million pounds and announced his plans to take it to Arizona. And then there were the Olympics, the Games of the XIX Olympiad, as they were officially known. For the first time ever, the Olympics were held in a developing (or

"Third World," as it was then known) country: Mexico. Both Avery Brundage, head of the International Olympic Committee, and Mexican President Gustavo Díaz Ordaz, were proudly present for the opening ceremony in Mexico City on October 12. They announced to the world's press that this would be the showcase not only of the world's best athletes, but of a country that had survived a revolutionary past to become the most stable of Latin American countries. There would be no Che Guevara in Mexico, no socialist upheaval. The Olympics would showcase the essentially democratic nature of this peaceful world neighbor.

Yet there was something strange about President Díaz Ordaz's smile, which was fixed and slightly maniacal. In fact, as few people knew at the time and few people outside Mexico remember today, it was a smile that hid a terrible secret—that ten days before, his army had murdered about three hundred sons and daughters of Mexico's middle-class in a plaza surrounded by residential apartment buildings, at a place called Tlatelolco, only a few miles from where the opening ceremony was taking place. Although the world news organizations had heard of these killings, the reports were murky. The headlines in the government-controlled Mexican press— "Foreign Interlopers Attempt to Damage Mexico's National Image" and "Criminal Provocation at Tlatelolco Meeting Causes Bloodshed"—seemed to indicate it was a local matter, and the number of dead, described variously as between twenty and thirty, both soldiers and "terrorists," was fairly low, especially for a "Third World" country. In any event, the journalists weren't there to report revolution: they wanted to see how American middle-distance runner Jim Ryun would fare in the thin air of Mexico City, if Czech gymnast Vera Caslavska

Mexico City in 1968. The city's university campus, the focus of student protests, was situated next door to the stadium hosting the Olympic Games.

would win four gold medals, and what results the introduction of the very first doping tests at the Olympics would have. So no one asked about Tlatelolco and, gradually, it was forgotten amid the bright lights and cheers of the Olympic Games.

THE FAMILY HOME

The massacre at La Plaza de las Tres Culturas (Plaza of the Three Cultures) in Tlatelolco, where Mexican soldiers and government agents opened fire on a crowd of between five and ten thousand peaceful men, women, and children, was Mexico's Kent State, its Tiananmen Square, a watershed event that brought to an end a decade of potential change and sent the Mexican left far underground. It can be argued that this was not a situation without precedent in Mexican history. So often in the country's past, just as it seemed that liberty was within reach of the Mexican people, it was snatched away. Banish the Spanish and the French step in. Banish the priests and the revolutionaries turn into little tin gods. However, starting in the early part of the twentieth century, leaders like Emiliano Zapata and Pancho Villa had helped foment a civil war, out of which, ultimately, the Mexican Republic and the constitution of 1917 were born. Subsequent Mexican presidents, starting with Alvaro Obregón, came to romanticize the history of the war, depicting it as a selfless revolution aimed at freeing the country. They pretended that the Revolution—always spelled with a capital "R"—was fought for a common goal, that the assassinated Zapata was a martyr, and that his enemy Venustiano Carranza was "the father of the 1917 constitution."

During the 1930s and 1940s, the Partido Revolucionario Institucional (PRI) became the dominant political party in the nation. It called itself "the family home." Its president, who was also the president of the country, presented himself as a father figure who could help his people solve their problems and live together in peace, adhering to the ideals of the Revolution. It was, as social critic Eric Zolov has pointed out, "a patriarchal ideology [superimposed] on a mythologized ... revolutionary struggle." But, as Zolov has also said, this cultural framework "was challenged and contradicted by everyday reality among Mexico's poor." The government's harping on the ideal of the family—Mother's Day became a state holiday—as well as the millions of pesos spent on erecting public monuments to the Revolution, helped to disguise the fact that the rich got richer as the poor stayed very, very poor.

After the Second World War, American culture invaded Mexico, as it was to invade most of the world. But it hit Mexico particularly hard. It wasn't just the Coca-Cola signs and the TV shows such as *Ozzie and Harriet*. Santa Claus appeared in his full red suit surrounded by reindeer in a land that seldom saw snow. Mexican movies began to take second place to American ones. At home, Mexican families began putting away the tequila and serving bourbon instead.

At first this was fine with the PRI. Mexico and America were allies, and the influx of American tourists and consumer goods helped the Mexican middle class to grow, as it did throughout the 1950s. But then an American import arrived that scared the PRI, because it could not be controlled or harnessed. That import was rock 'n' roll.

At first, rock 'n' roll seemed to the Mexicans to be just another style of swinging music, like the samba or fast jazz, and it was played by dance orchestras and it was mostly adults who swung their hips to it. Elvis Presley helped change that. His sneer, his forelock, his pelvic gyrations appealed to and were taken up by Mexican youth. Predictably, the family patriarchs of the PRI proclaimed that Presley was too feminine—a homosexual, in other words. In 1957, a story appeared in a Mexican newspaper claiming that Presley had said, "I would rather kiss three black girls than a Mexican," which in turn brought a storm of protest against the singer. The story was false and may even have been a deliberate smear planted in the press by an embittered government official, after Presley had turned down his request for the singer to appear at a private party. In any case, the PRI continued to make its position clear. A fight in a local theater during the showing of the Presley movie *King Creole* (whose title was translated into Spanish as *Sinister Melody*) gave the government-controlled press further opportunity to link rock 'n' roll to chaos and anarchy. As the 1950s turned into the 1960s, rock 'n' roll became a fact of life for Mexican youths—and a threat to the patriarchal nature of Mexican society.

Ironically, much of the "revolution" that ensued among Mexican teenagers in the 1960s was tame compared with what was happening in other countries at the time. When the music of the Beatles arrived in North America, and then filtered south to Mexico around 1964, Mexican youths treated the music—and that of the rest of the so-called "British Invasion"—with great reverence, so much so that the most popular local bands were those, such as Los Dug Dugs, Los Yaki, and Los Belmonts, who exactly replicated foreign music, right down to the inflections and words. The songs were played in English; imitation was, quite literally, the highest form of flattery. The Beatles and Rolling Stones and others did not come to Mexico; instead, these simulacrum bands played for screaming audiences in lieu of their godlike cultural heroes.

This did not mean that a real social revolution was not taking place in Mexico. So-called "youth clubs" began to become quite popular in Mexico City in the mid-1960s, and alcohol and drugs were part of the culture, as they were around the rest of the world. In early 1965, the government under the administration of President Díaz Ordaz launched a series of raids on some twenty-five clubs in the city, shutting them down as "centers of perversion and activities by evil-doing groups." But Ordaz's government had its hands full as it tried to hold back the influences that were threatening to overwhelm its idea of the Mexican family. As well as Mexican students, they had American hippies to deal with, who came to Mexico at first to search for the psilocybin mushroom in Indian villages in the highlands, but then to form communes near Acapulco and Mexico City. These "pernicious foreigners," as an official government press release called them, were ejected in large numbers but kept finding their way back into the country.

Add to this mix a burgeoning pop culture in Mexico that led upper-middle-class kids to grow their hair long and wear short skirts, refuse to go to school, avoid church, and stay out all night, and you had what came to be called "*La Onda.*" That means, literally, "the wave," but it meant more than that to Mexican youth counter-culture in the 1960s. It meant a sense of freedom, of movement, of being at the fore-front of ideas and cultural experimentation.

At the Universidad Nacional Autónoma de Mexico (UNAM), Mexico's constitutionally independent national university, *La Onda* met the radical left, and the seeds for the massacre of Tlatelolco were sown.

SUMMER OF '68 In July of 1968, a student National Strike Committee, the *Consejo Nacional de la Huelga* (CNH), was formed. This in itself was not unusual: in 1968, just after the spring upheavals on campuses and in cities around the world, it would have been strange if students had not organized. And UNAM students had a history of organizing—they had taken part in the massive union strikes that had hit the country in the late 1950s. One of the biggest causes of

TRIPPING OUT TO MEXICO

During the 1960s, Mexico had a reputation, especially among American students, as a place to go to get high on hallucinogenic mushrooms and commune with the universe. Few knew that this reputation was started by a New York banker named R. Gordon Watson, who, along with his wife and a photographer, visited the Indian village of Huautla de Jimenez in the Oaxaca highlands in 1955. There Watson, a daring traveler, ingested some of the hallucinogenic mushrooms the Indians called *los ninos santos*, which they used to treat physical and emotional illnesses.

Watson and his wife were the first foreigners to take *los ninos santos*, and they returned to New York with some. Spores from the mushroom, identified by Watson, an amateur mycologist, as *Psilocybin mexicana*, were taken to Paris by a scientist friend of Watson's, where they were artificially cultivated. Shortly thereafter, Swiss chemist Albert Hoffman created a synthetic hallucinogen, calling it psilocybin, which, in turn, became popular as LSD in the United States. But many students preferred the "natural" high of the mushrooms, and continued to travel to Mexico, despite the repressive regime of President Díaz Ordaz.

protest, from the students' point of view, was President Díaz Ordaz's massive publicity campaign as the Olympics approached. With the help of his PRI network, Ordaz was waging a campaign to show that there was no poverty in Mexico, no dissent, no crime. His secret police and student informers were everywhere, in the cafés, in the university, on the streets; you could trust no one.

At the end of July, what was essentially a smalltime gang fight between the students of two rival high schools was ruthlessly suppressed by Mexican police fearful that the slightest hint of unrest be picked up by the international press. When UNAM students marched to celebrate the anniversary of the Cuban Revolution, the police broke up the march with clubs. Naturally, this violence led to more student protest. Spreading out onto the streets, UNAM students spontaneously organized a general strike. Buses were captured and used to block intersections. High school students joined in, and the doors of several high schools were barricaded. In response, the use of force by the authorities escalated. Police even employed bazookas to blast their way into several high schools; in one such attack five students were wounded and a hundred arrested.

Up to this point, the uprising had been spontaneous and unplanned, but now the CNH stepped in and drew up a series of demands, which it presented to the government. Some were rights that were already, in theory, guaranteed by the constitution, such as the right to free speech, freedom from political persecution, and equality before the law—meaning that members of the police force and army should be prosecuted for any crimes they committed. The students also wanted the abolition of an infamous penal code, Article 145, which allowed anyone who dissented from the regime in word or action to be jailed indefinitely.

The student protests echoed others around the globe. In May in Paris, students protesting the Vietnam War had hooked up with other protest groups—workers, anarchists, even right-wing activists—and caused a nationwide strike. At the end of August, at the Democratic National Convention in Chicago, thousands of American students would attempt to derail a political process. In each case, authorities were quick to use violence to quell the unrest.

But although the Mexican students shut down UNAM and took over its Mexico City campus, they were generally more peaceful than their overseas counterparts. Significantly, an American observer at the time said that the occupation, compared with the similar occupations of universities such as Columbia and Berkeley, was "a discreet and decorous version of the Woodstock spirit." Poetry and political theater were performed; strikers painted murals and listened to rock music. This reflected the innocent and youthful spirit of *La Onda*—a spirit that was about to be crushed by massively repressive forces.

Previous pages: This photograph was taken on October 2, 1968, in the Plaza de las Tres Culturas, just seconds before the army began its savage assault on the student protestors.

TERROR IN TLATELOLCO
By the early fall, as the Olympics approached, the students left the campuses to begin a strike. They decided to make their message of protest public in the best way they knew how: by taking it to the streets. On September 13, twenty-five thousand people, a group that included students, members of various labor unions, writers, artists, and ordinary

citizens, marched in the "Silent Protest March." With their mouths taped over, they carried signs that implored people to listen to their message. They also peacefully took over various government spaces, such as large public squares where statues of revolutionary heroes stood, to reclaim, symbolically, their history. It was as if they were saying, "Our history belongs to us, too. We will not have it shaped by regime propaganda makers."

In mid-September, the army occupied the main campus of UNAM and several campuses of high schools affiliated with the university. This was an infringement of the Mexican constitution, which accorded complete independence from government interference (let alone armed occupation) to the university system, and the UNAM rector, Javier Barros Sierra, resigned in protest.

The tenor of the student strike then became noticeably more violent, as protestors battled soldiers on the UNAM campuses. Some members of the student strike committee started to carry guns and advocate violent government overthrow. It was established later that many were agents in the employ of the government, which, as was also later established, had heavily infiltrated the CNH, with some help from the American CIA.

A march was planned by CNH organizers for the afternoon of October 2, but when they got word that the army might be present they changed the time, to that evening, and the location, to a plaza situated in the middle of a large middle-class housing project. The plaza was centrally located and well known, an easy place for students from the various areas of the city to find, but by massing in this way the students unknowingly played right into the hands of the army.

The Tlatelolco housing project was a few miles north of the center of Mexico City, near the pre-Hispanic ruins that gave it its name. La Plaza de las Tres Culturas, where the students were to meet, was a large open area flanked by high-rise apartment buildings that were home to thousands of Mexican blue- and lower-level white-collar workers and their families. The balconies as well as the plaza itself were teeming with people; those who could see outside the plaza watched warily as armored vehicles and trucks filled with soldiers began to arrive.

The evening commenced with speeches, and applause from the crowd. Those giving the speeches were located on one of the fourth-floor balconies. Students passed through the crowd, soliciting donations for the CNH and selling posters. There was applause when a group of railway workers came into the crowd carrying a banner announcing solidarity with the students. Speakers criticized the government and the local press, at one point calling for a boycott of the daily *El Sol*, a government-controlled newspaper.

Then, at the moment when a student leader was announcing that a scheduled march out of the plaza to another campus would not take place because of the heavy military presence outside of Tlatelolco, a hovering army helicopter launched a flare. Immediately, shots were fired. The people trapped in the plaza began to run back and forth seeking an exit, as CNH organizers on the fourth-floor balcony called for them to be calm, saying that the soldiers were only firing into the air.

THE CIA IN MEXICO

According to documents obtained by the National Security Archive in 2003 under the Freedom of Information Act, the CIA, in response to Mexican concerns over security during the Olympic Games, suggested that the Pentagon send weapons and riot-control training material to the Díaz Ordaz administration. The CIA station in Mexico also sent daily reports to Washington, tracking developments within the university community. Six days before the massacre, both Secretary of the Interior Luis Echeverría Alvarez and Fernando Gutiérrez Barrios, head of federal security, told CIA station agents that "the situation will be under complete control very shortly."

The documents also revealed that student leader Socrates Camos Lemus may have been in the employ of the Díaz Ordaz government. After the massacre, Lemus appeared before the press and said that the students had been funded by dissident politicians, and that radical elements within the CNH had advocated firing on the troops at Tlatelolco. Everyone that Lemus charged denied this, and some student leaders suspected he had been tortured. Others thought he might be in the employ of the CIA.

The CIA memo released in 2003 seems to contradict this, merely indicating that Lemus was being used by an administration trying "to shift the blame for its inept handling of the affair." Lemus denied that he was influenced by anyone, and is currently a political official in Mexico.

But the soldiers were not firing into the air. In what was obviously a carefully planned and executed attack, soldiers on top of neighboring buildings and in the stairwells of the housing complex opened up with a hail of machine-gun and rifle fire. Men, women, and children dropped to the ground, cut down by bullets. Panicked people tried to escape through the open east side of the plaza, but were met by hundreds of troops pointing bayonets at them. They turned and ran back into the plaza and tried to sneak out through various alleyways, but bullets continued to rain down upon them.

Protestors noticed that certain members of the crowd wore white gloves on their left hands. One student heard a soldier call, "Don't shoot him, he's wearing a white glove," and realized that the students had been infiltrated by turncoats and police agents who wore the gloves as a means to identify themselves.

There was pandemonium in the plaza. A college professor ran down one of the enclosed stairwells and found her hands sticky. She looked down and noticed that there was blood on her hands and then saw that it was everywhere—on the railings, on the walls. The same woman saw a sixteen-year-old boy moving directly toward two men wearing white gloves who were shooting into a crowd. The boy may have thought they were students. She screamed a warning, but the boy kept going and the men turned and shot him.

Another student, running as fast as she could, made it to a street outside the plaza, just in time to see a young woman in a car being shot in the head. The woman's head fell against the car's horn and its blaring echoed down the alleyways as the student raced away from the scene.

"In a few moments," one student writer recalled, "the whole thing became a scene out of hell. The gunfire was deafening. The bullets were shattering the windows of the apartments and shards of glass were flying all over … the terror-stricken families inside were desperately trying to protect their youngest children." Indeed, some of the people killed at the plaza that night were simply onlookers who happened to live there.

After the massacre, the bitter smell of gunpowder hung over the plaza. Stained with blood, littered with posters and newspapers, it had the air of a battleground. One woman who lived in the Tlatelolco projects said later: "My daughter and I walked around the plaza and she kept saying, 'Look, Mama, here's where the tanks were … Look, here's where the dead bodies were.' The bullet holes have been repaired and the walls have been painted over. [I said to my daughter] 'Dear, I can't bear Tlatelolco one minute more, let's get out of here, let's go far away.'"

THE PLAZA OF SACRIFICES
The next day, the newspaper headlines blared that students had fired on police, had been fired on in return, and that there had been bloodshed. The official count of the dead was thirty-two. A Mexican Army general had been wounded, and one soldier killed. The testimony of onlookers makes it seem almost certain that these men were shot by their own troops.

The best count of the dead that has been put forward is around three hundred, with hundreds more wounded. (At the time, the U.S. State Department, relying on CIA informants, put the count of the dead at between 150 and 200, which included 40 military personnel.) The Mexican police cordoned off hospitals to keep those few journalists who were interested from making an accurate count. The police also arrested about one thousand students, some of whom they tortured. They were kept at a local military base, and in the notorious Lecumberri Prison. Many students immediately fled the country and did not return for years.

In the meantime, the Olympics began, and the world's attention turned in that direction. Vera Caslavska won her four gold medals, Jim Ryun failed in the 1,500 meters, and two black American athletes, Tommie Smith and John Carlos, having won medals, raised their black-gloved fists in a Black Power salute, and were

PUNISHING THE GUILTY

Since the year 2000, special prosecutors appointed by Mexican President Vicente Fox Quesada have been trying to punish those responsible for the massacre at Tlatelolco. Former president Luis Echeverría Alvarez, who in 1968 was secretary of the interior, has been the chief target of this probe. Although he has denied responsibility for planning the attack—blaming it instead on President Díaz Ordaz, who died in 1979—many suspect that he was the guiding hand behind what was obviously a carefully orchestrated assault.

Until 2006, the Mexican judicial system refused to allow Echeverría to be tried for the massacre at Tlatelolco, despite the fact that twenty-seven researchers contacted by the prosecutors wrote a report claiming that Echeverría and Diaz Ordaz were guilty of "crimes against humanity," and that the massacre was intended to "destroy a sector of society that [the 1968 Mexican administration] considered its ideological enemy." But in July 2006, in a politically charged move by President Fox, Echeverría was arrested on genocide charges. This may have come too late for the families of those killed, however. At the time of his arrest, Echeverría was eighty-four and in poor health—possibly too unwell to ever face trial.

banned from the Olympics for life. But no word was spoken of the massacre at Tlatelolco and on December 4, the CNH, with many of its leaders dead, underground, or in exile, officially disbanded.

For a moment, it seemed, Díaz Ordaz and the Mexican authorities had won. After a few brief mentions, the massacre at Tlatelolco was forgotten by the world media and even the American media, just a short distance away to the north (although countercultural publications such as the Boston *Phoenix*, the New York *Village Voice*, and *Rolling Stone* magazine published articles on it in the next few years). In the immediate aftermath of the brutal government attack, those participating students who were not in prison or in exile felt, as one wrote, "a sense of frustrated impotence." What could be done in the face of such violence? In the next few years, many students voiced both their powerlessness and their protest against the massacre by turning to drugs and harder rock music—"a way to scream," as one of them put it.

But the story of the massacre was kept alive in Mexico by writers such as the Nobel Prize winner Octavio Paz, who insisted that it not be forgotten, that it be seen as a seminal event in Mexican history. At the time of the killings, Paz was Mexico's ambassador to India. He resigned to protest the massacre. Seven years after Tlatelolco, he wrote: "It was as though the Mexico of 1968 were a metaphor of the Paris Commune or the attack on the Winter Palace." Mexican critic and novelist Carlos Monsivais, writing around the same time, said "there [has been] no Vietnam War for Mexican youth to confront." Instead, they had confronted a corrupt government and society. The massacre, according to Monsivais, changed "the consciousness of a generation and [signaled] the beginnings of the demystification of the country."

But change in Mexico would take time. Díaz Ordaz's successor as president in 1970 was Luis Echeverría Alvarez, secretary of the interior at the time of the massacre, whom many suspected of engineering the killings. In 1971, he presided over another massacre, when marching student protestors were attacked by a paramilitary squad called the *Halcones* ("Falcons"), who were trained by the government. Twenty-five students were shot or beaten to death. After the Corpus Christi Massacre, as this event became known, some wounded students were allegedly shot in their hospital beds.

By the late 1990s, however, politicians had begun to enter the public arena who had been students in the sixties. The Mexican president in that period was Ernesto Zedillo, who, as a student protestor, had been beaten by the police in the weeks before Tlateloco. He publicly acknowledged that the massacre had caused people to distrust the repressive government and long for democratic change. In 1997, Mexico's Congress also appointed a committee to investigate the massacre.

In 1998, the mayor of Mexico City decreed that flags would be flown at half mast on October 2. In 2000, Vicente Fox Quesada, the first non-PRI president of Mexico in history, ordered a probe into the Tlatelolco and Corpus Christi massacres, and demanded that those responsible face charges of murder. After much legal wrangling, Luis Echeverría was arrested on charges of genocide in July 2006.

Outside Mexico, the world remains oblivious. We know all about the four students killed at Kent State in 1969 and the hundreds cut down in Tiananmen Square in 1989, but have learned little about the dead of Tlatelolco. In Mexico, those students are never forgotten. Up until the late 1980s, votive candles would appear anonymously at Tlateloco every year on October 2. Then, on the twentieth anniversary of the massacre, veterans of the student movement erected a monument of pink sandstone, which, when it rains, turns the color of dried blood. There are two dozen names etched into the stone followed by the words "and many others whose names and ages we do not know." After briefly describing the massacre, the text on the monument precisely captures the sentiments of those who were involved, the still-open wound of Tlateloco: "Who? Who? Nobody … By the following dawn, the plaza was swept of the dead … On the television and the radio there was nothing. Not a moment of silence at the banquet (in fact, the banquet continued)."

Former president Luis Echeverría faces the press in 1998 after a state prosecutor called on him to account for his involvement in the actions that led to the massacre of October 2, 1968.

BIBLIOGRAPHY

Alexander, Edward. *A Crime of Vengeance: An Armenian Struggle for Justice*. Lincoln, Nebraska: iUniverse.com, Inc., 2000.

Alpern, Stanley B. *Amazons of Black Sparta: The Women Warriors of Dahomey*. New York: New York University Press, 1998.

Barber, Noel. *The War of the Running Dogs: How Malaya Defeated the Communist Guerillas, 1948–60*. London: Fontana Books, 1972.

Barnouw, Adriaan J. *The Pageant of Netherlands History*. New York, London: Longmans, Green & Co., 1952.

Black, Jeremy. *The Seventy Great Battles in History*. New York: Thames & Hudson, 2005.

Bridgman, Jon M. *The Revolt of the Hereros*. Berkeley, Los Angeles, London: University of California Press, 1981.

Chambers, James. *The Devil's Horsemen*. New York: Atheneum, 1979.

Chang, Iris. *The Chinese in America: A Narrative History*. New York: Viking, 2003.

Charney, Israel W., William S. Parsons, and Samuel Totten. *Century of Genocide: Eyewitness Accounts and Critical Views*. New York, London: Garland Publishing, Inc., 1997.

Chase, Marilyn. *The Barbary Plague: The Black Death in Victorian San Francisco*. New York: Random House, 2003.

Cummings, Bruce. *Korea's Place in the Sun: A Modern History*. New York, London: W.W. Norton & Company, 1997.

Dolnick, Edward. *Down the Great Unknown: John Wesley Powell's 1869 Journey of Discovery and Tragedy*. New York, San Francisco: HarperCollins, 2001.

Duffy, Eamon. *Saints and Sinners: A History of the Popes*. New Haven: Yale University Press, 1997.

Eggenberger, David. *An Encyclopedia of Battles: Accounts of Over 1,560 Battles from 1479 B.C. to the Present*. New York: Dover Publications, 1985.

Elegant, Robert. *Pacific Destiny: Inside Asia Today*. New York: Crown Publishers, 1990.

Fishbein, Seymour. *Grand Canyon Country*. Washington, D.C.: National Geographic Society, 1991.

French, Howard W. *A Continent for the Taking: The Tragedy and Hope of Africa*. New York: Alfred A. Knopf, 2004.

Frost, Orcutt. *Bering: The Russian Discovery of America*. New Haven & London: Yale University Press, 2003.

Gabriel, Richard A. *Subotai the Valiant: Genghis Khan's Greatest General*. New York: Praeger Publishing, 2004.

Gaustad, Edwin. *Roger Williams*. Oxford, New York: Oxford University Press, 2005.

Golway, Terry. *Irish Rebel: John Devoy and America's Fight for Irish Freedom*. New York: St. Martin's Griffin, 1998.

Greeley, Andrew M. *The Irish-Americans: The Rise to Money and Power*. New York, San Francisco: Harper & Row Publishers, 1981.

Hale, Christopher. *Himmler's Crusade: The Nazi Expedition to Find the Origins of the Aryan Race*. Hoboken, New Jersey: John Wiley & Sons, Inc., 2003.

Hamilton, Bernard. *The Leper King and His Heirs: Baldwin IV and the Crusader Kingdom of Jerusalem*. Cambridge, New York: Cambridge University Press, 2000.

Hughes, Robert. *The Fatal Shore: The Epic of Australia's Founding*. New York: Alfred A. Knopf, 1987.

Jardine, Lisa. *The Awful End of Prince William the Silent: The First Assassination of a Head of State with a Handgun*. New York: HarperCollins, 2006.

Jones, David E. *Women Warriors: A History*. Dulles, Virginia: Brassey's Books, 1997.

Kee, Robert. *Ireland: A History*. Boston, Toronto: Little, Brown & Company, 1980.

Kelly, John. *The Great Mortality: An Intimate History of the Black Death, the Most Devastating Plague of All Time*. New York, San Francisco: HarperCollins, 2005.

Levathes, Louise. *When China Ruled the Waves: The Treasure Fleet of the Dragon Throne, 1405–1433*. New York: Simon & Schuster, 1994.

McBrien, Richard P. *Lives of the Popes: The Pontiffs from St. Peter to John Paul II*. HarperSanFrancisco, 1997.

McBrien, Richard P. *Lives of the Saints: From Mary and St. Francis of Assisi to John XXIII and Mother Teresa*. HarperSanFrancisco, 2001.

Madden, Thomas F. *The New Concise History of the Crusades*. Revised Edition. Boulder, Colorado: Rowman & Littlefield, Inc., 2005.

Matsen, Brad. *Descent: The Heroic Discovery of the Abyss*. New York: Pantheon Books, 2005.

Moffit, Samuel Hugh. *A History of Christianity in Asia, Volume II: 1500–1900*. Maryknoll, New York: Orbis Books, 2005.

Morgan, David. *The Mongols*. Oxford, New York: Basil Blackwell, Ltd, 1986.

Nisbet, Jack. *The Mapmaker's Eye: David Thompson on the Columbia Plateau*. Washington: Washington State University, 2005.

Pakenham, Thomas. *The Scramble for Africa: The White Man's Conquest of the Dark Continent from 1876 to 1912*. New York: Random House, 1991.

Pelissier, Roger. *The Awakening of China 1793–1949*. New York, Toronto: G. P. Putnam's Sons, 1963.

Poniatowski, Elena. *Massacre in Mexico*. Columbia, London: University of Missouri Press, 1975.

Reader's Digest. *Great Adventures that Changed Our World: The World's Great Explorers, Their Triumphs and Tragedies*. Pleasantville: Reader's Digest Books, 1978.

Roberts, J. A. G. *A Concise History of China*. Cambridge, Massachusetts: Harvard University Press, 1999.

Rozario, Paul. *Zheng He and the Treasure Fleet, 1405–1433: A Modern-Day Traveller's Guide from Antiquity to the Present*. Singapore: SNP International Publishing, 2005.

Rozwadowski, Helen M. *Fathoming the Ocean: The Discovery and Exploration of the Deep Sea*. Cambridge, Massachusetts, and London, England: Belknap Press of Harvard University Press, 2005.

Ryan, Lyndall. *The Aboriginal Tasmanians*. 2nd ed. New South Wales: Allen & Unwin, Ltd, 1996.

Shorto, Russell. *The Island at the Center of the World: The Epic Story of Dutch Manhattan and the Forgotten Colony That Shaped America*. New York: Doubleday, 2004.

Skaggs, Jimmy M. *The Great Guano Rush: Entrepreneurs and American Overseas Expansion*. New York: St. Martin's Press, 1994.

Stevens, Peter F. *The Voyage of the Catalpa: A Perilous Journey and Six Irish Rebels Escape to Freedom*. New York: Carroll & Graf Publishers, 2002.

Warnes, David. *Chronicle of the Russian Tsars: The Reign-by-Reign Record of the Rulers of Imperial Russia*. London: Thames & Hudson, 1999.

Zolov, Eric. *Refried Elvis: The Rise of the Mexican Counterculture*. Berkeley, California: University of California Press, 1999.

ACKNOWLEDGEMENTS

I would like to thank everyone who helped bring this book to fruition, especially Will Kiester, incomparable publisher and brain merchant; Scott Forbes, whose astute and diligent editing saved me on many occasions; Peter Long, whose design makes the book such a visual pleasure; and Anne Burns and Amanda McKittrick, the intrepid photo sleuths.

PHOTOGRAPHY CREDITS